Separate Spheres No More

Separate Spheres No More

Gender Convergence in
American Literature, 1830–1930

Edited by Monika M. Elbert

THE UNIVERSITY OF ALABAMA PRESS

Tuscaloosa and London

1   2   3   4   5   6   7   8   9
07   06   05   04   03   02   01   00

Typeface: Bembo

∞

The paper on which this book is printed meets the minimum
requirements of American National Standard for Information
Science–Permanence of Paper for Printed Library Materials,
ANSI Z39.48-1984.

Library of Congress Cataloging-in-Publication Data

Separate spheres no more : gender convergence in American literature,
1830–1930 / edited by Monika M. Elbert.
        p. cm.
Includes bibliographical references and index.
    ISBN 0-8173-1036-3 (alk. paper)
    1. American literature—19th century—History and criticism. 2.
Gender identity in literature. 3. Literature and society—United
States—History—19th century. 4. Literature and society—United
States—History—20th century. 5. American literature—20th
century—History and criticism. 6. Sex role in literature. I. Elbert,
Monika M. (Monika Maria), 1956–
    PS169.G45 S47 2000
    810.9′353–dc21

                                00-008068

British Library Cataloguing-in-Publication Data available

For my parents, Paul and Maria Elbert

Contents

Preface

The idea for this collection emerges from my personal odyssey in the classroom, where, over the last decade, I have tried to make sense, both for my
students and for myself, of the many changing critical approaches to the
relationship between canonical American male writers and their "rediscovered" American female counterparts. In the spring of 1995, I chaired a
session entitled "Revitalizing the Canon: Separate Spheres No More" at the
Northeast Modern Language Association Convention in Boston, based on
my 1994 call for papers, "Separate Spheres No More." I was enthused by the
positive response—in the form of the many good papers I received, the
excellent turnout at the session itself (by male and female scholars), and the
exciting discussion that followed the panel presentations. I felt connected to
a community of teacher-scholars in a way I never have before, as classroom
politics became more real in the light of women's history and the rewriting
of women's history. And I felt less troubled as I saw other teachers grappling
with similar questions in a public arena.

The kind of community I experienced at the "Separate Spheres No
More" session continued with the community of writers in this volume.
E-mailing must be the late-twentieth-century version of quilting. I would
like to thank each contributor for participating in these conversations over
the last couple of years.

Of the many guides, teachers, and mentors I encountered along the way,
I would especially like to thank Donald B. Gibson, Frederick Newberry,
Leland S. Person, Jr., David Leverenz, and Heyward Ehrlich for their encouragement, their support, and their confidence in my projects. Indeed,
with their sensitivity to gender issues, they never made me feel stranded in
a separate gender sphere.

I am also grateful to Becky Redington, the guardian angel who helped me with last-minute technical support. And speaking of guardian angels, I would like to thank Rev. Msgr. Francis A. Reinbold, who, though now deceased, was very enthusiastic about my work.

My parents deserve special thanks for their undying patience and support, as does Wendy Ryden, who is always there for me. And heartfelt thanks to Stephen E. Foss, who constantly surprises me by making me see things anew.

Separate Spheres No More

Introduction

MONIKA M. ELBERT

Let us hear no more of "woman's sphere" either from our wise (?) [*sic*] legislators beneath the State House dome, or from our clergymen in their pulpits.
I am tired, year after year, of hearing such twaddle about sturdy oaks and
clinging vines and man's chivalric protection of woman. Let woman find out
her limitations, and if, as is so confidently asserted, nature has defined her
sphere, she will be guided accordingly; but in heaven's name give her a
chance!

—Louisa May Alcott to Maria S. Porter, 1874

When Margaret Fuller prophesied, in 1845, a "ravishing harmony of the
spheres" in *Woman in the Nineteenth Century* (37), her vision was based on
the shifting gender roles within her own time. The purpose of this collection is to show the intersecting or overlapping section of the "separate
spheres" of male and female experience and of public and private gender
roles. Admittedly, the concept of separate spheres still applies to nineteenth-
century literature to some degree, but recent critics have taken a more relaxed approach, especially in terms of the blurred or shifting boundaries
between the spheres. There is often no clear demarcation between the
male/public realm and the female/private realm, and thus binary oppositions dissolve. Post-deconstructionist, revisionist critics have enjoyed the
freedom in exploring a rather amorphous territory that includes experiences
common to both sexes.[1]

In her recent *Women in Public: Between Banners and Ballots, 1825–1880,*
historian Mary Ryan exposes the overlap of spheres and shows that women
had the opportunity to share in public spaces through many cultural events
and daily occurrences. The essays in this volume seek to revise or reassess
women's conventional position as a liminal public figure by looking at some
of the same liberating postures that Ryan's book exposes. This is not to say
that a separate sphere for women did not exist, or to suggest that the middle-
class ideology of the cult of domesticity was not emulated by the under-
classes to some degree, but that an essentialist, reductionist position is dangerous in coming to terms with the diverging experiences of different

2 · MONIKA M. ELBERT

kinds of women. Ultimately, issues of gender seem not as divisive or pressing as those of race and class, and certainly it is absurd to consider gender as
a category by itself—outside the attendant realms of race and class. This
volume seeks to redress that essentialist error common to earlier studies of
gender.

With nineteenth-century gender studies now permitting an emotional
study of public man gone private, it is time to examine the assertive and
rational side of private woman gone public. Indeed, the last half of the
twentieth century showed a radical shift in thinking—moving away from
the exclusionary 1950s concept of the great man in history, or the 1960s
separatist notion of (middle-class) women's history, to a reconciliatory and
eclectic vision of genders and classes interacting. As gender roles are being
questioned at the end of the twentieth century, more scholars are interested
in reassessing the gender roles of previous generations. Specifically, men are
being accepted as a kinder, gentler, more emotional breed, and women are
being perceived as more independent, assertive, and logical. Contemporary
masculinist critics and historians of nineteenth-century American manhood, roused and unfettered by the ideas of the 1960s feminists, have rewritten a new male history fraught with personal vulnerabilities and anxieties.[2]
At the same time, a new younger school of feminists is trying to reassess
women's history as less restrictive and oppressive and to position women in
a less vulnerable, more proactive role—so that women's story is not one of
victimization. Our changing concepts of men's and women's roles have affected the way we evaluate the relationships between men and women in
the past.

This book attempts to uncover and show the commonalities—the hopes,
fears, anxieties, aspirations, and historical roadblocks—shared by men and
women (and representative male and female authors) in nineteenth-century
America, both at home and in the marketplace, thus dissolving boundaries between public and private spheres and questioning or challenging the
stereotypical images of women as ineffectual or vulnerable within nineteenth-century society. Though this collection of essays does not deny the
existence of the separate spheres altogether, it shows the line between the
spheres to be much finer and the boundaries blurrier than was maintained
in the past. Indeed, to understand how men and women lived in the same
historical moment, it is more productive to see where and how their roles
converged and how their interactions created a national culture in flux
rather than to dwell on a separatist notion of the genders living apart or
without interaction. In such a way, the history of the American nineteenth-
century woman seems less oppressive and her influence over the public

realm much greater because of this newly recognized interdependence with men.

The essays in this collection examine these shifting boundaries of gender and genre and reassign new roles to women as an active force in social and political change. Thus, women's history is not perceived as a separate discipline; instead, the stories of both genders are interwoven. The contributors of these essays align female authors with male authors writing in a similar fashion or with similar concerns, or they address social issues that are shared by both men and women and which, at times, are disruptive or enigmatic to both genders. Such problems relate to class tensions and a shifting economic system; to the repercussions of slavery; to the Civil War and its aftermath; to alternative lifestyles, stemming from transcendentalist or utopian ways of thinking; to a new urban landscape; and to changing views of marriage, home, nationhood, and morality. All of the essays attempt to revise notions of male/female or public/private and to destabilize the myth of binary thinking as set forth in a "separate spheres" ideology.

For literary critics, it is illuminating and liberating to rethink categories of traditionally "male" and "female" ways of seeing and genres of writing. In rethinking gender roles, the critics in this volume also reevaluate the genres in which women write. Thus, for example, "sentimental" or "local color" writing, which has been devalued in the past, is seen as part of the larger and more "dignified" movements of transcendentalism or realism, often considered male-based; indeed, here too the boundaries are blurred as issues of canonicity are explored. There is no privileged genre or school of writing, nor is there a privileging of certain "canonical writers." Instead, there is a wide array of authors and texts explored—from familiar writers like Stowe and Dickinson to lesser-known writers like Susie King Taylor, Mary Gove Nichols, and Melusina Fay Peirce, and from novels and poetry to autobiographical writings, utopian fiction, and essays. This volume also differs from others in its field because of its appeal to both historians and literary critics (another shifting of boundaries): most essays cross boundaries by incorporating literary studies with historical issues (e.g., medical advances, economic development, the consequences of the Civil War, utopian movements).

I hope that the energies and vision of this collection will parallel pedagogical changes in the classroom—where, more frequently, male and female authors are being taught side by side in such courses as the "American Renaissance" or "American Literary Realism." The volume should assist in discussing the transition of mind-sets relating to changing gender paradigms —from a separatist manner of thinking that focuses on difference to a reconciliatory way of perceiving that takes into account similarities in gender experience. I have organized this introduction into three sections: first, a discussion of the "separate spheres" ideology as practiced, challenged, or subverted by nineteenth-century American women writers; second, an overview of feminist criticism (from the 1960s onward) of gender spheres, which shows a distinct move away from separatism; and third, a summary of the essays included in this volume. If I make much of the history of "separate spheres," it is to explain how we have arrived at the current moment of gender assessment.

I
Nineteenth-Century Notions of "Separate Spheres"

Historically speaking, the middle-class women writers who purportedly lived "the cult of domesticity" perceived the paradoxes involved in creating this separate space. From my opening epigraph, it becomes quite clear that Louisa May Alcott felt that there was a "world elsewhere"—beyond the home—for women. Although her best-known novels, such as *Little Women* or *Little Men,* seemed to reinforce the notion of separate spheres and affirm a vision of domesticity, in her personal life, paradoxically enough, Alcott remained single and never became a mother, though she performed both maternal and paternal duties for her family and for society. Her rediscovered works—in the shape of adult, sexual novels (*Moods*), thrillers with manipulating and strong heroines ("Behind a Mask"), and more serious works about woman's labor (*Work* and *Hospital Sketches*)—testify to Alcott's having perceived the power of women outside the home. In the latter two works, about the Civil War, Alcott obviously champions the public role of women and their ability to effect social change. But even in the forbidden sexual stories with the femme fatale as the heroine, Alcott imagines a feminine power outside the domestic experience, which was unspeakable in good company. And Alcott herself experiences the schizophrenic split between "little women" and public, outspoken women in her role as a writer. As she notes in a journal entry, after attending a predominantly male "Fraternity Festival," she felt strange being feted so vehemently for her *Hospital Sketches* by eminent male readers: "Had a fine time and was amazed to find my 'umble' self made a lion of, set up among the great ones, stared at, waited upon, complimented" (June 1864, *Journals* 130). She talks about this public adulation with ambivalence—"It was a very pleasant surprise and new experience," she notes—but ironically concludes with an allusion to Cinderella and fairy-tale princesses, a myth that has been the bane of women's dependence upon men: "I liked it, but think a small dose quite as much as is good for me, for after sitting in a corner, & grubbing a la Cinderella it rather turns one's head to be taken out & treated like a Princess all of a sudden" (June 1864).

Though Alcott seemed to be favoring the "rescued damsel" in this instance, it is clear from my epigraph that she scorns the notion that "nature has defined her [woman's] sphere" and attributes her restricted situation to a lack of education and opportunity. As one of the first advocates for the idea that gender traits are socially constructed rather than biologically determined, Alcott taunts the opposite sex with the injunction to educate women, so that "coming generations will know and be able to define more clearly what is a 'woman's sphere' than these benighted men who now try to do it" (Alcott to Maria S. Porter, 1874).

Margaret Fuller experienced the same contradictory feelings as Alcott over the notion of separate spheres, and she expressed them most eloquently in *Woman in the Nineteenth Century,* where she tries to break the binary code of male and female social roles through a discourse bordering on androgyny. As Whitman tried to queer the spheres and allow gender mobility through poetry, Fuller tried to collapse the spheres more prosaically—through a language of logic. Merging the traits often assigned stereotypically to either males or females, Fuller states that "there is no wholly masculine man, no purely feminine woman" (116). Just as "fluid hardens to solid, solid rushes to fluid," so gender traits "are perpetually passing into one another" (116). Accordingly, she advocates an education for both sexes that will unleash a "divine energy" so that "no discordant collision, but a ravishing harmony of the spheres, would ensue" (37). Though on a rational level she believes that this ravishing union is possible, she does finally preach a message of separatism, witnessed in her concluding image of the Virgin/Mother in her separate sphere; but this isolation appears to be a necessary though temporary state of being prior to an ultimately successful union (her motto being that there must be "units" before there can be "union"). However, as one of the earliest proponents of the personal realm being equal to the political, she suggested that consciousness-raising in men would come about through women's efforts—in personal relationships. Yet in her letters from Italy, after Fuller had become a mother, a cumbersome vision of maternal duties does seem to plague her. Similarly, though liberated writers like Fanny Fern and, later, Charlotte Perkins Gilman appear to have succeeded in the public realm through various public postures and voices as writers and as speakers, they always feel constrained by the obligation of maternity and are never free of the guilt and burden wrought by the cult of domesticity; the split between public and private selves could never be resolved for them, and it continued to haunt them throughout their writing careers.

The trends of early political feminist voices in the nineteenth century, such as Lydia Maria Child, Angelina and Sarah Grimké, and Catherine Beecher, reflect the development of the politics of the "separate sphere" claimants (or disclaimers) in the last three decades, from the 1960s onward. The rhetoric seems to emphasize woman's place in the home by showing its empowering or disempowering effect on women, or it attempts to reconfigure the spheres to emphasize the commonalities shared by men and women. Sometimes, more recently, the "spheres" rhetoric seeks to emphasize the divergent voices of women of the nineteenth century to debunk the notion of any one separate sphere.

Literary critics and historians of the 1960s and 1970s who analyzed woman's sphere were focused so myopically on middle-class women's separate sphere of the home that class wars or divisive economic factors were not acknowledged. Indeed, for working women the public space was always accessible, and for African-American women slaves, working side by side with African-American men did not cause any gender inequality. As Fuller already knew and acknowledged in her treatise on nineteenth-century women, one could not essentialize woman's position in society, for women of oppressed classes were always privy to the realm of male activity: "Not only the Indian Squaw carries the burdens of the camp, but the favorites of Louis XIV, accompany him in his journeys, and the washerwoman stands at her tub, and carries home her work at all seasons, and in all states of health. Those who think the physical circumstances of Woman would make a part in the affairs of national government unsuitable, are by no means those who think it impossible for negresses to endure field-work, even during pregnancy, or for sempstresses to go through their killing labors" (34–35). Ironically, this passage shows how women of the underclass, as prostitutes, servants, workers, and slaves, have more access to the public affairs of men than "privileged women" because they are in touch with their bodies, albeit their more physical presence among men also indicated a greater threat to their safety and well-being. Yet even middle-class women who had transgressed their boundaries by joining an illicit space, through participation in drama or in a sect, could achieve a type of freedom and voice not granted them in the domestic sphere. Fuller uses the examples of the empowered actresses and women Quaker preachers in her advocacy for women speaking in public. Moreover, like Mary Ryan's reappraisal of public women in American history, Fuller's 1855 treatise points to women's social interaction and public roles in "balls, theaters, meetings for promoting missions, revival meetings and others to which she flies, in hope of an animation for her existence commensurate with what she sees enjoyed by men" (35). Harking back to antiquity, Fuller points to women's appearance in public—in religious festivals, processions, dances, and songs (35)—and calls for this same kind of participation in her own time.

Where was the separate sphere demarcation for those below the middle class or for those daring to bend rules? Sarah Grimké first sympathized with the plight of middle-class white women because of their segregated positions in the household, but then decried the plight of the women of the leisure class by focusing on the women who were really suffering as a result not just of gender spheres but of class spheres. Thus, in Letter VIII of her "Letters on the Equality of the Sexes" (1837), she demonstrates that the woman of the "fashionable" world, when she shows any mental superiority, is "generally shunned and regarded as stepping out of her 'separate sphere,'" a sphere constructed by men (220). Grimké abandons the interests of the domestic realm of the middle-class woman to show a more pressing evil, the oppression of laboring-class women and slaves. She invokes the issue of inequality in pay for women working outside the home as compared to that of working men, as well as the degradation of slave women in the South, and asks how the American woman of leisure can remain apathetic. Indeed, she implicates American women in the degradation, trying to jolt them into accepting responsibility and taking political action. Yet her rhetoric, appropriately enough, is based upon what her readers would have been acquainted with, the language of the cult of domesticity: "Nor does the colored woman suffer alone; the moral purity of the white woman is deeply contaminated" (224). Thus, even in 1837, before Stanton and other suffragists became part of the larger political arena, a campaign was launched to make women politically accountable on an individual, personal basis.

In contrast to the enlightened and politically active Grimké or Fuller, there is a more traditional Catherine Beecher, who argues that woman's rightful place is in the home, where she can exert the most authority over her children and husband, thus leading to the progress of society. In her attack on northern abolitionists, Beecher clearly speaks out against public women: "Woman is to win everything by peace and love. . . . But this is to be all accomplished in the domestic and social circle" (*Essay on Slavery* 110–11). She takes a stand for passivity as she proclaims, "All who act on Christian principles in regard to slavery, believe that in a given period (variously estimated) it will end" (52).

Lydia Maria Child, an outspoken proponent of the rights of slaves and Native Americans, is perhaps most balanced in fostering a win-win situation for both genders, by advocating, like Fuller, a reeducation for both men and women. In her January 1843 "Letter from New York" (Letter XXXIV), she reacted coldly to a lecture by Emerson in which he exhorted women to abandon all their artifices, ornamentation, and frills and to "be, rather than seem." Though Child finds his advice sound, she feels thwarted by his condescending posture and by the double standard he is preaching. In Child's eyes, "*Men* were exhorted to *be,* rather than to *seem,* that they might fulfil the sacred mission for which their souls were embodied; . . . but *women* were urged to simplicity and trustfulness, that they might become more *pleasing*" (249). Child is clearly rebelling against woman's being a mere "helpmeet" to her partner. She finally suggests that in an effort to overcome woman's subordination, what is expected from women should also be expected from men, and both will share in the responsibilities from the respective spheres of domestic and worldly activity: "Women will not neglect the care and education of their children, but men will find themselves ennobled and refined by sharing those duties with them" (250–51). Men, in turn, will "receive . . . co-operation and sympathy in the discharge of various other duties, now deemed inappropriate to women" (251). This merging of the two spheres will ensure a better appreciation of home by men and of the business world by women. Using the prophetic tone characteristic of Fuller and other idealists, Child foresees the beginning of a new era: "The nearer society approaches to divine order, the less separation will there be in the characters, duties, and pursuits of men and women" (250).

Even traditionally patriarchal voices like Emerson's suggested that women's sphere was public, not exclusively private. Emerson feels that women are most talented in the art of conversation, and that conversation represents the highest form of art, the pinnacle of civilization: "Women are, by this [the art of conversation] and their social influence, the civilizers of mankind. What is civilization? I answer, the power of good women" ("Woman" 409). Emerson circles back to the domestic realm as women's locus of power, but he enlarges the sphere of influence from home to society, so that women do become political creatures. Emerson's message echoes that of popular advice manuals for women. *The Young Lady's Own Book* (1833), for example, noted the interdependent roles of woman as the keeper of domestic and social harmony: "Domestic life is a woman's sphere, and it is there that she is most usefully as well as most appropriately employed. But society, too, feels her influence, and owes to her . . . its balance and its tone" (Davis 75).

II
The Evolution of Feminist Thinking about Separate Spheres

Recent proponents of the separate spheres theory borrow the rhetoric of Catharine Beecher—with her emphasis on woman's power (and place) within the home. The other camp, who look outward to woman's public power, use some of the same rhetoric as Lydia Maria Child, the Grimkés, and Margaret Fuller. From the 1990s onward, there has been a tendency to conflate the two spheres. The evolution of the separate spheres theory can be best traced in the thinking of two historians, Nancy Cott and Mary Ryan, who retract their earlier positions of separatism and go the way of convergence.

In 1966 Barbara Welter coined the phrase "the cult of true womanhood" in a landmark essay bearing the same title and reprinted in her *Dimity Convictions*. For the last thirty years we have been reacting to this concept of woman's place in the home as an empowering or debilitating phenomenon. Welter did not invent the ideology of separate spheres, but she did accept the historical phenomenon as quite real, oppressive, and applicable to middle-class women of the nineteenth century. Welter, like other early feminist historians, points to the Industrial Revolution as the cause of the rift between public and private, since men's work took them outside the home and left middle-class women alone, stranded with housework and child-rearing duties, and eventually, later in the century, with increasingly more leisure time. Within the terms of the cult of domesticity, these early historians and literary critics perceived the home as a sacred refuge to which men, beaten down by the business world, could escape after a hard day's work. Successive feminist critics had to work within the parameters of this "cult of true womanhood," and their task, as they saw it, was to define the quality of the domestic space for women. Until recently, the domestic sphere was seen as either quite stifling (if thrust upon women) or as liberating (if constructed by women), and only in terms of how white middle-class women felt about this condition. As Carolyn Johnston describes the situation, "Paradoxically women were both empowered and trapped by being relegated to a separate sphere from men" (25). Similarly, G. M. Goshgarian maintains that the True Woman was both "sovereign" and "subordinate," "chastened and chastening" (59).

In a pivotal essay, "Separate Spheres, Female Worlds, Woman's Place: The Rhetoric of Women's History" (1988), Linda Kerber summarizes in great detail the changing attitudes toward the notion of women's "separate sphere." While it is not necessary to reiterate the extensive history she gives us, I would like to give a brief overview of the changing trends in defining women's sphere or women's space. There has been a move away from separatism to a reconciliation or a blurring of the spheres. Kerber rightly shows how "the boundaries" are becoming "fuzzier" (198), as she calls for an "interactive view of social processes" so as to consider how women's supposedly separate "sphere was socially constructed both *for* and *by* women" (171).

Carroll Smith-Rosenberg, in her influential essay "The Female World of Love and Ritual: Relations between Women in Nineteenth-Century America" (1975), became the spokesperson for the concept of "separate spheres" as a positive phenomenon and revealed the intense and emotionally fulfilling bond that middle-class women created with one other by sharing domestic experiences and duties. In an equally positive appraisal of women's separatism through the domestic sphere, Mary Ryan, in her early work *The Empire of the Mother* (1982), shows the influence of antebellum women on the patriarchal workplace and the "public" world because of their regal stronghold—in the home. As mothers and as authority figures in the private domain and, by extension, as political activists in reform associations, women could forever change the course of history by influencing their children and their husbands.[3]

The upshot of such thinking which promotes a separatist politics for women can be found in works by critics such as Joyce Warren and Josephine Donovan. This reflects an attempt, as Sandra Harding would see it, for "members of marginalized groups," like women, to "name their own experiences *for* themselves" in order to empower themselves (21). In an essay meant to integrate nineteenth-century women into the recognized canon, Warren actually allows the chasm between men and women writers to grow wider by insisting on a different school of writing for women. Arguing for two separate literary modes, with women following a sentimental tradition and men a more individualistic ethos, Warren asks us to "acknowledge the independent existence of their [women's] writings" (15), thereby perpetuating the ideology of separate spheres. Not only does her argument not allow for an overlap between sentimentality and individualism, but it equates the sentimental impulse with the communal impulse. Warren maintains, in a reductionist fashion, that the theme of nineteenth-century women writers' books "negates self-assertion and focuses on selflessness; the author values a sense of community and connectedness rather than the insular life that is portrayed in the novels of the solitary male quest" (15). The connectedness she envisions, in the mode of Smith-Rosenberg, is often not present, as witnessed in the non-communal and strongly individualistic experiences of Sarah Orne Jewett's and Mary Wilkins Freeman's solitary women, who actually flee from the dangers of claustrophobic and dangerous maternal or sisterly bonding.

Yet the myth of benevolent bonding is often perpetuated in separatist criticism to make it appear as if the female communities exist and are successful in women's writing, when they are actually fraught with tension. Josephine Donovan, for example, maintains that "the New England women created a counter world of their own, a rural realm that existed on the margins of patriarchal society, a world that nourished strong, free women" (3).

Donovan's "woman-identified" realism seems rather monolithic and ahistorical by today's standards. Moreover, both Warren and Donovan pit women's community against men's individuality, thereby obliterating any possibility of crossover. On the other hand, Ann R. Shapiro admits that there are differences between heroes of nineteenth-century male American literature and heroines of female American literature, but pointing to the example of unusual heroines, in the many shapes of "slave women and housemaids, rural matriarchs and dissatisfied wives, factory workers and middle-class professionals," she focuses on how they are amazingly similar: the heroines "exhibit the same urge to break with tradition, the same rejection of conventional values, and the same desire for adventure" as the male heroes (3–4). Similarly, Gillian Brown does not imagine such a large gap between male and female spheres as she revises the American concept of individualism in the light of domesticity.

Nuanced and balanced readings of women's sphere which show how the ideology behind the cult of domesticity was subtly subverted by middle-class women include recent works by Susan Harris and Susan Coultrap-McQuin. In *Nineteenth-Century American Women's Novels: Interpretive Strategies* (1990), Harris shows the need to read between the lines of nineteenth-century women's writings. She illustrates how nineteenth-century women authors veiled their critique of existing oppressive conditions for women and their strategies for emancipation under the acceptable and nonthreatening discourse of sentimentality and domesticity, and explains how nineteenth-century women readers would have interpreted these novels subversively. In her reconfiguration of nineteenth-century women writers, Coultrap-McQuin shows that, paradoxically, women authors were able to enter the public realm, represented by the paternalistic world of publishing, by adhering to behavior consistent with that of True Womanhood, that is, cooperation and moral stewardship. Her analysis builds upon that of Mary Kelley, who explored, early on, the intersections of public and private in writing women's lives: "Their perspective was private and familial, their allegiance was to the domestic sphere, but they were also women who, out of step with their culture's past, wrote in public and necessarily about private, domestic female lives" (ix).

Critics have recently contested or disclaimed the "Cult of True Womanhood." Frances Cogan has argued for a definition of "Real Womanhood" that encompasses the actual and not idealized experiences of nineteenth-century women. This other popular ideal—Real Womanhood, which coexisted with that of True Womanhood—fostered "intelligence, physical fitness and health, self-sufficiency, economic self-reliance, and careful marriage" and went outside the separate sphere of domesticity to claim "a unique sphere of action and duty for women . . . one vastly extended" (4). Similarly, in a most compelling recantation of her earlier work and introduction to her second edition of *The Bonds of Womanhood,* Nancy Cott admits that in the first edition she was so absorbed in gender constructions that she "succumbed to some extent to the universalizing pretensions of the discourse of domesticity" (xxii). To rectify her reading, she takes into account in her revisionist text more "complex self-definitions" of class, race, and ethnicity, which lead to "dissonance and subversion within the discourse of domesticity" and "multiple possibilities for action" (xxii).

Most recently, literary and historical critics have reexamined the paradox of separate spheres quite satisfactorily, and their readings show a way out of an essentialist perdition for women. For example, Nina Baym, in her *American Women Writers and the Work of History, 1790–1860* (1995), has shown that "public and private spheres were metaphorical rather than actual places, that public and private were different ways of behaving in the same space" (11). And she points out "the inadequacy of current gender-based distinctions between the public and private spheres (11). Indeed, in analyzing nineteenth-century women historians' works, Baym maintains that these authors were constantly eroding the boundaries between "domestic and public spheres" (1) and concludes that the history-writing women are "far from conforming to any paradigm of sequestered, submissive, passive domesticity that we might patronizingly attempt to impose on them according to some misguided millennial narrative of our own" (239). Historian Mary Ryan shares similar liberating patterns of thought when she discusses the fine line between public and private spaces in her recent study of nineteenth-century women, *Women in Public.* Such thinking that redefines public space has allowed critics to explore other opportunities women of varying classes had in the public realm, whether that be as laborers, actresses, reformers, political activists, prostitutes, or simply shoppers, theatergoers, or park-strollers.

Countless current histories have been written to accommodate this new image of a public woman. Even though some middle- and upper-middle-class women have been perceived as political activists, as members of reform movements and progressive societies, revisionist histories (e.g., Ginzberg, Scott) broaden women's political arena and show aspirations and social change that cut across class lines. Reconstructions of women's work (Boydston, Dublin, Porter) show how women of all classes were engaged in work outside the home more often than has been previously acknowledged and analyze how women's domestic work could be construed as political. As Jeanne Boydston points out, "Poor and working-class mothers and wives were ever-present and resourceful agents in the petty commerce of the streets" (88). Moreover, even some middle-class women, like their working-class counterparts, helped "bolster . . . their families' incomes by working in shops that their husbands presumedly owned and operated" (89). Dolores Hayden posits that most feminists at the end of the nineteenth century attempted to "overcome the split between domestic life and public life created by industrial capitalism" (4). Hayden asserts that there was no sharp delineation between women working on "public, or social, issues" and those working on "private, or family, issues" (4); feminists attempted to "increase women's rights in the home and simultaneously bring homelike nurturing into public life" (5).

Home seems to spill out into the streets in various accounts of women within urban spaces, such as Deborah Epstein Nord's *Walking the Victorian Streets* and Christine Stansell's *City of Women,* which try to decipher women's presence and activity on streets, as both spectacle and participant, and depending on men's view of them either as seductive or as sexually vulnerable, as a dangerous and endangered species. Considering that the term "public woman" was perceived in a dubious light, it is no wonder that, as Glenna Matthews asserts, there was no "real symmetry between public men and public women" (*Rise of Public Woman* 5). Barbara Bardes and Suzanne Gossett focus on similar themes in their reconstruction of a politically empowered nineteenth-century woman—"the intersection of the public and private spheres, the power of woman's voice, and the threat of the female body" (12)—elements which they perceive as intertwined.

Nineteenth-century women like Catherine Beecher and Harriet Beecher Stowe, who promulgated the metaphor of home as a social sphere of power, have their disciples in this century, but with a twist. "So uniformly accepted a symbol of middle-class values had the home become . . . by midcentury," asserts Glenna Matthews, "that it was a logical rallying point for those who wanted to change the world and, in particular, improve the lot of women" (*"Just a Housewife"* 44). In an obviously revised form, this metaphor has been revived, so that Elizabeth Barnes makes the connection between the construction of the family and the model of the ideal political state in *States of Sympathy: Seduction and Democracy in the American Novel.* Barnes analyzes sentimental literature to show "the ways in which aspirations of 'domestic' union (and the conflation of political and private spheres implicit in this concept) work to organize narratives of seduction and the extent to which seductive practices inform domestic stories" (13). Julia Stern, in *The Plight of Feeling,* also merges the realms of domesticity and politics as she reevaluates the emotional excess in eighteenth-century sentimental and gothic literature to prophesy the political rifts in the mid-nineteenth century. Similarly, Shirley Samuels shows how the political and domestic realms converge in *Romances of the Republic,* where she goes beyond the separate spheres concept to examine how "romances of the republic present women and the family paradoxically as at once embodiments and abstractions of national values" (14). Boundaries are perceived as "permeable," so that "the family was both made public and publicized" (16). Thus, the most recent reevaluations of women's and men's realms or private and public roles have focused on the intersecting spaces between spheres.

Nina Baym asserts that home became more of a "restraint and a constraint" after the Civil War and that there were fewer chances for women to effect change from the home (*Woman's Fiction* 50). But this change can be construed as positive, as Mary Ryan, in *Women in Public*, observes an increased activity of women in public rituals and processions in the late nineteenth century. Certainly, the number of recently published collections about women's activities in the Civil War (e.g., Yellin and Van Horne, Clinton and Silber) portray antebellum women as abolitionists or as members of antislavery societies, and women during the Civil War as spies, soldiers, nurses, and political activists. These myriad functions attest to the public role women played, whether it was a nurturing or aggressive role (cf. accounts by Hannah Ropes, nurse, and Sarah Rosetta Wakeman, soldier, in Brumgardt and Burgess, respectively).

Moreover, chronology is significant in the rendering of recent reconstructions of womanhood, especially of African-American women's experiences. Obviously, recent examinations of class and race have allowed us to go beyond the narrow confines of the white, middle-class woman's experience, and these explorations have helped to erode the framework of the cult of domesticity. Anne Boylan discusses the problems antebellum African-American women of the North encountered in their establishment of antislavery societies. Though these African-American women, most often segregated from the abolitionist groups of white women, "never endorsed standards of feminine respectability as fully as did white women," they did adopt certain standards "in order to establish their claim to feminine virtue" and "found themselves constrained by narrow definitions of appropriate behavior" (135). African-American women were in a double bind in feeling compelled to conform to and simultaneously rebel against the cult of domesticity. In accounts of post–Civil War freedwomen, one notes a common bond, albeit negative, with urban white women, that being their sexual vulnerability: "Emancipation escalated the degree of sexual violence to which they might be subjected" (Clinton 318). As Clinton points out, though, freedwomen did not have the "luxury" of finding protection within the domestic sphere (318). In her recent account of African-American women reinventing their lives in the Reconstructionist South, Tera Hunter comes up with a picture very similar to Carroll Smith-Rosenberg's image of sisterly bonding for white women in their separate sphere. Though burdened in their roles as domestic laborers, the freedwomen were able to construct their own community of work, recreation, activism, and protest. Thus, in some ways, the experiences of African-American women reflect those of white women trying to break away from a restrictive cult of domesticity.

To accommodate the many changes in the reassessment of shifting spheres, historians and literary critics have had to refashion and collapse the meanings of public and private. Mary Beth Norton has offered us the best revisionist definitions of public and private in her history of "Founding Mothers and Fathers" of American society. Though she bases her reformulations on colonial American history, her frame of reference could still pertain to the arbitrary nineteenth-century definitions of public and private. Apparently, colonial Americans did not equate the private realm with women or with family, but rather there was a gender difference between a "formal" and an "informal" public, with the former pertaining to the official authority of men (church, state) and the latter pertaining to the general community (18–24).

Using Jürgen Habermas's opposition between the public and official spheres, Nina Baym shows how nineteenth-century women were part of the "nonofficial public sphere" as a result of their ability to shape public opinion through their influence in the home (*American Women Writers* 6). Even early in her career, Baym tried to balance the gender equation by pointing out the misconceptions wrought by the concept of separate spheres and by revealing the intersections between the two realms, domestic and public. She maintained that the notion of "separate spheres" was more problematic to twentieth-century women than to the nineteenth-century women who had allegedly suffered through an oppressive and sequestered home life: nineteenth-century women authors "recognized that home and the world were different," but unlike the male observers of the time and the later generations of subjective critics, "they did not really see these as 'separate spheres'" (*Woman's Fiction* 48). Asserting that the home is not a "space" but rather "a system of human relations" (49), Baym suggests the possibilities for women's public influence: "If worldly values could dominate the home, perhaps the direction of influence could be reversed so that home values dominated the world" (48).

Many historians of American women have questioned the value of "a gendered public/private dichotomy," and new interpretations "explore how women's consciousness and political activities reflect the links between the public and private realms" (Helly and Reverby 2, 3). In her revisionist book of women's history (1994), Ann-Louise Shapiro states, "It has become clear that by keeping 'the private' from a political analysis, the public/private dichotomy has forestalled an analysis of relations between women and men" (7). Even as early as 1980, Michelle Zimbalist Rosaldo, in her anthropological study of gender roles, denounced the discourse of separate spheres and remarked upon the shortcomings of "models based upon two opposed spheres" which fostered a system whereby "women must be understood not in terms of relationship—with other women and with men—but of difference and apartness" (qtd. in Kerber 196).

III
Overlapping Spheres: The "Neutral Territory" of This Volume

The thirteen essays in this collection expose some of the problems created by bifurcating the world into separate spheres and present new ways of revising literary history to show how the separate spheres were not always so separate. The contributors consider the ongoing dialogue between male and female writers about gender, race, and class concerns, showing the intersections and deconstructing the boundaries between public and private, male and female, political and domestic, rational and intuitive, violent and passive, demonic and angelic, and any other split constructed by the fixed image of separate spheres. The essays make us question hard-and-fast definitions of literary genres and traditions; as they collapse the gender spheres, they expand the canon.[4]

One way to think of an organizing principle behind this collection would be to imagine how we teach our texts in a nineteenth-century American literature course. The general movement of the text is to challenge the stereotypes wrought by the separate spheres theory and the binary oppositions set forth by such thinking, and to reevaluate perceived differences by blurring or shifting the boundaries. There is an attempt to overlap, if not unite, the "separate" gender spheres of female domesticity and worldly male experience by including essays that emphasize the connectedness between old male canonical texts and new female or "other" canonical works. The vision of this book is in harmony with Paul Lauter's method of teaching by pairing up male and female authors to show "how radically similar their literary origins were, how they work with closely related assumptions, materials, and sentiments" (296).

The essays in this volume are organized into four sections, based upon the critics' thematic approaches to the overlapping spheres. In section one, "Intertextuality and Authorial Interconnectedness," the critics show how male and female authors converse with each other across the gender gap. The cultural materials with which male and female authors work are similar, and their sociopolitical interests intersect. Lucinda L. Damon-Bach's essay, "To

Be a 'Parlor Soldier': Susan Warner's Answer to Emerson's 'Self-Reliance,' "
explores how Warner's fiction both challenges and adapts some of Emerson's
ideals, in particular the ways in which women could be more self-reliant.
Novels like *Queechy* (1852), Damon-Bach argues, blur distinctions between
the "spheres" of men's and women's education and work, and in the end
reclaim and revamp Emerson's negative portrayal of those who are, by destiny or by choice, "parlor soldiers." Katharine Rodier, in "*Astra Castra:*
Emily Dickinson, Thomas Wentworth Higginson, and Harriet Prescott
Spofford," examines the triangular literary relationship between Dickinson,
Higginson, and Spofford. Enlarging upon Barton Levi St. Armand's discussion of Spofford's influence on Dickinson, Rodier explains how Higginson
is both a mediary figure and a reactive presence in this dynamic. Rodier
presents an interesting study of women's bonding and cross-influencing
through a male patron. In another essay that views Higginson as a pivotal
male figure in women's lives, Karen S. Nulton compares Susie King Taylor's
Reminiscences of the Civil War with Higginson's *Army Life in a Black Regiment* in "The War of Susie King Taylor." Nulton shows that Taylor is able
to gain "a political voice" not usually accessible to women through her
involvement in the war; moreover, as a black woman, Taylor can redefine
new boundaries of women's "proper" sphere. In the final essay of this section, "No Separations in the City: The Public-Private Novel and Private-
Public Authorship," Karen E. Waldron shows how three writers—Fanny
Fern, Rebecca Harding Davis, and Stephen Crane—cross gender and genre
boundaries by publicizing "the private" and "by reaching across and through
the presumed separation of spheres" in their journalistic sketches of urban
or industrial life. Emphasizing the shift in the debate from separate spheres
to social determinism and its accompanying tensions, Waldron shows how
critics must reformulate their critical methodologies so as not to ghettoize
works or genres.

In section two, "Body Politics: Framing the Female Body," the critics
analyze woman's empowerment through a growing level of comfort with
her body. These critics challenge the traditional notion and stereotype of
nineteenth-century woman as invalid, vulnerable, or sexless. Rather, they
depict woman taking charge of her body and ultimately of her life. Drawing from Mary S. Gove Nichols's sociological and physiological writings, as
well as from her best-known semi-autobiographical novel, *Mary Lyndon*
(1855), Dawn Keetley shows the intersections between public and private
woman by focusing on the politics of woman's body in her essay, "The Ungendered Terrain of Good Health: Mary Gove Nichols's Rewriting of the
Diseased Institution of Marriage." Keetley examines how Nichols sought to
improve women's health by "changing their view of their own bodies"—by

revealing how those bodies were fundamentally shaped by their social status and by "indissoluble marriage," the institution that was most responsible for enslaving women. Frederick Newberry treats a paradox of a similar nature between women and male medical experts in his essay, "Male Doctors and Female Illness in American Women's Fiction, 1850–1900." In questioning the model of invalidism that was allegedly imposed upon middle-class women by male medical doctors, he takes issue with the now customary view that male physicians helped create an ideology of invalidism among middle- and upper-class women. Newberry finds strong women characters who do not fit into the stereotypical invalid mode; moreover, the physicians, who do not subscribe to the cult of invalidism, are trustworthy, rational, and compassionate toward the female protagonists. Another kind of resistance to the mythmaking of woman's body, this time in terms of her sexuality, is revealed in Darby Lewes's "Gender-Bending: Two Role-Reversal Utopias by Nineteenth-Century Women." Lewes explores two contrasting views of "woman's place" as imagined by two rather obscure female utopian writers, Annie Denton Cridge and Mrs. J. Wood, who predated Charlotte Perkins Gilman's *Herland* (1915) by a good thirty years. The political ideologies expressed in the two utopian works are diametrically opposed and suggest the differing self-perceptions of nineteenth-century women.

In section three, "On the Home Front and Beyond: Domesticity and the Marketplace," the critics show women's traditional role in the household expanding to meet the demands of the marketplace world of men. One woman who goes public after the Civil War is social activist Melusina Fay Peirce, about whose cooperative venture Lisette Nadine Gibson writes in "A Homely Business: Melusina Fay Peirce and Late-Nineteenth-Century Cooperative Housekeeping." In Peirce's manifesto, "Co-Operative House-keeping," published in the *Atlantic Monthly* between 1868 and 1869 and revised in book form in 1884, she calls into question the underlying tenets of the ideology of separate spheres by arguing for a reformulation of work relations within the home and within the business world. Gibson maintains that Peirce was able to bring together the "public" and "private" by embracing two utopian ideals: that of the technological utopia and that of the domestic utopia. Debra Bernardi shows the blurring of domestic boundaries by examining the connections between national and international issues expressed in turn-of-the-century American literature. In "Narratives of Domestic Imperialism: The African-American Home in the *Colored American Magazine* and the Novels of Pauline Hopkins, 1900–1903," Bernardi examines how imperialism colors representations of the home—both national homeland and private household and shows how African-American formulations of home centered around images of violence and invasion "garnered from the imperialist, racial controversies of the day." In Hopkins's novels women are able to resist invasion by a type of "domestic imperialism" which Bernardi terms an "invasion of influence"—a type of gentle invasion that would empower African-American women. In the third selection of this section, "Public Women, Private Acts: Gender and Theater in Turn-of-the-Century American Novels," Jennifer Costello Brezina focuses on the theater as an urban site that merges or blurs boundaries between women's domestic and public spheres. In works published between 1890 and 1906 by Dreiser, Norris, Glasgow, and Dunbar, the private/public split is problematized by the use of "female characters in public space to embody the intense cultural shifts that modernity and rapid urbanization were bringing to American society."

In section four, "Sentimental Subversions," the critics show how women writers challenge notions of canonicity by subverting the sentimental genre imposed upon them. Indeed, their writing style and thematic concerns overlap with those of male authors. The sentimental female authors have much in common with their male contemporaries, and their work shares qualities of male trends in thinking and writing (i.e., transcendentalism, realism, naturalism). Thus, they go beyond the sentimental school of writing to which they have been traditionally relegated. The doubleness of woman's voice is seen in terms of "balance" in Mary Louise Kete's essay, "Gender Valences of Transcendentalism: The Pursuit of Idealism in Elizabeth Oakes-Smith's 'The Sinless Child,'" in which Kete gives proper recognition to the author Elizabeth Oakes-Smith, a true American Renaissance woman, and places her in the context of male transcendentalist writers. In her analysis of "The Sinless Child" (1841), Kete makes a case for reassessing transcendentalism by including female transcendentalist writers like Oakes-Smith in the canon and by paying attention to "the expression of romanticism carrying a feminine inflection." In "Sentimental Epistemologies in *Uncle Tom's Cabin* and *The House of the Seven Gables*," Marianne Noble, borrowing from Jane Tompkins's grouping of Hawthorne with sentimental writers, shows how sentimental writers such as Hawthorne, Stowe, and Fern were indebted to the Scottish Common Sense school of philosophy, which allowed them to "affirm an optimistic belief in an innate moral sense accessed through feelings." Through the example of Hawthorne's appreciation of sentimental writing, Noble maintains that "the separation of men's and women's spheres is, in many cases, a fiction produced by twentieth-century historiography." The book ends, appropriately, with a case study of how a woman's novel, Bess Streeter Aldrich's *A Lantern in Her Hand* (1928), considered a best-seller for many years, fell into oblivion and was then recanonized in the 1990s. Denise D. Knight's essay, "'I Try to Make the Reader Feel': The Resurrection of Bess Streeter Aldrich's *A Lantern in Her Hand* and the Politics of the Literary Canon," shows how Aldrich's blending of romanticism, realism, and naturalism challenges our assumptions about pigeonholing literature into "separate movements" and reveals the dangers of typing sentimental novels as women's domain.

It is my hope that the essays in this collection lead to a transfigured classroom, one in which converging male and female concerns in the overlapping section of gender spheres are addressed. As Tom Quirk and Gary Scharnhorst have pointed out, "The college classroom is the place where the canon is not only most importantly formed and perpetuated through the distribution of texts, but also where the circuit of repetition and perpetuation can be most effectively broken" (18). University professors have been blessed with the proliferation of women's readers on the market.[5] However, to do credit to the resurrected women writers, it would be wise to teach them not separately, but in relationship to their male counterparts. By marketing anthologies that basically ghettoize women writers, it might, unfortunately, be possible to perpetuate the separatist trend in the classroom—by offering courses only on nineteenth-century women writers, outside the common cultural context shared with male writers. And finally, since the literary and historical reassessments of gender are always in flux, the picture presented in this volume is subject to change. Nancy Cott summarizes the dilemma most eloquently in her preface to her revised edition of *The Bonds of Womanhood:* "Notions of gender are continually mutable—historical products always in the making and remaking—in every time and place being forged, disseminated, contested, reworked, and in some guise reaffirmed" (xxviii). Inevitably, the next generation's re-creation of woman's place in nineteenth-century literary history will reflect their personal understanding of gender and class in their own time.

Notes

1. Since I first wrote this introduction, several important works that accord with the vision of this volume have appeared, most notably Laura McCall and Donald Yacovne's *A Shared Experience: Men, Women, and the History of Gender* (1998), which seeks to analyze the "complementary lives of men and women" from a historical point of view and to show how women were "never confined exclusively to a domestic sphere," as historians of the past have insisted (2). See also Cathy Davidson's special issue of *American Literature,* "No More Separate Spheres," which actually has critics align themselves in a debate between the spheres paradigm of the past and the no-more-spheres paradigm of the present. Yet to set up another binary view is

dangerous; it is more productive to analyze the overlap of private and public, of female and male, than to create an artificial either-or situation.

2. See, for example, seminal works on men's history by Michael Kimmel, David Leverenz, and E. Anthony Rotundo, which allow us to see the other side of men's history—one fraught with tensions and anxieties about living up to some culturally imposed ideals about manhood. For another take on the personal side of men's history, see also the collection by Mark Carnes and Clyde Griffen. In many ways, the 1960s feminist rallying cry that the "personal is political" has evolved into an unspoken but nevertheless tacitly understood male manifesto that the political is indeed personal.

Most recently, Peter Stearns and Jan Lewis's *An Emotional History of the United States* attempts to make the emotional life as important as politics (and shows how they are interrelated). Essays in that collection also reveal the complementary aspects of men's and women's emotional lives (e.g., in mourning practices and marriage).

3. It may be that, as Fuller declared that women needed to be units before there could be a union of the sexes, the early stages of feminist criticism required this "separatist thinking." Early critics such as Barbara Harris and Rosalind Rosenberg felt it was only the unusual or educated woman who could overstep boundaries in the nineteenth or early twentieth century.

4. For discussions of the dissolution of boundaries in literary genre and gender, see Karen Kilcup's critical reader, which discusses the hybridity of women's literature, and Shirley Samuels's collection, which looks at the political implications of sentimental literature. In this volume, see especially essays by Brezina, Damon-Bach, Kete, Knight, Noble, and Waldron, who show the connections between men's and women's writing and between literary genres and movements.

5. See, for example, the recent anthologies by Karen Kilcup, Elaine Showalter, Barbara Solomon, and Glennis Stephenson. These works, the children of the Fetterley and Freibert and White anthologies, still seem to err in making women's stories exclusive and outside the realm of men's writing—thus the further ghettoization of women's literature and experiences for college students.

Like some other feminist critics, I find the notion of "difference" disturbing. In her early essay "What's New in Woman's History?" (1986), Linda Gordon prophetically discusses her fear that "difference is becoming a substitute, an accommodating, affable, and even lazy substitute for opposition" (27). She adds that "one of the worst things about the emphasis on difference is that it allows the development of new 'fields' and the adoption of new styles of critique that do not fundamentally challenge the structure of the disciplines" (27). Thus, the oppressive status quo is left intact. She suggests that we define women's studies so that there are not "pockets of women's literature, women's psychology, women's morality, and so forth" (27). As Dorothy Helly and Susan Reverby (1992) point out, "the oppression of women has been encoded or disguised by our employment of the concept of divided spheres" (1).

Works Cited

Alcott, Louisa May. *The Journals of Louisa May Alcott*. Ed. Joel Myerson and Daniel Shealy. Assoc. ed. Madeleine B. Stern. Boston: Little, Brown, 1989.

———. *The Selected Letters of Louisa May Alcott*. Ed. Joel Myerson, Daniel Shealy, and Madeleine B. Stern. Boston: Little Brown, 1987.

Bardes, Barbara, and Suzanne Gossett. *Declarations of Independence: Women and Political Power in Nineteenth-Century American Fiction*. New Brunswick, NJ: Rutgers UP, 1990.

Barnes, Elizabeth. *States of Sympathy: Seduction and Democracy in the American Novel*. New York: Columbia UP, 1997.

Baym, Nina. *American Women Writers and the Work of History, 1790–1860*. New Brunswick, NJ: Rutgers UP, 1995.

———. *Woman's Fiction: A Guide to Novels by and about Women in America, 1820–1870*. Ithaca, NY: Cornell UP, 1978.

Beecher, Catherine E. *An Essay on Slavery and Abolitionism, with Reference to the Duty of American Females*. New York: Books for Libraries P, 1970.

———. *A Treatise on Domestic Economy*. 1841. New York: Source Book, 1970.

Beecher, Catherine E., and Harriet Beecher Stowe. *The American Woman's Home, Or, Principles of Domestic Science*. Hartford: Stowe-Day Foundation, 1994.

Boydston, Jeanne. *Home and Work: Housework, Wages, and the Ideology of Labor in the Early Republic*. New York: Oxford UP, 1990.

Boylan, Anne M. "Benevolence and Antislavery Activity among African American Women in New York and Boston, 1820–1840." Yellin and Van Horne 119–38.

Brown, Gillian. *Domestic Individualism: Imagining Self in Nineteenth-Century America*. Berkeley: U of California P, 1990.

Brumgardt, John R., ed. *Civil War Nurse: The Diary and Letters of Hannah Ropes*. Knoxville: U of Tennessee P, 1980.

Burgess, Lauren Cook, ed. *An Uncommon Solider: The Civil War Letters of Sarah Rosetta Wakeman, alias Private Lyons Wakeman, 153rd Regiment, New York State Volunteers*. New York: Oxford UP, 1994.

Carnes, Mark C., and Clyde Griffen, eds. *Meanings For Manhood: Constructions of Masculinity in Victorian America*. Chicago: U of Chicago P, 1990.

Child, Lydia Maria. *Letters from New York*. 1845. Freeport, NY: Books for Libraries P, 1970.

Clinton, Catherine. "Reconstructing Freedwomen." Clinton and Silber 306–19.

Clinton, Catherine, and Nina Silber, eds. *Divided Houses: Gender and the Civil War*. New York: Oxford UP, 1992.

Cogan, Frances B. *All-American Girl: The Ideal of Real Womanhood in Mid-Nineteenth-Century America.* Athens: U of Georgia P, 1989.

Cott, Nancy F. *The Bonds of Womanhood: "Woman's Sphere" in New England, 1780–1835.* 2nd ed., with new preface. New Haven: Yale UP, 1997.

Coultrap-McQuin, Susan. *Doing Literary Business: American Women Writers in the Nineteenth Century.* Chapel Hill: U of North Carolina P, 1990.

Davidson, Cathy N., ed. "No More Separate Spheres!" Special issue. *American Literature* 70.3 (1998): 443–64.

Davis, David Brian, ed. *Antebellum American Culture: An Interpretive Anthology.* University Park: Penn State UP, 1997.

Donovan, Josephine. *New England Local Color Literature: A Women's Tradition.* 1983. New York: Continuum, 1988.

Dublin, Thomas. *Transforming Women's Work: New England Lives in the Industrial Revolution.* Ithaca: Cornell UP, 1994.

Emerson, Ralph Waldo. "Woman." *Miscellanies.* New York: AMS Press, 1968. 402–26.

Fern, Fanny. *Ruth Hall and Other Writings.* Ed. Joyce W. Warren. New Brunswick, NJ: Rutgers UP, 1988.

Fetterley, Judith, ed. *Provisions: A Reader from Nineteenth-Century American Women.* Bloomington: Indiana UP, 1985.

Freibert, Lucy M., and Barbara A. White, eds. *Hidden Hands: An Anthology of American Women Writers, 1790–1870.* New Brunswick, NJ: Rutgers UP, 1985.

Fuller, Margaret. *Woman in the Nineteenth Century.* New York: Norton, 1971.

Ginzberg, Lori D. *Women and the Work of Benevolence: Morality, Class, and Politics in the Nineteenth-Century United States.* New Haven: Yale UP, 1990.

Gordon, Linda. "What's New in Women's History?" *Feminist Studies, Critical Studies.* Ed. Teresa de Lauretis. Bloomington: Indiana UP, 1986. 20–32.

Goshgarian, G. M. *To Kiss the Chastening Rod: Domestic Fiction and Sexual Ideology in the American Renaissance.* Ithaca: Cornell UP, 1992.

Grimké, Sarah M. "Letters on the Equality of the Sexes and the Condition of Woman." *The Public Years of Sarah and Angelina Grimké: Selected Writings, 1835–1839.* Ed. Larry Ceplair. New York: Columbia UP, 1989. 204–72.

Harding, Sandra. "Starting Thought from Women's Lives: Eight Resources for Maximizing Objectivity." *Styles of Cultural Activism: From Theory and Pedagogy to Women, Indians, and Communism.* Ed. Philip Goldstein. Newark: U of Delaware P, 1994. 17–31.

Harris, Barbara J. *Beyond Her Sphere: Women and the Professions in American History.* Westport, CN: Greenwood P, 1978.

Harris, Susan K. *Nineteenth-Century American Women's Novels: Interpretive Strategies.* New York: Cambridge UP, 1990.

Hayden, Dolores. *The Grand Domestic Revolution: A History of Feminist Designs for American Homes, Neighborhoods, and Cities.* Cambridge, MA: Cambridge UP, 1985.

Helly, Dorothy O., and Susan M. Reverby. "Introduction: Converging on History." *Gendered Domains: Rethinking Public and Private in Women's History*. Ed. Dorothy O. Helly and Susan M. Reverby. Ithaca: Cornell UP, 1992. 1–27.

Hunter, Tera W. *To 'Joy My Freedom: Southern Black Women's Lives and Labors after the Civil War*. Cambridge: Harvard UP, 1997.

Johnston, Carolyn. *Sexual Power: Feminism and the Family in America*. Tuscaloosa: U of Alabama P, 1992.

Kelley, Mary. *Private Woman, Public Stage: Literary Domesticity in Nineteenth-Century America*. New York: Oxford UP, 1984.

Kerber, Linda K. "Separate Spheres, Female Worlds, Woman's Place: The Rhetoric of Women's History." *Toward an Intellectual History of Women*. Chapel Hill: U of North Carolina P, 1997. 159–99.

Kilcup, Karen, ed. *Nineteenth-Century American Women Writers: A Critical Reader*. Malden, MA: Blackwell, 1998.

———, ed. *Nineteenth-Century American Women Writers: An Anthology*. Malden, MA: Blackwell, 1997.

Kimmel, Michael. *Manhood in America: A Cultural History*. New York: Free P, 1996.

Lauter, Paul. "Teaching Nineteenth-Century Women Writers." *The (Other) American Traditions: Nineteenth-Century Women Writers*. Ed. Joyce W. Warren. New Brunswick, NJ: Rutgers UP, 1993. 280–303.

Leverenz, David. *Manhood and the American Renaissance*. Ithaca: Cornell UP, 1989.

Matthews, Glenna. *"Just a Housewife": The Rise and Fall of Domesticity in America*. New York: Oxford UP, 1987.

———. *The Rise of Public Woman: Woman's Power and Woman's Place in the United States, 1630–1970*. New York: Oxford UP, 1992.

McCall, Laura, and Donald Yacovne, eds. Introduction. *A Shared Experience: Men, Women, and the History of Gender*. New York: New York UP, 1998. 1–15.

Nord, Deborah Epstein. *Walking the Victorian Streets: Women, Representation, and the City*. Ithaca: Cornell UP, 1995.

Norton, Mary Beth. *Founding Mothers and Fathers: Gendered Power and the Forming of American Society*. New York: Knopf, 1996.

Porter, Susan L., ed. *Women of the Commonwealth: Work, Family, and Social Change in Nineteenth-Century Massachusetts*. Amherst: U of Massachusetts P, 1996.

Quirk, Tom, and Gary Scharnhorst, eds. *American Realism and the Canon*. Newark: U of Delaware P, 1994.

Rosenberg, Rosalind. *Beyond Separate Spheres: Intellectual Roots of Modern Feminism*. New Haven: Yale UP, 1982.

Rotundo, E. Anthony. *American Manhood: Transformations in Masculinity from the Revolution to the Modern Era*. New York: Basic Books, 1993.

Ryan, Mary P. *The Empire of the Mother: American Writing about Domesticity, 1830–1860*. New York: Harrington Park P, 1985.

——. *Women in Public: Between Banners and Ballots, 1825–1880.* Baltimore: Johns Hopkins UP, 1990.

Samuels, Shirley, ed. *The Culture of Sentiment; Race, Gender, and Sentimentality in Nineteenth-Century America.* New York: Oxford UP, 1992.

——. *Romances of the Republic: Women, the Family, and Violence in the Literature of the Early American Nation.* New York: Oxford UP, 1996.

Scott, Anne Firor. *Natural Allies: Women's Associations in American History.* Urbana: U of Illinois P, 1993.

Shapiro, Ann-Louise, ed. and intro. *Feminists Revision History.* New Brunswick, NJ: Rutgers UP, 1994.

Shapiro, Ann R. *Unlikely Heroines: Nineteenth-Century American Women Writers and the Woman Question.* New York: Greenwood P, 1987.

Showalter, Elaine, ed. *Scribbling Women: Short Stories by Nineteenth-Century American Women.* New Brunswick, NJ: Rutgers UP, 1996.

Smith-Rosenberg, Carroll. *Disorderly Conduct: Visions of Gender in Victorian America.* New York: Oxford UP, 1985.

Solomon, Barbara H., ed. *Rediscoveries: American Short Stories by Women, 1832–1916.* New York: Mentor, 1994.

Stansell, Christine. *City of Women: Sex and Class in New York, 1789–1860.* Urbana: U of Illinois P, 1987.

Stearns, Peter N., and Jan Lewis, eds. *An Emotional History of the United States.* New York: New York UP, 1998.

Stephenson, Glennis, ed. *Nineteenth-Century Stories by Women: An Anthology.* Lewiston, NY: Broadview Literary Texts, 1993.

Stern, Julia A. *The Plight of Feeling: Sympathy and Dissent in the Early American Novel.* Chicago: U of Chicago P, 1997.

Tompkins, Jane. *Sensational Designs: The Cultural Work of American Fiction, 1790–1860.* New York: Oxford UP, 1985.

Warren, Joyce A. "Introduction: Canons and Canon Fodder." *The (Other) American Traditions.* Ed. Joyce Warren. New Brunswick, NJ: Rutgers UP, 1993. 1–28.

Welter, Barbara. *Dimity Convictions: The American Woman in the Nineteenth Century.* Athens: Ohio UP, 1976.

Yellin, Jean Fagan, and John C. Van Horne, eds. *The Abolitionist Sisterhood: Women's Political Culture in Antebellum America.* Ithaca: Cornell UP, 1994.

PART I

Intertextuality and
Authorial Interconnectedness

To Be a "Parlor Soldier": Susan Warner's Answer to Emerson's "Self-Reliance"

LUCINDA L. DAMON-BACH

We are afraid of truth, afraid of fortune, afraid of death, and afraid of each other. Our age yields no great and perfect persons. We want men and women who shall renovate life and our social state. . . . Our housekeeping is mendicant, our arts, our occupations, our marriages, our religion we have not chosen, but society has chosen for us. We are parlor soldiers. We shun the rugged battle of fate, where strength is born.
—Ralph Waldo Emerson, "Self-Reliance" (161)

The thought of his words had given her courage, or strength, to go beyond her usual reserve in speaking . . . and she thought her words had done good.
—Fleda, in Susan Bogert Warner's *Queechy* (615)

In the winter of 1846–47, just a year prior to the period of extreme poverty that would force Susan Bogert Warner literally to take her fate in her hands and begin writing *The Wide, Wide World,* Susan and her sister Anna spent two months with the Bruen family in Boston, during which they talked and dined with many notable nineteenth-century figures. Warner's journal entries and letters home indicate that she especially enjoyed the intellectual stimulation of her extended visit; she was, in particular, "glad of the practice in *arguing*" which her time in Boston afforded (her emphasis). In particular, discussion concerned "mental equality or inequality between the sexes."[1] "[The visit] has really been excellent in this point," she stressed in one of her many letters to her father and aunt back in Cold Springs, New York, "teaching me to hear absurdity, falsehood, and mischief propounded, in various forms, degrees, and modifications . . . and [to] reply with some measure of patience and moderation; virtues which, you know, in old times I was by no means wont to exercise on similar occasions" (*SW* 251).

In the same letter in which she celebrates the pleasingly argumentative nature of her visit, Warner describes a dinner party for eighteen that included "Catharine Sedgwick, Mr. and Mrs. Minot [publisher of the *North American Review*] . . . Mr. and Mrs. (Mayor) Quincy, Mr. Agassiz the great naturalist, and Mr. Emerson the great schoolmaster" (*SW* 251). Elaborating on this particular occasion, her initial meeting with Agassiz and Emerson, Warner added, "Mr. Agassiz is a perfectly charming man, really most agreeable in his whole appearance and manners. Mr. Emerson I didn't fancy" (*SW* 251–52).

An avid amateur botanist—Susan and Anna owned a microscope and skillfully drew studies of their local flora—Warner had several lengthy conversations with Agassiz over the next few months and grew to admire him greatly, but this dinner party seems to have concluded her face-to-face encounters with Emerson. Whether Warner was put off primarily by Emerson's appearance, his manners, or his ideas, she does not specify; that he may have been one of those with whom she "practiced arguing" seems evident in the book she began composing a year later, in which her apparent antipathy is played out through her punningly named character Miss Fortune Emerson. Throughout *The Wide, Wide World* (1850), the heroine, Ellen Montgomery, is tried both physically and spiritually by her aptly named aunt, who seems to be a caricature of Emersonian ideals, especially those expressed in "Self-Reliance" (1841). In his interpretation of Miss Fortune Emerson's name, David Leverenz reasonably concludes that Warner's aim is parody: "Any woman would find it a 'misfortune' to be an Emerson, self-reliant, taking responsibility for her own life" (181). Yet, as James Albrecht suggests in his recent look at Ralph Ellison's allusions to Emerson in *Invisible Man,* such satire may not be a rejection of Emerson's individualism but instead a "dual gesture of critique and affiliation" (47). Like Ellison, Warner seems, in Albrecht's words, to "reject canonical Emersonianism . . . in order to appropriate the ethical possibilities of a more pragmatic [and, I would add, *Christian*] Emersonian individualism" (47). Leverenz's reading of Warner's parody overlooks the fact that Fortune Emerson is proud of her self-reliance: "She got tired of setting [Ellen] to work; she liked to dash around the house alone, without thinking what somebody else was doing or ought to be doing" (340).

Warner's objection is that Miss Fortune Emerson takes self-reliance to an extreme. She is not simply self-reliant, but alienates herself from the rest of her community; she is also, significantly, without faith—not a Bible-reading Christian like the women in the novel who become Ellen's role models. Yet Warner does not simply reject what Miss Emerson stands for: paradoxically, she too is a model for Ellen, the one who initiates Ellen into the world of women's work and instructs her on how to be useful. As the dual readings of her name suggest, life with her aunt is both a "misfortune" and a "fortune" for Ellen: the hardships of rural farm life with her distant and at times cruel aunt make Ellen's life miserable but at the same time push her to become more self-reliant and more reliant upon her newfound Christian faith; in addition, Fortune teaches Ellen skills that increase her competence and her confidence in herself. Mid-novel, Ellen is indeed "changed," having mastered her "misfortune" through a combination of skill and faith (352). To Warner it is only a "misfortune" to be an Emerson if one is without a "Christocentric" religion and if one loses track of the "importance of a relational identity as well as the need for self-expression" (Hovet and Hovet 12).

Warner's second novel, *Queechy* (1852), readdresses—even celebrates—the self-reliant ideals that initially seem spoofed in *The Wide, Wide World,* making it clear that Warner's response to Emerson's ideas was far from simple dismissal. In her own time, Warner was known for both *The Wide, Wide World,* which became the first American best-seller, and *Queechy,* published two years later, which was nearly as popular as its precursor.[2] In *Queechy,* Warner ambitiously continued to build on ideas and scenes introduced in *The Wide, Wide World,* producing a novel that is at times radically different from its predecessor, especially in terms of her heroine's increased self-reliance. Cynthia Schoolar Williams (1990) and Susan Harris (1990) began the important work of drawing *Queechy* out of the shadow of its predecessor. In both books Warner explores the relationship between Christianity and self-reliance in a woman's life, but in *Queechy* she repeats and revises several key scenes from her first novel, featuring the heroine as the agent of change rather than the object of change. While *The Wide, Wide World* expresses Warner's initial response to Emerson, *Queechy* functions as an extension of her thinking, continuing the exploration of what is liberating as well as limiting for women in the doctrine of self-reliance.

The ambiguity inherent in Warner's response to Emerson is symptomatic of her complex understanding of the possibilities and limitations of a woman's place in nineteenth-century America. In both of her first two novels, and in *Queechy* in particular, Warner can be read as quietly arguing with Emerson—with "some measure of patience and moderation," as she might put it—testing his ideas against the realities of nineteenth-century women's lives. So her novels highlight the clash between religious, reliable, working women's lives and the often unpredictable life of (male) intellect described by Emerson; but they also explore the possibility of a more balanced blending of lives when beliefs and actions are in alignment.

Significantly, Emerson's own essays display considerable ambivalence toward the ideas of self-reliance he seems to be championing. On the one hand, he challenges men to develop their higher selves by cultivating originality, self-reliance, and nonconformity, obeying the whim of genius and, when necessary, even shunning family responsibilities: "I shun father and

mother and wife and brother when my genius calls me. I would write on
the lintels of the doorpost, *Whim*" (150). Yet, paradoxically, Emerson also
declares that "In manly hours we feel that duty is our place. The soul is no
traveler; the wise man stays at home" (164). "Why are there frequently two
voices in an Emerson essay?" asks Sharon Cameron. "Why two voices that
seem deaf to each other's words? In an essay like 'Experience' [1844] are
claims voiced, repudiated, and differently iterated so that the self that can
say words and the self that can hear them may be brought into relation and
implicitly reconciled with each other?" (17). Likewise, to Stephen Whicher,
Emerson seems less intent on capturing "the Pegasus of our inner power
and more to ride our whole nature, as equestrians in a circus balance on two
horses at once" (123). In Whicher's reading, Emerson is—perhaps unwit-
tingly—seeking a balance, attempting to straddle both horses, just as Warner
strives to create heroines who are self-reliant but still womanly—something
which, as we shall see, is for her a complex ideal.

I
Accepting One's Given "Plot of Ground": Warner's Christian Heroines

Why, then, did Warner not express a greater sense of kinship to Emerson?
Most obviously, Emerson's intellectual universe was predominantly phallo-
centric. In "Self-Reliance," women are mentioned directly only three times
—twice in passing remarks as the wife or mother who gets left behind and
as the girl delighted with her studies of botany (150, 163), and most significantly in his call for "men and women who shall renovate life and our
social state" (161). But in the same passage in which he includes women in
his renovations, Emerson alludes to women in a derogatory way by referring to those who are not independent thinkers or actors as "parlor soldiers." Could a woman, then, whose domain was primarily the household,
be self-reliant? Could she be a nonconformist in the parlor? That this was a
struggle is evident from one woman's wry remark in a letter to her friend
Elizabeth Stoddard. "I think of Emerson when I do my washing," she
writes, obviously a woman in the process of ensuring that her housekeeping
was indeed *not* "mendicant."[3]

Yet Emerson's description in "Self-Reliance" of the "time in every man's
education" when he must assess his life and work with what he has been
given, could serve, with the gender of pronouns in the passage switched, as
a précis of the main plots of Warner's first two novels. Both heroines in *The
Wide, Wide World* and *Queechy* must pause to assess their lives, each literally
accepting her given "plot of ground" and committing her individual

power: "There is a time in every [wo]man's education when [she] arrives at the conviction that . . . [she] must take [her]self for better or worse as [her] portion; that though the wide universe is full of good, no kernel of nourishing corn can come to [her] but through [her] toil bestowed on that plot of ground which is given to [her] to till. The power which resides in [her] is new in nature, and none but [she] knows what that is which [she] can do, nor does [she] know until [she] has tried" ("Self-Reliance" 148). Both books are types of *Bildungsromane,* tracing the lives of the heroines from childhood through—or close to—marriage. And in both novels the heroine's first step toward evolving fully is indeed accepting and working on her given "plot of ground," which for Ellen Montgomery means adjusting to life—and learning how to be useful—on her Aunt Fortune's remote farm, and for Fleda Ringgan means taking charge of her grandfather's failing farm and returning it to a flourishing business. Warner hypostatizes Emerson's metaphor, giving her heroines ground to till, both physically and spiritually. But in order to accept her "ground," and her self, Warner makes clear, each heroine needs to choose her religion—to become a Christian.

As Ann Douglas has shown in *The Feminization of American Culture,* the process of growing up for nineteenth-century women was synonymous with becoming a Christian. Citing Rev. Horace Bushnell in a letter to his daughter in 1845, Douglas identifies the antebellum womanly ideal: "A woman should be a Christian . . . [her] character can be finished only by assimilation to God" (44). Although Warner, after her debates in Boston, believed Bushnell must have a "rather . . . erratic mind," her books suggest that she would have been in full accord with this ideal (*SW* 248). She would also have agreed wholeheartedly with another minister of the time, writing in 1832 for *Ladies Magazine,* who advised women even more strongly: "Religion is far more necessary to you than self-sufficient men. In you it would be not only *criminal,* but *impolitic* to neglect it" (minister's emphasis, qtd. in Douglas 44).

Warner's heroines indeed need religion more than "self-sufficient men" because the men in her fiction (and in her own life, as well)—"self-sufficient" lawyers, investors, and businessmen—often are, even choose to be, unreliable sources of support to their wives and daughters. Convinced that they will survive or find financial solutions better elsewhere, bankrupt Captain Montgomery, Ellen's father in *The Wide, Wide World,* and Fleda's insolvent guardian Uncle Rolf Rossitur in *Queechy* both abandon their families. These men are perhaps types of the self-reliant man described by Emerson, who may leave unexpectedly to follow their genius on a whim, shunning not only "father and mother and wife and brother" but daughters and orphaned nieces when they go. Uncle Rossitur takes the family's re-

maining money with him to speculate on land in Michigan, and his depar-
ture is duly noted by one of *Queechy*'s hardworking and reliable Christian
women: "So much security any woman has in a man without religion!"
(252). And, as Beverly Voloshin confirms, "male self-reliance, though valued,
also led to the amorality, materialism, and aggressiveness of the public realm
and required the counter-balance of 'woman's sphere,' of the institution of
the home as the source of affectional bonds and ethical relations" (298).

Leaving home and family, whether to pursue one's genius or to run away
from problems, was not a possibility for nineteenth-century women. Unlike Emerson's wanderer, Warner's heroines never entertain the option of
leaving home—as Jane Tompkins points out, "one cannot run away in the
world of nineteenth-century women's fiction" (593). When left alone to
fend for themselves and for their families, nineteenth-century women, and
the heroines in the fiction that describes them, needed a source of inner
strength with which to carry on their lives (and through which to nurture
others). Christianity both dictated that a woman's duty was to remain in
the home and at the same time often gave her the strength to stay there. In
Warner's novels, the heroine's moral courage surfaces not in leaving home to
seek her fortune elsewhere, but in staying home to face it and to work with it.

"What do you want with Miss Fortune, little one?" asks a villager of
eight-year-old Ellen, who has just asked directions to her aunt's farm. "I
expected she would meet me here, sir," replies Ellen, and in a way, she does;
Ellen's life at her severe aunt's is initially a far cry from fortunate (90). Yet
Ellen's time at her aunt's serves a moral purpose—to develop her Christian
faith—so during her stay she is repeatedly told, "All things mend with your
own mending," the first step of which is to pray (154). With the support of
several Christian mentors, Ellen learns how to rely on her newfound faith,
and through it, how to increase her self-command. She has some self-control
before she becomes a Christian, but, Warner argues, grounding herself
through faith in God can help her to reinforce her sense of self and enable
her to access her self-command more readily. "Try to compose yourself,"
Mrs. Montgomery tells her hysterical young daughter at the beginning of
the novel, when Ellen first learns that they will be separated, and Ellen responds: "Exerting all her self-command, of which she had sometimes a good
deal, she *did* calm herself . . . and listened quietly" (13, emphasis Warner's).
But although Ellen makes considerable headway throughout the novel in
this battle with herself and her fate, at its close she is still learning the lesson
that will liberate her from dependence on others to an inner self-reliance.
In the novel's final scene, Ellen wonders aloud whether her minister "brother"
John Humphreys—now her fiancé—will mentor her when they are finally
reunited: "and then you will keep me right?" But he replies, "I won't promise you that, Ellie, . . . you must learn to keep yourself right" (565).

Warner's images of mending and righting oneself recall Emerson's definition of self-reliance. "The bended tree recovering itself from the strong wind," he states, is a demonstration "of the self-sufficient and therefore self-relying soul" (275–76). Warner extends this analogy as she describes each of her first two heroines, using the image of a plant or flower not only to convey their different levels of maturity and independence but to reinforce the correlation between the level of each girl's faith and her capacity for self-reliance. Using an analogy of the stages of a plant's growth, Warner reports on Ellen's development in the last paragraph of *The Wide, Wide World:* "The seed so early sown in little Ellen's mind, and so carefully tended by sundry hands, grew in course of time to all the fair structure and comely perfection it had bid fair to reach—storms and winds that had visited it did but cause the root to take deeper hold;—and at the point of its young maturity it happily fell again into those hands that had of all been most successful in its culture" (569). Here Warner strikes what seems to be a crucial balance for her heroine: though she is self-reliant at various times during the novel, at this concluding moment the metaphor reinforces the idea that Ellen is merely a vessel for the "seed" of Christianity, and still reliant on hands other than her own—those of a capable gardener—for her cultivation.

By way of contrast, Miss Fortune Emerson lacks this balance: in her insistence on doing everything herself, she overdoes it, and makes herself sick: she "had overtasked [*sic*] her strength; and by dint of economy, housewifery, and *smartness,* had brought on herself the severe punishment of lying idle and helpless" (355). While in his image of "the bended tree recovering itself" Emerson conflates the terms "self-sufficient and therefore self-relying soul," through Miss Fortune Emerson's situation Warner makes an important distinction between the two. In general, the term *self-reliant* suggests relying on one's own powers, not clinging to another or being dependent (especially not to the point of converging or losing one's self in an other), but being individually strong and acting independently. Self-reliance can be seen as courageous, though in nineteenth-century terms it could be seen as irreligious if one relied on self rather than God within oneself. The term *self-sufficient,* however, as the minister's implicit criticism of "self-sufficient men" suggests, carries several negative connotations. It suggests not only that one is "able to supply one's needs oneself," as in growing one's own food so that one is self-supporting as well as independent (which is what Aunt Fortune is admired for), but "in an unfavorable sense [it also suggests] having excessive confidence in oneself, [and in] one's powers . . . characterized by overweening or self-conceited opinion or behavior" (*OED*); it perhaps even suggests a sense of not "needing" other people. Though she has rare moments of generosity, Fortune's "smartness," and Warner's overall parody of her intense self-reliance, suggests her critique of Emerson's occasional privileging of intellect over heart, and of the self over family or community (339). Warner would not, however, reverse the equation; in both *The Wide, Wide World* and *Queechy* it is clear that she believes in a blend. Her goal for Ellen is not only that she learn to keep herself "right," but that she become a useful, Christian woman, and this moment of Fortune's illness provides Ellen with the opportunity to demonstrate that she has begun to change in both these areas.

Neither, in itself, is sufficient, in Warner's view. At the end of *The Wide, Wide World,* even Ellen's now solid faith and impending marriage to a minister do not constitute maturity. Though she is a Christian, according to Warner Ellen's character is still not "finished." Ellen has yet to demonstrate that she has the power to "right" herself on her own, or, in Emersonian terms, to "recover" herself despite "strong wind." Thus, *The Wide, Wide World* concludes with Ellen at her irreligious grandmother's house, where she will endure "three or four more years of Scottish discipline," rather than comfortably back in America with those "she best loved" (569). Thus far, her Christianity has helped her to stake out a territory for herself, and she has even disobeyed her grandmother in order to obey her own, higher truth. Fifteen-year-old Ellen stands up for her right to read the Bible, not only because she considers it a Christian duty, but because, significantly, she wants "some time to myself" (541). When we last see Ellen, she has ventured out to attend church by herself: "with a singular feeling of pleasure . . . she entered the church alone." Emphasizing Ellen's peaceful solitude—"she was alone, quite alone in the midst of that crowd"—Warner uncannily echoes another of Emerson's remarks, again, with the gender of the pronouns shifted: "It is easy in the world to live after the world's opinion; it is easy in solitude to live after our own, but the great [wo]man is [she] who in the midst of the crowd keeps with perfect sweetness the independence of solitude" ("Self-Reliance" 267).

II
The Power of the Word

> There is at this moment for you an utterance brave and grand . . . but different. . . . [I]f you can hear what the patriarchs say, surely you can reply to them in the same pitch of voice.   —Emerson, "Self-Reliance" (282)

> For God did not give us a spirit of timidity but a spirit of power and love and self-control.   —Timothy 1:17

While *Queechy*, like *The Wide, Wide World,* is a female *Bildungsroman*, *Queechy* can be read more accurately as a double *Bildungsroman*, since it traces the growth of both Fleda and her future partner, Guy Carleton, from their youths to maturity, in this case through their marriage. Despite the difference in their ages—Fleda is eleven and Carleton twenty when the novel opens—both are still in the process of growing up: Fleda's physical immaturity is paralleled by Carleton's spiritual immaturity. Though she is already a sturdy Christian, Fleda is too young for him and needs to grow up intellectually and physically, while Carleton has not yet converted and is thus spiritually young.

In "The Lost Brother, the Twin: Women Novelists and the Male-Female Double *Bildungsroman*," Charlotte Goodman suggests that the double *Bildungsroman* is a "form that offers a critique of patriarchal society's gender divisions; the fracture of an androgynous self. Only in the final scene . . . is the fragmentation of self momentarily healed as male and female protagonists are reunited" (36). As a "critique of patriarchal society's gender divisions," the double *Bildungsroman* form is useful in Warner's project to talk back to Emerson, providing her with the means to explore the differences and the possible balance between men's and women's self-reliance. The structure of this type of novel, Goodman points out, differs from the linearity of the typical *Bildungsroman* plot and is instead more circular: the male and female protagonists share a childhood where they exist as equals; as adolescents they are separated—the male seeks his fortune, the female is left behind; and as adults their reunion "turns away from adult experiences and celebrates their shared childhood when the male and female were undivided" (36). To a certain extent, *Queechy* shares this overall pattern, but with two significant differences, both having to do with the revisionary independence of the female protagonist.

In a scene near the beginning of *Queechy*, Warner returns to the plant analogy with which she described Ellen to suggest Fleda's more developed strength and independence. In this scene, one of many parlor scenes in the novel in which current societal "standards" are challenged, several male characters are debating the "finer qualities of a woman's nature" (68). Comparing Marie Antoinette, for instance, to an exotic hothouse flower that would lose its beauty and droop "in the strong free air," Carleton asserts that the strength of a wildflower is his ideal. Without referring to her by name, Carleton suggests that eleven-year-old Fleda "is a flower of the woods, raising its head above frost and snow and the rugged soil where fortune has placed it, with an air of quiet patient endurance;—a storm wind may bring it to the ground easily—but if its gentle nature be not broken, it will look up again unchanged, and bide its time in unrequited beauty and sweetness to the end" (68). The differences between Ellen's and Fleda's character descriptions highlight the shift in Warner's thought as she approached her sec-

ond novel. Described in active rather than passive terms, this flower has will
and agency; similarly, what Ellen struggles to learn throughout most of *The
Wide, Wide World,* Fleda is already able to do as a young girl at the opening
of *Queechy.* The key difference between the two girls is Fleda's already secure faith, which gives her the courage to be assertive and the strength to
be creative.

Warner confirms Fleda's agency early on, in another scene that reverses
a similar scene from *The Wide, Wide World.* When the novel opens, Guy
Carleton is a type of Emerson's whimsical man, shunning his home to follow his genius. He has left his estate in England and is roving from place to
place in America, "trying . . . in vain, to soothe the vague restlessness that
called for a very different remedy" (112). He is wandering "Not mali-
ciously,—not wilfully,—not stupidly;—rather the fool of circumstance,"
Warner emphasizes, pointing out that these circumstances are in part his
mother's fault: a wealthy "lady," and a "woman of the world" rather than a
Christian, she is unable to impart to him the values he needs to find his
purpose in life, to recognize his duty (107). Blinded by an "eye sensitively
fond of . . . the extreme of elegance, in everything," he is unable to see that
the "mental and bodily wretchedness among the ignorant poor" of his own
estate in England is within "his power to do away [with] or alleviate" (112).

The "remedy" is Fleda; more precisely, Fleda's faith. Following the death
of Fleda's grandfather, Carleton escorts her to Paris, where she will live until
her uncle becomes bankrupt. On board the steamer to Europe, in a scene
that exactly reverses Ellen's conversion on board the ferry en route to her
aunt's, Fleda begins Carleton's conversion. In *The Wide, Wide World,* an older
gentleman reads hymns to Ellen and helps her to understand and accept the
challenges of Christianity; in *Queechy,* by contrast, Fleda actively ministers
to Carleton, significantly initiating the necessary transformation of the man
who will, nine years later, become her lover (135). Thus, to reverse Joanne
Dobson's apt phrase, she effectively begins to "educate herself a husband."

Warner's epigraph to *Queechy* telegraphs that the distinction begun in
The Wide, Wide World has now become her main theme: "I hope I can speak
of woman without offence to the ladies." Although Ellen aspires to be a
lady and a Christian like her mother (240), providence and her father's loss
of fortune situate her at a farm, where she, a "fallen *possible* lady," becomes
a working woman. The phrase is Catharine Maria Sedgwick's (another of
the attendees at the 1847 dinner party), and it comes from her didactic tract
Live and Let Live; or, Domestic Service Illustrated (1837), a book owned both
by Warner and Emerson (v). The situation Sedgwick describes is both
Warner's and her heroines' and highlights what can happen in financial circumstances when "a *lady* must perform the primitive offices of women, or

her family must be comfortless" (v, emphasis Sedgwick's). Fleda, too, has the potential to be a lady, and when she marries Carleton she will in fact become a titled lady—"Lady Carleton"—co-leader of Carleton's English estate. But before she can realize this position she must demonstrate her ability to work—to do both "women's" and "men's" work. In both Sedgwick's and Warner's fiction, women work; ladies, on the other hand, are often criticized in these novels for their inability to work as well as for their shallow education. A woman, Warner suggests—a great woman, in Emersonian terms— would be a nonconformist on both counts.

By selecting as her epigraph a sentence that opposes "woman," singular, to "ladies," generally, Warner calls attention to the larger scope of her project—she is not writing only for an elite subgroup of "ladies," in the same way, it seems, Emerson aimed to write for all men. Both Ellen and Fleda cross the nineteenth-century social boundary between "woman" and "lady" by engaging in manual labor, not only out of perceived duty but for "pay," which was considered degrading to an aspiring nineteenth-century lady. Warner shared Sedgwick's deep concern that "a great many ladies are of no use in the world," especially those who are unwilling or unable to work in order to provide for their families, even when their circumstances and their Christian obligation to their families demand it (*Live* 200). Mrs. Rossitur, Fleda's aunt, is an example of a useless lady, one who has not been taught how to help out in basic ways. Following her husband's financial failure, Mrs. Rossitur "wearied herself excessively with doing very little" (228), which Fleda excuses because her aunt "isn't strong"; but Barby, their hired but unpaid housekeeper, has a different impression: "Nor don't want to be, does she? I've heerd tell of her. Mis' Plumfield, I should despise to have as many legs and arms as other folks and not be able to help myself!" (239–40). To Barby, Mrs. Rossitur's apparent unwillingness to help herself or others reads as an unreasonable whim, and in a way, she is right: in essence, Mrs. Rossitur is "leaving" her home to others, and absenting herself from society, as well, because of superficial concerns about her worn-out wardrobe. The wanderer may be Emerson's extreme; the useless lady is Warner's: both, ultimately, are *not* self-reliant but completely dependent that others will carry on while they are "gone." Because the realities of women's lives, especially in the 1830s, often placed them in reduced circumstances, part of Warner's mission was to challenge received divisions between ladies and women. She consistently offers heroines who combine the capabilities of both "ladies" and "women," and suggests that a woman's education could enable her to bridge that societal divide.

Warner is well aware that some of what Emerson assumes for men—that will enable them to be self-reliant—cannot be assumed for women whose informal education did not necessarily include reading history, much less Emerson's essays. Most women, whose families could afford it, were tutored in French and taught embroidery and dancing—it was assumed that they would need little else since they were not expected to participate much in the running of the country. Warner was not alone in her concern that not only future "ladies" but all women needed a more complete education.

Sedgwick, too, advocated a practical as well as a cultural education for women. In her preface to *Live and Let Live,* she maintains that it is "imperative . . . [for] American mothers to qualify their daughters to superintend their domestics, and to prepare the future housewife for the exigencies that await her," since a lady might have to do these things herself. "French, Italian, drawing, music, . . . these are the ornaments and luxuries of education; but let not the *necessaries* be omitted" (v, emphasis Sedgwick's). Yet beyond adding a practical dimension to girls' training, both writers call for a rigorous and thorough intellectual education, not limited to the "luxuries," but including, as well, history (both ancient and political), philosophy (religious and "natural"), sciences, and math—subjects usually reserved for nineteenth-century boys. Interestingly, it is in the parlor—that most public space of a private home—that Warner's characters confront conventional beliefs about women's education, so crucial to their possible self-reliance.

In *Queechy,* Carleton, who is one of Warner's "parlor soldiers," articulates the author's progressive position that women ought to be educated so that they could be the intellectual equals of—even superior to—their husbands. Refuting another man who claims that since a woman's destiny is the home, she should "have nothing to do with books," Carleton argues, "The wealth of a woman's mind, instead of lying in the rough, should be richly brought out and fashioned for its various ends, while yet those ends are in the future, or it will never meet the demand. And for her own happiness, all the more because her sphere is at home, her home stores should be exhaustless—the stores she cannot go abroad to seek. . . . It were [*sic*] ungenerous in man to condemn the *best* half of human intellect to insignificance merely because it is not his own" (385, emphasis Warner's). Significantly, Carleton suggests that a woman's education is not primarily for the benefit of her children, but for herself: she should be surrounded with books "for her own happiness." Using the familiar gardening metaphor to represent a woman's mind, he continues: "The man knows little of his own interest . . . who would leave that ground waste, or would cultivate it only in the narrow spirit of a utilitarian. He needs an influence in his family not more refreshing than rectifying; and no man will seek that in one greatly his inferior. He is to be pitied who cannot fall back upon his home with the assurance that he has there something better than himself" (386).

Carleton's comment that a woman's conversational influence—at least in the home—can be not only "refreshing" but "rectifying" reveals his alignment with Emerson that women can indeed be "the civilizers of mankind." Though, as Monika Elbert notes, "Emerson circles back to the domestic realm as woman's locus of power," to him, and to Warner, woman's sphere was "not exclusively private" (8). Here Warner importantly emphasizes the step necessary for women to become "civilizers" both within and beyond the home. The education of women that Carleton advocates Warner has already illustrated, to different degrees, through her heroines' upbringings, which blend learning from both spheres. Though neither attends school, both girls pursue a classical (male) as well as an "ornamental" and practical (female) education. With some guidance from John and Alice Humphreys, her informally adopted family, Ellen diligently studies not only the ladylike "ornaments" of French and drawing, but religion, geography, literature, history, English, "natural philosophy," and math. Her future husband, John, adds riding, his favorite hobby. Self-taught Fleda, on the other hand, despite a lack of guidance, still achieves an impressively thorough education. Warner provides an excerpt of Fleda's reading log, culled from her own the year she, too, began tutoring herself, which includes *Histoire de France* (five volumes, in French); Johnson's *Incidents of Travel;* Goldsmith's *Animated Nature;* Marshall's *Life of Washington;* Paley's *Natural Theology; Paolo e Virginia* (in Italian); *Memoirs de Sully;* Milner's *Church History;* and her favorite, Spenser's *Faerie Queene* (180–83).[4] Because, mid-novel, she takes over the management of the Queechy farm, Fleda's reading also includes farming manuals and catalogs, a distinctly male domain. In the same way that Emerson blurs the boundaries between male and female, public and private spheres, acknowledging that "in manly hours . . . the wise man stays at home" (164), an act that "transvalue[s]" that domestic space (Zwarg 22), Warner suggests that a Christian woman's duty may require her to cross over into what was considered male territory (both intellectual and physical) and ultimately begin to "transvalue" certain public spaces. Fleda anticipates her success in both agriculture and business with an Emersonian proclamation: "One can do anything, with a strong enough motive!" (320).

Having classically and politically educated herself through books and newspapers, Fleda demonstrates that she has, in fact, mastered the art of conversation Emerson so admires and is aware of her possible social and political influence. At various points in *Queechy,* Fleda adroitly discusses the Mexican War, abolition, the education of the poor, religion (including subcategories such as obedience of wives to husbands, power, and duty), patriotism, republicanism, and even gives a nod toward women's rights. Though the parlor—where Fleda and Ellen speak most publicly—is indeed a liminal place, it is clearly also a place of power for Warner's heroines, as evidenced by their male listeners' reactions to their words. But while Ellen's intellect is admired by educated men at the end of *The Wide, Wide World* (when she is fifteen), her intelligence is never seen as a threat to them, as Fleda's is to some. Carleton is not threatened by Fleda's knowledge—in fact, he admires all of it—but other men in the novel are more ambivalent. "She's as clever a girl as you need to have," remarks one of Fleda's farmhands (330). That such women might need to be controlled is suggested by Dr. Gregory, a favorite family friend, who, despite being impressed with Fleda's wide range of learning by her early teens, putting his library at her disposal, and even helping in her subsequent tutoring, couches his admiration in terms that suggest she might run away, intellectually. Twice he expresses concern to her uncle as if she were a potentially wild horse: "If that girl ever takes a wrong turn with the bit in her teeth, you'll be puzzled to hold her. What stuff will you make the reins of?" (185).

The horse metaphor recalls Stephen Whicher's image of Emerson as circus rider, seeking to "balance on two horses" and thus "ride [one's] whole nature." Obviously, Fleda is not horse but rider, in an even more complex balancing act. Striving to balance her "male" and "female" knowledge as well as her private and public voices, well-educated Fleda does not just read and talk, she writes. And, significantly, many of her acts of self-reliance—publishing poems to earn money, traveling alone to New York City to find her uncle (who has deserted the family)—serve to connect her further to her family and to the community at large. Driven to write in the hopes of earning much-needed cash during the family's bankrupt return to Queechy (a situation that absolutely parallels Warner's own experience), Fleda has several poems published under the pseudonym "Hugh," her cousin's name. As Mary Kelley has shown in *Private Woman, Public Stage,* nineteenth-century women writers were very ambivalent about the public aspects of their careers, and often initially published anonymously (like Sedgwick) or with a pseudonym (Warner's was her grandmother's maiden name, "Elizabeth Wetherell"). Though Fleda claims that she would never have picked up the pen if magazines did not pay because she believes that a woman should not "display" herself in this public manner, dire necessity forces her hand and "excuses" her public act. In this light, Fleda considers it acceptable to write and to work in other modes (even publicly) for money. That she disguises herself as a man in this instance raises some interesting questions and emphasizes Warner's blurring of the gendered boundaries of publishing. Fleda's use of a male pseudonym does two things at once: by using it, Fleda is literally "passing" as a man and, as such, may gain easier access to the "worldly sphere" of publication; but at the same time, by choosing her cousin's name and revealing herself as the author to her immediate family, she is also emphasizing her personal connection to them. Once again, Fleda's Emersonian act of self-reliance paradoxically increases her interconnectedness with others and enables her to occupy both public and private realms of experience simultaneously.

For Warner, as for Lydia Maria Child, actively fulfilling "the sacred mission for which [one's] soul is embodied" is both men's and women's work (Child 249). While not always based upon public work, fulfilling one's sacred mission often required public acts, such as Fleda's trip alone to New York City, her raising and selling of produce and flowers, and her management of male workers. Significantly, a self-reliant, Christian woman, Warner suggests, should work—and write—even if she does *not* need the money, because it is her duty not only to believe, but to be a "doer of the word" (James 1:19), to use her talents for the benefit of others as well as for her own spiritual growth. Once the initial unladylike hurdle was crossed and their work was published, writers like Warner could rationalize their continued desire to write through its missionary effects. As Anna Warner notes, many readers wrote to Susan and traced their conversion to Christianity to having read *The Wide, Wide World* (SW 264). Others made similar claims about *Queechy*.

For Warner, Emerson, and Child as well, it is not enough to "seem" *or* to "be"; one must "do" (see Elbert 8). These objectives are conflated in one of Fleda's window reveries, when, after a taste of intellectually and emotionally stimulating New York City society, she returns to the Queechy farm, reassesses, and reaccepts her Emersonian "plot of ground": "She made up her mind she was glad to be back again among the rough things of life, where she could do so much to smooth them for others and her own spirit might grow to a polish it would never gain in the regions of ease and pleasure. 'To do life's work!'—thought Fleda clasping her hands,—'no matter where—and mine is here. I am glad I am in my place again—I was forgetting I had one'" (452). While a Christian was to do the work assigned to her to do, not only to help others but to "polish" her own spirit, she was also to remain "unspotted by the world" (James 1:26), which is Fleda's mother's special prayer for her daughter, used as a refrain throughout the novel.[5] This stipulation often limited the options for the kinds of work a ladylike Christian woman could do.

But Fleda, in fact, turns the cultivating metaphor on its head, becoming the cultivator, rather than, like her predecessor Ellen, the cultivated. In the middle portion of *Queechy*, the section Susan Harris has identified as the locus for "ideological disruption" in many nineteenth-century women's novels, Fleda's life rewrites both Ellen's and Miss Fortune's lives, as she manages not only the farmhouse, but the farm. She may be "in her place again," but she is also creating a new space at the same time, one that blends public and private, male and female spheres. Following her uncle's desertion, Fleda takes matters into her own hands and not only reads manuals to learn current methods of planting corn and harvesting hay, but democratically introduces these new methods to her farmhands, and subsequently increases production to such an extent that her overseer enthusiastically declares that she is "the best farmer in the state" (456). Significantly, Fleda's achievement goes beyond researching ways to increase the yield of corn or improve the preservation of hay; she succeeds because of the way she manages the men who work for her. Rather than acting as though they are beneath her, or assuming authority through force (strategies that failed for her uncle), she speaks with the men as equals, with respect, rallies experts around her, and introduces new methods as mutual "experiments" (346).

But in these ways Fleda is very aware that she has again crossed into male territory. "Not that in the least she doubted her own ability and success; but her uncle did not deserve to have his affairs prosper under such a system and she had no faith that they would" (324). Warner's novel illustrates Baym's claim that nineteenth-century women saw home not so much as a "space" separate from a more worldly "sphere," but as "a system of human relations" (49). Fleda's discomfort here may highlight Warner's own ambivalence about the implications of profound self-reliance. In this instance, especially, her novel indeed seems a "dual gesture of critique and affiliation" in her possible "conversation" with Emerson (Albrecht 47). Fleda does not doubt her abilities, but questions whether "such a system"—of a woman managing a farm, presumably—*ought* to succeed. And indeed, when her uncle returns two years later (still penniless, following his whimsical rovings in Michigan), he is appropriately embarrassed that she has achieved so much. In another parlor scene, Uncle Rolf addresses his son, a captain in the army, and exclaims:

> "Look at what this slight frame and delicate nerves have been found equal to, and then tell me if the broad shoulders of all your mess would have borne half the burden or their united heads accomplished a quarter of the results." . . .
>
> "Uncle Rolf," said Fleda gently,—"nerves and muscles haven't much to do with it—after all you know I have just served the place of a mouth-piece. Seth was the head, and good Earl Douglass the hand." (445)

Although Fleda's cousin has been a soldier fighting beyond the "parlor" in the Mexican War, her uncle recognizes that she is more of a soldier, winning her struggle with fate on the home front.

Curiously, just at this moment of triumph for Fleda, her attempt to ease her uncle's discomfort that she, a woman, has been successful in his domain contradicts her earlier resolution when she first decides to accept this challenge: "I will try farming myself," she tells her cousin, "I will get Earl Douglass or somebody else to play second fiddle, but I will have but one head on the farm and I will try what mine is worth" (319–20). Warner's apparent ambivalence about Fleda's achievements actually reveals her double project: not only to show that women are capable contributors in many "spaces" or "spheres," but also to correct Emerson and emphasize that duties should be shared. Women both should not and physically cannot (for extended durations—no one could) do all by themselves. And so Fleda, like Aunt Fortune but with an entirely different motive, overextends herself and gets sick. She suffers from occasional, incapacitating migraines, significantly, when she is burdened with what should, according to Warner, be either a man's tasks or at least shared work. Uncle Rossitur shirks his duty, which transfers the burden of both raising money and running the household onto the women, but because Aunt Rossitur is a "useless lady," both responsibilities are then passed along to Fleda. Fleda, the self-reliant wildflower whose spiritual strength should enable her to "recover herself" from these strong winds, is eventually weighed down to such a degree that even her faith is shaken. But since Fleda's future husband, Guy Carleton, has converted to Christianity eight years earlier and diligently studied the Bible during that time, by mid-novel he is spiritually mature and thus able to help Fleda recover, both physically and emotionally. He has, in effect, become Emerson's "wise man," ready and able to stay at home.

In this situation, Warner is making two crucial distinctions. First, there is an important balance of work and caring for others that needs to be achieved. Both Fortune and Fleda overdo it. Though both are self-reliant, one is too selfish and the other too selfless, and both are doing work that needs to be shared with others, men in particular. Second, in Warner's more balanced ideal world, not only would both men and women work, they would nurture each other. Carleton is Warner's representative man because he is able and willing to minister to Fleda both spiritually and physically. Because he is now a Christian, he can support her through religious conversation; he also, significantly, nurses her physically during her migraine headaches, providing her with a restorative (an aromatic vinegar that he purchases especially for her) and making the strong coffee that seems to help her. He is thus Warner's model of a self-reliant Christian man, one who recognizes women's intellectual capacity and the need for a balanced inter-dependency within a marriage and therefore acts responsibly.

Does the self Fleda has cultivated through her extraordinary accomplishments mid-novel—the site of *Queechy*'s "ideologic disruption" created by Fleda's agency—suffer "obliteration under the aegis of a dominating husband" by the novel's close, as Susan Harris claims (79)? The exchanges between the two throughout the novel, and especially while they are engaged near its close, suggest a much more balanced future partnership, one that reveals Warner's Emersonian ideal. While each contributes differently to their relationship, there is a mutuality to their exchanges: older, Carleton assumes the role of her physical protector, as Harris has noted, but Fleda is his moral instructor. Because they are both Christians, they recognize their individual obligations to act. As Kelley has noted: "For many nineteenth-century protestants, piety involved more than an inner conviction and passive devotion. If the involvement was private and personal, the commitment was social. One served God by lovingly and actively serving others" (292–93). By the end of the novel, Fleda's ministry has worked, and Carleton has not only become a Christian but accepted that Emersonian "manly" work and responsibilities are at home.

That home turns out literally to be Carleton's: Fleda joins him in England, thus closing the circle of the double *Bildungsroman*. Yet this does not mean that Fleda will give up her hard-won self-reliance. Though others expect that Fleda, upon marrying this wealthy nobleman, will have a new life of ease, she thinks differently and declares, "I expect to have a great deal to do; if I don't find it, I shall make it" (618). In fact, she has already suggested one possibility to Carleton: "There might be a great deal of pleasure in raising the tone of mind and character among the people,—as one could who had influence over a large neighborhood," which he then reveals is the very work he has been doing for the last eight years (570–71). Fleda's uneasy laugh here conveys her awareness of what Warner has been suggesting all along: that a Christian woman's duty may require her to cross into male domain, and to act unconventionally.

In its conclusion, Goodman observes, "the male-female double *Bildungsroman* differs most significantly from that of the traditional *Bildungsroman*: instead of facing the future, as do the protagonists of the more conventional *Bildungsroman*, the male protagonist returns to the world of his childhood by embracing his female counterpart, allowing the male and the female halves of the divided self to be joined once again" (43). Her implication is that the male and female protagonists typically grow up in the same town; thus the male returns to where the female has stayed "instead of facing the future." Warner rewrites this ending; the male protagonist does go home, but Fleda does not, which also breaks the pattern Pratt and White have observed typical of female *Bildungsromane*. Unlike her male counterpart, they observe, "the female protagonist does not *choose* a life to one side of society after conscious deliberation . . . rather she is ontologically or radically alienated by gender-role norms from the very outset" (36). Fleda, on the other hand, deliberately, and unconventionally, chooses to join Carleton in England (622).

In a manner more typical of the male *Bildungsroman,* by the end of the novel Fleda is prepared for society and introduced to the world—literally, a new country—rather than, like Ellen, returned to a version of her old childhood home. And similar to Emerson's "great man," she too is able to keep "with perfect sweetness the independence of solitude" even in the midst of those who disapprove of her nonconformity, thus becoming Warner's version of a "great woman." Fleda has harvested real corn, by the bushel, and metaphorical corn—knowledge, spirituality, love, even money—by the wagonload as well. In this manner *Queechy* significantly revises *The Wide, Wide World* and offers a nineteenth-century Christian woman's version of Emersonian self-reliance. In her own act of self-reliance, Warner began her second novel before her first was even published, hoping that it would help her support herself, as well as her sister, father, and aunt. That it did echoes the comment of one of her characters: "I don't believe the world would go now . . . if it wa'n't for women" (*Queechy* 299).

For Warner, Christianity was empowering and liberating for women, and could allow—almost require—them to be nonconformists, both secret and public rebels. Warner's revision of Emerson's classic remark, "Whoso would be a man, must be a non-conformist" (265), would be, "Whoso would be a woman must be a Christian and *thus* a non-conformist." While Emerson seems to condemn those (men) who stay home, who are only "soldiers" in "parlors," Warner's novels highlight the moral courage and strength of those who had to stay home, who had no choice. By taking charge of their own lives—developing their capacity for self-command, to use a Warnerian term—and by helping others to strengthen their faith and self-reliance, Warner's heroines convert Emerson's insult into a mission: that women could not only be "parlor soldiers," taking on "the rugged battle of fate" within their own homes, but that they could have influence beyond the parlor as well. Ultimately, Warner would agree with Emerson "that a greater self-reliance must work a revolution in all the offices and relations of men"—and *women,* Warner would add—"in their religion; in their education; in their pursuits; [and in] their modes of living" (279). Remarkably, to varying degrees, each of Warner's heroines takes on the challenges set forth by Emerson in "Self-Reliance," confronting early-nineteenth-century expectations of women's roles, not only in "housekeeping," but "arts . . . occupations . . . marriages . . . [and] religion."

Notes

1. Entry for 12 January 1847 in Anna Warner, *Susan Warner* 248. Further citations from this source will be abbreviated *SW* with page number.

2. Warner was known in her own time for both *The Wide, Wide World* and *Queechy,* as well as for novels that followed, including *The Hills of the Shatemuc, The Old Helmet, Daisy, Diana,* and *My Desire.* It is estimated that *The Wide, Wide World* sold 1,000,000 copies between 1850 and 1922. While sales records are incomplete—usually low prior to copyright laws—in its first year alone *Queechy* sold 19,000 copies in America, as well as thousands in England, France, and Germany. In England the book sold particularly well—62,000 copies in its first two years. One railway bookstall alone sold 10,000 copies. The Constitution Island Association (formed following Anna Warner's death in 1915 to preserve the Warner house and manuscripts) has counted fifty editions in the novel's first fifty years, a figure that does not include the many pirated, cheaper editions both here and abroad (Constitution Island Association Archives).

Following the success of *The Wide, Wide World* and as a result of many readers' requests, the Warner sisters then wrote a number of children's books for a series called "Ellen Montgomery's Bookshelf."

3. Elizabeth G. Martin in a letter to Elizabeth Stoddard, 17 January 1866. Elizabeth Drew Barstow Stoddard Manuscripts, New York Public Library.

4. This list can be found in Warner's journal for the year 1837–38 (the year her family moved from New York City to their farmhouse on the Hudson River, when she was eighteen) in the Constitution Island Association Archives.

5. This phrase is perhaps borrowed from Sedgwick's *Redwood,* which Warner read as she was still planning out *Queechy.* In *Redwood,* Charles Westall's father dies when his son is only four, before which he prays that Charles will be kept "unspotted from the world" (1:196).

Works Cited

Albrecht, James M. "Saying Yes and Saying No: Individualist Ethics in Ellison, Burke, and Emerson." *PMLA* 114 (1999): 46–63.

Baym, Nina. *Woman's Fiction: A Guide to Novels by and about Women in America, 1820–1870.* Ithaca: Cornell UP, 1978.

Cameron, Sharon. "Representing Grief: Emerson's 'Experience.'" *Representations* 15 (Summer 1986): 15–41.

Child, Lydia Maria. *Letters from New York*. 1845. Freeport, NY: Books for Libraries P, 1970.

Dobson, Joanne. "The Hidden Hand: Subversion of Cultural Ideology in Three Mid-Nineteenth-Century American Novels." *American Quarterly* 38.2 (1986): 223–42.

Douglas, Ann. *The Feminization of American Culture*. New York: Knopf, 1977.

Elbert, Monika. Introduction. *Separate Spheres No More: Gender Convergence in American Literature, 1830–1930*. Ed. Monika Elbert. Tuscaloosa: U of Alabama P, 2000.

Emerson, Ralph Waldo. *Selections from Ralph Waldo Emerson*. Ed. Stephen E. Whicher. Boston: Houghton Mifflin, 1960.

Goodman, Charlotte. "The Lost Brother, the Twin: Women Novelists and the Male-Female Double *Bildungsroman*." *Novel: A Forum on Fiction* 17.1 (1983): 28–43.

Harris, Susan. *Nineteenth-Century American Women's Novels: Interpretive Strategies*. Cambridge, England: Cambridge UP, 1990.

Hovet, Grace Ann, and Theodore R. Hovet. "Identity Development in Susan Warner's *The Wide, Wide World:* Relationship, Performance, and Construction." *Legacy* 8 (1991): 3–16.

Kelley, Mary. *Private Woman, Public Stage: Literary Domesticity in Nineteenth-Century America*. New York: Oxford UP, 1984.

Leverenz, David. *Manhood and the American Renaissance*. Ithaca: Cornell UP, 1989.

Pratt, Annis, and Barbara White. "The Novel of Development." *Archetypal Patterns in Women's Fiction*. Bloomington: Indiana UP, 1981. 28–45.

Sedgwick, Catharine Maria. *Live and Let Live; or, Domestic Service Illustrated*. 1837. New York: Harper & Bros., 1861.

———. *Redwood: A Tale*. 1824. New York: Putnam, 1850.

Tompkins, Jane. Afterword. *The Wide, Wide World*. By Susan Bogert Warner. 1850. New York: Feminist P, City U of New York, 1987. 584–605.

Voloshin, Beverly R. "The Limits of Domesticity: The Female *Bildungsroman* in America, 1820–1870." *Women's Studies* 10 (1984): 283–302.

Warner, Anna B[artlett]. *Susan Warner ("Elizabeth Wetherell")*. New York: Putnam, 1909.

Warner, Susan [Bogert]. *Queechy*. 1852. Philadelphia: Lippincott, 1900.

———. *The Wide, Wide World*. 1850. Afterword by Jane Tompkins. New York: Feminist P, City U of New York, 1987.

Whicher, Stephen E. Introduction to "1839–1840: Society and Solitude." *Selections from Ralph Waldo Emerson*. Boston: Houghton Mifflin, 1960. 122–23.

Williams, Cynthia Schoolar. "Susan Warner's *Queechy* and the *Bildungsroman* Tradition." *Legacy* 7 (1990): 3–16.

Zwarg, Christina. *Feminist Conversations: Fuller, Emerson, and the Play of Reading*. Ithaca: Cornell UP, 1995.

2

"Astra Castra": Emily Dickinson, Thomas Wentworth Higginson, and Harriet Prescott Spofford

KATHARINE RODIER

Before she began to jot excuses to her brother and his wife for missing social occasions at their home, the Evergreens, Emily Dickinson had enjoyed salon-style evenings there in the late 1850s, reportedly replete with "wild games of battledore and shuttlecock" and Dickinson's inimitable piano improvisations, "one she called the Devil being particularly applauded" (Bianchi, *Life* 64). Her sister-in-law, Susan Huntington Gilbert Dickinson, also her passionate friend and literary confidante, recounted somewhat quieter evenings when the *Springfield Republican*'s editor, Samuel Bowles, added outside perspectives to these apparently private affairs: " . . . now some plot of local politics rousing his honest rage, now some rare effusion of fine sentiment over an unpublished poem, which he would draw from his pocket, having received it in advance from some fascinated editor. I especially remember two such, 'Pomegranate Flowers,' by Harriet Prescott . . . and a little unpublished poem of Mrs. Browning's" (qtd. in Bianchi, *Face* 282–83). Many critics have assessed Emily Dickinson's admiration for and artistic indebtedness to Elizabeth Barrett Browning. But because of extant references to Dickinson's reading of "Circumstance," studies of her interest in Harriet Prescott Spofford focus largely on Spofford's fiction, notably in commentary by Barton Levi St. Armand and Jerrald Ranta, and in passing by Van Wyck Brooks.[1] In fact, Dickinson's appreciation of Spofford's writing may have been wider and deeper, as Susan Dickinson's account seems to hint: an aesthetic fusion of the nominally separate nineteenth-century spheres of public and private influence.

Moreover, Dickinson may have appreciated Spofford as a visible and visibly successful protégée of Thomas Wentworth Higginson, the reformer and man of letters whom Dickinson chose to pursue as a correspondent. His expectations for "public" women artists like Spofford helped shape his responses to the reticent, stubborn, and idiosyncratic Dickinson and her work, but his renowned advocacy of emerging women writers like Spofford undoubtedly encouraged Dickinson to approach him in the first place. His mediation in such matters, however direct or indirect, further blurs claims that rigidly gendered spheres of influence defined the work and workings of these authors. Tensions in Higginson's own poetry and his posthumous editing of Dickinson's poems suggest that he may have associated both Dickinson and Prescott as radically compelling writers, if ostensibly under his tutelage, despite the anomalous nature of his "preceptorship" with Dickinson, which as he admitted, "it is almost needless to say did not exist" (*Carlyle* 267).

After her letter of April 15, 1862, inaugurating what would become a twenty-year correspondence, Dickinson cryptically responded on April 25 to Higginson's prompt reply, apparently referring to a comment in his letter: "I read Miss Prescott's 'Circumstance,' but it followed me, in the Dark—so I avoided her—" (L#261, p. 404). According to Jay Leyda, within a few months of this exchange, Dickinson scissored from the *Atlantic*'s pages the running title of Prescott's review, "The Author of 'Charles Auchester,'" and Prescott's reference to the reclusive author Elizabeth Sheppard's novel, *Almost a Heroine* (2: 60), perhaps to include with her scrapbook "Treasures" or in one of her collage-style compositions. Other hints of Dickinson's interest in Spofford's writing surface in comments by Susan Dickinson, herself a crucial influence upon the poet's work, as Martha Nell Smith elaborates in *Rowing in Eden: Rereading Emily Dickinson*. In truth, Dickinson began to write to Higginson at a vulnerable point in her life when her needs, literary or emotional, could be the priority of neither of her sometime confidants, Susan or the man credited with introducing their literary circle to Harriet Prescott's "Pomegranate-Flowers," Samuel Bowles. In addition, Bowles had excerpted "Pomegranate-Flowers" in the May 11, 1861, issue of the *Springfield Republican,* Dickinson's local paper, which Higginson's family also read.[2]

As Susan Coultrap-McQuin discusses in *Doing Literary Business,* publishing in the heyday of the "Gentleman Publishers" (28) came to offer nineteenth-century women an ambiguous if limited sanction to unveil their writing through the agency of genteel, accommodating men espousing "cultural aims" ahead of economics (48). If reassured by the chivalrous pretext of committing their literary business into the hands of such purportedly high-minded entrepreneurs, women writers may have appreciated even more the doubled distance from commercial concerns afforded by the intervention of those less professionally identified mentors or consultants who also served as liaisons or go-betweens like Higginson, who was not literally an editor of the *Atlantic* when Prescott first published there in 1859 or when Dickinson began her correspondence with him after reading his "Letter to a Young Contributor" in its pages. As an intermediary, a male promoter could offer female writers the illusion of continued invisibility even as these efforts would expose a heretofore private pastime to the eyes of the world.[3]

Furthermore, the paradoxical role of both old-world protector of femininity and new-world pitchman of marketable goods may have appealed strongly to men of letters whose own prestige and vocational security in an industrializing culture were by no means assured.[4] Both backward-looking and foresighted, Higginson transmuted a conventional role, the fatherly authority, a friend to women in their socially prescribed frailty, into one that his mainstream culture could consider radical. His efforts played on the deeply patriarchal basis of artistic patronage in a fashion that strikes twentieth-century feminists as conservative if not insulting. Yet this assistance enabled women of his acquaintance to aspire to be heard, seen, and read as had only recently begun to seem respectable or even conceivable. With Helen Hunt Jackson, Spofford stands as one of Higginson's greatest successes, making both a living and a public career of writing, a venue Dickinson never admittedly sought or had to pursue out of financial necessity.

Harriet Prescott's acquaintance with Higginson began literally as a teacher-student relationship, Prescott appearing in the role that Dickinson would also claim by July 1862, as his "Scholar" (L#268, p. 412). After losing his pulpit in 1849 at the First Religious Church and Society in Newburyport, Massachusetts, because of his fervent abolitionist preachings, Higginson remained for several years in the manufacturing town. As he recalled, "I had a large and intelligent class of factory girls, mostly American, who came to my house for reading and study once a week. In this work I enlisted a set of young maidens of unusual ability, several of whom were afterward well known to the world . . . [including] Harriet Prescott, afterward Mrs. Spofford; . . . I never encountered elsewhere so noteworthy a group of young women" (*Yesterdays* 129). Spofford's biographer, Elizabeth Halbeisen, attributes the growing intensity of Prescott's "literary incursions" (43) to her involvement in Higginson's poetry group and to her teaching night classes in his program for workers. In a memoir of Spofford, Rose Terry Cooke notes that Higginson "developed by kindly counsel and generous encouragement the dormant genius his penetration had discovered" in "this brilliant girl" (529), herself new to Newburyport, having moved there from Maine in 1849 to stay with an aunt when Prescott's father had left the family to seek wealth in Oregon. Prescott won an essay prize in a series that Higginson had founded; he schooled the young writer, who had published hymns, critical works, and blank-verse dialogue in her school paper, to read Emerson, Shakespeare, Thoreau, and Bettina Brentano von Arnim. In Mary Thacher Higginson's 1914 biography of her husband, Spofford glows: "Mr. Higginson was like a great archangel to all of us then and there were so many of us! Coming into the humdrum life of the town, he was like some one from another star" (95–96). This aura of hero worship seemed acceptable to all involved: Thacher Higginson notes that Spofford "incidentally . . . speaks of his great personal beauty. This last impression was confirmed by Wendell Phillips, who, while listening to a lecture by Higginson, said to his companion, 'Is it not glorious to be handsome!'" (96).

The full text of the letter that Thacher Higginson quotes, written sometime between Higginson's death in 1911 and the biography's 1914 publication, shows the intimacy that Spofford, by then nearly eighty years old, recalled from her youthful friendship with her former teacher. After Spofford consoles her hero's widow, the warmth of her affection rekindles brightly, even after decades, despite her claim that her memories are "trifling":

Deer Island Near Newburyport
My dear Friend:

I hope the summer has healed your hurt, as far as it *can* be healed. We go through life, after this loss, like some one hopelessly maimed. We *have* to "get used to it." With me, as time goes on, I feel more and more sure of reunion, and I am confident that one way of gaining that assurance is by *assuming* it. . . .

I will look over all my letters, and all that I find I will send you, although I doubt if there are any that would be particularly illustrative to your work.

But I have some, written very very long ago, which I would like to read over with you, and talk about, some time when you have leisure,—just encouraging letters to a young girl. . . . My own reminiscences are very personal (to *me*), and too trifling to assist you,—his interest in the schools and visits there—his Shakespeare class to which it was such an honor to belong,—the Evening School,—his giving me the prize for an essay on Hamlet, a gold Eagle in a little mesh purse,— his employing me to copy a lecture on Mohamad [*sic*],—his arranging the Floral Processions for Fourths of July, and robbing me of my Oleanders which I had secured for the Greece float, and giving me the first raspberries in their place, having been up at four in the morning to go for them, (I *cried,* but I had been up *all night!*)—his lying on a bank watching the clouds all one afternoon, his rowing on the river, —and long afterwards all of us girls sitting together in woody places reading his "Out-Door Paper" as they came out,—his great personal beauty. I was deeply in love with my husband at the time, . . . but Mr. Higginson was like a great archangel to all of us then, and there were so many of us! Coming into the humdrum life of the town, he was like some one from another star.[5]

While Dickinson recorded no surviving impression of Higginson's physical appearance, Susan Dickinson had asked Samuel Bowles to procure a picture of Prescott's "archangel" for her even before her sister-in-law had begun to write to Higginson, perhaps suggesting both Dickinsons' interest in owning an image of this man whose writings Emily had admired. Moreover, not unlike Spofford, after Dickinson gained his acquaintance, she would repeatedly refer to him as a man who "saved [her] Life" (L#621, p. 649).

Whether or not Harriet Prescott, or Dickinson for that matter, upheld the stereotype that the nineteenth-century male-female mentoring relationship required on one hand "the lovesick lady" (Marchalonis xv), Prescott would send Higginson "immense letters" (*Letters and Journals* 104) after he moved to Worcester in 1852. In May 1854 he wrote cordially to his young friend in Newburyport of his new ministry: "Would you like to look in at the Free Church? The people are bright and earnest, rather than cultivated. . . . Worcester is a great thoroughfare, and there are always many strangers, and many Nicodemuses there are, who come by night only" (qtd. in Thacher Higginson 122). During these years after Higginson's move to Worcester, Prescott had begun to write up to fifteen hours a day to help support her invalid parents, in one case writing all night until "her hand and arm were swollen from incessant use . . . and . . . after all, she did not receive the prize" (Halbeisen 50). The image recalls the self-imposed ambidexterity of Louisa May Alcott, whose 1877 *A Modern Mephistopheles,* published in the anonymous "No-Name Series" by Roberts Brothers, would be widely guessed to be Spofford's creation. Like Alcott, Prescott and her sister Mary N. Prescott were both compelled to seek publication out of financial urgency.

Lured by the lucrative possibility of publishing in a new journal, the *Atlantic Monthly,* first printed in November 1857, Prescott submitted her detective story, "In a Cellar." Upon its publication in February 1859, Higginson wrote to his mother of Prescott's acceptance and the intrigue surrounding the author's identity, smugly prefiguring Spofford's autobiographical story of 1882, "Miss Wildrose," in which a rector verifies the heroine's authorship of a particular tale (Halbeisen 53–54).[6] "Do you remember a Newburyport girl named Harriet Prescott . . . whom I think a wonderful genius? She has just sent to the 'Atlantic' a story, under an assumed name, which is so brilliant and shows such an extraordinary intimacy with European life that the editors seriously suspected it of being a translation from some first-class Frenchman, as Balzac or Dumas, and I had to be called in to satisfy them that a demure little Yankee girl could have written it: which, as you may imagine, has delighted me much" (*Letters and Journals* 104). This acceptance launched a series of *Atlantic* publications for Prescott which Dickinson undoubtedly read, as her comments on "Circumstance" ambiguously affirm, a popularity that flourished even as critics like Henry James began to object to Prescott's "description for the sake of description" that was "true to nothing" (qtd. in Halbeisen 74), as he wrote of her novel *Azarian: An Episode* in the January 1865 *North American Review.*

More charitably, Higginson had written of the same novel in the October 1864 *Atlantic:* "If one opened the costly album of some rare colorist, and became bewildered amid successive wreaths of pictured flowers, with hues that seemed to burn, and freshness that seemed fragrant, one could hardly quarrel with a few stray splashes of purple or carmine spilt heedlessly on the pages; . . . if few are so lavish and reckless with their pigments as Harriet Prescott, it is because few have access to such wealth" (515). But even Prescott's great champion expressed reservations about aspects of his protégée's writing, blaming her tendency toward "melodramatic" plots, "morbid" characters, and "overdone" descriptions in part on "the American public, so ready to flatter early merit" and "the fatal cheapness of immediate reputation" (516). His comments faulting popular tastes and their negative influence may not have been lost on an *Atlantic* reader—and relatively invisible writer—like Emily Dickinson who eschewed the demands of celebrity. In contrast, besides such vivid appearances in prose, as author and as subject, Harriet Prescott Spofford published over three hundred poems in more than thirty-five magazines between 1860 and 1921 (Halbeisen 142), many of which the Dickinson family received regularly. She first collected her poems in 1882, four years before Emily Dickinson died, eight years before Higginson co-edited the first edition of Dickinson's verse.

Higginson's correspondence with *Atlantic* editor James T. Fields reveals his even more profound investment in Prescott's emerging career. Beyond his concern to champion Prescott's art and to place her stories in this prestigious market, Higginson's letters to Fields document his meticulous entrepreneurial skills and his intent to wield them. While obviously upholding the contemporary ideology of the male prerogative to shield women from worldly worries, Higginson also exposes the man-to-man machinations that underlay Coultrap-McQuin's overtly genteel world of "Gentleman Publishers." On August 16, 1860, after the phenomenal reception of Prescott's first *Atlantic* stories, "In a Cellar," "The Amber Gods," and "Circumstance," Higginson wrote to Fields from Pigeon Cove to press his protégée's apparent advantage:

> I want to suggest to you the expediency of paying Miss Prescott more than the ordinary $5 per page. It seems to me that such persons as she & Rose Terry ought not to be permitted to stray off into Harper & the Knickerbocker! Which they would have no disposition to do if treated with only equal liberality & promptness in the Atlantic. Miss Prescott's father is an invalid & she is the eldest of a considerable family, who looks largely to her for support, so she cannot afford to indulge any disinterested enthusiasm for the Atlantic.

Stressing Prescott's scrupulous character, her loyalty to Fields's magazine, her viability in other markets, her altruism in supporting her family, and the exigency of the matter, Higginson asks not only that Fields recognize these issues but that he grant Prescott special remuneration. If not in fact planning to start a bidding war among literary journals on this young woman's behalf, Higginson wanted Fields to realize that Prescott represented a commodity worth such competition.

Shortly thereafter, writing again to Fields from Worcester on September 6, 1860, Higginson pushed Prescott's interests further, and more explicitly:

> I wished to see you in passing through Boston, to show you a letter from Harriet Prescott about her compensation; it was so simple & honest. I find that she has written another story for Harper & one for the Cosmopolitan Art Journal which last she didn't want to do, but couldn't afford not. She should infinitely prefer to write for the Atlantic. And it turns out that she did not know the difference between the Harper & the Atlantic page—or thought it lay on the other side. Harper only offered eight dollars a page & wished stories both for the monthly & weekly.
>
> Now the Harper page is more than one third larger, so that this really is only equal to $6 per page for the Atlantic. If I were you I would pay her at the rate of $7 for the story which is now in Lowell's hands.—at least that. And whatever the increase is, I will see that a hint goes with it that the Atlantic has the refusal of what she may write hereafter—paying as high as anybody will pay as you said to me.
>
> She is a thoroughly honorable person, in the very best sense, & she feels that to have her compensation raised at all "seems as if she had

got into company where she had no right to be." "That is on one side. On the other is the fact that it would be the most inconceivable relief not to be forced to write & that I should then do better, & that I need all & every cent I can earn—not at all for myself though"—she is afraid of doing something dishonorable & so leaves it in my hands.

Now that you know just how it is, you can just see that the check is filled out for her, next time, to whatever amount you think best, & no farther correspondence will be needed from you, either by her or by me, about it. You are too busy.

Once again stressing Prescott's innocence of the pecuniary details of publishing, Higginson steps in with zeal, ready to nickel-and-dime a profitable deal with Fields in her name. His ambiguous remark that "she is afraid of doing something dishonorable & so leaves it in my hands" seems unintended to call his own honor into question. Confident of appearing above reproach, he rushes to propose what seems an obvious conclusion, urging Fields to accept his advice literally by signing on the dotted line. In his exuberance, Higginson may have miscalculated his mastery of the situation, or consciously exaggerated it, for in truth, what had he to lose? His own reputation seemed to him not at stake.

But a year later, on August 19, 1861, he wrote to Fields to acknowledge a disappointment of his efforts: "As for Miss P's story, I feel very badly about it, for know you wd. not hv. done such an unpleasant duty twice, save from necessity. I hv. heard nothing of it, & she does not write me so often, naturally, as before the advent of a nearer confidant." While concerned for Prescott's prospects, Higginson also knew when to acquiesce to the editor's ultimate control. Here he appears to have shifted allegiance, identifying more strongly with Fields than with the unfortunate "Miss P." As Dickinson had admonished her correspondent in her first letter to him, "Honor is it's own pawn" (L#260, p. 403).[7] His letters to Fields about Harriet Prescott are instructive, suggesting how Dickinson could imagine that an advocate of women writers like Higginson might assume a cooperative role in her own art, if not a managerial one, even if she never actually broached that less delicate subject with him. Such negotiations also reflect the aspects of public exposure for her writing that Dickinson may have most dreaded.

Throughout their friendship, Higginson persisted in constructing Spofford as an ingenue, an unworldly girl who needed and appreciated his help, often casting her in literary terms. He compared to Frances Burney's equally wide-eyed Evelina the wide-eyed young Prescott, awed to attend the *Atlantic* dinner honoring Harriet Beecher Stowe—the only other woman who joined the assembled male literati of Boston on this occasion. When Higginson quizzed Prescott on her conversation with the great lady, she reported that they said "Nothing, except that she once asked me what o'clock it was, and I told her I didn't know" (*Yesterdays* 176–78). At another point, he compared Prescott to Burney herself, the demure writer who had ascended into the eighteenth-century literary court of Samuel Johnson; Higginson later mentioned Burney as a stylistic exemplar of sorts in "Letter to a Young Contributor" (406). Clearly, he delighted in the apparent incongruity between Prescott's phenomenal success and her modest demeanor, her intense writing and her deferential deportment, and enjoyed the avuncular role he played in advertising the proceedings, perhaps seeing the contrast as a way to mainstream such "sensation" writing for a broader readership. Higginson's tendency to include critical remarks on his protégées' looks may have derived from a concern to extinguish any trace of eroticism from his depictions of these relationships, often rendered for his invalid wife or his mother, much as Spofford's fond letter to Higginson's widow reflects a similar concern for blameless appearance.

Notably, Higginson also sketched Dickinson as a literary figure, writing to his first wife upon meeting the poet at her home in Amherst that "if you had read Mrs. Stoddard's novels you could understand a house where each member runs his or her own selves" (Leyda 2: 151). Elizabeth Stoddard's *The Morgesons* opens with the brilliantly paced line, " 'That child,' said my aunt Mercy, looking at me with indigo-colored eyes, 'is possessed' " (5). A typically wry exchange between Stoddard's characters reads:

> "Suppose you had been fed mostly on Indian meal, with a herring or a piece of salted pork for a relish, and clams or tautog for a luxury, as I have been, would you be as tall and as grand-looking as you are now? And would you be covering up your face, making believe worry?"
>
> "Maybe not. You may tell mother that I am coming." (132)

Following Dickinson's own self-promotional leads, Higginson would also depict her as a character bordering on the gothic, a construction perhaps intended to help sell her books. Quite simply, Higginson's obviously doting and paternal literary portraits of Harriet Prescott may contrast so strikingly with his evocation of Dickinson because, as Tilden G. Edelstein puts it, "Other women writers took his advice" ("Mentor" 41).

However, after Dickinson's death, Higginson may have connected the self-professed "only Kangaroo among the Beauty" (L#268, p. 412) with this less "Wayward" protégée, despite his apparently incompatible imaginative constructions of their personae. Not long after Dickinson died, he wrote a wistful sonnet, titled "Astra Castra," in which the speaker is haunted by an elusive female spirit:

Somewhere betwixt me and the farthest star,
Or else beyond all worlds, all space, all thought,
Dwells that freed spirit, now transformed and taught
To move in orbits where the immortals are.
Does she rejoice or mourn? Perchance from far
Some earthly errand she but now has sought,
By instantaneous ways among us brought,
Ways to which night and distance yield no bar.
Could we but reach and touch that wayward will
On earth so hard to touch, would she be found
Controlled or yet impetuous, free or bound,
Tameless as ocean, or serene and still?
If in her heart one eager impulse stirs,
Could heaven itself calm that wild mood of hers? (qtd. in Lease 98)

Edelstein, Richard Sewall, and Benjamin Lease all suggest that Higginson's memory of Emily Dickinson inspired this meditation, published in 1889. Higginson also imposed "Astra Castra" as his title for Dickinson's poem #524, "Departed—to the Judgment," published in his first edition of her work in 1890. Among Higginson's papers in the Galatea Collection at the Boston Public Library is a handwritten card, the ink now purple with age, that bears simply his signature, the phrase "Astra castra, numen lumen," and underneath those words the designations "Cambridge" and "Jan. 12, 1880." While he identifies "Astra Castra" as a "mediaeval motto" ("Portfolio" 8), it also served to subtitle the concluding section of one of Prescott's most famous tales, "The Amber Gods," serialized in the *Atlantic* early in 1860. St. Armand calls the story "a florid exercise in posthumous reverie" ("Died" 101) and contends that the narrator's realization at the story's end—that she has died—undoubtedly inspired Dickinson's use of a similar narrative perspective in many of her poems.

St. Armand also notes that Higginson further linked these two writers by later assigning the second phrase of Prescott's subtitle, "Numen Lumen," to introduce Dickinson's poem #463: "I live with Him—I see His Face," a study of eternal union in death printed in the 1896 third edition ("Died" 118 n. 15). Whether the phrase held a cultural resonance for Higginson and Prescott, as Alfred Bendixen suggests (219), whether Higginson associated it with Prescott's story, or whether in fact she had drawn it from some previous interchange with him, Higginson's borrowings of the title from Prescott's previously published work not only recall that story as an authorial precedent for both his own composition and his editorial gestures, but affiliate it and its writer with the subject of both projects, a juxtaposition apparently to his mind not ultimately incongruous.[8]

Each of these writers was also drawn to the concept of evanescence, an attraction perhaps reinforced for Dickinson and Spofford by Higginson's usage in the *envoi* for the April 1862 "Letter to a Young Contributor": "Yet, if our life be immortal, this temporary distinction is of little moment, and we may learn humility, without learning despair, from earth's evanescent glories" (410).[9] Later, "evanescence" would become one of Dickinson's totem words. About 1879, she may have based her poem "A Route of Evanescence" (P#1463) on Higginson's description of a hummingbird in the December 1862 *Atlantic* essay "The Procession of the Flowers," which Spofford also knew. Dickinson had not only read this Higginson piece but had mentioned it in her letters (L#280, p. 424). According to Thomas H. Johnson, Dickinson circulated copies of this poem to five or six different recipients who ranged from family members to Higginson to Helen Hunt Jackson and to an editor, Thomas Niles. Higginson received his copy in November 1880, while Mabel Loomis Todd received one in thanks for a painting of a wildflower, the Indian-pipe, in late 1882.[10]

Interestingly, a poem entitled "Evanescence" by Harriet Prescott Spofford had appeared in *Harper's New Monthly Magazine* in February 1875. According to Jack Capps, the poet's sister Lavinia referred in 1851 to *Harper's New Monthly* as her "usual magazine" (128), a propensity she may have maintained through 1875 and which Emily Dickinson may have shared.[11] While Spofford's poem makes no mention of a hummingbird, its unconventional revision of a *carpe diem* motif would not be foreign to Dickinson's sensibility:

> What's the brightness of a brow?
> What's a mouth of pearls and coral?
> Beauty vanishes like a vapor,
> Preach the men of musty morals!
>
> Should the crowd then, ages since,
> Have shut their ears to singing Homer,
> Because the music fled as soon
> As fleets the violet's aroma?
>
> Ah, for me, I thrill to see
> The bloom a velvet cheek discloses

Made of dust—I well believe it!
So are lilies, so are roses!

Spofford's comic rhyme in the second stanza, "Homer" and "aroma," while a cruder version of the irreverent wit that Dickinson enjoyed, highlights the unsentimental approach this poet takes to reclaim with contemporary irony a sensual poetic tradition from those "men of musty morals" who would deny its validity. Moreover, a reader like Dickinson might have appreciated the knowing voice that Spofford gives to her poem's acerbic persona.

Spofford's own later writing further triangulates the three writers, equally subtly, but strikingly compressed into a single piece. Her June 1892 article in *Harper's Bazar*, "Pomegranate Flower and Apple Blossom," celebrates the "ethereal delicacy" of New England spring flowers over the ostentatious blooms of the "fabled tropics" (451). Here it is Spofford's phrase "this processional parade of flower and bud" that echoes Higginson's 1862 *Atlantic* essay, "The Procession of the Flowers." Perhaps coincidentally, Spofford describes the "cypripedium, exquisite beyond the power of a pencil to produce" (451), a flower placed in Dickinson's coffin at her burial service which Higginson had attended in May 1886 (Longsworth 243). Spofford also describes a mass of flowers as an "encampment," one translation of the Spofford-Higginson-Dickinson connective "castra." More definitely, she reveals her familiarity with Higginson's co-production of Dickinson's poetry, mentioning Dickinson by name: "the Indian-pipe, shows itself on small heaps of moulds, sometimes of a faint rose-color and sometimes pallid and ghastly enough to warrant its name of corpse flower, in which capacity perhaps it shines upon the covers of Emily Dickinson's wondrous verses" (450). Mabel Loomis Todd, Higginson's co-editor, had contributed the cover art for Dickinson's posthumous collection of poetry, based on the painting that Todd had given the poet during her lifetime. Higginson's second wife, Mary Thacher Higginson, would also evoke the curious beauty of this parasitic plant in a 1900 sonnet, "Indian-Pipe, Corpse-Plant, Ghost-Flower" (Nims 116).

While the Indian-pipe is the ultimate flower that Spofford celebrates in her catalog of northern wonders, her ambiguous treatment of Dickinson—a writer of "wondrous" poetry also evoked as "pallid," "ghastly," and suggestive of a "corpse"—seems especially significant in a text in which the writer seems to renounce her own earlier "florid" preferences for more restrained, more local, and less "ostensible" miracles (Dickinson, L#316, p. 450). As Bendixen notes (xix–xx), at this point in Spofford's career, her writing had absorbed more realistic components, perhaps shaped by post–Civil War cultural demands, perhaps in response to Henry James's objections to what became known as "the Azarian School," as well as to Higginson's gentler but as widely circulated critique of that novel. Yet in 1891, one critic still remembered Spofford as "A Flaming Fire Lily among the Pale Blossoms of New England" (qtd. in Halbeisen 1), echoing Rose Terry Cooke's 1888 description of the "tropic-souled fire-lily" who had given to the *Atlantic* the 1859 sensation "In a Cellar" (531). In 1914 Spofford would remark, "But although I like to write realistic stories, . . . I cannot say I am in sympathy with any realism that excludes the poetic and romantic" (qtd. in *Amber* xix). Whether or not her "procession" of the flowers encodes an apology for her movement toward realism, it does comprise an awareness that Dickinson could enjoy a "wondrous" immortality through publication after her death, a fact owing to Higginson's agency, as did Spofford's own art and career. Significantly, the title "Pomegranate Flower and Apple Blossom" also recalls the vivid poem which had appeared in 1861 at the height of Harriet Prescott's *Atlantic* career, several years before James's harsh assessment of *Azarian*.

Poems, Spofford's first collection of poetry, published in 1882, may also reveal her anxiety over trying to accommodate changing popular tastes, the marketplace condition that Dickinson both acknowledged and defied in her experiments with alternative publication, which included her correspondence with Higginson. Of her many previously published poems, Spofford included mostly those in which "the rare colorist" reverts to simpler meditations on life, love, and death (Halbeisen 143), excluding the sensational "Pomegranate-Flowers," which the Dickinson circle had so admired. Whether Spofford or an editor determined her table of contents, the 1861 *Atlantic* publication is absent.[12] Of "Pomegranate-Flowers," Paula Bennett argues: "Of the many nineteenth-century poems by women centering on autoerotically-based female sexual desire, none is more striking. . . . Spofford, a writer of extravagant, not to say reckless, stylistic effects, devotes twenty-seven stanzas to a young woman's ecstatic response to a pomegranate tree, the gift of a now absent lover. . . . What is beyond question . . . is that alone and abandoned in her 'small room' (575, line 94) this girl still possesses notable erotic resources of her own" (194). Bennett quotes one stanza to illustrate (196):

> Now, said she, in the heart of the woods
> The sweet south-winds assert their power,
> And blow apart their snowy snoods
> Of trilliums in their thrice-green bower.
> Now all the swamps are flushed with dower
> Of viscid pink, where, hour by hour,
> The bees swim amorous, and a shower

Reddens the stream where cardinals tower.
For lost in fern of fragrant stir
Her fancies roam, for unto her
All Nature came in this one flower (575, ll. 93–132)

While it is hard to imagine that an unorthodox stylist like Emily Dickinson would be drawn to Prescott's poem by the quintuple identical rhymes that center each stanza, Dickinson nonetheless read and enjoyed all manner of conventional popular writing. But any contemporary reader of this poem most likely would register its coded but relentless eroticism. This earlier treatment seems to repudiate Spofford's 1892 floral lesson in "Pomegranate Flower and Apple Blossom" of preferring what is local and understated to the offerings of "the fabled tropics" ("Blossom" 450). In the essay, the pomegranate, a plant native to western Asia, grown in this country mostly in the southernmost states, does not appear, except in the title. A tension between Spofford's aesthetics of past and present may have informed the decision to leave this provocative poem out of her first collection. While the book did include the exotic tribute "The Granadan Girl's Song," it featured more subdued verses like "The Violet," "The Hyacinth," "The Rose," and "The Lily," among others.[13]

At least one reader regretted the exclusion. In 1903, Susan Huntington Dickinson wrote to the *Springfield Republican* from Rome:

> I am extremely glad to see in your weekly issue, just read, an article of warm admiration and suggestion regarding the literary work of Harriet Prescott of the early Atlantic days, as well as the well-known writers of to-day. For several years I have wondered why everything of hers was not gathered up and represented to the public, and have many times thought to write her and urge the matter upon her attention.
>
> As usual, your paper is alert upon the trail of genius. That she has genius I am sure no one can deny who has known her work. Her vivid imagination is a refreshing protest to those who still revolt from a literature of materialism. She was the very tropics of those old high-flavored Atlantic monthlies, the Atlantics of Holmes and Longfellow, of Thoreau and Emerson, of Whittier, Lowell, and Higginson, and I remember with what distinct disappointment I used to put down the current number, if there was no kindling touch of hers found in them. The late Mr. Bowles keenly felt her originality and power and frequently sent the brief extracts from her manuscripts given him by his friends in the editor's sanctum.

>   Among these are none more beautiful than a few stanzas from
> "Pomegranate Flowers." (19)

Susan Dickinson goes on to affiliate Spofford's name with that of her by
then renowned sister-in-law, a juxtaposition often quoted by twentieth-
century scholars wishing to reintroduce Spofford's writing to a literary
world that had come to overlook it:

>   I missed in your citation of her early work to find no mention of
> "Circumstance," the most highly imaginative and thrilling tale I have
> ever read. I cannot understand the ignorance I find of it everywhere.
> . . . After first reading it, I sent it at once to my sister-in-law, Emily
> Dickinson. Immediately she wrote me:—
>   Dear S. That is the only thing I ever saw in my life that I did not
> think I could have written myself. You stand nearer the world than I
> do. Send me everything she writes. (19)

In revisiting through publication the site where Bowles had introduced
"Pomegranate-Flowers" to the *Republican* readership, Susan Dickinson's description valorizes not only Spofford's writing but her own role in supply-
ing her sister-in-law with material to inspire her imagination. Her further
comments celebrate the fantastic or thrilling qualities of Spofford's writing,
associated with the early *Atlantic Monthly* that Susan here nominally links
to Higginson. Would a poem like "Pomegranate-Flowers"—shared between two passionate female friends, eventually published in a journal that
both Dickinsons associated with Thomas Wentworth Higginson, remembered by Susan Dickinson into the twentieth century—not also have engaged Emily Dickinson?

Dickinson's impressions of the poem are unknown, but a memoir by
Martha Dickinson Bianchi hints that Harriet Prescott's "Pomegranate-
Flowers" may have inspired Bianchi's aunt in at least one way. Recalling
Dickinson's amazing conservatory, with its Cape jasmine, heliotrope, and
ferns (*Face* 4), Bianchi also remembered its summer relocation outdoors: "In
pleasant weather both aunts used to sit on the retired little side piazza, where
we joined them. . . . The giant *Daphne odora,* moved out from the conservatory, stood at one end with the Cape jasmine" (39). The Cape jasmine
served as "the crowning attention" (42), but according to Bianchi, Dickinson's pomegranates became "a butterfly Utopia" (39). Under the poet's hand,
the tropical pomegranate not only survived indoors the New England winter, but blossomed outside as her family gathered there to enjoy a more
agreeable season. Perhaps, like the protagonist of Harriet Prescott's 1861

poem, Dickinson luxuriated that "All Nature came in this one flower." But unlike Prescott's unnamed heroine, Dickinson could witness at least seasonally her plants' liberation from an interior confinement, "close shut beneath a roof" (578, l. 243). Ironically, this enclosure permits the tree of the poem, and its owner's reverie, to thrive. In further contrast, in Prescott's poem, many of Dickinson's cherished creatures appear only in the hothouse domain of dreams:

> No humming-birds here hunt their fruit.
> No burly bee with banded suit
> Here dusts him, no full ray by stealth
> Sifts through it stained with warmer wealth
> Where fair fierce butterflies salute. (578, ll. 271–75)

While a test to Dickinson's gardening skills, cultivating pomegranates also may have served the poet's transformative imagination as a silent tribute to another woman writer, one whom she had encountered in a largely unspoken configuration of influence that also encompassed their mutual "Preceptor," Higginson. Not surprisingly, Dickinson once again managed to surpass the limitations of her apparent inspiration.

To an unknown recipient, Spofford inscribed a copy of the 1882 *Poems,* now held in the Barrett Collection at the University of Virginia:

> My Dear Sir,
>   May I once again knock at your door with my verse?
>   If you do not wish for it, kindly let me have it again soon that I may use it while it is still seasonal?

Known to share his letters from Dickinson with others, Higginson may have chosen his friend Spofford as one so privileged. Her note evokes the wit and indirection that Dickinson typically deployed in her dispatches to him, synchronously gracious, arch, and challenging. Whether inspired by Dickinson's evasive style or simply quite capable of producing her own memorable personal prose, both puzzling and charming, Spofford anticipated as well that even her private dedications might find a greater readership, as her performative inscription here suggests. Perhaps Dickinson contrived her letters to a public figure like Thomas Wentworth Higginson with much the same assumption. Through the voices of her published writing, her relish of exotic and even violent motifs that flower from domestic realms, Harriet Prescott Spofford clearly shared affinities with Higginson's "only Kangaroo." Moreover, their connections through the "fair," the "fierce," and the "morbid" flourished within and beyond an evanescent intertextuality that swept these figures together across ideologically separate spheres, a dynamism fusing restraint, appreciation, and resistance in ways that all three writers may only have sensed.

Notes

1. I thank the Houghton Library of Harvard University for permission to quote from unpublished letters identified hereafter. I also wish to acknowledge the Boston Public Library for permission to quote from material in the Galatea Collection, and the Barrett Library at the University of Virginia for permission to quote Spofford's inscription from its edition of her *Poems*. Complete references follow as these works are cited.

In this essay, references to Thomas H. Johnson and Theodora Ward's edition of Dickinson's letters will be made by number (L#) followed by the page. Poems are also indicated by Johnson's numbers (P#).

In *Emily Dickinson and Her Culture*, St. Armand addresses Dickinson's response to "the Dark," a reference to Spofford's story "Circumstance" (173–80). He summarizes Dickinson's inspiration by Spofford: "It was the poet's genius to condense and crystallize, to distill and domesticate this spasmodic exuberance through the folk form of her verse, tempering the lush sensuousness and exotic word-painting of the Azarian school with the stern angularity and stark abstraction of 'homespun' Puritan discipline. From Spofford Dickinson learned a vocabulary of passion associated with tropical flowers, rich stuffs, fabulous jewels, and fantastic colors, but she also managed to contain such a vocabulary within a unique artistic medium that was purely her own" (186).

Ranta discusses how Dickinson "adjusts" (85) Higginson's ideals and language from "Americanism and Literature" in the January 1870 *Atlantic* to express in P#1167, "Alone and in a Circumstance," a woman's loss of intellectual property.

In the 1940 study *A New England Indian Summer, 1865–1914*, Brooks notes that "phrases and images . . . by Mrs. Spofford . . . seem to have left their traces in Emily Dickinson's mind. . . . One of Mrs. Spofford's heroines had 'sherry-colored eyes' before Miss Dickinson discovered that her eyes were like the sherry in the glass that the guest leaves" (nn. 156–57). Significantly, Dickinson included the "sherry" reference in one of her early letters to Higginson (L#268, p. 411). But in fact, the protagonist of Spofford's "The Amber Gods" qualifies the description of the elusive color of her eyes: "Some folks say topaz, but they're fools. Nor sherry" (*Amber* 38).

Brooks's impressions may be apt, but his documentation of another work by Prescott is incorrect. *Sir Rohan's Ghost* was not serialized in the *Atlantic*, although James Russell Lowell did review that novel in the February 1860 issue, the same issue that included the conclusion of Prescott's "The Amber Gods." Of Spofford's poetry, Higginson thought "Ballad" or "The Night Sea" from *Sir Rohan's Ghost* her signature pieces (Higginson and Boynton, *Reader's History* 263–64).

2. For a discussion of Dickinson's possible motivations for turning to Higginson as correspondent, see my 1995 dissertation, "'A Career of Letters': Emily Dickinson, T. W. Higginson, and Literary Women."

For Bowles to have access to a forthcoming *Atlantic* publication like "Pomegranate-Flowers," the *Springfield Republican* editor may have had closer professional ties to the prestigious monthly than has been previously assessed, suggesting further Dickinson's interest in corresponding with Higginson, whose work was so strongly associated with that magazine.

I thank Paula Bennett for pointing out that Bowles had also introduced parts of the poem for a print audience in the *Republican*. Many of Bennett's other insights inform this essay, and I appreciate her sharing with me in manuscript her article "The Spider, the Weaver, and the Seamstress: Dickinson and Her Nineteenth-Century American Women Poet Peers." I also thank Margaret R. Higonnet for her comments upon reviewing my essay in draft.

3. Interestingly, Dickinson's correspondence with Elizabeth Holland, wife of writer and publisher J. G. Holland, may also reflect a version of this dynamic of indirect transmission.

4. On the literary marketplace, see especially Michael T. Gilmore. See also Ann Douglas, *The Feminization of American Culture,* for more on Higginson's cultural context as minister and as literary man. On Ralph Waldo Emerson's parallel quest for vocation, see Henry Nash Smith.

Because of his own sense of failure as a poet, Higginson decided, "I must be content to enjoy instead of creating poetry" (Thacher Higginson 65). Despite this renunciation, he did continue to write and to publish poems, later collaborating on a collection with his second wife.

5. The recipient of this letter from Spofford (Houghton file Ms Am 1162.10, #895) is cataloged as Thomas Wentworth Higginson, but Judith C. Breedlove argues that it seems in fact to be directed to his second wife and biographer, Mary Thacher Higginson. Besides the content of the letter itself, evidence from Thacher Higginson's own biography indicates to me that Breedlove is indeed correct. I am profoundly grateful to this generous colleague for sharing her insights and her transcriptions of several Houghton letters with me.

6. I wish to thank Paula Kot for reminding me of this reference to the story that Halbeisen calls "The Song of the Morning Stars," published in *Our Continent* on March 8, 1882. Kot's work on Spofford has been invaluable to my study.

7. Again, I thank Breedlove for alerting me to these letters from the Higginson file at the Houghton Library. I reproduce her transcriptions here of letter Ms Am

1162.10, #686 (not the complete text), letter #689 (complete), and letter #721 (not complete).

Although Higginson knew many women whom he could call "Miss P," Harriet Prescott became engaged to Richard Spofford by 1860 and did not marry him until 1865. In abbreviated form, this letter seems to express a concern for the young writer's welfare not incompatible with the previously quoted letters to Fields. The apostrophe in Dickinson's quotation and the text of Susie King Taylor's letter that follows are reproduced as they appear in manuscript.

On March 11, 1902, Taylor, who had served the 1st South Carolina Volunteers, the Union army's first authorized black regiment, as a laundress, nurse, and teacher, appealed to Higginson, the unit's former commander: "I now write to let you know that I have nearly completed my manuscripts of the book that I am writing now about the my life in the Regiment. And of which I spoke to you of. I would be very grateful to you If [sic] you could review my manuscript & kindly give me your opinion upon it—whenever it is convenient to you. You can let me know & I await your reply with interest. And if you find it to your approval I would be very grateful for your signature" (Houghton Ms 1162.10, #914). Without defining what interventions Taylor may have hoped that Higginson might make on her behalf, not unlike Dickinson forty years earlier, she left the execution up to him, which by 1902 may have become for him simply a matter of routine. And in truth, Taylor's approach met with a different immediate response than did Dickinson's oblique inquiry. On November 18 (Houghton Ms 1162.10, #915), Taylor wrote to thank Higginson for his preface to the volume, published later the same year as *Reminiscences of My Life in Camp with the 33rd U.S. Colored Troops, Late 1st South Carolina Volunteers*.

8. In an undated letter, composed sometime after Higginson's commission as colonel in the Union army and Spofford's residence at Deer Island, she writes to him: "And thank you for the quotation! It made me proud to be so used! It made me, also, recall how much you had to endure of my young enthusiasms" (Galatea Collection, Boston Public Library). While Spofford does not indicate which of her works Higginson might have quoted nor in what capacity or forum, she clearly understood that his gesture had represented a tribute to her writing.

Thomas and Maria Teresa Prendergast translate "astra castra, numen lumen" as "starry field, divine light" (pers. comm.). Brian Striar reads these words all as nouns: "stars"; "military encampments or fortresses"; "godhead" or "divine command"; "light" or "glory" (pers. comm.). St. Armand proposes "cut star, numinous light" ("Died" 118), while other scholars offer "the stars my camp, the deity my guide" (Lease 97). Bendixen proposes "the star is cut, the power is the light" (219).

9. The first installment of Prescott's "The South Breaker" ran in the next issue in May (vol. 9, no. 55), while its conclusion and the review that Dickinson seems to have cut out, "The Author of 'Charles Auchester,'" ran immediately thereafter in June (vol. 9, no. 56).

10. This relatively wide dissemination of a poem suggests that Dickinson thought the subject or treatment would appeal to a range of readers, or as Johnson proposes, may "indicate the assurance ED felt about its quality" (*Poems* 1011). Johnson explains that Dickinson may have drafted the poem at Helen Hunt Jackson's request, sending her a copy in the summer of 1879.

11. Jack Capps specifically lists the following issues of *Harper's New Monthly Magazine* as holdings in the Dickinson collection at Harvard University: June 1850– May 1886; May 1853; January and September 1869; May 1870 (175). He finds "no indication that the subscription was ever allowed to lapse" in the Dickinson home (129). Jay Leyda notes that the words "George Sand" and "Mauprat" have been cut from the May 1870 issue, as has the phrase "it will prove a dangerous book" (2: 148). The latest issue in this collection dates from the month that Emily Dickinson died.

"Evanescence" was reprinted in Spofford's 1882 volume of *Poems* (38).

12. For an argument that Dickinson's correspondence with Higginson represented the poet's most daring experiment with alternative publication, again see my dissertation.

Despite Higginson's influence, the publisher of Spofford's book of poetry, Houghton, Mifflin, would decline to print Higginson and Todd's selections of Dickinson's poetry, a task which Roberts Brothers eventually undertook in 1890.

In her bibliography of Spofford's works, Halbeisen lists no subsequent publication for this poem.

13. Interestingly, Spofford's "The Lily," while not openly a celebration of the sensual, subtly juxtaposes a meditation on the sacred with an appreciation of transcendent pleasures:

Lift thine eyes, against the deepening skies
All the sacred hills like altars glow,
Waiting for the hastening sacrifice
Ere the evening winds begin to blow.

Lift thy heart, and let the prayer depart
To meet the heavenly flame upon the height,
Till all thy shadows to effulgence start,
And the calm brain grow clear with still delight!

"Flower-Songs," of which the "The Lily" is the concluding poem, first appeared in *Harper's New Monthly Magazine* November 1868: 833.

When Higginson met Dickinson in Amherst in August 1870, he described his new acquaintance in a letter to his first wife, Mary Channing Higginson: "She came to me with two day lilies which she put in sort of a childlike way into my hand & said 'These are my introduction'" (L#342a, p. 473). Although Dickinson may not have anticipated Spofford's eventual reputation as a "fire-lily," and while her choice of a flower of "introduction" may have simply reflected its seasonal—and local—availability, it may also represent a tribute, conscious or unconscious, to the 1868 publication by Higginson's protégée.

Works Cited

Bendixen, Alfred. Introduction and Explanatory Notes. Spofford, *"The Amber Gods" and Other Stories* ix–xxxiv, 217–22.

Bennett, Paula. " 'Pomegranate-Flowers': The Phantasmic Productions of Late-Nineteenth-Century Anglo-American Women Poets." *Solitary Pleasures: The Historical, Literary, and Artistic Discourses of Autoeroticism.* Ed. Paula Bennett and Vernon A. Rosario II. New York: Routledge, 1995. 189–213.

———. "The Spider, the Weaver, and the Seamstress: Dickinson and Her Nineteenth-Century American Women Poet Peers." Unpublished essay, 1998.

Bianchi, Martha Dickinson. *Emily Dickinson Face to Face.* Boston: Houghton Mifflin, 1932.

———. *The Life and Letters of Emily Dickinson.* New York: Biblo and Tannen, 1971.

Brooks, Van Wyck. *A New England Indian Summer, 1865–1914.* New York: Dutton, 1940.

Capps, Jack. *Emily Dickinson's Reading.* Cambridge: Harvard UP, 1966.

Cooke, Rose Terry. "Harriet Prescott Spofford." *Our Famous Women: An Authorized and Complete Record of the Lives and Deeds of Eminent Women of Our Times.* Hartford, CT: Hartford Publishing Co., 1888. 521–38.

Coultrap-McQuin, Susan. *Doing Literary Business: American Women Writers in the Nineteenth Century.* Chapel Hill: U of North Carolina P, 1990.

Dickinson, Emily. *The Letters of Emily Dickinson.* Ed. Thomas H. Johnson and Theodora Ward. Cambridge: Belknap of Harvard UP, 1986.

———. *The Poems of Emily Dickinson.* Ed. Thomas H. Johnson. Boston: Belknap of Harvard UP, 1955.

Dickinson, Susan Huntington [S. H. D.]. "Harriet Prescott's Early Work: A Reader Who Agrees with Us That Mrs. Spofford Should Republish." *Springfield Republican* 1 February 1903: 19.

Douglas, Ann. *The Feminization of American Culture.* New York: Knopf, 1977.

Edelstein, Tilden G. "Emily Dickinson and Her Mentor in Feminist Perspective." *Nineteenth-Century Women Writers of the English-Speaking World.* Ed. Rhoda B. Nathan. Westport, CT: Greenwood P, 1986.

———. *Strange Enthusiasm: A Life of Thomas Wentworth Higginson.* New Haven: Yale UP, 1968.

Gilmore, Michael T. *American Romanticism and the Marketplace.* Chicago: U of Chicago P, 1985.

Halbeisen, Elizabeth K. *Harriet Prescott Spofford: A Romantic Survival.* Philadelphia: U of Pennsylvania P, 1935.

Higginson, Mary Thacher. *Thomas Wentworth Higginson: The Story of His Life.* Boston: Houghton Mifflin, 1914.

Higginson, Thomas Wentworth. "Azarian: An Episode. By Harriet Prescott Spofford." *Atlantic Monthly* October 1864: 515–17.

———. *Carlyle's Laugh and Other Surprises.* Boston: Houghton Mifflin, 1909.

———. *Letters and Journals of Thomas Wentworth Higginson, 1846–1906.* Ed. Mary Thacher Higginson. Boston: Houghton Mifflin, 1921.

———. "Letter to a Young Contributor." *Atlantic Monthly* April 1862: 401–11.

———. Ms Am 1162.10, #686; #689; #721. Unpublished letters. Houghton Library, Harvard University.

———. "An Open Portfolio." *The Recognition of Emily Dickinson.* Ed. Caesar R. Blake and Carlton F. Wells. Ann Arbor: U of Michigan P, 1968. 3–10.

———. Unpublished letters. The Galatea Collection, Boston Public Library.

———. *The Writings of Thomas Wentworth Higginson.* Vol. 1: *Cheerful Yesterdays.* Vol. 2: *Contemporaries.* Vol. 6: *Out-door Studies.* Boston: Houghton Mifflin, 1900.

Higginson, Thomas Wentworth, and Henry Walcott Boynton. *A Reader's History of American Literature.* Boston: Houghton Mifflin, 1903.

Lease, Benjamin. *Emily Dickinson's Reading of Men and Books.* New York: St. Martin's P, 1990.

Leyda, Jay. *The Years and Hours of Emily Dickinson.* 2 vols. New Haven: Yale UP, 1960.

Longsworth, Polly. *Austin and Mabel: The Amherst Affair and Love Letters of Austin Dickinson and Mabel Loomis Todd.* New York: Farrar, Straus, Giroux, 1984.

Marchalonis, Shirley, ed. *Patrons and Protégées: Gender, Friendship and Writing in Nineteenth-Century America.* New Brunswick, NJ: Rutgers UP, 1988.

Nims, John Frederick, ed. *Western Wind: An Introduction to Poetry.* New York: Random House: 1983.

Ranta, Jerrald. "Dickinson's 'Alone and in a Circumstance' and the Theft of Intellectual Property." *ESQ* 41.1 (1995): 64–95.

Rodier, Katharine. "'A Career of Letters': Emily Dickinson, T. W. Higginson, and Literary Women." Ph.D. diss. U of Connecticut, 1995.

Sewall, Richard B. *The Life of Emily Dickinson.* 2 vols. New York: Farrar, Straus & Giroux, 1974.

Smith, Henry Nash. "Emerson's Problem of Vocation." *NEQ* 12 (March 1939): 52–67.

Smith, Martha Nell. *Rowing in Eden: Rereading Emily Dickinson.* Austin: U of Texas P, 1992.

Spofford, Harriet Prescott. *"The Amber Gods" and Other Stories.* Ed. Alfred Bendixen. New Brunswick, NJ: Rutgers UP, 1989.

———. Ms Am 1162.10, #895. Unpublished letter. Houghton Library, Harvard University.

———. *Poems.* Boston: Houghton Mifflin, 1882.

———. "Pomegranate Flower and Apple Blossom." *Harper's Bazar* 4 June 1892: 450–51.

———. "Pomegranate-Flowers." *Atlantic Monthly* May 1861: 573–79.

———. Unpublished letter (undated). The Galatea Collection, Boston Public Library.

St. Armand, Barton Levi. *Emily Dickinson and Her Culture.* New York: Cambridge UP, 1984.

———. "'I Must Have Died at Ten Minutes Past One': Posthumous Reverie in Harriet Prescott Spofford's 'The Amber Gods.'" *The Haunted Dusk: American Supernatural Fiction, 1820–1920.* Ed. Howard Kerr, John W. Crowley, and Charles L. Crow. Athens: U of Georgia P, 1983. 99–119.

Stoddard, Elizabeth. *The Morgesons and Other Writings.* Ed. Lawrence Buell and Sandra A. Zagarell. Philadelphia: U of Pennsylvania P, 1984.

Taylor, Susie King. Ms Am 1162.10, #914; #915. Unpublished letters. Houghton Library, Harvard University.

3

The War of Susie King Taylor

KAREN S. NULTON

There are many people who do not know what some of the colored women did during the war. . . . These things should be kept in history before the people. There has never been a greater war in the United States than the one of 1861, where so many lives were lost—not men alone but notable women as well.

—Susie King Taylor

When war is the sphere of men; when you are both free and fighting for freedom; when you must be careful what you say but you are determined to speak; when you write as a woman and a soldier and a dissident; when you retell the history you are making; what text stands as the final result? For Susie King Taylor, the answer is *Reminiscences of My Life in Camp with the 33rd U.S. Colored Troops, Late 1st S.C. Volunteers.* Taylor scholar Willie Lee Rose declares, "There is nothing even vaguely resembling Susie King Taylor's small volume of random recollections in the entire literature of the Civil War" (Romero and Rose 7). Taylor's readers—though perhaps disagreeing with Rose's characterization of her prose as "random"—will likely identify with his enthusiasm. *Reminiscences of My Life* is an unparalleled portrayal of a newly freed black woman's "wonderful revolution" which provides avenues for both personal growth and political expression.

Taylor holds the copyright to the 1902 edition of her autobiography. Her preface succinctly sets the stage for her decision to publish her work:

In 1900 I received a letter from a gentleman, sent from the Executive Mansion at St. Paul, Minn., saying Colonel Trowbridge had told him I was about to write a book, and when it was published he wanted one of the first copies. This, coming from a total stranger, gave me more confidence, so I now present these reminiscences to you, hoping they may prove of some interest, and show how much service and good we can do to each other, and what sacrifices we can make for our liberty and rights, and that there were "loyal women," as well as men, in those days, who did not fear shell or shot, who cared for the sick and dying;

women who camped and fared as the boys did, and who are still caring for their comrades in their declining years.

The juxtaposition of self-abnegation and ego in Taylor's preface echoes that of countless women writers enmeshed in a "literary double bind" who had to speak to be published and speak to be truthful.[1]

Taylor's authorial tightrope-walk is particularly apparent when we realize that she is explicitly revisioning war as it is put forward by Thomas Wentworth Higginson, to whom she dedicates her work. It is not uncommon to find two published works delineating one shared experience. These paired texts are always interesting for what they reveal about authorial voice, perspective, and agenda. When these texts are written by an army commander and an army laundress, respectively; when one author is born to a world of letters and the other lays claim to literacy as she does freedom; and when the central event in the narratives in the American Civil War in which both participants play unusual roles—then the pairing of these texts becomes more than an interesting genre study. This chapter will examine the inherent interweaving of race and gender in two texts of the American Civil War, and will explore Taylor's unique position as a woman writing about war, a traditionally male construct.

Higginson, familiar to many as a friend and correspondent of Emily Dickinson, spent two years as the commander of the 1st South Carolina Volunteers; he recorded his memories of this experience in *Army Life in a Black Regiment* (1869). Though it is impossible to construct a literary history without deconstructing others, Taylor's position as historian is more precarious than most. To tell her story—the "truth" of life in the 33rd Regiment—is radically to revision Higginson's (already published and acclaimed) text. As a colonel, Higginson was able to hold his social role of gentleman even as he tells of his decision to champion unconventional troops. He is a leader and a humanitarian, two roles that do not unfit him for the social role he plays during and after the war. The authorial niche Taylor must carve for herself is rather more constrained. In one volume, she claims that (1) women no less than men helped to win the Civil War; (2) she was able to view carnage and death without shuddering, and yet did not lose her essential femininity; (3) Reconstruction has failed miserably; and (4) Higginson got it wrong.

Just who was this woman who lived and wrote about life with the 33rd U.S. Colored Troops? Taylor, as she tells us early in her autobiography, was "born under the slave law in Georgia, in 1848," and gained her freedom in the capture of Fort Pulaski by Union troops on April 12, 1862 (29). She spent the Civil War in the South with the first company of African-American

Union troops, eventually marrying a sergeant in the company, Edward King. As she seeks to "tell a true story," Taylor does not offer her reader the angst-laden confessions that characterize much of twentieth-century auto-biography. A product of slavery, Taylor is well aware of the horrors of being possessed by another; her autobiography testifies to her determination to keep part of her inner life free from an all-consuming public. "For these black women," comments one critic, "to expose themselves in the market-place would require an amnesia powerful enough to blot out the horrific memory of the block" (Taylor xiv). Here, too, we see racial and gender concerns intermingled in Taylor's text; though she participates in the dominant culture, Taylor also participates in a distinct cultural subsection that guides her writing in particular ways. As Darlene Clark Hine suggests,

> Because of the interplay of racial animosity, class tensions, gender role differentiation, and regional economic variation, Black women, as a rule, developed and adhered to a cult of secrecy, a culture of dissem-blance, to protect the sanctity of inner aspects of their lives. The dy-namics of dissemblance involved creating the appearance of disclosure, an openness about themselves and their feelings, while actually re-maining an enigma. Only with secrecy, thus achieving a self-imposed invisibility, could ordinary Black women accrue the psychic space and harness the resources needed to hold their own. (915)

Because of this "dissemblance," Taylor retains a fundamental possession. Thus she conceals even as she reveals. Her first husband and marriage are introduced simultaneously; she records the men engaged in an early skir-mish, and adds, "Charles O'Neal was an uncle of Edward King, who later was my husband and a sergeant in Co.E., U.S. I" (Taylor 39). Her husband's death and the birth of her only son are accorded equally brief dispatches: "In September 16, 1866, my husband Sergeant King, died, leaving me soon to welcome a little stranger alone" (124). Of her second marriage nearly thirteen years later we are only told, "I next lived with Mrs. Gorham Gray, Beacon Street, where I remained until I was married, in 1879, to Russell L. Taylor" (124). Critics such as Willie Lee Rose, who bemoans, "What were the thoughts of a young mother-to-be upon the sudden and accidental death of her husband, the reader must only guess," ask Taylor to reveal as-pects of her private life and implicitly demand that she hand over power to her reader, a demand that she is unwilling to gratify (Romero and Rose 19).

Although her autobiography was not published until 1902, when Taylor was fifty-four, what she calls attention to both in the title and text of her narrative is the Civil War, in which she is between fourteen and eighteen years old. Her autobiography keeps the Civil War as its touchstone even when it rails against current social injustices; indeed, what allows Taylor to critique her society so thoroughly is the actual and implied presence of war, a construct that destabilizes and radicalizes prevailing social constructs.

Before exploring Taylor's textual relationship to Higginson, it is necessary to examine how writing about war shapes Taylor's text. War serves, in the words of Czeslaw Milosz, to redefine what is "natural" in life; tasks that would be considered unnatural—unfeminine and outside the boundaries of proper social behavior—for women during times of peace can become "natural," feminine, and socially acceptable during war (513). Of course, what was "socially acceptable" for black women differed radically from what was acceptable for upper-class whites. Still, like their white counterparts, southern black women lived in communities that accepted certain female roles and rejected others.[2] By writing about war, Taylor lays claim to a sphere of influence and action unavailable to her in times of peace. The Civil War allows Taylor to agree that only "those who had occasion to be in it" can know of the war, even as she declares, "I have seen the terrors of that war" (119). Writing herself out of the myth of passive and domesticated womanhood, Taylor reveals her own public and powerful agenda: "Let us not forget that terrible war, or our brave soldiers who were thrown into Andersonville and Libby prisons," she exhorts her reader.

Taylor's claim that "I have seen the terrors of war" rips through traditional delineations of war and peace. Historically, "because women are *exterior* to war, men *interior*, men have long been the great war-story tellers, legitimated in that role because they have 'been there' or because they have greater entree into what it 'must be like'" (Elshtain 212). Since this construction reduces women to mere onlookers to war rather than participants in war, their war literature is often characterized as secondary in importance to men's firsthand war texts. Consequently, "part of the female absence has to do with how war gets defined (where is the front?) and with who is authorized to *narrate*" (213). By writing about war, women writers alter traditional images of home and family. As they merge the iconography of public war with that of private life, they transform our perception of what constitutes war. In this way the idea that war is men's business to which women are exterior becomes "shattered by history" (Ruddick 219). Taylor's text forces us to question the artificial dichotomies between public and private, home and battle, protector and protected, and allows her to project a social and political voice that is muted in times of peace.

Because of the voice that war grants Taylor, it is easy to understand why she broadens "war" to include both the discrete event of the Civil War and the ongoing battle for civil rights, why she segues from describing her role in the Civil War to critiquing her limited social role in the years following. This dual war allows her to describe herself as a patriotic American who fights for the integrity of the Union while simultaneously revealing the ongoing battle for equality.[3] Her penultimate chapter, titled "Thoughts on Present Conditions," begins succinctly: "Living here in Boston where the black man is given equal justice, I must say a word in the general treatment of my race, both in the North and South, in the twentieth century" (61). For Taylor, "present conditions" are part of the story of the Civil War. The war does not end at Appomattox Courthouse, but continues in the lives of black Americans who are unfairly vilified and discriminated against. She muses, "I wonder if our white fellow men realize the true sense or meaning of brotherhood? For two hundred years we toiled for them; the war of 1861 came and was ended, and we thought our race was forever free from bondage . . . but when we read almost every day of what is being done to my race by some whites in the South, I sometimes ask, 'Was the war in vain? Has it brought freedom, in the full sense of the word, or has it not made our condition more hopeless?'" (61). Freedom "in the full sense of the word"—not simply the nebulous freedom of a law outlawing slavery—is what Taylor demands from her country. She knows, and wants her reader to know, just how far from possessing "full" freedom she and other African Americans are.[4]

Taylor was already writing without a net when she lay claim to being an authority on war; her narration becomes even more complex as she simultaneously revises Thomas Wentworth Higginson's *Army Life in a Black Regiment*. Her personal and literary relationships to Higginson (whose history of life with the 33rd had been unchallenged for thirty-three years before her work was published) were necessarily convoluted. Higginson, who offers a social "letter of introduction" to Taylor by writing the introduction to her work, offers generous, if qualified, praise for her work. He concludes that descriptions of military life in a black regiment "have never before been delineated from the woman's point of view," which gives "peculiar interest" to Taylor's "little volume" (Taylor xi). In contrast to Taylor's "little" work, Higginson refers to his own "volume," which was "long ago translated into French by the Comtesse de Gasparin under the title 'Vie Militaire dans un Regiment Noir'" (xi).

Higginson, who understandably looms large in his own telling of life with the regiment, is left almost completely out of Taylor's narrative. She tells us that he was the commander of the 33rd, and then does not mention him again until she remarks, "Colonel Higginson had left us in May of this year, on account of wounds received at Edisto. All the men were sorry to lose him. They did not want him to go, they loved him so. He was kind and devoted to his men, thoughtful for their comfort, and we missed his genial presence from the camp" (Taylor 32). In contrast, Taylor praises commander Trowbridge extensively, remarking that "We thought there was no one like him, for he was a 'man' among his soldiers. . . . I shall never forget his friendship and kindness toward me, from the first time I met him to the end of the war" (45). "No officer in the army," she claims, "was more beloved than our late lieutenant-colonel, C. T. Trowbridge" (46). Because of this uneven praise of Higginson, and given her need for him to review her work favorably, it is difficult not to question the sincerity of Taylor's flattery. Certainly, some of Higginson's descriptions of the 33rd Regiment must have pained Taylor. While his sincere belief in the abolitionist cause can hardly be questioned, and though he willingly gave two years of his life to help freed slaves fight for their freedom and country, Higginson was also as racist as many of his contemporaries. In describing "this mysterious race of grown-up children with whom my lot is cast," he unquestioningly asserts that mulattos are more intelligent than "pure" blacks: "When the Rebels evacuated this region they probably took with them the house-servants, including most of the mixed blood, so that the residuum seems very black. But the men brought from Fernandina the other day average lighter in complexion, and look more intelligent, and they certainly take wonderfully to the drill" (Higginson 17, 10). Looking over the camp one day, he notes that "my young barbarians are all at play" (8). He describes these men as "simple, docile, affectionate almost to the point of absurdity" (10). And, while watching their off-duty relaxation one day, Higginson announces that it is characterized by "such infinite guffawing and delight, such rolling over and over on the grass, such dances of ecstasy, as made the 'Ethiopian minstrelsy' of the stage appear a feeble imitation" (11). However much she may have respected Higginson's intentions toward her race, comments such as these must have rankled Taylor. In her work, in contrast, there is no "guffawing" and no vestige of an "Ethiopian minstrelsy." Instead, Taylor reaffirms the basic dignity and courage of both herself and the men with whom she lived and worked; she tells how "One night, Companies K and E. on their way to Pocotaligo to destroy a battery that was situated down the river, captured several prisoners. The rebels nearly captured Sergeant King [Taylor's husband], who, as he sprang and caught a 'reb,' fell over an embankment" (Taylor 27). She continues, "In falling he did not release his hold on his prisoner. Although his hip was severely injured, he held fast until some of his comrades came to his aid and pulled them up. These expeditions were very dangerous. Sometimes the men had to go five or ten miles during the night over on the rebel side and capture or destroy whatever they could find" (27). Just as Taylor blurs the spheres of men's and women's roles in war, she blurs the demarcations between the roles of black and white, soldier and civilian, protector and protected. If Higginson saw "young barbarians" when he viewed his troops, Taylor saw men who volunteered to go on "extremely dangerous" missions. We can only understand what Taylor is doing if we acknowledge that she and Higginson both participated in a culture that, while it stratified gender and racial roles, existed precisely because of their complex interdependence.

If we needed only one argument why there should be "separate spheres no more" in teaching nineteenth-century American literature, the following example might serve. In her book, Taylor retells a pivotal moment in Higginson's text and U.S. history: the reception of Lincoln's Emancipation Proclamation by the 33rd Regiment. The markedly different ways in which Taylor and Higginson interpret the proclamation argues pointedly for a conflation of male/female, black/white literatures. While it is clear that Higginson and Taylor view the event differently, what is also clear is the unity of their perception of society that underscores and allows these differences. Taylor's recapitulation is made possible by her understanding of and participation in the prevailing social constructs that marked the day as out of the ordinary. What differentiates the stories of Higginson and Taylor is the degree to which each author *believes* the history he or she is creating. For Higginson, the rhetoric of freedom that permeates the day stands for real freedom; his telling of the day imbues it with nearly sacred proportions. He tells of the proclamation's announcement, then continues,

> Then followed an incident so simple, so touching, so utterly unexpected and startling, that I can scarcely believe it on recalling, though it gave the key-note to the whole day. The very moment the speaker had ceased, and just as I took and waved the flag, which now for the first time meant anything to these poor people, there suddenly arose, close beside the platform, a strong male voice (but rather cracked and elderly), into which two women's voices instantly blended, singing, as if by an impulse that could no more be repressed than the morning note of the sparrow.—

> "My country, 't is of thee,
> Sweet land of liberty,
> Of thee I sing!"

Higginson believes, and wants his reader to believe, that the moment of the proclamation changes history fundamentally. It was for him not symbolically, but literally, a new beginning for a people who, "for the first time," had a flag that "meant anything" to them. Though Higginson views Lincoln's proclamation as a boon that allows the words "My country, 't is of thee" to take on new and auspicious meaning, Taylor points out repeatedly that her family fought to bring this country into existence. What is more, as she reminds us in her text, she and the others at the event are active agents working for their own freedom, not a people surprised by gratitude at a sudden gift of freedom.

Higginson continues,

> People looked at each other, and then at us on the platform, to see whence came this interruption, not set down in the bills. Firmly and irrepressibly the quavering voices sang on, verse after verse; others of the colored people joined in; some whites on the platform began, but I motioned them to silence. I never saw anything so electric; it made all other words cheap; it seemed the choked voice of a race at last unloosed. Nothing could be more wonderfully unconscious; art could not have dreamed of a tribute to the day of jubilee that should be so affecting; history will not believe it; and when I came to speak of it, after it was ended, tears were everywhere. (55)

In contrasting his "stupid words" with the "wonderfully unconscious" song of the spectators, Higginson relegates the soldiers and their families to a more natural, unconscious level of experience and elevates himself and the other whites whom he "motioned to silence" to a civilized, lettered, and fundamentally aware state of being. Here, too, Higginson carefully separates the experience of white and black; if the "whites on the platform" wanted to join in the lyrical tribute, Higginson would have none of it; the role he sets for himself is to watch, record, and analyze those around him—not to commingle with them. Distancing himself and the other whites from this "choked voice of a race at last unloosed," Higginson first reduces the reaction of the African Americans in the audience to an idealized combination of simplicity and gratitude, and then asserts that he can adequately interpret this response for his less knowledgeable reader. Thus, if he worries that "history will not believe" his interpretation of events, Higginson is also empowered to author a history that he finds acceptable.

Finally, the reader (one who would understand the "quaint" and "innocent" aspects of the scene and reminisce benevolently about "Old Tiff," we might imagine), is directly addressed, and exhorted to "think of it":

> If you could have heard how quaint and innocent it was! Old Tiff and his children might have sung it; and close before me was a little slave-

boy, almost white, who seemed to belong to the party, and even he must join in. Just think of it!—the first day they had ever had a country, the first flag they had ever seen which promised anything to their people, and here, while mere spectators stood in silence, waiting for my stupid words, these simple souls burst out in their lay, as if they were by their own hearths at home! When they stopped there was nothing to do for it but to speak, and I went on; but the life of the whole day was in those unknown people's song. (40–41)

The degree to which Higginson plays on the racial instincts of his reader is apparent when he remarks that "a slave-boy, almost white . . . even he must join in." The "even he" reminds his reader that Higginson expects the spontaneous song from the darker slaves, but must exclaim that this "almost white" child also joined in. Further, it reiterates how Higginson views the day as marking a fundamental, dramatic change in the world of the southern blacks. If on this day "even" the "almost white" slave must join in, it is because the song is, in his view, a cathartic epiphany, the voice of a race "at last unloosed." It changes history, and marks a history changed.

History does not change quite so dramatically on that particular day in Taylor's estimation. The "slave-boy" may be called free after the celebration, but he leaves with the same people who brought him. The flag may have "promised" much to her "people," but many of those promises were as empty as the coffers designated to pay the soldiers with whom Taylor fought. Words mean less—and more—to Taylor than they do to Higginson. Words that promise she views with suspicion; but the power of words to make and change history Taylor the author and teacher knows well. In her autobiography, she tells us of her birth and then skips right to a lengthy discussion of her early schooling in reading and writing; she explains that her husband can read and write, and highlights the hunger of the troops for words: "I taught a great many of the comrades in Company E to read and write, when they were off duty. Nearly all were anxious to learn. My husband taught some also when it was convenient for him" (Taylor 21). Higginson's assessment of the literacy of the same troops is worth noting; he writes, "Their love of the spelling-book is perfectly inexhaustible,—they stumbling on by themselves, or the blind leading the blind, with the same pathetic patience which they carry into everything. . . . But the alphabet must always be a very incidental business in a camp" (Higginson 25). For Higginson, literacy is a luxury that may or may not be given to his soldiers; for Taylor, however, literacy is part of the freedom for which she fights.[5] Words matter for Taylor, because without access to them Higginson can define her as a creature of pure emotion, natural—and uncontemplative—as a sparrow.

Consequently, when she retells the story of the proclamation day, Taylor deemphasizes the importance of Lincoln's proclamation (indeed, her reaction to the reading of the proclamation is not even mentioned) and emphasizes instead the celebration of a simple holiday:

> On the first day of January, 1863, we held services for the purpose of listening to the reading of President Lincoln's proclamation by Dr. W. H. Brisbane, and the presentation of two beautiful stands of colors, one from a lady in Connecticut, and the other from Rev. Mr. Cheever. The presentation speech was made by Chaplain French. It was a glorious day for us all, and we enjoyed every minute of it, and as a fitting close and the crowning event of this occasion we had a grand barbecue. A number of oxen were roasted whole, and we had a fine feast. Although not served as tastily or correctly as it would have been at home, yet it was enjoyed with keen appetites and relish. The soldiers had a good time. They sang or shouted "Hurrah!" all through the camp, and seemed overflowing with fun and frolic until taps were sounded, when many, no doubt, dreamt of this memorable day. (49–50)

The song that Higginson found so moving is not even mentioned by Taylor, and—pointedly—Higginson's speech is not discussed. (In Charlotte Forten Grimké's account of the same day, by contrast, Higginson's crafted rhetorical performance is described as central and moving.) Possibly Taylor, aware that no speeches represented an African-American voice that day, decided to ignore rhetoric entirely. In her narrative, the celebration is depicted as a pleasant holiday rather than as a momentous and inspiring occasion: the "crowning event" of the day is a "grand barbecue" (one described in a wonderful display of ownership and vigor as "not served as tastily or correctly as it would have been at home") and not, as we would expect, Lincoln's proclamation or the attendant speeches. Indeed, Taylor ends the chapter titled "Camp Saxton—Proclamation and Barbecue" by remarking how she "taught a great many of the comrades in Company E to read and write" (21). As Taylor posits herself and her husband as not only literate but *teachers* of literacy to colleagues who were "anxious to learn," she repudiates the unlettered and uncontemplative voice ascribed to her by Higginson. According to Higginson, silence or emotional exuberance represents the African-American voice equally well. In contrast, Taylor refuses to pretend that silence can stand for voice, and so fills the interstices of Higginson's text with voices celebrating a "grand" (though imperfect) barbecue.

Of course, by deemphasizing the importance of Lincoln's proclamation, Taylor also highlights the promises made to her and other African Americans that remain unfulfilled. If Higginson values the rhetoric that promises freedom to African Americans, Taylor denies the ability of mere words to change the reality of her social and political predicament. She neither misunderstands nor participates in the history Higginson creates. Rather, she questions his history, quietly insisting that the emperor has no clothes even while she applauds politely at the parade. Thus Taylor, "born free in the sight of God," argues that her rights of citizenship predate Lincoln's proclamation. She does not characterize herself or the soldiers as "simple souls" whose voices are "quavering" with gratitude, but instead denies the ability of mere words to grant a freedom that birthright and long service have already guaranteed—and, what is more, that ensuing years have denied.[6]

As she corrects Higginson's account of the celebration, Taylor merges her awareness of Reconstruction with that of the day itself. The woman who writes later in her narrative that "my people are striving to attain the full standard of all other races born free in the sight of God. . . . Justice we ask,—to be citizens of these United States, where so many of our people have shed their blood with their white comrades, that the stars and stripes should never be polluted," brings her awareness of the inadequacy of words alone to effect change to her telling of the day (75–76).

Another revealing retelling of Higginson's book comes when Taylor shifts the emphasis of the capture of Robert Defoe, the first black prisoner of war in the regiment. In Taylor's rendition of the story, Defoe is captured and imprisoned for his country for twenty months, and yet dies unrewarded. In contrast, Higginson tells of Defoe's capture without once mentioning his name, and says nothing of his poverty and death. He mentions how there was a party of men out tapping the telegraph wires, including "our adventurous chaplain and a telegraphic operator," at which point "a squad of cavalry was sent in pursuit, and our chaplain, with Lieutenant Osborn, of Bryant's projected regiment, were captured; also one private,—the first of our men who had ever been taken prisoner" (231). In Higginson's telling, the "adventurous" chaplain, who "enjoyed every minute" of his capture, is central; Defoe, who is unnamed, matters not as an individual man but as a representative of his race. At this point the narrative begins to play out like a B-grade adventure movie in which, once again, the African-American character is a foreign and unknowable counterpart to a brave, "commanding" white presence. "After his return," reminisces Higginson, "I remember [Chaplain Fowler] gave the most animated accounts of the whole adventure, of which he had enjoyed every instant, from the first entrance on the enemy's soil to the final capture. . . . But he told me nothing so impressed him on the whole trip as the sudden transformation in the black soldier who was taken prisoner with him" (231). Higginson records this "transformation" with a fascinating mixture of understanding and condescension:

> The chaplain at once adopted the policy, natural to him, of talking boldly and even defiantly to his captors, and commanding instead of beseeching. He pursued the same policy always and gained by it, he thought. But the negro adopted the diametrically opposite policy, also congenial to his crushed race,—and all the force seemed to go out of him, and he surrendered himself like a tortoise to be kicked and trodden at their will. This manly, well-trained soldier at once became a slave again, asked no questions, and, if any were asked, made meek and conciliatory answers. He did not know, nor did any of us know, whether he would be treated as a prisoner of war, or shot, or sent to a rice-plantation. He simply acted according to the traditions of his race, as did the chaplain on his side. In the end the soldier's cunning was vindicated by the result; he escaped, and rejoined us after six months, while the chaplain was imprisoned for a year. (231–32)

Higginson seems to feel mingled respect and repugnance for this man who "simply acted according to the traditions of his race, as did the chaplain on his side." While acknowledging that Defoe "did not know, nor did any of us know, whether he would be treated as a prisoner of war, or shot, or sent to a rice-plantation," Higginson still feels betrayed that such a "manly, well-trained soldier" (trained and molded into manhood by Higginson's command, we can assume) allows himself to lapse into a "tortoise to be kicked and trodden upon" by his foe. Defoe's "cunning" (which implies sly, instinctual thought) is contrasted with the chaplain's drawn-out—but properly military—release. As Higginson comments later in his narrative, "One half of military duty lies in obedience, the other half in self-respect. A soldier without self-respect is worthless" (259). Because he views self-respect and soldiering as inextricably intertwined, Higginson expects Defoe to act within codes of military honor that place a man's pride above his personal safety—even as he acknowledges the very real barriers to this behavior.[7] When Defoe acts within the boundaries of manhood defined by slaves such that he can be a man even while providing his captors/masters with lip-service docility and subservience, Higginson is at a loss to place him in the human spectrum he understands. Thus, just as the spectators at the celebration became as natural as "sparrows" in Higginson's account, Defoe is reduced to a subhuman, elemental animal, a "tortoise" who uses foxlike "cunning" to survive.

Not surprisingly, Higginson does not mention the subsequent death of the unpaid Defoe. Taylor, in contrast, focuses on the realities of Defoe's life after he has given his safety and health for his country, and questions Higginson's statement that Defoe escaped after six months; she asserts that "Robert Defoe was confined to jail at Walterborough, S.C. for about twenty months" (63). The particulars of where he was imprisoned and for how long serve as a counterpoint to the silence surrounding the man in Higginson's text; it matters to Taylor where and for how long Robert Defoe was imprisoned—just as it matters that he be fully named. She does not question how Defoe acted toward his captors in order to stay alive while inside Confederate lines, but focuses on the debt owed to Defoe and to his heirs.[8] "He had not been paid," Taylor reveals, "as he had refused the reduced pay offered by the government. Before we got to camp, where the payrolls could be made out, he sickened and died of small-pox, and was buried at Savannah, never having been paid one cent for nearly three years of service" (63).[9] In this way a named and unrewarded hero replaces the downtrodden "tortoise" of Higginson's text. Once again, Taylor's autobiography becomes a place where she can retell Higginson's history of the Civil War and substitute for it the realities of the war experienced by herself and fellow African Americans.

In all of her revisionings of Higginson's narrative, one of Taylor's principal concerns is how little the American public recognizes the contribution of African Americans to the Federal war initiative. Published nearly forty years after the close of the Civil War, Taylor's narrative highlights active black Americans fighting for their own freedom, thus repudiating white-centered accounts of slaves as placid contraband fought over by whites. James McPherson, in *The Negro's Civil War*, reveals how widespread the misconception of passive blacks is; he explains that "the belief still persists among many laymen and some historians that the slave was a passive, docile, uncomprehending recipient of freedom in 1865, and that the four and a half million Negroes in the United States played no important or effective role in the tragic drama of the Civil War" (xvi).[10] A wonderful passage from a 1928 biography of General Grant breathes life into this observation: "The American negroes are the only people in the history of the world, so far as I know, that ever became free without any effort of their own . . . [the Civil War] was not their business. They had not started the war nor ended it. They twanged banjos around the railroad stations, sang melodious spirituals, and believed that some Yankee would soon come along and give each of them forty acres of land and a mule" (qtd. in McPherson xv). Far from twanging banjos or singing spirituals in Taylor's account, African Americans are shown fighting for their country even when that country refuses them uniforms, pay, and respect. She tells of the taking of Charleston, and how "the 'rebs' had set fire to the city and fled, leaving women and children behind to suffer and perish in the flames" (Taylor 42). At this point, Taylor records how "our regiment went to work assisting the citizens in subduing the flames. It was a terrible scene. For three or four days the men fought the fire, saving the property and effects of the people, yet these white men and women could not tolerate our black Union soldiers, for many of them had formerly been their slaves; and although these brave men risked life and limb to assist them in their distress, men and even women would sneer and molest them whenever they met them" (42). These "brave men" who "risked life and limb" are not thanked (or paid), but are accosted and denigrated by those they help. It matters to Taylor that the magnanimity of these "black Union soldiers" be recorded and celebrated.

While the tone of the portion of her text centered on the war itself is often instructive (for instance, as she explains daily routines with which her audience would be unfamiliar), Taylor's last two chapters are personal and defiant. Early chapters that explain how she and other African Americans served their nation during the Civil War are followed by chapters that demand acknowledgment of how unjustly they are treated in the years following it. In many ways, Higginson's relationship to war ends when he leaves the 33rd Regiment; Taylor's time with the 33rd, however, is the beginning of a larger war for respect and recognition. Of the Spanish war she comments, "there were black soldiers there too. At the battle of San Juan Hill, they were in the front, just as brave, loyal, and true as those other black men who fought for freedom and the right, and yet their bravery and faithfulness were reluctantly acknowledged, and praise grudgingly given" (63). She continues, "All that we ask for is 'equal justice,' the same that is accorded to all other races who come to this country, of their own free will (not forced to, as we were), and are allowed to enjoy every privilege, unrestricted, while we are denied what is rightfully our own in a country which the labor of our forefathers helped to make what it is" (63). In a sentence that throbs with anger and defiance, Taylor returns to the message that the privileges of citizenship "rightfully" belong to the black Americans whose "forefathers" helped to establish and preserve the Union. She does not ask for grudging concessions from her reader and her nation, but rather demands the dues that belong to her as a citizen. At this point, her autobiography moves from an individual to a collective narrative; it becomes "a public rather than a private gesture, [as] me-ism gives way to our-ism and superficial concerns about individual subjection usually give way to the collective subjection of the group" (Benstock 70).

Taylor, who lives in Massachusetts, arguably the most liberal of the states at the time, relates a journey that she takes to Louisiana to see her son who was "just recovering from a severe hemorrhage" (71). Taylor wants to bring him home to Boston to recuperate, but Jim Crow laws that would not permit him a berth on a sleeper car prevail: "I might have brought him home, but as I could not I was forced to let him remain where he was. It seemed very hard, when his father fought to protect the Union and our flag, and yet this boy was denied, under this same flag, a berth to carry him home to die, because he was a negro" (71–72). Again and again, Taylor reminds her reader that equality is not a gift to be granted by the United States government at its convenience, but a right both entrusted by God and earned by sacrifice in service to the Union. She tells us that the Civil War is only the beginning of a larger civil rights war; although Higginson may believe that Lincoln's proclamation guaranteed freedom for black Americans, Taylor knows that Jim Crow laws contributed to her son's death. As she explores the privileges that are "denied" to her in particular when she cannot bring her son home, Taylor also examines the privileges that are denied to her race as a whole.[11] The movement in her narrative is from the particular to the collective, from the story of one woman's experience of the Civil War to that of a broader racial discrimination. Higginson's text can remain an individual's story; Taylor's history seeps into the lives of her compatriots.

Finally, Taylor angrily denounces a call by the Daughters of the Confederacy to ban the play *Uncle Tom's Cabin*. She explains how the memory of slave sales and their horrific emotional consequences will never desert her and then adds in disgust,

> I read an article, which said the ex-Confederate Daughters had sent a petition to the managers of the local theatres in Tennessee to prohibit the performance of "Uncle Tom's Cabin," claiming it was exaggerated, (that is, the treatment of slaves), and would have a very bad effect on children who might see the drama. . . . Do these Confederate Daughters ever send petitions to prohibit the atrocious lynchings and wholesale murdering and torture of the negro? Do you ever hear of them fearing this would have a bad effect on the children? Which of these two, the drama or the present state of affairs, makes a degrading impression upon the minds of our young generation! In my opinion it is not "Uncle Tom's Cabin," but it should be the one that has caused the world to cry "Shame!" It does not seem as if our land is yet civilized. (66)

Taylor's final claim, that "it does not seem as if our land is yet civilized," reverses the logic of the Confederate Daughters and makes their attitude, rather than the banned play, a sign of barbarism. More, it transforms the unlettered drawl of a character in Higginson's book into her own crafted, powerful language. In *Army Life,* Higginson tells of an African-American soldier in his regiment who had told him he would leave the South after the war was over because "I'se made up my mind dat dese yer Secesh will neber be cibilized in my time" (266). In the amused slang in which he records this speech, Higginson portrays the soldier as illiterate and naive. In revisioning the history of the 33rd, however, Taylor strips any naïveté from the statement that "It does not seem our land is yet civilized." Instead, she drops each word with powerful anger, daring her reader to question her rhetoric or authority to speak.

Thus, just as much of black writing glances at identity from both individual and group perspectives, Taylor's narrative reveals a doubled awareness of self articulated both on personal and national levels. In one respect, the author identifies herself as an American who has a national enemy to fight; in another respect, she defines herself as an American who has a national enemy to expose.

All of Taylor's Civil War narrative is crafted to demonstrate how the war ultimately did not grant African Americans true freedom. As do other women who write about war, Taylor takes advantage of a time of social upheaval to expand her social and political voice and to revision the history put forth by Thomas Wentworth Higginson. Like Phillis Wheatley before her and Zora Neale Hurston after her, Taylor views herself not as voiceless spectator of war but as a woman with vested interest in the fight for national interests and racial equality. Since the Civil War fed a hunger for freedom in black Americans, King Taylor fought for racial equality by merging this objective with that of Unionism. In this view, to fight for the goals of the United States was also to fight for minority rights.

Notes

1. The unique constraints autobiography imposes upon women whose texts blur the public/private boundaries are well documented. Some secondary texts that elucidate this issue particularly well are Bell and Yalom; Benstock; Fowler and Fowler; and Stanton.

2. For more detailed analyses of these roles, see Fox-Genovese; Gaspar and Hine; Friedman, Hawks, and Skemp; Hine; Morton; White; and Weiner.

3. The path for Taylor's resistance runs back to Phillis Wheatley's revolutionary poetry. Wheatley supported the American claim to autonomy but questioned the place of slavery in a new, free society. Consequently, she asks leave to "paint fair freedom's charms" in her poem "On the Death of General Wooster," but does not stop with asking for divine freedom's help in the battle; instead, she chastises her

reader and her country, asking, "But how presumptuous shall we hope to find / Divine acceptance with th' Almighty mind— / While yet (O deed Ungenerous!) they disgrace / And hold in bondage Afric's blameless race?" (149). As her poetry supports the American Revolution, Wheatley reminds her reader to examine the rhetoric of "freedom" to which she aspires, and to create a new nation in which the rhetoric and the reality coincide for black as well as white Americans. Her struggle is not simply for the freedom of a nation, but for the freedom of a nation's people.

4. In a sharp denunciation, Taylor questions the reality left behind in the aftermath of the Civil War: "In this 'land of the free' we are burned, tortured, and denied a fair trial, murdered for any imaginary wrong conceived in the brain of the negro-hating white man. There is no redress for us from a government which promised to protect all under its flag. It seems a mystery to me. They say, 'One flag, one nation one country indivisible.' Is this true? Can we say this truthfully, when one race is allowed to burn, hang, and inflict the most horrible torture weekly, monthly, on another? No, we cannot sing, 'My country 't is of thee, Sweet land of Liberty'! It is hollow mockery. The Southland laws are all on the side of the white, and they do just as they like to the negro, whether in the right or not" (61–62). Her pointed references to the flag under which "the most horrible torture" is inflicted on blacks castigate a government and people that claim moral superiority for the "freedoms" the flag symbolizes and underscores the relationship between the Civil War and the war of racial oppression.

5. Thomas Webber's *Deep Like the River* helps to situate Taylor's quest in a broader historical perspective.

6. Her work places her life in both religious and historical contexts; she claims that both natural freedom (she is "born free in the sight of God") and patriotic debts owed her family (five of her great-uncles fought in the Revolutionary War) validate her claims for the full rights of citizenship denied her during Reconstruction. Like Cooper, who in *The Pioneers* has his hero adopted by Native Americans to validate his claims to the land, Taylor tells her reader in her first paragraph that not only did her family fight in the Revolution, but her great-great-grandmother was "half Indian" (5). Thus, instead of agreeing that the Civil War granted her freedom and citizenship, Taylor claims that she was a (vilified and unjustly treated) citizen prior to the war.

7. In his study *Honor and Violence in the Old South,* Bertram Wyatt-Brown concisely defines this vision of honor: "The chief aim of this notion of honor was to protect the individual, family, group, or race from the greatest dread that its adherents could imagine. That fear was not death, for dying with honor would bring glory. . . . Rather, the fear was public humiliation" (viii). Wyatt-Brown continues, "This vulnerability was distressing not only in itself, but, and more important, because it forced the vulnerable party to admit the shame to himself and to accept the full implications. With his loss of autonomy, he had betrayed kinfolk and man-

hood, in fact, he had betrayed all things held dear" (viii). While Higginson was not a southerner, the basic tenets of honorable conduct were shared by many northerners as well. This emphasis on personal honor that reflects on family and race helps to explain Higginson's horror at Defoe's decision to value personal safety above the abstract values of honor and valor.

8. Although black troops were originally promised full pay, this was reduced to half pay, and even this scant money was not regularly forthcoming. Many soldiers refused the half pay out of principle, joined by a great number of white commanders in the belief that they deserved the full pay promised them as Union soldiers.

9. In his defense, Higginson was a vocal and active campaigner for the pay owed to black soldiers both during and after the war (see letters in appendix to *Army Life*).

10. Ironically enough, while McPherson's text is dedicated to placing black soldiers in the center of the Civil War, his book also serves to validate Susie King Taylor's claim that there are "many people who do not know what some of the colored women did during the war." While McPherson quotes from Taylor extensively in his study, her actual life and history as a woman appear to have held little interest for himself or for his editors. In both his 1960 original edition of *The Negro's Civil War* and the 1991 reissue, McPherson claims that "One of the estimated 500,000 slaves who escaped or came within union lines was Susie King Taylor . . . Miss King (she later married a Negro soldier named Taylor) had secretly learned to read" (56). However, as even the most superficial reading of Taylor's autobiography attests, she was born Susie Baker and was later married twice; first to Sergeant Edward King, and later to Russell Taylor (who was not, as far as we are told, a soldier).

11. Yellin and Van Horne's *The Abolitionist Sisterhood* offers productive grounding in the larger political concerns touched upon by Taylor.

Works Cited

Bell, Susan Groag, and Marilyn Yalom, eds. *Revealing Lives: Autobiography, Biography, and Gender.* Albany: State U of New York P, 1990.

Benstock, Shari. *The Private Self: Theory and Practice of Women's Autobiographical Writings.* Chapel Hill: U of North Carolina P, 1988.

Elshtain, Jean Bethke. *Women and War.* New York: Basic Books, 1987.

Fowler, Lois J., and David H. Fowler. *Revelations of Self: American Women in Autobiography.* New York: State U of New York P, 1990.

Fox-Genovese, Elizabeth. *Within the Plantation Household: Black and White Women of the Old South.* Chapel Hill: U of North Carolina P, 1985.

Friedman, Jean E., Joan V. Hawks, and Sheila Skemp, eds. *Sex, Race, and the Role of Women in the South.* Jackson: UP of Mississippi, 1983.

Gaspar, David Barry, and Darlene Clark Hine, eds. *More Than Chattel: Black Women* and *Slavery in the Americas (Blacks in the Diaspora)*. Bloomington: Indiana UP, 1996).

Higginson, Thomas Wentworth. *Army Life in a Black Regiment*. Boston: Beacon P, 1962.

Hine, Darlene Clark. "Rape and the Inner Lives of Black Women in the Middle West: Some Preliminary Thoughts on Dissemblance." *Signs* 14.4 (1989): 915.

McPherson, James M. *The Negro's Civil War*. New York: Ballantine Books, 1991.

Milosz, Czeslaw. "The American Ignorance of War." *Ourselves Among Others: Cross-Cultural Readings for Writers*. Ed. Carol J. Verburg. N.Y.: Bedford, 1991.

Morton, Patricia, ed. *Discovering the Women in Slavery: Emancipating Perspectives on the American Past*. Athens: U of Georgia P, 1996.

Romero, Patricia W., and Willie Lee Rose, eds. *Reminiscences of My Life: A Black Woman's Civil War Memoirs*. By Susie King Taylor. New York: Markus Weiner, 1988.

Ruddick, Sara. *Maternal Thinking: Towards a Politics of Peace*. New York: Ballantine Books, 1989.

Stanton, Donna C. *The Female Autograph*. Chicago: U of Chicago P, 1984.

Taylor, Susie King. *Reminiscences of My Life with the 33rd U.S. Colored Troops, Late 1st South Carolina Volunteers*. Reprinted in *Collected Black Women's Narratives*, ed. Henry Louis Gates, Jr. New York: Oxford UP, 1988.

Webber, Thomas. *Deep Like the River: Education in the Slave Quarter Community, 1831–1865*. New York: Norton, 1981.

Weiner, Marli Frances. *Mistresses and Slaves: Plantation Women in South Carolina, 1830–80*. Champaign: U of Illinois P, 1997.

Wheatley, Phillis. *The Collected Works of Phillis Wheatley*. Ed. John C. Shields. New York: Oxford UP, 1988.

White, Deborah Gray. *Ar'n't I a Woman? Female Slaves in the Plantation South*. New York: Norton, 1985.

Wyatt-Brown, Bertram. *Honor and Violence in the Old South*. New York: Oxford UP, 1986.

Yellin, Jean Fagan, and John Van Horne, eds. *The Abolitionist Sisterhood: Women's Political Culture in Antebellum America*. New York: Cornell UP, 1994.

4
No Separations in the City: The Public–Private Novel and Private–Public Authorship

Karen E. Waldron

TO THE READER

I present you with my first continuous story. I do not dignify it by the name of "A novel." I am aware that it is entirely at variance with all set rules for novel-writing. There is no intricate plot; there are no startling developments, no hair-breadth escapes. I have compressed into one volume what I might have expanded into two or three. I have avoided long introductions and descriptions, and have entered unceremoniously and unannounced, into people's houses, without stopping to ring the bell. Whether you will fancy this primitive mode of calling, whether you will like the company to which it introduces you, or—whether you will like the book at all, I cannot tell. Still, I cherish the hope that, somewhere in the length and breadth of the land, it may fan into a flame, in some tried heart, the fading embers of hope, well-nigh extinguished by wintry fortune and summer friends.

—Fanny Fern

Fanny Fern's 1855 preface to *Ruth Hall* provides dramatic evidence of how both nineteenth-century fiction and attempts by readers and reviewers to characterize writing as "manly" or "womanly" participated in an ongoing, volatile, and conscious debate over the nature of public discourse.[1] As Fern's message to the reader and the delicious paradox of her publicly private literary identity as "The" Fanny Fern document, writers often negotiated the supposedly simple ideological and social boundaries between public and private, or manly and womanly, with self-reflexive dexterity. Fern's preface highlights the contradiction inherent in any representation of the privacy where womanhood supposedly resides with an ironically public and female authorial voice. Operating in the liminal space between writer and reader, the preface explains its motive—and the story's: to publicize the private, by reaching across and through the presumed separation of spheres. The preface also claims to be creating a new kind of public as it constitutes a network of shared hope among those who share texts. It relies on the particularity of one pseudo-gendered authorial position—the in-between identity of the narrating persona—for this effect. The position evokes not just a communal readership but a fiction "at variance with all set rules for novel-writing." Fern's prefatorial disdain for the intricate plot, authorial proclamation that her text enters unceremoniously into people's houses, and insistence that the text creates its own community argue simultaneously for the fiction's realism, status as new kind of novel, and agency. *Ruth Hall* proclaims itself a public-private novel by means of an authorial preface and pseudonymic persona that mediate between private and public, feminine and masculine, and imagined and real discourses. As it does, Fern the journalist textualizes a new kind of literary consciousness.

Fern's private-public voice came spectacularly to novelistic fiction through her fame in the burgeoning periodical press. Along with the novel, other kinds of narratives, including reform tracts, dime fiction, chapbooks, religious testimonials, slave narratives, and sketches of scenes and persons, developed and proliferated with the periodical phenomenon.[2] Within these texts, concepts of public and private, masculine and feminine—dichotomous vehicles for discussing proper discourses as well as relations between discourses and persons—operated as both subject matter and constructive means for evolving forms of authorial voice and journalistic authority. Fern's prefatorial insistence on the tangible reality of her blended public and private identities calls attention to the increasing impact of such proliferating democratic discourses and rapidly altering journalistic styles on "novel-writing."

Thus what Mary Poovey calls the dual directionality and ideological work of gender, even *as* discourse, forms but one element in the construction and analysis of an authorial identity like Fanny Fern's and its effect on the novel. Edgar Allan Poe and Margaret Fuller, who both shepherded new literary material, knew striking formal developments could result from discursive contestation and blurred linguistic boundaries. As literary critic for Horace Greeley's *New York Tribune* and editor of the *Dial,* Fuller was in a position to claim that newspapers and magazines could and would become both a force for positive public action and a location of literary excellence (137–39). Greeley's own editorial "sermon" on democratic discourse in the July 4, 1845, edition of the *Tribune* implied a clear relation between private and public that presumably anyone could recognize: "Let men feel in their private lives more than in public measures must the salvation of the country be" (qtd. in Ryan 140). Editors like Fuller, critics like Poe, and scribbling women like Fanny Fern suggest developing, complex, public-private forms of discourse arising from democratic eloquence. They do so by responding directly to the medium of Greeley's message—the periodical that constituted private-public authorship.

Fern's fiction, along with that of Rebecca Harding Davis and Stephen Crane—authors spanning the second half of the nineteenth-century who all conceived of themselves at one time or another as journalists—articulates the contestation and formal potential inherent in presenting a journalistic authorial identity through novelistic publication. In the process, all three writers develop narrative strategies and perspectives that reshape the American novel. Private and public discourses comment on one another in works that set gendered stories in the city, where private lives occur amidst bustling public activity. Fern's, Davis's, and Crane's novels complicate the assured nativist authority Greeley postulates for private democratic virtue, as well as its manifestation in fictional voicing. Their authorial personae and consequent public-private novels deliberately blur boundaries between discursive spheres. They also textualize—manifest in the consciousness and form of their narratives—multiple interactions between fiction and reporting. American novelistic representations of the city, for which the widely divergent works of Fern, Davis, and Crane provide only an initial case study, provide a fertile ground for examining the contested rhetoric of "separate spheres" on its own terms, in its own time, and as part of the discursive and formal history of the environmentally gendered and "sketch"-dominated American realistic novel.[3]

I
The Infamous Fanny Fern, Public Discourse, and Fictional Voicing

To observe that Fanny Fern's writing drew focus from her position and profession as a columnist for the *New York Ledger,* or that her novels dramatically manifest a shift toward realism in their encounter with the city, is not new. Nor is the claim that Fern articulates her private-public identity as participating in a discourse that deconstructs while reinforcing simple dichotomies of gender.[4] These points have been made primarily in a context of nineteenth-century *women's* novels, however. I wish to suggest another way of looking at Fern's domesticating realism and authorial positioning, through the context of the debate over democratic discourse, public language, and the achievement of a public voice by many new social groups— identified by gender but also by race, ethnicity, religion, class, and political concerns. With her initial sketches, *Ruth Hall,* and later work in the *Ledger,* Fern took the sentimentalization of style with which Dickens had portrayed social issues in England into this hotly contested discursive realm. All Fern's writings utilized a journalistic stance that highlighted links between idealized discourses of gendered or economic separations and romantic (fictional) representation. *Ruth Hall,* as novel, emphasizes discourse, voice, and authorship in a plot that focuses on and textualizes the emergence of vocal power. Ruth Hall the heroine, an initially silent character operating amidst a cacophony of argumentative vocal positions, both finds a means to speak and achieves serial and book publication with a private-public persona. And the first "realistic" view the protagonist has of gender, class, ethnicity, religion, and her own subjective, potentially authorial, position occurs when she moves into the city.

Fern's *Ruth Hall* in fact took fictional shape from the city, not only with the prefatory and communal "To the Reader," but as fictional writing from the pen of a spectacularly popular newspaper columnist who had been published for several years. Fern had written for Boston's *The Olive Branch* and *True Flag* (1851–53), the *New York Musical World and Times* (1852–53), and the Philadelphia *Saturday Evening Post* (1853–54) before taking the break from column-writing requested by the publishers (Mason Brothers) who solicited her first novel. Fern's pen name had also provoked constant public speculation about her gender and "private" life. Letters to editors wondered aloud whether Fern the columnist was male or female by vociferously debating the masculine and feminine qualities in her writing. Interest in the private identity of this author also came from a style that drew strength and authority from titillatingly intimate experience and the willingness to provoke. Fern's "uncommon discourse," as Joyce Warren has styled it, ranged widely through subjects as divergent as "Woman's Wickedness" (1852), "Soliloquy of a Housemaid" (1852), "Children's Rights" (1853), and after *Ruth Hall,* "Leaves of Grass" (1856), "How I Read the Morning Papers" (1867), "The Working-Girls of New York" (1868), "The History of Our Late War" (1868), and "Legal Murders" (1870).[5] But in every piece there was the unique private-public narrator who constantly publicized the private "I": "I never want to *touch* a baby except with a *pair of tongs!*" ("Sunshine and Young Mothers," 1852), "That is all I have to say about *that*" ("House-Furnishing by Proxy," 1859), "Is my article for the *Ledger* ready? No, sir, it is not. With my hair standing on end, I tell you, it is NOT!" ("Voice from Bedlam," 1861), and "you labor under the hallucination that I felt *merry* when I wrote all that nonsense! *Not a bit of it;* it's a way I have, when I can't find a razor handy to cut my throat!" (*Olive Branch* 31 January 1852; Warren, *Fanny Fern* 100). Readers responded by showing how real the private-public persona was to them, both in criticisms labeling Fern "vulgar" and those claiming she was "a kind, loving sister."[6] Two volumes of her reprinted columns were already best-sellers before *Ruth Hall* was produced, and imitations of her style frequently led her to publicly claim the illimitable "mark" of her voice (Warren, *Fanny Fern* 113).

Fern's pseudo-gendered journalistic persona constantly commented on discursive relations mediated through the supposedly separate spheres of public and private and/or men's and women's activities. Fern further capitalized on the private-public paradox by often textually representing herself in the third person. She drew direct attention to discourse and the language of social categories by placing key words, including the real names of authors (Charlotte Brontë) and pseudonyms of editors (Apollo, Mr. *Tribune*), in quotes, using italics and capitalization, and deconstructing words and phrases like "old maid" (*Ruth Hall* 230), "independence" (314), "reasonable being" (317) and "masculine" (372). Both readers and editors called for a novel from the pen of the infamous Fanny Fern in response. Fern's authorial identity, voice, and vibrant vernacular style (120, 334–35 n. 2) successfully generated interest in both her fiction and her personal story.[7] *Ruth Hall* was marketed as an autobiographical novel and roman à clef as soon as the vengeful editor from the *Olive Branch,* having lost her column, revealed Fern's identity (Warren, *Fanny Fern* 123).

Like Fern as journalist, *Ruth Hall* protests its genre and separating rhetorical categories from within—and not only by naming its author as Fanny Fern and its subject as people's houses. The story of a young, publicly voiceless, private woman opens with many of the conventions of novel-writing and gender significantly intact, including a third-person narration, idealizing tone, and romance. At first the heroine sits separate from public life and the city in her protected feminine boudoir: "The city's busy hum had long since died away; myriad restless eyes had closed in peaceful slumber; Ruth could not sleep. This was the last time she would sit at that little window. The morrow would find her in a home of her own. On the morrow Ruth would be a bride" (13). A series of questions distinguishes Ruth as silent object of attention from the narrator who addresses the reader. The technique both romanticizes Ruth's situation on the eve of marriage and puts what is clearly sentimentalism in broader context. Ruth wonders about those romantic values ascribed to her situation: "Would a harsh word ever fall from lips which now breathed only love? . . . As time, with its ceaseless changes, rolled on, would love flee affrighted from the bent form, and silver locks, and faltering footstep?" (13).

Setting up its heroine with idealistic but legitimate longings, *Ruth Hall's* first chapter also details the difficult childhood circumstances that make her "craving" for love understandable yet problematic. Though beginning with a sentimental plot—Ruth's mother is dead, her father selfish and unsympathetic, and her brother, Hyacinth, the recipient of constant attention while she is sent off to boarding school—the novel soon presents scenes that challenge the idealized vision of feminine privacy. At boarding school, Ruth shares a room with "four strange girls" who ridicule her for being an old maid. Ruth only gains positive attention on composition day. And significantly, at this stage Ruth sees her power as deriving not from *her* love for books or writing, but her ability to inspire *others'* love (15).

Ruth's initial, "sentimental" power gives her no authority in the private life where she remains object and text. Marriage moves Ruth to the home of her in-laws, where she finds precious little privacy or domestic bliss. Witnessing to the challenges of a post-marriage sentimental plot, the narration shifts style, tone, and journalistic method. "Unceremoniously" thrust into the elder Halls' home, readers learn about the predominantly silent Ruth by listening in on the conversations of her in-laws. Mrs. Hall's commentary to her husband highlights and critiques Ruth's idealized feminine delicacy: "I've been peeping into her bureau drawers to-day. What is the use of all those ruffles on her under-clothes, I'd like to know?" (18). When husband Harry is out, the "old lady" instructs Ruth: "You should avoid everything that looks frivolous; . . . And Ruth, if you should feel the need of exercise, don't gad in the streets." There's even the literary comment: "I hope . . . that you don't read novels and such trash" (20–21). While Ruth's lack of privacy becomes ever more apparent, her socially and fictionally appropriate and necessary dream of domestic bliss remains. But the birth of a baby and additional intrusions of the nurse start to prod Ruth to forge new relations to the dream she soon gets to try out in an Edenic country home of her own—until the in-laws move next door. Events as well as persons invade the supposedly idyllic private and pastoral realm. After two more daughters and the loss of her firstborn, Ruth travels mournfully with her husband to the "artificial atmosphere" of a hotel where there is "room for everything but—thought" (50). Unfortunately, the "artificiality" of public life quickly becomes Ruth's reality when Harry contracts typhoid and dies.

The public reality of Harry's death provides both Ruth's and the novel's motives to survive and develop in a less separated world. Public exposure begins with the family, as Ruth's in-laws comment: "She has been a spoiled baby long enough; she will find earning her living a different thing from sitting with her hands folded, with Harry chained to her feet" (60). Placement of the remark both builds sympathy for sentimental ideals and shows their lack of usefulness in Ruth's situation. Since Harry's parents want to take Ruth's children, but will not support their mother, Ruth must move back to the city to try to find work. This time Ruth does not simply gaze out at a sleepy urban scene. Narratively, another few threads of her tenuous relation to privacy unravel, exposed to dirt, disorder, and *bad language:*

> In a dark, narrow street, in one of those heterogeneous boarding-houses abounding in the city, where clerks, market-boys, apprentices, and sewing-girls, bolt their meals with railroad velocity; where the maid-of-all-work, with red arms, frowzy head, and leathern lungs, screams in the entry for any boarder who happens to be inquired for at the door; where one plate suffices for fish, flesh, fowl, and dessert; where soiled table-cloths, sticky crockery, oily cookery, and bad grammar, predominate; where greasy cards are shuffled, and bad cigars smoked of an evening, you might have found Ruth and her children. (73)

After the third-person narrator locates Ruth in the city, another shift into dialogue shows her again subject to intrusive gazes. A "low-browed, pig-faced, thick-lipped fellow" and his companion, Jim, muse on Ruth's "nice form" and potential for kissing; Jim goes so far as to say he likes widows—but would not want to marry one. The now public gazes and voices further develop the fiction and its revolutionary public-private plot. Necessitating a formal shift, they create a textual need for Ruth to move out of her subject position. Clearly, home in the city is not where Ruth as domestic object belongs, for it is not "home"—as daughter Katy notes plaintively to her mother (75). Yet Ruth's position as visual urban object, need to find employment, and city dwelling force her out of the private idyll to look for work, see an insane asylum, and listen to the discourse of the streets. Signaled narratively by the city's juxtaposed scenes and voices, Ruth's experiences reconstitute her as a private-public writer for the newspapers—as the "Floy" who operates, like Fern's novel, to garner attention but also reach troubled hearts. Ruth's city life, her subjective exposure to "a decrepit old woman" (90) or a "wan and haggard face" at a tenement or brothel window, finally articulates what she has been experiencing all along, the voyeuristic invasion and language which prove there is no protected private sphere. The result is authorship. From tramping streets, meeting strangers in public, and asking for work in the city, Ruth and the novel create a private-public, professional, narrating identity and consciousness that have more power, in and beyond the text, than Ruth's simply gendered private voice.

As a novel, *Ruth Hall* insists on being *fictionally* connected to Fanny Fern's construction of an authorial identity. The narrating persona mediates, through story, not only between the arenas identified rhetorically as private and public, but the ongoing current of debate over appropriate language, access to the public sphere, and especially the nature, purpose, and strategies of public (including fictional) discourse. In response, Fern's journalistic work both highlights issues of gender and perversely indulges the inclination to polarize men and women. Fern even engages in literary cross-dressing by suggesting women ignore foolish idealizations of femininity and saying she occasionally wears a suit for walking. Her articles claim men are often just as "womanly" as women, and that women and men share environments, frivolities, and needs—as, for example, in "Thoughts on Dress" (1851), "A Law More Nice Than Just" I and II (1858), and sketches in which the narrating "I" resists the fiction of fashion. The fictional result of her private-public discursive identity is what Mark Seltzer, writing on Crane, calls an emergent and *narrative* "logistics of realism." *Ruth Hall*, with its journalistic backdrop and authorial reference point, signals a formal fissure in the gendering rhetoric of domesticity, coincident with the rise of the American city and an increasingly diverse and vocal mass culture, that shifts authorial positioning in tandem with novelistic and narrative style. *Ruth Hall* and the periodical press pave the way for an incipiently realistic fiction in which gender dichotomies participate in the ideological work not only of gender but class, race, ethnicity, and discourse itself.

In turning to the later and more explicitly urban-focused works of Rebecca Harding Davis (*Life in the Iron Mills*, 1860) and Stephen Crane (*Maggie: Girl of the Streets*, 1893), the remainder of this essay focuses on additional ways in which nineteenth-century journalistic imperatives interact with the fictional impulse to textualize the public-private novel and its discursive consciousness. Davis and Crane use urbanized settings to simultaneously render both apparently essentialized gender roles and the economic, social, and discursive forces constructing and transforming them. Important tensions within and between these realist works of the city and its languages raise ongoing questions about the ways fiction evolves as it reinforces while also contesting cultural assumptions, public discourse, the American novel, and its own discursive logistics.

II
Embedded in the City, Embedded in the Text:
Rebecca Harding Davis's Private-Public "I"

Rebecca Harding Davis's unnamed narrator in her first published piece, *Life in the Iron Mills*, also proclaims a private-public "I"—a voice gendered only, and at times perversely, by the assumptions readers bring to the text and the text's manipulation of those assumptions. In a setting which is in fact not the city, but a town with a factory, the text and its movement toward the novelistic form probe growing tensions between urban or more properly industrial life, gender roles and obligations, class distinctions, and language. The urban environment interacts with gender to shape a narrative form in which gender is only one element of a developing discursive context that manipulates and challenges rhetorics of gender, class, power, ethnicity, religion, and race. Deriving, as did Fern's *Ruth Hall* and Crane's later *Maggie: A Girl of the Streets,* much of its discursive impact from the tensions between fiction and sketch, Davis's text may have been a sensation in part because of its formal challenges. *Life in the Iron Mills* participates actively in a complex public discourse, mediated through a private-public narrative "I," in the constant process of relocating and re-creating categories. Since Davis initially called her work "an article" (86), the later naming of *Life in the Iron Mills* as fiction also dramatizes the way in which sketches became novels in the move toward linguistic realism.

Davis's later sketches, like Fern's columns, show a wide range of concern for and consciousness of the problematics of gender polarization. Yet in Davis's case, the production of fiction was unsolicited, unmarked as "story," and constitutive of her *later* journalistic analysis of gender and economic separations. For *Life in the Iron Mills,* the cityscape was primary and gendered spheres a deconstructive tool for reexamining the relationship of art to life. *Life in the Iron Mills* immediately insists the reader become part of the text by using the direct address so common to nineteenth-century fiction to highlight its realistic authority: "A cloudy day: do you know what that is in a town of iron works?" (11). The narrator challenges as well as invites, constantly demanding reader involvement and discursive analysis: "What do you make of a case like that, amateur psychologist?" (12). Confounding private and public, she stresses the story's location with graphic elements that should make it "real": "I am going to be honest. This is what I want you to do. I want you to hide your disgust, take no heed to your clean clothes, and come right down with me,—here, into the thickest of the fog and mud and foul effluvia. I want you to hear this story. There is a secret down here, in this nightmare fog, that has lain dumb for centuries: I want to make it a real thing to you" (13–14).

Like Fern's preface, Davis's beginning lines allude to a historical memory the narrator's private life and public consciousness have exposed her to: "My story is very simple,—only what I remember of the life of one of these men." Constituted as both private and public, the narrator's memory of immigrant realities reads an urban setting against the backdrop of periodical literature. Personal memory becomes a means of dramatizing interactions between what are clearly ideological, ethnic, and class-based "spheres" that predetermine who and what forms might be considered artistic or empowered to speak. There are no separations between spheres in this incipient city for the protagonists Hugh and Deborah Wolfe; their "lives were like those of their class: incessant labor, sleeping in kennel-like rooms, eating rank pork and molasses, drinking—God and the distillers only know what; with an occasional night in jail, to atone for some drunken excess" (15). Reformers, according to the narrator, go among them "with a heart tender with Christ's charity, and come out outraged, hardened." But while the text's initial sympathy might be with a sentimental and assimilating salvation plot, the narrator quickly moves to redirect it toward the Wolfes, whose lives make the dream of domestic privacy and consequent "salvation" a mockery. Character descriptions emphasize the futility of discursive idealism in their world: Hugh suffers passions of soul-hunger, his "fierce thirst for beauty" choked by a "vile, slimy life" (25); while his cousin Deborah, a "ghastly" and "deformed" woman with watery eyes, must consume a "dainty repast" of cold boiled potatoes and ale. When the "stimulant" which might be love or hope or need is gone, both are likely to "take to whiskey" (17). The text strives to create a conscious need for a new discourse with the narrator's constant questions and demand for understanding: is there "nothing worth reading in this wet, faded thing"? (21).

Davis's narrator insists that the industrialization producing cities from towns generates a possibly national, certainly institutional, and definitely controlling discourse, "the vast machinery of system by which the bodies of workmen are governed" (19). And she documents that world to those who have not seen or heard it. The narrator's journalistic stance thus presumes and creates her private-public identity and a joint immersion of reader and narrator in the evolving public sphere. Hugh's artistic inclination and "meek, woman's face" (24) along with Deborah's mocked womanliness expose misreadings generated by assumptions about gender, discourse, and "private" experience in the cityscape. The urban world evolves metaphorically from the mills: "Deborah looked in on a city of fires, that burned hot and fiercely in the night. . . . It was like a street in Hell" (20). And Deborah's love for Hugh, set against her deformity, allows the private-public and obviously middle-class narrating "I" to challenge the reader's desire for a separate female sphere and fiction. "You laugh at it?" she queries; "Are pain and jealousy less savage realities down here in this place I am taking you to than in your own house or your own heart?" (23).

Continuing with Hugh, the narrator introduces the possibility of a script and discourse not present in what I call sentimentalism's or realism's "available plots." Romantic and artistic desires confront the language of work: "With all this groping, this mad desire, a great blind intellect stumbling through wrong, a loving poet's heart, the man was by habit only a coarse, vulgar laborer, familiar with sights and words you would blush to name" (25). The same private-public authority highlights the misreadings and limited discourse of those who come to visit the mills but cannot see beyond the surfaces of system, machinery, and workers' bodies to recognize the soul-hunger and discursive potential of the mill hands. Though the narrative strategy marks Hugh Wolfe differentially as "artist," it also makes him a potential representative of all others who might have either the artistic or romantic desire that enables subjective resistance to social and fictional plots. By the end of the text, the private-public persona and discursive attention to Hugh's and Deborah's longings allow the narrator to claim "private" and fictional individuality for an entire class (64). Davis's private-public authorial persona makes the public-private novel into an argument about social conditions maintained by discursive and narrative patterns. *Life in the Iron Mills* also highlights the journalist's agency in discursive battle. The narrator of Davis's "article," embedding the self-reflexivity of Fern's preface through its private-public authorial voice, further textualizes a realistic impulse that blurs boundaries between fiction and reporting while focusing attention on discursive separations.

Although at times her works center on the particularized dilemmas of women ("The Wife's Story," "Anne," "The Story of Christine," "Dolly," "A Day with Dr. Sarah," and "Marcia," among her short stories, highlight women's names and roles, while "The Middle-Aged Woman," "Women in Literature," and "The Newly Discovered Woman" identify social and especially literary issues by gender), after *Life in the Iron Mills* Davis wrote just as frequently of men, race, and class. "John Lamar," "David Gaunt," and "Blind Tom" name male figures as central, while the essay "Men's Rights" makes clear that her developing private-public persona and authorial form recognize gender roles in a process of transition and the rhetoric of separate spheres as a trap. Like Fern's, Davis's periodical narrator utilizes the first person and comments on language with a comic, self-mocking touch: "I have always had a perverse inclination to the other side of the question, especially if there was little to be said for it" (Pfaelzer 343). Davis's journalistic persona challenges the effect of gendering discourse by highlighting city women and then shifting focus and tone:

> For instance: this question of Woman's Wrongs, or Woman's Needs, as I prefer to call it. It is a truth so self-evident, so weighty, that it is too late for argument about it. It finds tacit, terrible words of its own in the envious, hungry eyes of the lean women crowding in the evenings into the doors of slop-shops and arsenals; in that other mob of women, born pure as you or I, who, later in the night, stand at the street-corners, waiting—waiting; in every fresh sweet girl who carries her soul and body into the market for a husband. It is a tragedy more real to me than any other in life.
>
> But its reality oppresses us sometimes: takes away our breath like

the pele-mele bloodiness of Hamlet. Is there no wholesome comedy left in the world? One's heart is so sore looking at women, that it is a relief to turn to the tyrants—men, who are accused with all this misery, to find if they have not a word to plead on their side. (Pfaelzer 343)

The complex private-public nature of Davis's narrating and journalistic "I," like the plot structure and overheard dialogue of Fern's means for moving her fictional heroine to voice, underscores the significance of *Life in the Iron Mills's* discursive moves. Interacting forms and discourses show how necessary it is for this narrator to reflect contemporary debate and move among gendered and social positions rather than reify a particular category or role. At the same time, there is the distinct proclamation of gender identity and allegiance ("us"). A further careful itemization of what is claimed to be "truth" and "tragedy" illustrates a common strategy of both reporters and novelists to blend so-called objective reality with interpretive storytelling. The private life of the narrator everywhere feeds into and provides material for her public presentation: it is her unnamed neighbor who has provoked the question she brings before the public, her identity as a woman and public writer that makes her claim alliance with streetwalkers ("that other mob of women, born pure as you or I"), and a similar subjectivity that allows her to differentiate herself with "I prefer." Assumptions about gender are both confining and critically relevant. The serious then lighthearted narration and ironic tragicomic movement of the entire essay deconstruct as much as they reinforce standardly unquestioned assumptions about private, public, and gendered separations. In "Men's Rights" the city allows Davis's private-public narrator to be both part of and separate from the group "women" which so mixes generations, classes, and concerns. Like Fanny Fern's, Davis's private-public narrator positions herself in the midst of a discourse about gender which insists that while "women" may be a legitimate category, women's spheres of action derive from a complex range of social variables. "Men's Rights" significantly concludes with a call to stop focusing on gender when the issue, especially in a country swollen with immigration, urbanization, and an "excess" population of women, is work (361).

Davis's private-public authorial identity serves as a means of narrating and negotiating the both-and of a gender identification that resists essentialism, the polarization and separation of private and public realities and concerns, excessive "sex-consciousness" (405), and the determination of narrative structure and voice by primarily gendered identifications. The city inspires a narrative persona that utilizes the rhetoric of private and public to move between and show the interrelationships of those positions, as well as the constantly contested nature of public discourse about them. Urbanization thus allows Davis's work to participate in the ideological work of gender, politics, and narrative in complex and culturally constructive as well as deconstructive ways. And this establishment of Davis's journalistic authority in a private-public narrating "I" derives from the strategy and complications of the journalistic and fictional impulses in *Life in the Iron Mills.* Although the setting of the "article" is a town rather than a city, the narrator directs attention to the processes of storytelling and urbanization that industrial growth and immigrant labor made discursively transformative for Ruth Hall and Fern's novel. Davis's form claimed that urban American scenes could not be seen simply as representations from the underside or pleas to the reform impulse. With Davis's both voyeuristic and identifying narrative experience with the discursive world of urbanization's teeming and complexly evolving locus of public concern and culture, the effect is particular: a highlighting of the diversity of discourses, identities, and persons contributing to the relation of art and life constituting American realism's public-private novels.

III
Narrative Fiction as Separation?
Stephen Crane's *Maggie,* the Logistics of Realism, and Gender in the City

The full impact of the effect of urban settings on the representative ideology of separate spheres requires a presentation of Fern's and Davis's preliminary moves next to those of explicitly realist writers as diversely interested in the city, gender, journalism, the economics of environments, public life, and problems of representation as Mark Twain, Henry James, William Dean Howells, and Stephen Crane. Additional differences can be marked by Sarah Orne Jewett and Mary Wilkins Freeman from the New England countryside, Charles Waddell Chesnutt, Paul Laurence Dunbar, and Alice Dunbar Nelson from the black South, and others classified more often as regionalists. The differences provide readers—indeed, one might argue that the genre of "local color fiction" did much of this cultural work—with broader contexts for conceiving of male and female, private and public, and urban and rural roles and identities than those articulated by discursive attention simply to the signified. Focus on particular settings, language patterns, regions, and dialects provided another means of expressing the tension between perspectives that defined American realism's representational, narrative, and social strategies. As Amy Kaplan notes, realist fiction documents a need to determine what *is* real in a world of striking class differences set next to mass discursive culture. Thus realism "explores and bridges the perceived gap between the social world and literary representation" through the relation of narrator and text (9). The outsider, viewing an environment, makes the realist author akin to the journalist who could be directed by Greeley's editorial nativism or Fuller's related sense of the newspapers' formal potential. Certainly works focusing on cities and gender like Howells's *The Rise of Silas Lapham,* James's *The Bostonians,* and Phelps's *The Silent Partner* all highlight the conflict between perceived public and private identities with subtextual analyses of journalistic representation.

Stephen Crane, however, like Fern and Davis, explicitly merged fictional and journalistic techniques through his narrative position. He also resisted idealizing tendencies with an emphasis on environmental determinism. While realism was yet forming as a self-conscious mode of fictional representation, the tension between idealistic and naturalistic goals, dramatized by continuing debates over the cause and reality of private and public lives, began manifesting the contradictions of realism as narrative and representational system. Kaplan's, Brodhead's, and Lang's work, alongside Crane's own essay "Howells Fears Realists Must Wait" (1894; reprinted in Stallman, *Omnibus* 169–72), suggest these tensions arise at least in part out of conflicting discourses of domesticity, private and public spheres, gender, regionalism, mass culture, and nationalism that the public–private journalistic novel exposes. Crane's *Maggie: A Girl of the Streets* moves the insights of *Ruth Hall* and *Life in the Iron Mills* about the discourse of separate spheres to a city where even the hope that *Life in the Iron Mills* ends with—marked, significantly, by "clover-crimsoned meadows," "long years of sunshine, and fresh air" (63)—disappears. Maggie's is an expanded and isolating urban world that makes mockery of "natural" gender inclinations, domesticity, and the presumed purity of private life. There are no separations possible in the city *Maggie* details, and none through either narrative personae (as with Fern's pseudonym) or narrative interpretation (the Christian pastoral rhetoric of *Life in the Iron Mills*). As a result, there is no way for the female protagonist to outlast her text, as Ruth and Deborah eventually did, by moving finally into a privatized domesticity deriving from separate male and female, work and home, city and country, and/or public and private spheres.

Crane subordinates the ideological work of gender in *Maggie* to the power of an urban environment under the influence of mass culture along with increasing immigration, poverty, and industrialization. No longer are concerns of class veiled in a voyeuristic peering into the city; the tentative experiences of the character Ruth Hall and Davis's narrator, the need to frame stories with a private–public authorial identity that claims simultaneous identification with and the power to describe and categorize the other (as perceived significantly not by gender but class, ethnicity, physical location, and economic status), disappears. Embedded in the third-person point of view of the text, the narrator's presumed familiarity with such different spheres manifests as a matter of style rather than proclamation. *Maggie* textualizes as narrative consciousness, not narrative voice, a realism that declines the idealistic and egoistic tendency to overtly highlight the mind and presence of the private-public writer. As the city becomes the authorial vehicle, transforming the center of consciousness to the fictional text that implies but does not speak of its author, realism's discursive paradoxes evolve. What the city created as discursive contradictions and debates through shifts in voice in *Ruth Hall* and *Life in the Iron Mills* finds another formal locus: a fictional style that plays ideals and reality against each other in the plot.

Tension begins with Crane's title. "A Girl of the Streets" and the subtitle "A Story of New York" delineate the protagonist as caught between gendered and classed identities, text and world. Within the text, the streets, like the novel written from a journalist's notebook, have the narrative force of both author and character. The streets also publicize and make general any private dimension there might be to Maggie's subjective experience of her gendered, economic, ethnic, or regional positions. Discourses of the public sphere and a sex-consciousness that fails to recognize them—as well as the narrative stance—overpower Maggie's few attempts to claim subjectivity within the text. She never reaches the status of heroine, nor does she become, like Fern's Ruth or Davis's narrator, a character whose existence outlasts the end of the story. Maggie barely has a voice, and loses even this when she "goes to the devil." First sexual object, she later becomes a streetwalker, then dies on the streets without speaking a word, while businessmen and drunken vagrants remark on her presence (Stallman, *Omnibus* 102). Crane's narration in *Maggie* entangles cause and effect in a message of despairing recognition that private and public, as well as male and female, constitute one another through a process of discursive conversation controlled by economic and social, rather than individual, language (Seltzer makes a similar point in "Statistical Persons"). Gone is the hope, shared by Horace Greeley, Fanny Fern, and to some extent Rebecca Harding Davis, that the private discourse of an individual might express public consciousness and political agency. All social impact must come from the novel's textualization of discursive conflicts.

Crane's novel realizes and highlights tensions present in the works of Fern, Davis, and others, showing their relation to a more internally focused narrative form. But the novel's power still comes from the dialectical production of a journalist writing fiction. Crane's journalism does not take form in his prefaces or narrative posture; it seems more like an approach than a means of personifying views. A journalist (though anonymously so) while still in college, his father a preacher whose books recommended the Bible and violently opposed novel-reading (Stallman, *Crane* 15; Benfey 27), Crane may have been predisposed to write reportorially. Yet *Maggie* and the less-well-known *George's Mother,* which he had to publish himself, were early fictional experiments predating Crane's later fame as war correspondent and author of *The Red Badge of Courage.* Crane also drafted the novel before doing his reportorial checking of the manuscript in New York's Bowery (Stallman, *Crane* 66; Benfey 61). His concerns as a writer were not restricted to the city (he also produced, concurrently with *Maggie,* the *Sullivan County Sketches*), and his journalism did not highlight gender, although utilizing it as one discourse among many. *Maggie* simply and profoundly makes use of the polarization and discursive power of gendering and other discourses *of* the public to highlight their jarring connection to the material lives a novelizing journalist might record.

Maggie insists on attention to discourse—as did *Ruth Hall* and *Life in the Iron Mills*—by including a significant amount of dialogue capturing particular qualities of voice easily linked to ideology, economics, religious or other beliefs, gender, ethnicity, social position, region, and environment. The novel records this dialogue as if it has been heard, directly, in the tenement or on the street. The urban setting brings the several identifiers of public language together, collapsing their particulars in a force so overwhelming that individuals are not able to conceptualize beyond their "sphere." Thus in Maggie's New York, spheres have no form; there is no surrounding, protective, demarcating bubble between public and private, male and female, home and work. The novel, like the public space, inevitably locates contesting words and scripts. Spheres determine not the "proper" realm of actions and discourses (as, presumably, the ideology of separate private and public, women's and men's spheres set out to do) but the overpowering influence manifested by the material setting on discursive and conceptual debates.

The New York environment's economic realities, defining the spaces within which characters move, also shape their discursive world. Only the narrator, significantly not present as a mediating "I," even bothers to articulate that the street fight with which the novel opens occurs on a "heap of gravel" (*Prose* 7). Jimmie and Maggie Johnson, children at the outset of the story, speak to each other in terms imaginatively limited by their surroundings and circumstances. New York encircles the Irish gamins with a world of discourse, but presents little opportunity for them to be aware of discursive choices. Maggie begins to reach haltingly toward new linguistic possibilities when she meets the successful bartender Pete, her "beau ideal of a man" (26). Her language barely changes, however. Limitations on her dialogue generate tension and trap her just as she begins to gain self-consciousness. At first Maggie starts to see her city surrounds differently: "Turning, Maggie contemplated the dark, dust-stained walls, and the scant and crude furniture of her home. A clock, in a splintered and battered oblong box of varnished wood, she suddenly regarded as an abomination. She noted that it ticked raspingly. The almost vanished flowers in the carpet-pattern, she conceived to be newly hideous. Some faint attempts she had made with blue ribbon, to freshen the appearance of a dingy curtain, she now saw to be piteous" (28). But she does so within the context of a gendered consciousness which unfortunately adds to her unconscious acceptance of simplistically gendering discourse. Her dreams become those that circulate in the culture: "She began to see the bloom upon her cheeks as valuable" (34). Even the narrative's language ("raspingly," "piteous") calls attention to the distance between Maggie's conceptualization of possible scripts for her future and the actual details of the strangling collar and cuff factory and domestic "abominations" of her dawning awareness.

The most poignant moments of the novella despairingly dramatize links of length and style between the nature of the reportorial mode and the futility of predictive scripts. Maggie dreams of a future whose only "reality," completely fictional, comes to her through the melodramatic typing and linguistic manipulations of theater: "She rejoiced at the way in which the poor and virtuous eventually surmounted the wealthy and wicked. The theatre made her think. She wondered if the culture and refinement she had seen imitated, perhaps grotesquely, by the heroine on the stage, could be acquired by a girl who lived in a tenement house and worked in a shirt factory" (37). Pete takes Maggie to several shows, each more seedy than the last, but even without this progression the reader knows to suspect the danger for Maggie in always departing "with raised spirits from the showing places of the melodrama" (36). The narrative's language signals Maggie's acceptance of crowd values and lack of a new discourse: she has perceived a "transcendental realism" in the theater. An insistent shift in tone, additional irony, and emphatic mocking of the common languages of imitative reality point out how mythical and destructive the notion of separate discursive spheres can be. By invoking her imagination and stereotypical gender roles, the theater simply blinds Maggie further to her reality.

The fiction even invites readers to see Maggie and Jimmie as temporarily reinforcing essentialized notions of gender embedded in and through the discourse of separate spheres. Jimmie is a tough, while Maggie is a flower blossoming in a mud puddle (24); his future is about machinery and work, while her visions focus on romantic notions of love, domesticity, and heroism. She is represented as the natural nurturer and as innately resisting the alcoholic and separate spheres–deconstructing rages of "the" mother and father, parents who become tyrannical and violent under the influence of drink. But Maggie is not the only female character in the novel, and her counterparts—her alcoholic and brutalizing mother, the successful prostitute Nell, even the withered women in her factory—clearly emphasize the role of other forces besides domesticity and romantic idealization, most dramatically language, power, and place, in determining gender expectations and realms of action.

Gender realities in *Maggie,* merged with those of class, ethnicity, and environment, thus both reinforce and reconfigure gendering discourses. There is certainly no private space in *Maggie* to aid her in reinscribing separate spheres. Maggie and Jimmie's home life proclaims their poverty, Irish immigrant status, and the determining role of the character-like tenement, block, and streets in their plots. When the family fights, the neighbors call out; when Maggie spends a night with Pete, her behavior becomes a matter of public scorn in her building, potential but failed power in Pete's nightclubbing realm, and experiential self-defeat. The ideology and limiting discourses of gender produced by romantic fantasies and reinforced by mother and neighbors leave Maggie unable to craft a position like that of the powerful call woman Nell. Maggie has neither the discourse nor the script, certainly no textual model, for overcoming the determining power of public fictions. The question of her character can only be addressed by examining her discursive options. With the realization of city as controlling, discursively complex, and almost unreadable character (*Maggie* as "A Story of New York"), the private-public voice of the narrator both reframes the textualization of realism as consciousness in the public-private novel and dramatizes the discursive limits of a totalizing environmental determinism in this form.

As with *Ruth Hall* and *Life in the Iron Mills,* the publication history of *Maggie* provides crucial contextual information about the novel's private-public voice, production, and readership. Crane wrote *Maggie,* critics have argued, under the influence of Zola, his father's preaching, his mother's death, and a compulsion to visit the New York Bowery. While this may be true, Crane's novelizing took him out of the realm of the lurid reformist exposé legitimized by journalistic realism and sensationalized by religious motivation. Language and scenes common to reformist tracts were not acceptable in the form of the novel—or at least, the novel as represented by "reputable" publishers. Yet although Crane ended up putting the book out himself, and suffered significant disappointment at the novel's reception, there were trickles of interest—most focusing on the novel as slum fiction —that allowed Crane to republish the work in a cleaned-up version. Reviews of both editions were mixed, with many focusing predictably and contradictorily on the power of Crane's realism and its lack of moral vigor. Playing by the rules of novel-writing, Crane exposed the paradoxes at the heart of realism.

The presence in *Maggie* of both "animalism" and a sentimentalized plot captures the complexity of the discursive move into realism through the reformist lens of cityscape representations as well as the need to move beyond a study of the novel that reifies separate spheres. Eric Solomon argued in 1966 that *Maggie* is a parody of popular (i.e., feminized and sentimental) nineteenth-century fiction about the fate of young girls ("Love and Death in the Slums," 22–26). Such reductionist discussions of gender and formal stereotypes led up and in to the wave of analyses of a female tradition within the nineteenth-century novel that has dominated the past twenty years of scholarship. But the tensions such discussions highlight can also be examined from a non-essentializing position that links the texts of female and male writers, sentimentalism and realism, together. Like *Ruth Hall* and *Life in the Iron Mills, Maggie* is both sentimentally satisfying and realistic; the elements of melodrama take discursive form and comment upon themselves. Examining the actual representation of the city in this text, as well as the complex consciousness of the narrative's posture, reveals contradictions created by and regenerative of a level of discursive tension present in the larger world to which the novel's words contribute. Powerfully addressed with an aesthetic complicated not simply by realism and idealism, but sordid realities and genteel pretensions, the reporting of news and the creation of stories, Crane's text, like Fern's and Davis's, captures the private-public contradiction as that of a journalist-author.

The necessarily ambivalent answer to the question of whether Fern, Davis, and Crane are literally journalists productively signals the complex position of many nineteenth-century novelists. Contemporary critics recognized all three writers' affinities with the style of the journalistic sketch. For example, while condemning Crane's novel for its false representation of life in the slums ("there is little to choose between hollow sentimentality and lurid melodrama"), Edward Bright commended the author for using "his note-book to good effect" (Crane 1979, 153). However, the same critics left largely unaddressed the way the journalistic representation of city scenes invoked a particular and richly productive set of discursive and artistic tensions for the novelist. Contemporary critics also often overlook the way those paradoxes constitute a realism of textualized formal tension and consciousness. Material that was perfectly acceptable in a reformist tract or newspaper report had a very different effect when embedded in fiction. The fictionalization of reportorial urges produced new hybrids of the novel. Common acknowledgments of the shift from romanticism and sentimentalism to realism, regionalism, and naturalism in nineteenth-century American novel-writing discuss the disillusioning impact on the genre of the Civil War, Reconstruction, the failures of reform, immigration, and the rise of visible urban and industrial poverty along with mass culture. However, the history of the novel as journalistic should also be placed in the context of the rapidly shifting discursive surrounds of fictional representations. The material analyses Fern's, Davis's, and Crane's public-private novels call for highlight discursive tensions not only as a way of reading their fictions but as constitutive historical, artistic, and authorial contexts. Such analyses show the shift from separate spheres to social determinism as a constant and complex discursive debate. The American novel's ongoing contestations of public discourse show the need to reformulate those critical methodologies that ghettoize works in categories that inherently disallow the discursive complexities manifested in democratic debate and textual consciousness.

Notes

1. Historians and literary scholars focused on the discursive debates relevant to this study include Ann Douglas (1977), who drew attention to the immense cultural power of America's ministers and "scribbling women"; Mary Kelley (1984), who articulated the private-public dilemma women writers faced; Carroll Smith-Rosenberg (1985) on visions of gender; Linda Kerber (1988) on separate spheres; Kenneth Cmiel (1990) on democratic eloquence; David Reynolds (1988) on the "other" texts of the American Renaissance; Mary P. Ryan (1990) and Glenna Matthews (1992) on women in public; and Amy Kaplan (1988) and Richard Brodhead (1993) on the social contexts of American realism. Jane Tompkins's notion of the "cultural work" of American women's fiction (1985) and Mary Poovey's attention to "the ideological work of gender" in Victorian literature (1988) provide additional theoretical background for the conceptualization of the public-private novel developed here.

2. Kenneth M. Price and Susan Belasco Smith's *Periodical Literature in Nineteenth-Century America* provides a useful addition to more general sources on technological developments, the history of the book, and authorship.

3. Other authors whose publications ranged from newspaper sketches to novels, who wrote significantly about cities, and whose writings reveal a conscious crafting of that mediated presence I am calling a private-public identity include Lydia Maria Child, Edgar Allan Poe, Herman Melville, Elizabeth Stuart Phelps, Mark Twain, and scores of editors, journalists, and critics. Less-well-known authors, particularly those detailing cities not centralized by the Northeast's dominant publishing terrain, provide an important counterpart to this investigation and a different angle on the private-public identity as an element of literary presentation.

4. I was first compelled toward a more complicating view of gender, textuality,

and separate spheres in the process of co-presenting Fern's *Ruth Hall* to a nineteenth-century American literature class at Brandeis University with Amy Curtis Webber. While I drew attention to the circumstances that produced voice for Fern's protagonist, Curtis Webber focused on how the same scenes dramatized class concerns. Together, we articulated a movement within the novel that highlighted the interaction of a woman's voicing—the participation in public discourse both within the novel and of the novel itself—with an increasingly realistic representation of city scenes and sketches. Amy Schrager Lang's "Class and the Strategies of Sympathy" highlights, in a critically important way, assumptions about class in the discourses of domesticity, while Joyce Warren's comprehensive biography of Fanny Fern goes a long way toward illuminating the private-public identity of a writer whose very name signals her conscious mediation of separate spheres. Ann Douglas's *The Feminization of American Culture,* Susan Coultrap-McQuin's *Doing Literary Business,* and Gillian Brown's *Domestic Idealism* provide important insights into both the gendering discourse of domesticity and the relationship of literary discourse to public language debates and the professionalization of writing.

5. All pieces cited have been reprinted in *Ruth Hall and Other Writings.*

6. From the *Olive Branch:* 31 January 1852; 19 April 1852; and 28 August 1952; cited in Warren, *Fanny Fern* 100.

7. Fern's articles, including a satirical essay ("Apollo Hyacinth" for the *New York Musical World and Times* [1853]) about her brother N. P. Willis, a well-known poet and editor, continually invited belief in a real but private person who knew and saw through the public identities of others.

Works Cited

Benfey, Christopher. *The Double Life of Stephen Crane.* New York: Knopf, 1992.

Brodhead, Richard H. *Cultures of Letters: Scenes of Reading and Writing in Nineteenth-Century America.* Chicago: U of Chicago P, 1993.

Brown, Gillian. *Domestic Individualism: Imagining Self in Nineteenth-Century America.* Berkeley: U of California P, 1990.

Cmiel, Kenneth. *Democratic Eloquence: The Fight over Popular Speech in Nineteenth-Century America.* Berkeley: U of California P, 1990.

Coultrap-McQuin, Susan. *Doing Literary Business: American Women Writers in the Nineteenth Century.* Chapel Hill: U of North Carolina P, 1990.

Crane, Stephen. *Maggie: A Girl of the Streets (A Story of New York).* Facsimile of 1st ed. Ed. Donald Pizer. San Francisco: Chandler, 1968.

———. *Maggie: A Girl of the Streets.* Ed. Thomas Gullason. New York: Norton, 1979.

———. *Prose and Poetry.* New York: Library of America, 1984.

Davis, Rebecca Harding. *Life in the Iron Mills and Other Stories.* Ed. Tillie Olsen. New York: Feminist P, 1972, 1985.

Douglas, Ann. *The Feminization of American Culture.* New York: Knopf, 1977.

Fern, Fanny. *Ruth Hall and Other Writings.* Ed. Joyce Warren. New Brunswick, NJ: Rutgers UP, 1986.

Fuller, S. Margaret. "American Literature." Vol. 2. *Papers on Literature and Art.* London, 1846 (2 vols.). Rpt. New York: AMS, 1972. 122–63.

Kaplan, Amy. *The Social Construction of American Realism.* Chicago: U of Chicago P, 1988.

Kelley, Mary. *Private Woman, Public Stage: Literary Domesticity in Nineteenth-Century America.* New York: Oxford UP, 1984.

Kerber, Linda. "Separate Spheres, Female Worlds, Women's Place: The Rhetoric of Women's History." *Journal of American History* 75 (June 1988): 9–39.

Lang, Amy Schrager. "Class and the Strategies of Sympathy." *The Culture of Sentiment: Race, Gender, and Sentimentality in Nineteenth-Century America.* Ed. Shirley Samuels. New York: Oxford UP, 1992. 128–42.

Matthews, Glenna. *The Rise of Public Woman: Woman's Power and Woman's Place in the United States, 1630–1970.* New York: Oxford UP, 1992.

Pfaelzer, Jean, ed. *A Rebecca Harding Davis Reader: "Life in the Iron-Mills," Selected Fiction, and Essays.* Pittsburgh: U of Pittsburgh P, 1995.

Poovey, Mary. *Uneven Developments: The Ideological Work of Gender in Mid-Victorian England.* Chicago: U of Chicago P, 1988.

Price, Kenneth M., and Susan Belasco Smith, eds. *Periodical Literature in Nineteenth-Century America.* Charlottesville: UP of Virginia, 1995.

Reynolds, David S. *Beneath the American Renaissance: The Subversive Imagination in the Age of Emerson and Melville.* New York: Knopf/Random House, 1988.

Ryan, Mary P. *Women in Public: Between Banners and Ballots, 1825–1880.* Baltimore: Johns Hopkins UP, 1990.

Seltzer, Mark. "Statistical Persons." *Diacritics: A Review of Contemporary Criticism* 17.3 (1987): 82–98.

Smith-Rosenberg, Carroll. *Disorderly Conduct: Visions of Gender in Victorian America.* New York: Knopf, 1985.

Solomon, Eric. *Stephen Crane: From Parody to Realism.* Cambridge: Harvard UP, 1966.

Stallman, R. W. *Stephen Crane: A Biography.* New York: George Braziller, 1968.

——, ed. *Stephen Crane: An Omnibus.* New York: Knopf, 1952, 1961.

Tompkins, Jane. *Sensational Designs: The Cultural Work of American Fiction, 1790–1860.* New York: Oxford UP, 1985.

Warren, Joyce. *Fanny Fern: An Independent Woman.* New Brunswick, NJ: Rutgers UP, 1992.

——. "Uncommon Discourse: Fanny Fern and the *New York Ledger.*" *Periodical Literature in Nineteenth-Century America.* Ed. Kenneth M. Price and Susan Belasco Smith. Charlottesville: UP of Virginia, 1995. 51–68.

PART II

Body Politics:
Framing the Female Body

5

The Ungendered Terrain of Good Health: Mary Gove Nichols's Rewriting of the Diseased Institution of Marriage

DAWN KEETLEY

Mary S. Gove Nichols was perhaps the most prominent woman in the antebellum water-cure movement, a popular health reform that rejected the invasive methods of regular physicians in favor of drinking and soaking in water and, more broadly, educating people about their own bodies. In the 1840s and 1850s, Nichols lectured tirelessly on women's anatomy and physiology and wrote extensively for the popular *Water-Cure Journal,* including a series of articles, "Mrs. Gove's Experience in Water-Cure," which were later published as a book. She herself practiced as a water-cure physician, ran several establishments, and along with her second husband started the American Hydropathic Institute in New York, a college for male and female students of the water cure. Still more radically, Nichols's concern for women's health led her to denounce marriage at a time when even women's rights activists were reluctant to criticize the institution. For Nichols, to be intent on improving women's health was of necessity to oppose an indissoluble marriage that confined women to an unnatural and unhealthy role as the private property of men. In *Marriage,* which she co-authored with her husband in 1854, Nichols devotes her section to the stories of women's illness, including her own, as a means of exposing the untold truth about marriage as a "terrible institution," a system of enslavement, and "an abyss of evil" (246, 192–93). She contends that in order to preserve their well-being, women should break the bonds of the immolating domestic realm, and that in contradistinction to all mandates about appropriate femininity, they should be free to choose the father of their children and to indulge their sexual appetite. Her best novel, *Mary Lyndon,* a thinly fictionalized autobiography written a year later, continues Nichols's critique of marriage by telling her own story more fully; it tracks the heroine's progress from a debilitating childhood, through an oppressive marriage, to a healthy public life as a social reformer.[1]

A reviewer for the *New-York Daily Times* excoriated *Mary Lyndon*. He was clearly shocked by Nichols's unremitting condemnation of marriage and by her insistence on the bodies and health of women as the locus of the asymmetrical power relations of marriage and of the potential overthrow of the institution. Caricaturing Nichols's attention to the body and her demands for women's right to inhabit the public realm, he indulges in an extended metaphor for *Mary Lyndon* that figures it as a deformed and grotesque body on unseemly public exhibition. He writes that the novel is akin to "the numerous displays of physical deformity which disgust us daily in the public streets." It is, he continues, like a "man with a fever sore, or distorted by epilepsy [who] considers himself entitled to public compassion, and feels comforted by the . . . dolorous sighs which the public exposure of his afflictions excites." The reviewer's excessive contempt (he goes on to call her a "child of hell") evinces the revolutionary nature of Nichols's work for women and of her representations of womanhood ("A Bad Book" 2). Moreover, his anxious reiterations about the book's being a "public" disgrace suggest that he objected in particular to the fact that Nichols's revolution involved her publicizing of "private" issues such as women's health and sexuality—disclosing both to be imbricated in ideologies and social practices. Indeed, above all, Nichols believed that the truly deformed and grotesque body (metaphorically substituted for her book by the reviewer) is the privatized and "enslaved" body of the married woman. Her agenda is to show women the way to health by changing their view of their own bodies—and to do so she reveals how those bodies did not exist in a natural enclave sealed off from culture but were fundamentally shaped specifically by indissoluble marriage. For Nichols, the seemingly private body is instead the repository of oppressive power relations and also the potential site of social transformation.[2]

Before turning to Nichols's politics of the body, this chapter will first explore the ways in which women's bodies were described and defined in antebellum America by both "regular" or allopathic physicians and by health reformers—two groups whose biological diagnoses were inseparable from gendered cultural prescriptions in general and the ideology of separate spheres in particular.[3] Dominant medical discourse, in an unexamined circular process, tended to infer notions of appropriate femininity from purportedly debilitating reproductive organs and functions while at the same time ascribing conventional feminine characteristics to the organs and functions of the body. In so doing, medicine worked to map damaging cultural categories—such as the notion of women as essentially private, static, and interior creatures—onto biological matter and simultaneously to legitimate those same cultural categories by claiming their biological foundation: pre-existent cultural categories were "discovered" to be immanent in the body. Health reformers, on the other hand (and I am focusing here on proponents of the water cure in particular), suggested a more socially determined conception of the body and of health and illness, one that demystified the ways in which *a priori* cultural categories impressed themselves on the body. In the second part of the chapter, I will turn to Nichols's writings, primarily *Mary Lyndon,* in order to show how they draw upon water-cure reform to resist the models of womanhood disseminated by the medical establishment and to counter its claims about what is "natural." Nichols adapted the tenets of the water cure to posit an architecture of the body and of the self as shaped by culture and not by biology; femininity, she argued, is inscribed *on* and not inherent *in* the body. More specifically, both *Marriage* and *Mary Lyndon* insist that the institution of indissoluble marriage with its privatization of women serves as both the primary reinforcer of femininity and the primary cause of women's ill-health. As she contests the reigning medical construction of the female body and its accepted etiology of women's ill-health, Nichols effectively challenges those more intangible cultural ideals that are founded on the allegedly frail female body—ideals such as the organization of women's experience into private traits and spaces separate from the public realm, and women's purity and lack of sexual desire.[4] *Mary Lyndon* and *Marriage* both recognize how the female body is always already public, always saturated with ideological prescriptions—how it is, in Moira Gatens's words, an effect "not of genetics but of relations of power" (131). Working from this most local and concrete effect of culture, Nichols's writings show that an effective way to reform reigning institutions and ideologies is to begin by redefining the bodily structures in which they are grounded and from which they draw their power as "natural."[5] Addressing the apparently private body, in other words, reveals not only its permeation by public institutions and relations but also discloses it as a site through which those institutions can be changed.

In the nineteenth century, the belief that American women were "a nation of invalids" was so pervasive that it crossed ideological lines and garnered agreement from conservative "regular" physicians to health reformers and from proponents of domesticity to women's rights activists.[6] One of the primary causes, according to established medicine, for women's ill-health was innate physiological weakness, especially during the "critical periods" of puberty, menstruation, menopause, and pregnancy (and at a time when most women married and had no reliable form of birth control, most of a woman's adult life could be a "critical period"). As physician Edward Dixon claims, "woman" is particularly vulnerable "from the time when her organism asserts the distinctive peculiarity of her sex, to its often eventful close, when she drops prematurely into the grave, the victim of some of those numerous ills incident to that period in which she is fulfilling the great end and object of her existence" (5). Dixon's sketch of the "perilous" times of a woman's life represents the extreme view of woman's inherent physical frailty, which tended simply to equate her reproductive system with infirmity. Women's physiological processes were thus redefined by the medical profession as events needing professional supervision and intervention: in a two-stage process, doctors asserted that the reproductive organs were, in physician John Wiltbank's words, "pre-eminent"—exercising a "controlling influence on her entire system" (7)—and then they constructed them as disabling.[7] Since any undue mental or physical exertion on the part of women during their enervating "critical" or "perilous" periods could purportedly lead to permanent and serious damage, medicine effectively legitimated the conservative status quo as far as women's role was concerned—most notably in their encouraging women's exclusion from any work outside the home.

Demonstrating the extensive reach of the medical model of womanhood, many domestic texts also describe a frail female body and correlate it to woman's "natural" place within the private sphere. Mrs. L. G. Abell, in *Woman in Her Various Relations* (an 1851 book that purports to explain the "allotments" of "Woman, in her own *appropriate* sphere"), writes that "weakness" is "common to American females" and that their bodies are "so delicately, so wonderfully, so fearfully made, requiring so much care" (iii, 257, 270). In *Woman in America* (1850), Maria McIntosh argues that the "different spheres of action appointed to man and to woman" are "dependent upon physical organization" and that woman is a perfect "help-meet" to man in her "allotted work" as spiritual guide, because "a feebler physical organization" has kept her on the verge of death and thus closer to God and his ministerings (23, 26). As many commentators have pointed out and as McIntosh's discussion of woman's being closer to God exemplifies, domestic renderings of woman's weaker body did serve to elevate women, at least in moral and spiritual terms, above men. However, they simultaneously functioned along with dominant medical representations to foreclose women's activity in the public arena.

Not just ideologically confined by their physiology *within* the home, women were concomitantly defined *as* both biologically and socially "interior" creatures. As Dr. William H. Holcombe writes in 1869: "Mentally, socially, spiritually, [woman] is more interior than man. She herself is an interior part of man, and her love and life are always something inferior and incomprehensible to him" (qtd. in Smith-Rosenberg and Rosenberg 14).

While Holcombe writes metaphorically about women as interior, his metaphor drew its force from a tendency in scientific discourse to divide and to gender the body's structures and functions—specifically, to conflate the interior spaces of the human body with the "feminine." The embryonic science of genetics, for example, held that the mother determined the internal organs and the father the external structure of the fetus. In 1854, Alexander Harvey published an extended analysis of hereditary transmission in humans based on agricultural efforts at selective breeding. The article explains the role of each parent in the transmission of characteristics to the fetus: the male parent, Harvey argues, "chiefly determines the external characters, the general appearance, in fact, the outward structures and locomotive powers of the offspring (e.g., the brain, nerves, organs of sense, and skin, and likewise the bones and muscles more particularly of the limbs)." The female parent, on the other hand, "chiefly determines the internal structures and the general size and quality, mainly furnishing the vital organs (e.g., the heart, lungs, glands, and digestive organs), and giving tone and character to the vital functions of growth, nutrition, and secretion" (108).[8] Those functions which the male passes on are, Harvey claims, "all that can properly be regarded as essential to any animal," while those which the mother transmits "have no other objects in the economy than the preservation and maintenance of the animal organs." Since the male determines the "sentient being" and invests it with a sense of voluntary control over the world, he "must be regarded as the proper representative" of the species (116–17). The female's role, conversely, is strictly supportive, since the organs and functions she bequeaths are not sufficient for sentience and bestow no "voluntary power"; they are, in fact, no different from "vegetables." Furthermore, while the "masculine" inheritance establishes "the relations of this being to external objects," the "feminine" biological legacy is strictly confined to the interior of the body. "Proof" of the female's transmission of the merely supportive and internal structures, Harvey claims, lies in the fact that it is, after all, "in keeping with what is obviously the subordinate character of these functions, subordinate . . . in relation to the order of nature in the animal economy" (117). What is subordinate, in other words, must be associated with the female. A corollary to his attribution of what is primary and what is merely subordinate is Harvey's more covert mapping of the gendered qualities of separate spheres ideology onto the body: the male principle is representative, sentient, voluntary, and external/public, while the female principle is nurturing, supportive, involuntary, and internal/private.

The actual structure of the antebellum home, in some cases, reinscribes this medically constituted body. As historians of mid-nineteenth-century domestic architecture have suggested, planners of the middle-class house incorporated into their designs the increasing specialization of women's role, becoming especially preoccupied with the separation of gendered "public" and "private" spheres. And just as the feminized organs and functions of the body were decreed to be interior, the private spaces of women's domestic work, such as kitchens, were often secluded in the recesses of the home.[9] Catharine Beecher, a major proponent of the virtual professionalization of women's place in the home, contributed to the division of the social realm along highly differentiated lines of gender. For instance, a floor plan proposed by Catharine Beecher and Harriet Beecher Stowe in *The American Woman's Home* (1869) confirms that the areas designated for women's work were the more private spaces—and that they formed an interiorized nucleus at the center of and below the home: a plan of a basement indicates its use as a laundry room and storeroom, and on the level above, the kitchen is confined to the rear-middle (40). Like the internal viscera of the body, these "private" spaces and the work done in them remain subordinate, functioning "unseen" to maintain the more visible outer structures. The public spaces of the home, akin to the "masculine" organs and functions of the body, are in a privileged and conspicuously exterior location; the library, for example, which shapes (in Harvey's words) the "sentient being," was typically placed on an outer edge of the home. Women's places are not only interiorized—placed behind and below the public spaces of the antebellum home—they are also often explicitly concealed. Illustrations from *The American Woman's Home* show how the artifacts of women's domestic labor should always be contained within something else, and Beecher and Stowe's explanations of the inside of the home are rife with descriptions of drawers, boxes, barrels, shelf-boxes, pockets, bags, trunks, closets, and recesses.[10]

Despite the ubiquity of the bodily architecture described by regular physicians, and despite its predominance in shaping conceptions of woman's "nature" and sphere, medicine was by no means a homogeneous institution in the 1850s. One of the most popular alternatives to regular medicine during the mid-nineteenth century was the water cure, or hydropathy. Hydropathy not only offered an alternative to regular medicine at a time when it was not very effective and frequently painful, but also provided a different way of explaining the causes of disease and of conceiving of the body. In treating both women and men, water curists traced the etiology of infirmity not to the body but beyond it—perhaps the greatest difference between the regular physicians and the reformers. As Mary Louise Shew proclaims in *Water-Cure for Ladies:* "Disease is not a living thing within, as many seem to suppose, which may be killed and driven out" (22). For hydropathists, physical manifestations of disease were merely the symptoms and not the origins of disease. Looking beyond rather than within the body for the cause of illness, hydropathists did the same in their treatments, applying their non-invasive cures to the body's surface. "We remark the careful withdrawal of all stimulants from internal parts," writes John Forbes, M.D. (in a lead article in one of the early issues of the *Water-Cure Journal*). He continues that almost all of the measures of the water cure "are applied to the surface" and that it "deals with outward instead of inward parts" (6–7). Unlike regular medicine in that it turned outward rather than inward both to understand the etiology of disease and to treat it, the water cure promoted a shift from the belief in the determining power of internal organs to understanding illness as a more fluid set of influences beginning outside the body.

Deeply involved in the water-cure movement, Mary Gove Nichols consistently depicted health as an effect of surrounding circumstances rather than of the body's inherent frailty. At the same time, she moved beyond the individualistic bent of many health reformers, who often focused on women's deleterious voluntary habits. She launched a systemic critique—showing how gendered assumptions and the institutions that materialize them, primarily marriage, inhibit women's self-determination and as a consequence make them ill. Hence the good health of the nation's women requires changes in (if not the abolition of) current marriage law—especially its insistence that wives remain the permanent and private property of husbands. In *Marriage,* for instance, Nichols figures marriage as the origin of disease—using the stories of sick women, including herself, to portray it as a "terrible institution" because it forces all people to adhere to an unbreakable bond and because it abrogates women's self-ownership and their freedom to define their own sphere of action (246). In one of a string of cases recounted in *Marriage,* a woman writes to her husband to demand a separation because she can no longer bear to live with him. The husband is apparently aware of his wife's feelings but attributes them to her ill-health. His wife insists, to the contrary, that "it is this perpetual struggle within me to seem the being I am not, which has made me ill. My feelings have caused my illness. This is the secret why physicians are so puzzled as regards my disease" (259). Reversing her husband's causal explanation of her illness, the woman asserts that both cohabiting with her husband and the constant struggle to meet society's demands for her marriage has caused her chronic sickness (a cause, she adds, that is invisible because unthinkable to the medical profession). In response to this woman and the many women like her, Nichols claims that to cure the symptoms of disease is not enough; in fact, to introduce the patient to the principles of the water cure and then send her back to her marriage is no cure at all. "You may alleviate this suffering," Nichols writes, "but you cannot cure, while the cause remains. . . . I will always relieve suffering whilst I can, but my business now is to dig up the root of this giant evil—this universal disease of woman" (222–23). Unlike other hydropathists who tended to focus on such evils as drinking tea and inhaling impure air, Nichols asserted one universal "disease," one "root" of the many evils women suffered: the institution of indissoluble marriage, where disease began and thrived.

The first half of Nichols's fictional autobiography, *Mary Lyndon,* addresses the sick childhood, early marriage, and subsequent complete breakdown of its heroine—highlighting marriage as the fundamental ground of women's ill-health. Despite the fact that Nichols follows a traditional linear narrative in telling the thinly disguised story of her life, the narrator does not assert "I was born" until the start of the second chapter (14). In the first chapter, she tells the story of two marriages—that of her own parents and that of the Wilmots, parents to her girlhood friend Eva; she thus gives textual priority to the institution of marriage, placing it before her birth and locating it as her own beginning—as the reason she is compelled to write: "I was born in sickness—amidst almost death-pangs" (14–15). Nichols reveals the ill female body to be an effect specifically of the mind-body split inherent in the unequal positioning of the sexes within marriage, and she decries the two dominant and embodied ideologies that defined married women: the laborer, tied to excessive amounts of work within the home; and the decorous object, compressing her body with stays, corsets, or other tight clothing and effectively rendering herself spectacularly useless. Both ideologies structured a bifurcated world of public men and women shaped for their personal use in private spaces.[11] Depicting both forms in the first chapter of *Mary Lyndon,* Nichols exemplifies domestic labor in Mary's mother and self-display in her friend's mother, Mrs. Wilmot. Traversing both of these positions, and only implicit in this early part of *Mary Lyndon,* is the compelled sexual labor of women—the most pernicious way, according to Nichols, in which women were reduced to their bodies within marriage. As Nichols argues in *Marriage,* sex was an inevitable part of both domestic labor and women's self-commodification, serving as "a condition of support" for women within antebellum marriages (200).

Never doing anything constructive in her home, Mrs. Wilmot produces only herself—as a figure of excessive femininity. Before she married, she enjoyed pursuits separate from her husband in a rich city community, but after they married she and her husband wished "to escape from all the world, and live only for and with each other" in "isolation and absorption" (11). Mrs. Wilmot's marital "isolation" and the couple's mutual "absorption" suggest a relationship in which both gender and sex roles are sharply dichotomized—to the exclusion of other modes of acting and being: Mrs.

Wilmot is utterly "absorbed" into playing the total sexual and social female. Commenting on the inevitable consequences of adopting such a role, the narrator remarks that the "isolation and absorption in which they had lived, had produced the usual results. The lady was 'nervous' and ill, and her husband very anxious and over indulgent." Giving a scene "illustrative of their wedded bliss, in their isolation," the narrator recounts how Mrs. Wilmot begs her husband not to go out one day, insisting that their daughter is sick and that their son has swallowed a pin: "I am so anxious and troubled that I can not have you leave me, and—and *I* am not well, Henry, dear." Mr. Wilmot agrees to stay home with his "baby wife" and to pander to her "morbid feeling," as the narrator calls it: "Illness in my family," Mr. Wilmot says, "is a sufficient reason for my absence [from work]" (11). The problem, however, is that illness is endemic to his family—is, in fact, endemic to the reigning cultural construction of the wife and family as sanctuary—as a haven marked off from the world. Mrs. Wilmot has no employment but "to love her husband and children; consequently her love became a very morbid passion" (12). She has no work but the labor of love and nurturance, no pastime but to decorate with her very body her family's home. The result is her own illness, her conviction that her children are ill, and her inculcation of anxiety and stress in her husband. Such a marriage, according to *Mary Lyndon,* may be utterly conventional, but it is also a breeding ground for sickness.

The marriage of Mary's parents demonstrates similar problems. Mary's mother is, like Mrs. Wilmot, confined to the body, but her part is not that of self-display but of domestic labor. The narrator says of Mary's mother that "she was no dreamer, but a most alarming worker." Her father, on the other hand, "had a rich endowment of mental material. . . . He was a philosopher, a village disputant, a politician" (10). Nichols narrativizes her parents within the split between the practical woman, immersed only in concrete household details, and the impractical man, evading daily life through the world of both reason and fantasy. Having no understanding of Mary's need for a life of the mind, her mother prohibits her from reading and forces her to work in the house: "That a child of hers should, from any cause, be exempt from labor . . . was to her the depth of degradation" (20). Her lack of sympathy with her daughter stems from her own immersion in the body, from "the bitterness of wearing labor, anxiety, and care" (21). As marital labor constitutes Mary's mother as a "machine," she thoughtlessly repeats the pattern on her daughter.

Nichols at times partakes of the reformist strain of thought that located illness in voluntary habits, a view evident in *Mary Lyndon* when the narrator occasionally blames Mary's mother and other female characters for their own and their daughters' debility. But the narrator portrays them most of the time as themselves caught within the unhealthy power relations that constitute marriage. She writes, for instance, that Mary's mother's ignorance is a "plague," implying that it is less individual and freely chosen than it is a pervasive and invasive condition over which she has little control (14). Later in the narrative, Mary gives a lecture on "woman's sphere," and she is careful to delineate the power of institutions to shape individual women's behavior: "Ministers and laymen have attempted to define and limit her sphere, but as yet no individual woman has been left free to do this for herself. . . . If a woman leaves the towpath of custom, or, in vulgar parlance, goes out of her sphere," she continues, "ministers and laymen stand ready to lash her back with the scorpion whip of public opinion" (165). The ubiquity of "ignorant" mothers who pass on their unhealthy practices to their daughters has less to do with women's "voluntary" self-determination than with a cultural insistence that woman keep to her already-defined place.

The result of the Lyndons' division of labor along gendered lines is written on the bodies of their daughters—Emma and Mary. Even though Emma and Mary are unmarried, they are nevertheless biologically shaped by the institution that precedes their birth and organizes their early lives. To make this point, Nichols had only to turn to her culture's widely accepted belief in the hereditary transmission of acquired traits: at midcentury the medical establishment held that not just essential genetic matter but also learned values and characteristics could be passed from parents to offspring.[12] Nichols had, in fact, adapted this belief in the hereditary transmission of learned characteristics to her central argument in *Marriage,* in which she claims that the "evils" of marriage are transmitted to the children born within its confines. It is precisely the inherited sufferings of those born in an indissoluble marriage that constitute "the great argument" against it: "From generation to generation the evils of sensual and unloving marriage pass onward" (264). Marking her difference from dominant scientific beliefs and medical practice, then, Nichols is not concerned with the hereditary transmission of organs and functions that are inscribed as "feminine" and "masculine" but with the transmission of a whole "internal life [that] is a foul rotting ulcer." Cultural ideals of gender are relevant to this process of transmission only in that it is largely women's assigned place within marriage, and the broader ideology of separate spheres, that creates the "rotting" interior that parents pass on to their children. In what reads almost as a gloss on her own subsequent portrayal of Mary and Emma in *Mary Lyndon,* Nichols insists, in *Marriage,* that the "hereditary evils to children born in a sensual and unloving marriage are everywhere visible. They are written in every lineament of the Present,—sensuality, sickness, suffering, weakness, imbecility, or outrageous crime" (223). In the case of Emma and Mary, the pernicious effects of marriage are very graphically "written in every line-ament" of their bodies in that their particular diseases embody their cause—conventional and corporeal feminine roles.

Mary's sister, Emma, is an attractive young woman whose life is given over to clothes and to her active social life, both of which prove fatal after she contracts consumption; the narrator blames her death on her fashionable dress and life—on her production, in other words, as a feminine body made only for exhibition. During one outing, for instance, to a party on a New England winter night, her dress leaves her "half-naked," and, Nichols comments, "her waist was laced so tightly, that its hour-glass form proclaimed the sands of life fast ebbing" (34). Emma's dress and corsets create a body distinctly marked as a sexual object of display, one that is to be bought and sold on the marriage market. This transaction, however, involves the figura-tive and often the literal "consumption" of the vitality of the female self that consumes such deadly attire. In an article for the *Water-Cure Journal,* Nichols explicitly identifies the intersections of fashion, sexual servitude, and women's illness and death, proclaiming that the "present style of dress" is endorsed "by those who wish women to be weak, sickly, and dependent—the pretty slave of man" ("The New Costume" 30).

Woman's location as "body" within the system of marriage is exem-plified differently by Mary, primarily because, unlike Emma, she is not considered attractive and thus not an appropriate object of display. In de-scribing herself as a child, Nichols seems obsessed by her ugliness: "I knew my own ugliness full well. My mother told me that I was a fright; that my skin was yellow as a squash, my nose large enough for two, and that my eyes were not mates." Because of her ugliness, her parents agree that she will never "catch a beau" (9). Although her own marriage seems out of the question, her parents do expect Mary to care for her father and to take on her mother's role as domestic laborer. However, Mary is, in her words, "nei-ther useful nor ornamental" (21), and her continuing inability to adopt either of the available feminine identities leads to a paralysis that contrib-utes to her disastrous first marriage to Albert Hervey, a man much older than herself and for whom she feels no affinity. The narrator has difficulty expressing why she agrees to marry Hervey, blaming a "moral paralysis" caused by "law and custom" and her own "fearful weakness" in the face of it (125). Again, her earlier *Marriage* serves to gloss her fictionalized self-portrayal in *Mary Lyndon,* as Nichols argues in the former text that women have as little responsibility for their "decision" to marry as slaves have for their en-slavement. Speaking of her own first marriage, she writes: "I was as much kidnapped as thousands of slaves and married women have been, and will be again—and I gave as little my consent to the transaction" (193). Her marriage is the action of somebody who feels she has no volition, who has been raised without the legal right to self-possession and the skills for rational self-determination.

Mary enacts her inheritance of the gendered power relations of marriage in her own marriage—the culmination of the influences of her young life. Represented as the logical result of Mary's training in corporeal womanhood, like her mother before her Mary enters marriage "full of the spirit of self-abnegation" and unthinkingly obeys the instructions of her husband "even as a machine obeys the hand that guides it" (126–27, 129). Guided solely by the demands of her husband, Mary becomes an automaton—her position invoking the genetic paradigm in which the "feminine" is all that is involuntary and the "masculine" all that is necessary for "sentience." Of her marriage, the narrator claims, "I cultivated that spirit of entire self-abnegation. . . . I knew Hervey's temper—and I bowed myself before it. . . . I never disobeyed him in the veriest trifle" (126). "I strove to have no will," she continues; "some one has said, 'Women have no rights; they have only duties.' This was the doctrine I believed and acted upon" (127). Despite the explicit passivity described in the narrator's confessions, they contain an underlying and subversive sense of agency: she says, for instance, that she "determined" to be sacrificed, that she "cultivated" selflessness, "acted" as if she had no rights, and "strove" to have no will. In her retelling of her story, the narrator writes that she willed—or "acted"—her obedience, a rhetorical strategy that empties all the "nature" out of her situation. Far from its being natural for her to be utterly obedient and to "have no rights," Mary had to work very hard at inhabiting such a position. Wives without a mind or a will of their own, the narrative suggests, are not born but are created in the act of attempting to comply with cultural and social mandates.

Mary had to endure "severe and cruel labor" in her marriage to Hervey, and the text hints that her labor is, among other things, sexual (127). Her husband insists that she obey him "in all things," and the narrator writes that as a result she came to believe that "marriage without love was legalized adultery" (128, 137). In *Marriage,* Nichols had explicitly identified the institution as promoting sexual slavery. In return for economic support and "protection" under the marriage laws, she writes, a wife must go "shuddering and loathing to the bed of the drunkard, or any diseased monster, or any honest and good man whom she does not love" (198). While *Mary Lyndon* is not explicit about the sexual relations between Mary and her husband, Mary's physical disgust is revealed in the illness that her marriage precipitates, one of the symptoms of which is that she goes into convulsions whenever Hervey comes near her—a covert revolt against her enforced sexual submission.

This final illness, the nadir of Mary's marriage, is hysteria. Demonstrating the subjection of her self to a body saturated with laws and cultural ideologies, the narrator writes that "I had a stony feeling all over me, and particularly in my head. I knew that my eyes were open, and yet I could not see. All my limbs were rigid like wood" (138–39). Her organs of sentience—brain and eyes—will not function, and she can feel only the inert heaviness of her body. Such symptoms, like Emma's consumption, are exaggerated versions of woman's interiorized and corporeal role within marriage—isolated, confined to physical sensation, unable to move, with no connection to or even glimpse of the outside.[13] Mary's illness also encodes, however, an emergent resistance. One of the first signs of Mary's hysterical attack is that, becoming devoid of "consciousness," she walks out of the house, continuing for several miles (138). And every time her husband approaches or touches her "a convulsive shudder ran over my whole system, giving me indescribable pain. I could not overcome it" (137). While both of these symptoms disclose their cause (in their absence of "consciousness," they disclose Mary's enforced embodiment), they also evince a simultaneous impulse to reject corporeal servitude, as Mary physically abandons her home and repulses her husband's touch.

Mary's hysteria is a turning point in the narrative: in terms of the plot, it signals the beginning of a recovery that starts with her separation from her husband; Nichols's strategy for critiquing marriage and for helping women to health also changes. As I have argued, the discourse of the water-cure movement provided Nichols with a means to write about the illnesses of the female body as an effect of an external cause (marriage) and thus to condemn that cause. However, by inscribing the body simply as effect within *Mary Lyndon,* Nichols reduces her heroine to just an ill body—albeit a body that makes visible the pernicious results of cultural ideologies and institutions. To illustrate the outcome of marriage on the body is certainly to effect some change, in that it demystifies accepted understandings of woman and her "natural" place—but it is also a strategy finally dependent on the continued sickness and even death of women. In *Marriage,* Nichols presents what can be seen as another gloss on her tactic through the first half of *Mary Lyndon.* There is, Nichols writes, "an exposition of indissoluble marriage" at the Medical College in Albany, an exhibit that "should be studied by all those who begin to see that a legalized union may be a most impure, unholy, and, consequently, unhealthy thing." Nichols describes an array of uterine tumors, weighing from one-half to *twenty-four* pounds, tumors caused by the "amative excess" that is legal, even enforced, within marriage (207). Such an "exposition"—like the representations of chronically ill women in *Mary Lyndon*—may be an effective way to unmask the power of marriage to damage women, but the point is made on female bodies that are sick and still others that are dead and eviscerated.

In offering a different way of conceiving the structure of the body, water-cure discourse, however, provided the terms of an alternative to—as well as a critique of—the dominant and debilitating models of embodied womanhood. Refusing the dominant medical tendency to trace women's illness back to their irreducibly gendered reproductive system, hydropathists downplayed sexual difference; the causes of debility, in their view, cut across the lines of gender; sick people had transgressed the "universal laws" of life, and the water cure could restore what its proponents insisted was "the human system." Hydropathy was attractive, in fact, precisely because of its "universality"—because the laws of health that it promoted applied equally to everyone (T. L. Nichols, "The Curse Removed" 171). In water-cure discourse, woman's body was more "human" than it was irreducibly "female," and this view of the body seeped into health reformers' formulations of the social arena, which were similarly unstructured around sex as determinant. Insisting on women's equal right to learn about and practice the laws of health and thus their right to inhabit the public as well as the private sphere, advocates of the water cure were some of the most committed proponents of women's becoming physicians. Water cure's assumptions about the fundamental "humanness" of the body, along with its seeking the causes of illness in habits that crossed gender lines, were translated into a vision of social spaces and functions that were similarly ungendered.

The connection between the biological and social norms in medical discourse is exemplified in a story told repeatedly in the pages of the *Water-Cure Journal*. As described by both reformist doctors and patients, pregnant women under the treatment of regular physicians were confined for months to their homes, often to their beds. These same women, however, once they adopted the tenets of the water cure, gained freedom and mobility before and after parturition. Joel Shew, editor of the *Water-Cure Journal,* cites the case of Mrs. C—, who had received "bad treatment during pregnancy and confinement," and who "had always been confined to her bed for eight or ten weeks after her accouchment." After she converts to the water cure, Shew remarks, she "walked often in the open air, and walked several miles a day up to the time of confinement" (168). While the principles of regular medicine, grounded in women's "unique" physiology, resulted in a literal "confinement" that symbolized woman's social confinement to separate functions and spaces, women's bodily freedom from constraint under the water cure figures the movement's general endorsement of women's social freedom beyond the domestic sphere.

Just as the sex-differentiated "internal" and "external" biological structures described by established medicine are reiterated in domestic structures, the biological structures implicit in hydropathic discourse, primarily their ungendered character, are repeated in the social architectures that reformers constructed. In 1851, for instance, Nichols and her husband opened the American Hydropathic Institute in New York, a school that they described as "for the instruction of qualified persons of both sexes, in all the branches of a thorough medical education" ("American Hydropathic" 91). The Nicholses boarded their male and female students in one residence, "making a pleasant family circle" (T. L. Nichols, "Medical Education" 65). They thus founded a home and a "family" that consisted not of a single male and female couple, each with separate functions and spheres, but a heterogeneous group of both sexes who shared public and private spaces and work equally: the curriculum, for instance, included social gatherings at the residence that merged private pleasure and labor—that "join[ed] to the acquisition of science the genial and refining influences of society" (T. L. Nichols, "Medical Education" 65). Structures of the body and of buildings in the water-cure movement thus reflect its resistance to both the specialization and the spatialization of social and cultural forms on the basis of gender.

This resistance is also part of the transformative function of *Mary Lyndon,* which challenges the assignment of appropriate activity and "sphere" on the grounds of traditional gender conventions. The first place that Mary lives after leaving her husband is open, with only permeable boundaries separating interior and exterior, and her room is always radiating the sunshine and moonlight of outside. As the narrator describes it, it is a repudiation of the structural association of women with interiority and enclosed spaces: "No pictures hung against the walls, hoarding a treasured loveliness; . . . no little table was half hidden in a corner, draperied with white network and covered with choice books and souvenirs; no curtains, except the climbing plant, covered and ornamented the windows; . . . no couch, with an Oriental display of cushions" (193). Here, in contrast to Stowe's and Beecher's insistence on covering and concealing domestic instruments, the narrator depicts an absence of the "hoarded," the "hidden," the "draperied," the "covered," and the "ornamented"—stressing instead an openness that leaves everything visible to the eye and that hints, in the image of the climbing plant, at a connection between indoors and outdoors rather than their strict demarcation.

Yet the openness of Mary's room is compromised when she falls in love with the English radical Mr. Lynde, who boards with her parents for some time. The couple meets often in Mary's room, and, worried about being seen holding hands with him, Mary agonizes over putting up curtains to shut out her prying neighbors—already suspicious of a woman who has left her husband. The curtains become a moral dilemma for Mary, because she sees them as representing her neighbors' insistence that she give "obedience to their standard of morality." She writes that she "deliberated upon the curtains," but adds: "O the intense shame to humanity, of a social state, where there is espionage and tyranny *everywhere* over the most sacred relations of life!" (210). The curtains (which Mary does finally put up) represent the coercion of her feelings and desires by the weight of public opinion; expectations about appropriate feminine behavior serve to confine her to hidden and interior places.

Still later in *Mary Lyndon,* Mary establishes a household in New York with some other reformers, both men and women. The house is both a structural and an ideological divergence from the conventional: "There was a want of common prudence, an utter dislocation of our lives from all worldly wisdom in the forming of this household" (310). The rooms are equally divided among the inhabitants, with none of the traditional gendered divisions. Mary mentions, for instance, that she has turned what had been parlors into classrooms in which she teaches women about their health, conducting her public "business" in her private home (311). Finally, the house, including its spatial designations, is formed around the dictates of health and not of gender: "This home had at the very first assumed the character of a 'cure'"—and so one of its most notable rooms is the gymnasium (311). The spaces that women occupy in this house are neither private (they are gyms and classrooms) nor repressed and "concealed." They represent, in fact, both the blurring of public and private—of women's spheres and men's spheres—and the translation of women's activity into the open. They thus function to redefine "home" as ungendered and as "cure" rather than pathology.

Having intervened in the twinned construction of gendered bodies and social spaces, Nichols then makes an opposing but equally strategic move— she posits an alternative "natural" woman, re-embodying a distinctly different womanhood than that formulated in dominant medical discourse. Nichols's "natural" woman seems a product of a tactical rather than of an ontological essentialism, however.[14] The first part of *Mary Lyndon,* after all, has disabused the reader of any notion that the female body is some sort of irreducible foundation that exists beneath and that determines social constructions. Representing the body as an effect of existing institutions, Nichols has already shown that it is constructed, and thus always potentially fluid and subject to change. In the second half of the narrative, however, Nichols adopts a different strategy, choosing to position the body as "natural" in a purposeful feminist move that shows what the female body might be were it not for the distorting overlay of culture. Using a tactical biological determinism and a strategically "natural" female body as the ground of a radical revolution of social institutions, Nichols undermines cultural prescriptions about both women's fragile bodies and their expected submissive position within marriage.

Nichols's most radical claim about the "natural" woman was her startling statement (for the time) that women experienced strong sexual desires: a "healthy and loving woman," she writes in *Marriage*, "is impelled to material union as surely, often as strongly, as man" (202). Just when the medical establishment was most intent on providing physiological grounds for women's lack of sexual desire and was even constructing female desire as disease, Nichols asserted that women were innately desiring beings.[15] In *Marriage* she goes on to argue that women's desire is destroyed by marriage: in "marriage as it presently exists," she writes, "the instinct against bearing children and against submitting to the amative embrace, is almost as general as the love for infants after they are born. The obliteration of the maternal and sexual instinct in woman is a terrible pathological fact. It has not been defined," she adds, "by theologians, physicians, or political economists" (201–2). Whereas the pain and disease that seem to be inevitable complements to reproduction have, according to Nichols, a myriad of external causes, she attributes the elimination of women's sexual desire only to a culture that enforces irrevocable marriage: "The apathy of the sexual instinct in woman is caused by the enslaved and unhealthy condition in which she lives" (202). Since women's "senses" and "instincts" are driven out of them because they are always someone else's private property, always forced to submit, they can have no sense of ownership—even ownership of their own desires—and thus no understanding of their own active sexuality.[16]

Nichols's arguments about sexuality in *Marriage* are manifest in her self-representation in the latter part of *Mary Lyndon*. Her two loves—for Mr. Lynde, who dies, and for Mr. Vincent, whom she finally marries—are very physical. Her desire for each man, expressed outside of marriage, is both embodied and spiritual and intellectual, thus inverting the traditional marriage relationship in which mind and body are dissevered—attached, respectively, to man and woman. Mary is first attracted to Lynde and Vincent on a cerebral plane—because of their radical opinions; she admires Vincent, for instance, as a writer before she even meets him. When she does meet him, though, she has an utterly physical response; on his touching her hand, a "strange fire shot through my nerves and veins" (340). Similarly, when she describes her earlier love for Lynde, she says: "I knew that his love possessed my being, that every globule of my blood, every fiber and filament of body and spirit were instinct with new, and delicious, and divine life" (213). For Mary, the almost literal "circulation" of love through her body, like blood, is an effect of her self-transformation. She writes that she "had always been a lover," but, before and during her marriage, she had "warred against" her nature by "striving to crush and kill my loves," believing that if love were not legally sanctioned by marriage it was sinful; thus she perpetually suffocated her "life's life" (210–11). Having recognized and thrown off the conditions of ill-health and excavated such "natural" traits as desire, Mary has found that true love is of the body—not of either man's or God's law—and that it is as fundamental and as physical as blood.

From the posited ground of this re-embodied female subject, Nichols intervenes in the cultural concepts that form and deform women's desires and subjectivities. The concepts of "virtue" and "purity" in particular depended on and promoted a repressed female body. While antebellum women's own claim to purity and virtue was in many ways empowering for them, lending them moral if not economic and legal superiority, such a strategy came with a price: body and desire. Nichols advocates an alternate route. Rather than either rehearsing or rejecting dominant ideas of disembodied and sexless virtue and purity, she reformulates them and founds her call for the transformation of marriage upon those reformulations. Contrary to the dominant view, in which purity and sexuality can coexist only in marriage, Nichols argues that indissoluble marriage actually violates a woman's purity: a wife may be "subjected to more amative abuse than any paid harlot, less liberty of refusal and of self-protection, as much loathing, and not even the chance of choice that the unmarried prostitute has" (*Marriage* 203). Nichols distinguishes "legal purity," in which women are coerced into unwanted sex by their husbands (and which is actually no purity at all) from "true" purity. She redefines purity and virtue as much more than "a name and a regulation"; they are, instead, qualities inherent only in the "emancipate" and "healthy" woman, who is free to say no to sex, to choose the father of her children (even out of wedlock), and to feel sexual desire (205). Nichols calls for a "revolution of pure principles," suggesting that the end point of her agenda, which began with rethinking the healthy female body as sexual, is to transform society—liberating women from traditional marriage and from their systematic ownership by men: "we will yet reach freedom, purity, self-ownership" (214).

While Nichols's strategic essentialism deconstructs cultural prescriptions about women's bodies and place, her ability to imagine a female body that inhabits the liminal territory outside the rigid binaristic logic of separate spheres ideology is dependent, however, on another essentialism that seems less strategic and more of a blind spot produced by her race and class position. Nichols construes the bodies of women other than white middle-class women as static entities. Indeed, her argument that white womanhood has been socially and culturally constructed (and can thus be deconstructed and reconstructed) rests on the fixed ground of women of color and poor women who serve to figure the opposing intractable states of absolute victimization and absolute health—seemingly contradictory states that are joined by virtue of their both being located beyond history. If white middle-class women, in Nichols's writings, are able to move along a continuum of health and of shifting corporeal representations, women of color and poor women inhabit the immutable poles that fix the continuum. They constitute the stable states to which white women are analogized, to which middle-class white women are potentially subject, but in which they are not irretrievably entrenched. Like many transformative projects, Nichols's vision is limited by a simplified model of power and resistance structured by gender alone; it is about women's resistance to men's power, and it obliterates class and race oppression.[17]

The only times Nichols mentions African-American women in *Mary Lyndon* or in *Marriage* is to draw an analogy between slaves and married (white) women. She frequently calls marriage a "slavery" and "bondage" (*Mary Lyndon* 129, 130), and at one point in *Mary Lyndon* she insists on her right to see "a parallel to the institution of marriage in that of slavery"; she insists on the literal truth of women's "enslavement" and thus erases actual slaves (269). The inertness of the slave in Nichols's discourse is highlighted at one point in *Marriage* when she says the connection between marriage and slavery is becoming partially mitigated by married women's accrual of property rights (193). The emancipation of married white women is thus gauged by the extent to which they move away from the oppression of the slave—conceived as invariable in this book even though it was written at the height of the (unmentioned) abolitionist movement. Nichols also refers, in her "Experience in Water-Cure," to those women "who live in want and hard labor," who, along with those women who live in "luxury and idleness," are the "most diseased and the most wretched" (36). Directing all her advice toward the latter group of women, who are materially able to change their habits, Nichols does not address how poor, laboring women can achieve a state of health. She describes going to see two very poor women in New York—her "cases among the ignorant poor"—and the advice she gives them is that their own ill-health has caused the ill-health of their babies and that the latter will die if their mothers do not leave the city, go to the country, eat, exercise, and dress correctly and, presumably, leave off their excessive labor (36–37). Not once in her discussion of "the ignorant poor" does

Nichols suggest that their ability to control their own health and that of their families is constrained by their economic situation; she proffers them the same advice she would give a middle-class or wealthy woman and refuses responsibility for the poor women and their children should they not follow her advice. Like the slave, then, poor women in her argument are stranded in an intractable state of victimization and disease, their bodies unable to acquire the healthy, liminal characteristics of white middle-class women.

Nichols's rhetoric also espouses the common view that women who were not "civilized" were more healthy and experienced little pain in childbirth. In "The Curse Removed," Nichols's husband writes about "the women of nature" as a state that "civilized" (white, wealthy) women have lost. He argues that "the women of savage life, the negro slave, [and] the healthy and hardy peasantry of Europe" are exempt from painful labor, adding that "the Indian woman, living in the open air, a stranger to the weakening refinements of civilization," knows nothing of either labor pain or illness in general (168). In writing of women's illness, Nichols herself virtually always addresses herself to "civilized" women and thus, like her husband, relies on the "women of savage life" as the unspoken proof of the possibility of white women's return to health. They are the ever-present and yet never-present gauge against which "civilized" women are measured; absent in reality, their metaphorical presence guarantees the possibility of Nichols's radical agenda.

The ending of *Mary Lyndon* may come as something of a surprise in the light of Nichols's sustained critique of marriage: Mary gets married for a second time. This marriage is grounded in the transformed body, though—healthy, sexual, and "emancipate," and it reflects and effects a transformed social structure. Mary's re-embodied self necessitates that she also reconceive the conventional marriage vows, and she only marries after claiming a sexual and intellectual freedom within marriage. She asserts her right to her own name and her own room and insists on her power to leave if she ceases to love her husband. The last pages of *Mary Lyndon,* which detail the courtship of Mary and Vincent, are told in an epistolary form, portraying the mutuality of the relationship. The voices of the two lovers are given equal time, and neither one is subordinated to the other; they coexist, rather than one telling the story and one being told.

While they try—like some other radical antebellum couples, most notably Lucy Stone and Henry Blackwell—to change the institution of marriage from within, Mary and Vincent are now inescapably subject to the laws of the land, which points up still another difficulty with Nichols's emancipatory vision: in her concluding emphasis on a singular woman's potentially revolutionary actions, she does not completely escape a liberal individualism that finally qualifies her self-declared social revolution. The heroine of *Mary Lyndon,* despite all her opposition to marriage and despite all of Nichols's claims about how it "enslaves" women, chooses to enter the same institution that most endangers the healthy body and the free mind—which has done most to ensure that both remain confined and debilitated. Aside from the questions this raises about Mary's possible self-delusion—about her perceived "free" choice to enter marriage and freedom within it—in this ending Nichols ultimately envisions a heroine who seems able to enter marriage from *beyond* its ideological constraints and who is depicted as unentangled by those constraints. Despite her sophisticated critique of the body's permeation by sociocultural ideologies, Nichols ends by suggesting that such ideologies, which she on the one hand indicates are constitutive of the very foundation of subjectivity, can also be circumvented. Such is the liberal vision—which promotes a self unencumbered by relations of power, able to inhabit with *personal* freedom institutions acknowledged as oppressive. Since *Mary Lyndon* ends at this point, in the time-honored tradition of nineteenth-century women's fiction, the reader is left to guess at the efficacy of Nichols's concluding liberal agenda for transforming society.

Notes

1. For discussions of Nichols's life and writings, see Baym 255–58, Blake, Burbick 87–95, Danielson, and Myerson.

2. In their unflinching attention to the body, Nichols's writings pose an alternative to domestic fiction, which, according to several recent critics, apotheosized woman as "disembodied"—as, in Richard Brodhead's words, "something separate from or opposed to bodily life and force" (50). See also Brown 64–67 and Armstrong 76, 95. For discussions of domesticity that consider its body politics, see Bromell, Romero 70–88, and Thomson.

3. In addressing the ways in which medicine and health reform both drew upon and promoted the ideology of separate spheres, this chapter partakes of a dismantling of separate spheres as an exclusive rubric for explaining nineteenth-century literature and culture; it does so by being concerned, in Cathy Davidson's words, "with evaluating the larger social system that collaborates in the creation of interlocking ideologies of the separate spheres" (451). It highlights separate spheres rhetoric as a construct, not as natural.

4. In a recent intriguing essay on women's reform efforts, embodiment, and disability, Rosemarie Garland Thomson focuses on the essentially conservative mobi-

lization of the body in women's domestic writing and social practice. She argues that as women extended their roles as custodians of the body into the public sphere, they "accepted a mandate to police and extirpate from the social body" their own "frail, sensual, vulnerable, and venal bodies" (130). I suggest that Nichols, on the other hand, is less interested in removing the spectacle of the sick or disabled body per se than in removing the sociocultural causes of ill-health disability.

5. My argument has been influenced by Moira Gatens's work on female embodiment, as well as by the work of Elizabeth Grosz and Judith Butler.

6. For discussions of women's illness in the mid-nineteenth century, see Smith-Rosenberg, "Puberty to Menopause" and "The Hysterical Woman"; Smith-Rosenberg and Rosenberg; Wood; Morantz; Donegan, esp. chapter 4; and Cayleff, esp. chapter 2. For literary approaches to the predominant ideology of women's illness in nineteenth-century America, see Herndl. For Beecher's view of women's ill-health, in particular, and also for a discussion of the racial overtones of the laments about the debility of primarily white, middle-class women, see Burbick 97–104.

7. Echoing Dixon, Wiltbank proclaimed in 1854 that "Woman's reproductive organs are the source of her peculiarities, the centre of her sympathies, and the seat of her diseases" (7).

8. Harvey's article was published in a British medical journal, but, as with all British and European medical research at this time, its influence was quickly felt in America—and his views on hereditary transmission are repeated almost verbatim in, for example, Pallen 495 and Willard 192.

9. As historian Clifford Clark puts it: "Some spaces were clearly private. It was important, said the new housing promoters, that the service aspects of the house be hidden from the eyes of visitors. Kitchens were usually placed to the rear of the house, sometimes even in the basement" (42). See also Brown 76–77.

10. Brown discusses and illustrates Beecher's containing, compartmentalizing, and labeling of domestic implements as a sign of her highly "systematic" domestic economy (19).

11. Nancy Armstrong has identified these two conventional corporeal roles for women—woman as displayed artifact and as laborer (76). For an insightful discussion of how the mind-body split was not only gendered but racialized, see Romero 77–86.

12. For discussions of the transmission of acquired characteristics, see Rosenberg and Zirkle. For a medical view contemporaneous with Nichols, see Pallen; for a more popular example, see Pendleton.

13. As in my reading of Mary Lyndon's illness, Gillian Brown has suggested that hysteria was for nineteenth-century America the "most dramatic manifestation" of the "dissociation of self from bodily activity" and that it seems to "exemplify the pathological potential in work, the negative effects of the dissociation between self and body that makes housekeeping the transcendent activity Beecher celebrates" (65).

14. For interesting discussions of "strategic" essentialisms, see Spivak 197–221, and Fuss 31–37.

15. The pervasive view of women at midcentury was that they were, to quote Nancy Cott, "passionless"; the ideology of Victorian "passionlessness," which had its roots in evangelicalism, was taken over by American physicians at mid-nineteenth century as they "attempted to reduce the concept to 'scientific' and somatic quantities" (164).

16. Nichols's claim that women felt sexual desire and her still more radical view that extramarital sex was perhaps a more natural outlet than marital sex are both startling. As Ellen Carol DuBois and Linda Gordon have argued, feminists "remained committed to the containment of female sexuality within heterosexual marriage" (15). Moreover, nineteenth-century feminists were only "relatively 'pro-sex,'" and most of them, like social reformers in general, believed in harnessing, rather than celebrating, sexuality (16–17).

17. In a recent article on domesticity, Amy Kaplan makes the brilliant argument that when "domestic" is counterposed against the "foreign" (rather than the typical private/public split) not only does it *not* separate men and women but it in fact joins them in a common imperialist project. My reading of Nichols suggests that even efforts to *dismantle* domesticity and separate spheres ideology, when those efforts see only gender politics, can be similarly implicated in potential racism.

Works Cited

Abell, Mrs. L. G. *Woman in Her Various Relations: Containing Practical Rules for American Females.* New York: Holdredge, 1851.

Armstrong, Nancy. *Desire and Domestic Fiction: A Political History of the Novel.* New York: Oxford UP, 1987.

"A Bad Book Gibbeted." *New-York Daily Times* 17 August 1855: 2.

Baym, Nina. *Woman's Fiction: A Guide to Novels by and about Women in America, 1820–70.* Urbana and Chicago: U of Illinois P, 1993.

Beecher, Catharine E., and Harriet Beecher Stowe. *The American Woman's Home: or, Principles of Domestic Science.* New York: J. B. Ford, 1869.

Blake, John B. "Mary Gove Nichols, Prophetess of Health." Leavitt 359–75.

Brodhead, Richard H. *Cultures of Letters: Scenes of Reading and Writing in Nineteenth-Century America.* Chicago: U of Chicago P, 1993.

Bromell, Nicholas K. *By the Sweat of the Brow: Literature and Labor in Antebellum America.* Chicago: U of Chicago P, 1993.

Brown, Gillian. *Domestic Individualism: Imagining Self in Nineteenth-Century America.* Berkeley: U of California P, 1990.

Burbick, Joan. *Healing the Republic: The Language of Health and the Culture of Nationalism in Nineteenth-Century America.* New York: Cambridge UP, 1994.

Butler, Judith. *Bodies That Matter: On the Discursive Limits of "Sex."* New York: Routledge, 1993.

Cayleff, Susan E. *Wash and Be Healed: The Water-Cure Movement and Women's Health.* Philadelphia: Temple UP, 1987.

Clark, Clifford Edward. *The American Family Home, 1800–1960.* Chapel Hill: U of North Carolina P, 1986.

Cott, Nancy. "Passionless: An Interpretation of Victorian Sexual Ideology, 1790–1850." *A Heritage of Her Own: Toward a New Social History of American Women.* Ed. Cott and Elizabeth H. Pleck. New York: Simon and Schuster, 1979. 162–81.

Danielson, Susan Steinberg. "Alternative Therapies: Spiritualism and Women's Rights in *Mary Lyndon: or, Revelations of a Life.*" Diss. U of Oregon, 1990.

———. "Healing Women's Wrongs: Water-Cure as (Fictional) Autobiography." *Studies in the American Renaissance: 1992.* Charlottesville: U of Virginia P, 1992. 247–60.

Davidson, Cathy N. "Preface: No More Separate Spheres!" *American Literature* 70 (1998): 443–63.

Dixon, Edward H. 1855. *Woman and Her Diseases from the Cradle to the Grave: Adapted Exclusively to Her Instruction in the Physiology of Her System, and All the Diseases of Her Critical Periods.* New York: A. Ranney, 1857.

Donegan, Jane B. *"Hydropathic Highway to Health": Women and Water-Cure in Antebellum America.* New York: Greenwood P, 1986.

DuBois, Ellen Carol, and Linda Gordon. "Seeking Ecstasy on the Battlefield: Danger and Pleasure in Nineteenth-Century Feminist Sexual Thought." *Feminist Studies* 9 (1983): 9–25.

Forbes, John, M.D. "The Water-Cure." *Water-Cure Journal* 6 (1848): 5–10.

Fuss, Diana. *Essentially Speaking: Feminism, Nature, and Difference.* New York: Routledge, 1989.

Gatens, Moira. "Power, Bodies, and Difference." *Destabilizing Theory: Contemporary Feminist Debates.* Ed. Michele Barrett and Anne Phillips. Stanford: Stanford UP, 1992. 120–37.

Grosz, Elizabeth. "Bodies and Knowledges: Feminism and the Crisis of Reason." *Feminist Epistemologies.* Ed. Linda Alcoff and Elizabeth Potter. New York and London: Routledge, 1993. 187–215.

Harvey, Alexander, M.D. "On the Relative Influence of the Male and Female Parents in the Reproduction of the Animal Species." *Monthly Journal of Medical Science* August 1854: 108–18.

Herndl, Diane Price. *Invalid Women: Figuring Feminine Illness in American Fiction and Culture, 1840–1940.* Chapel Hill: U of North Carolina P, 1993.

Kaplan, Amy. "Manifest Domesticity." *American Literature* 70 (1998): 581–606.

Leavitt, Judith Walzer, ed. *Women and Health in America: Historical Readings.* Madison: U of Wisconsin P, 1984.

McIntosh, Maria J. *Woman in America: Her Work and Her Reward.* New York: Appleton, 1850.

Morantz, Regina Markell. "Making Women Modern: Middle-Class Women and Health Reform in Nineteenth-Century America." *Journal of Social History* 10 (1977): 490–507.

Myerson, Joel. "Mary Gove Nichols' *Mary Lyndon:* A Forgotten Reform Novel." *American Literature* 58 (1986): 523–39.

Nichols, Mary Gove. *Mary Lyndon; or, Revelations of a Life. An Autobiography.* New York: Stringer and Townsend, 1855.

———. "Mrs. Gove's Experience in Water-Cure." *Water-Cure Journal* 7 (1849): 40–41, 68–70, 103, 135–37, 165–68; 8 (1849): 7–11, 35–38, 98–100.

———. "The New Costume." *Water-Cure Journal* 12 (1851): 30.

Nichols, T. L. "The Curse Removed." *Water-Cure Journal* 10 (1850): 167–73.

———. "Medical Education. The American Hydropathic Institute." *Water-Cure Journal* 12 (1851): 65–66.

Nichols, T. L., and Mrs. Mary S. Gove. "American Hydropathic Institute." *Water-Cure Journal* 11 (1851): 91.

———. *Marriage.* Cincinnati: Valentine Nicholson and Co., 1854. Rev. ed., 1855.

Pallen, Montrose A., M.D. "Heritage, or Hereditary Transmission." *St-Louis Medical and Surgical Journal* November 1856: 490–501.

Pendleton, Hester. *The Parent's Guide for the Transmission of Desired Qualities to Offspring and, Childbirth Made Easy.* New York: Fowler and Wells, 1856.

Romero, Lora. *Home Fronts: Domesticity and Its Critics in the Antebellum United States.* Durham, NC: Duke UP, 1997.

Rosenberg, Charles E. "Factors in the Development of Genetics in the United States: Some Suggestions." *Journal of the History of Medicine* 22 (1967): 27–46.

Shew, Joel, M.D. "Case of Child-Birth." *Water-Cure Journal* 2 (1846): 168–69.

Shew, Mrs. M. L. *Water-Cure for Ladies.* New York: Wiley and Putnam, 1844.

Smith-Rosenberg, Carroll. *Disorderly Conduct: Visions of Gender in Victorian America.* New York: Oxford UP, 1985.

———. "The Hysterical Woman: Sex Roles and Role Conflict in Nineteenth-Century America." Smith-Rosenberg 197–216.

———. "Puberty to Menopause: The Cycle of Femininity in Nineteenth-Century America." Smith-Rosenberg 182–96.

Smith-Rosenberg, Carroll, and Charles Rosenberg. "The Female Animal: Medical and Biological Views of Woman and Her Role in Nineteenth-Century America." 1973. Leavitt 12–27.

Spivak, Gayatri Chakravorty. *In Other Worlds: Essays in Cultural Politics.* New York: Methuen, 1987.

Thomson, Rosemarie Garland. "Crippled Girls and Lame Old Women: Sentimental

Spectacles of Sympathy in Nineteenth-Century American Women's Writing." *Nineteenth-Century American Women Writers: A Critical Reader.* Ed. Karen L. Kilcup. Malden, MA: Blackwell, 1998. 128–45.

Willard, Elizabeth Osgood Goodrich. *Sexology: Implying Social Organization and Government.* Chicago: J. R. Walsh, 1867.

Wiltbank, John. *Introductory Lecture for the Session, 1853–54.* Philadelphia: Edward Grattan, 1854.

Wood, Ann Douglas. "'The Fashionable Diseases': Women's Complaints and Their Treatment in Nineteenth-Century America." 1973. *Clio's Consciousness Raised: New Perspectives on the History of Women.* Ed. Mary S. Hartman and Lois Banner. New York: Harper and Row, 1974. 1–22.

Zirkle, Conway. "The Knowledge of Heredity before 1900." *Genetics in the Twentieth Century: Essays on the Progress of Genetics during Its First Fifty Years.* Ed. L. C. Dunn. New York: Macmillan, 1951. 35–57.

6
Male Doctors and Female Illness in American Women's Fiction, 1850–1900

FREDERICK NEWBERRY

It might be supposed that Charlotte Perkins Gilman's "The Yellow Wall Paper" (1892), featuring a host of cultural conflicts involving a woman's mind and body as perceived by male doctors, would have a discernible lineage in American women's fiction of the nineteenth century. After all, the gradual and highly successful efforts of men to secure control over medical care in nineteenth-century America often took place in public arenas and thus brought with them a fair amount of social controversy. But it would seem to be a fact that Gilman's story does stand rather resolutely alone in pointing a finger of blame at male physicians for their failure to understand, let alone diagnose with some degree of accuracy, the physiological and psychological conditions of female patients. The apparent fact must therefore appear strange to anyone even vaguely familiar with the contrast between the positive representation of male physicians in women's fiction and the frequent negative opinion of them expressed throughout the century.[1] Probably more than anyone else, male physicians were historically responsible for proselytizing the outlook that women were physically and mentally inferior to men.[2] As adumbrated some years ago by Ann Douglas Wood, and more recently by Diane Price Herndl, this outlook led a lot of women to consider themselves as physiological, psychological, and intellectual weaklings.[3] From our vantage, of course, there would seem to be no accident in the timing of this male-encoded pathology. At the very moment in the 1840s and early 1850s, when women were being accorded a certain measure of power through the entangled and exalting paradigms of the "cult of true womanhood," at the very moment, furthermore, when the feminist and suffragette movements were accelerating, the vast majority of male doctors in the nation were pronouncing women as inherently frail.[4]

At roughly the same moment, however, there also existed quite a different view of women, one that Frances Cogan incisively and wittily presents in *All-American Girl: The Ideal of Real Womanhood in the Mid-Nineteenth Century*. According to a substantial amount of evidence assembled by Cogan, a good number of enlightened medical and cultural spokespersons—both men and women—advocated physical and mental equality, or virtual equality, between the sexes. This advocacy became all the more compelling were women to become especially informed about such matters as diet, exercise, dress, hygiene, menstruation, and preparation for the practical needs of living either a married or single life (Cogan 29–100). Implicit throughout Cogan's study lies the point that women would have served themselves better by ignoring the advice books and medical opinions of those men who simultaneously heralded their weakness and elevated them into the nether region of maternal beatitude. In other words, middle- and upper-class women had to resist the ideology of invalidism that accompanied the cult of domesticity.[5]

Whether the latter half of the nineteenth century actually witnessed a prevalence of weak, sickly, neurasthenic women remains somewhat uncertain. Herndl, who offers the fullest literary study to date on the subject, takes the precaution of qualifying her thesis in the light of Cogan's study (Herndl 22). Nevertheless, like others, she proceeds to select examples from fiction that specify numerous females afflicted with assorted ailments—both physical and mental, real and imagined. In all of these instances, girls and women evidently subscribe to the historically dominant view of them on the part of most male physicians: that women were in fact delicate and thus prone to illness. As far as I am aware, no major study other than Cogan's challenges the wide-scale application of this literary point of view,[6] one that entails gathering culturally inscribed data from the historical record and then discovering analogous examples in fiction that seem to confirm the validity of the paradigms suggested by the data.

Despite my general admiration for Herndl's methodology, one incompatibility between the historical record and the fictional case deserves remark. In medical histories on the nineteenth century, abundant evidence reveals that many women, as well as some men, were not at all sanguine about the steady rise to preeminence of male doctors who had scant if any knowledge of women's physiology and who, for the most part, practiced a kind of "heroic" or allopathic medicine that more often than not inflicted greater suffering on the ill than did the symptoms of illness in the first place (Rothstein 65–78). As a result, it was not at all uncommon for men, but especially women, to choose to suffer rather than to consult a doctor; for male physicians were often considered frightening, ghoulish monsters because of their ignorance, incompetence, and insensitivity. No accident, therefore, that many women not residing in the cities, where male doctors initially solidified their professional status, continued to call on midwives, consulted with female herbalists, and initiated various self-help programs and health reforms that were especially relevant to their gender.[7] No accident, too, that a cry went out, "Send us a woman physician" (Abram).[8]

A survey of major novels written by women during the last half of the century, however, reveals few examples not only of invalid women but also of the historical suspicion and denigration of male doctors. The husband of the narrator in "The Yellow Wall Paper," along with the historical figure of S. Weir Mitchell—famous in his day and now infamous in ours because of the story—can be cited as exceptional instances.[9] And I suppose that no one would want to exclude the father-in-law of Ruth Hall—in the novel so named by Fanny Fern—from the list of exceptions, though I'm not sure that Dr. Hall, when we bear in mind his cruel and shrewish wife, would qualify as a banner-waving advocate of women's demure and fragile nature. But these examples are the only ones that I have thus far discovered in my reading of the fiction in which women seem beset by physical or mental symptoms for which a male doctor is consulted.

Accordingly, questions arise. If, in the latter half of the nineteenth century, all of the ostensibly ailing or seemingly neurasthenic females in women's fiction necessarily reflect an unavoidable cultural inscription, as Herndl would have it, why does that fiction not echo, even on a minor scale, an equivalent cultural inscription: a negative portrayal of male physicians? Did women writers choose to accept the diagnosis that women are liable to illness; and by such acceptance, did they thereby not only valorize the demeaning opinion of women on the part of male physicians but also, inadvertently or not, aid in the deliberate effort of men to control the medical profession by excluding women? Or did they accept the diagnosis while ignoring the widespread opinion, especially outside the South, that male doctors were basically ignorant of women's physiological and psychological condition? And finally, what role or function do male doctors actually play in women's fiction? In the following survey of American women's fiction from the 1850s until the end of the century, I should like to engage these questions by examining female characters who *do not* conform with the model of invalidism advanced by Herndl and others, and by pointing to male doctors who *do not* reveal, whether scarcely or indisputably, a condescending, patriarchal view of women.

Marie Susanna Cummins's *The Lamplighter* (1854) presents a physician to whom women in need of medical attention might turn as an exemplary doctor and to whom women lacking such need might turn as a model of manhood. No one can read the novel without observing how it teems with disease and death; and hence at first glance it might seem to support the outlook of women's inherent fragility. But a careful consideration of the cases reveals that Herndl's thesis on invalid women does not have any substantive application to the book. Instead, Cummins evidently represents the extratextual world we all take for granted: people get sick, and people die, either from illness or old age. For instance, when early in the book young Gertrude is cast out into a cold winter's night without proper clothing, there's nothing fashionable or imagined about the fever she develops that results in her lying abed, semiconscious and delirious, for several weeks. Significantly enough, Trueman Flint, who has adopted Gertrude, does not call upon a physician to administer to the girl but cares for her himself. As Cummins puts it, Flint "knew a good deal about sickness; was something of a doctor and nurse in his simple way; and, though he had never had much to do with children, his warm heart was a trusty guide, and taught him all that was necessary for Gerty's comfort" (Cummins 16). Such care on the part of Flint contrasts with an episode recounted by Mrs. Sullivan that offers one of the few fictional examples of the low esteem in which doctors were held at midcentury. In the course of explaining to her son Willie the reason for her father's apparent sour disposition, Mrs. Sullivan reminisces: "Mother was taken down with her death-stroke, and there was a quack doctor prescribed for her, that father always though[t] did her more hurt than good" (39).

If anyone in *The Lamplighter* might qualify as a candidate endorsing the thesis on female invalidism, it would be Emily Graham, who seems vulnerable to periodic bouts of illness. Not until late in the book, however, does the reader learn that her physical ailments no doubt stem from a psychological trauma suffered years earlier. Moreover, Cummins emphatically addresses Emily's supposedly delicate constitution by essentially denying it: "The invalid girl, if we may call her such (for, in spite of ill health, she still retained much of the freshness and all the loveliness of her girlhood)" (394). Still, Cummins's most cogent point does not bear on the number of persons who suffer ailments or die so much as it does on the kind of care received by those who are genuinely ill or dying. In terms of nursing, the most important care issues from the love and sympathy extended by man or woman —the kind of care that Trueman Flint and Mrs. Sullivan give to Gertrude and that Gertrude in turn gives to Emily Graham. But in terms of professional medical care, Dr. Jeremy represents the ideal physician, for his mind and feelings are attuned to the physical and emotional needs of his patients. After Dr. Jeremy prescribes medication for the dying Mrs. Sullivan, for example, the woman remarks about him to Gertrude that he is "so different

. . . from common doctors . . . so sociable and friendly! Why, I felt, Gertrude, as if I could talk to him about my sickness as freely as I could you" (163). Married to a woman with whom he shares an equal, mutually respectful, and loving relation, Dr. Jeremy assumes both a sympathetic and steadying force in the novel, obviously sensitive to the culturally inscribed burdens of women and just as obviously impatient with—and thus a splenetic vehicle through which Cummins vents her bile at—the sometimes tyrannical Mr. Graham, the patriarchal ogre who must undergo a kind of feminizing tutelage in order to become transformed into the sort of man, sensitive to women, that Dr. Jeremy is. Apparently having no children of his own, Dr. Jeremy serves as a romanticized father physician, similar to the one that Fanny Fern creates in *Ruth Hall*.

Although Fanny Fern excoriates one doctor in *Ruth Hall* (1855), she also reflects the variety of medical practitioners in the nineteenth century by including several others. Two of these are of note. The first is a Mrs. Waters who "styled herself a female physician. She kept a sort of witch's cauldron constantly boiling over the fire, in which seethed all sorts of 'mints' and 'yarbs,' and from which issued what she called a 'potecary odor.' Mrs. Waters, when not engaged in stirring this cauldron, or in various housekeeping duties, alternated her leisure in reading medical books, attending medical lectures, and fondling a pet skull, which lay on the kitchen dresser" (113). Whether this somewhat unattractive characterization of Mrs. Waters hints at Fern's general opinion of traditional women herbalists or at an unsavory figure in Fern's life cannot be determined. But in happy opposition to this mixed characterization of Mrs. Waters appears another physician who registers an alternative to the heroic medicine practiced by Dr. Hall and the herbal remedies brewed by Mrs. Waters. In the boardinghouse where Ruth first wins fame as a writer resides the mysterious Mr. Bond, to whom she turns after her youngest daughter, Nettie, becomes seriously ill. Mr. Bond turns out to practice homeopathic medicine, thereby reflecting Fern's awareness at midcentury of that popular alternative to the aggressive, heroic medicine endorsed by most male physicians.[10] In the light of Ruth's earlier experience with three male physicians, including Dr. Hall, who have been unable to prevent the deaths of her first daughter and her husband, well might the reader imagine that Ruth would feel some reluctance in consulting Mr. Bond. Having nowhere else to turn, however, Ruth allows Mr. Bond to see Nettie; and he successfully prescribes a dosage for the child. Significantly, Ruth senses that Mr. Bond "was a man of refined and courteous manners. . . . Ruth felt glad he was so much her senior; he seemed so like what Ruth had sometimes dreamed a kind father might be" (127).

In this highly charged remark, which throws into relief Ruth's relations with her uncaring father and horrific father-in-law, Ruth echoes Mrs. Sullivan's opinion of Dr. Jeremy in *The Lamplighter.* Taken together, both opinions record an attitude toward the bedside manner of Dr. Jeremy and Mr. Bond that contradicts the manner endorsed by most male physicians throughout the latter half of the nineteenth century. As Mary Roth Walsh argues, "Sternness, control, efficiency, strength, and organization were terms late nineteenth-century doctors liked to use to describe themselves" (139). Such terms served not only to reflect men's threatened conception about themselves as professionals but also to help erect a patriarchal barrier against increasing numbers of women who sought to become doctors and who had quite a different conception of professional behavior.[11] Cummins and Fern suggest this conception—taking up in their role as novelist the historical function of women physicians—to feminize the profession. It therefore seems to me that, more than anything else, the positive characterization of male physicians in women's fiction serves as an idealized projection of the qualities that women would like not only doctors but also men in general to possess: a sympathy and understanding altogether free from condescension toward women. Hence the paternal kindness that Mrs. Sullivan detects in Dr. Jeremy or that Ruth senses in Mr. Bond should not be confused with a patriarchal power to which women are constrained to submit.

At first glance, Elizabeth Stoddard's *The Morgesons* (1862) appears to confirm the popular notion that many women in the latter half of the nineteenth century gravitated toward the culturally induced condition of invalidism. Veronica, the bizarre though interesting youngest daughter, often seems ill or indisposed. In a book that pays more attention to food than does Thomas Wolfe's *Look Homeward, Angel,* Veronica eats little and is probably anemic, in remarkable contrast to her sister Cassandra, the narrator of the novel, who regularly stuffs herself or suffers from hunger. At times, the source of Veronica's ailments and reclusiveness appears to be psychological. A reader might especially get the impression that the girl feigns illness as a means of gaining the very attention that she ostensibly intends to spurn, or of simply getting her own childish way. But I think it inadvisable to rely on this impression, because the "mysterious disorders" that afflict Veronica may in fact have a physical cause. Surely we are invited to consider the physiological basis of these disorders when, just beyond the middle of the novel, Cassandra describes the symptoms of one of their attacks in terms fairly graphic yet still somewhat puzzling. During the night, Veronica has fainted several times while being attended at her bedside by Cassandra and Temperance, the devoted housemaid.

> Veronica could not speak, but she shook her head at me to go away. Her will seemed to be concentrated against losing consciousness; it

slipped from her occasionally, and she made rotary motions with her arms, which I attempted to stop, but her features contracted so terribly, I let her alone.

"Mustn't touch her," said Temperance, whose efforts to relieve her were confined to replacing the coverings of the bed, and drawing her nightgown over her bosom, which she often threw off again. Her breath scarcely stirred her breast. I thought more than once she did not breathe at all. . . . Suddenly she turned her head and closed her eyes. Temperance softly pulled up the clothes over her and whispered: "It is over for this time; but lord, how awful it is! I hoped she was cured of these spells." (Stoddard 146–47)

That Veronica's attacks are "real" acquires further credence from a remark that Cassandra makes earlier in the novel, but hardly understandable at that point, when she comments on her sister's experience with illness from the vantage of the narrator privileged with the knowledge of her story's conclusion: "Verry was educated by sickness; her mind fed and grew on pain, and at last mastered it" (59).

Although Cassandra includes scattered references to doctors attending to Veronica, she offers no information on what their diagnosis of Veronica might be. This lapse does not apply, however, to herself. At one point when she is paying an extended visit to her cousin Charles and his wife, Alice, in Rosville, an unnamed physician is called to examine Cassandra.[12] She feels no particular ailment, but she does feel lethargic, lacking the energy or motivation to get out of bed. After the doctor concludes a brief examination, he and Cassandra enter into the following exchange:

"Nothing serious," he said; "but, like many women, you will continue to do something to keep in continual pain. If Nature does not endow your constitution with suffering, you will make up the loss by some fatal trifling, which will bring it. I dare say, now, that after this, you never will be quite well."

"I will take care of my health."

"You wont—you can't. Did you ever notice your temperament?"

"No, never; what is it?"

"How old are you?"

"Eighteen, and four months."

"Is it possible? How backward you are! You are quite interesting."

"When may I get up?"

"Next week; don't drink coffee. Remember to live in the day. Avoid stirring about in the night, as you would avoid Satan. Sleep, sleep then, and you'll make that beauty of yours last longer."

"Am I a beauty? No living creature ever said so before."

"Adipose beauty."

"Fat?"

"No; not that exactly. Good-day." (84)

Stoddard incisively poses Cassandra's enervation against her vibrant and confused sexuality, what the doctor euphemistically alludes to in his reference to her "temperament." Though Cassandra is only dimly aware of her sexual nature, as if conforming to a prim conception of Victorian womanhood, her alluring beauty is certainly not lost on Charles, who struggles against an unmistakable desire to seduce Cassandra, while she on her part faintly recognizes his desire and evidently teases him. Nevertheless, what most cogently compels attention in the doctor's comments to Cassandra, beyond his astonishment over her sexual naïveté, is his prediction of (or is it possibly a challenge for her to ward off?) her becoming like other women with whom he is familiar by imagining she is afflicted with all sorts of maladies. It would seem clear enough that the doctor is critical of the culturally inscribed and/or self-induced syndrome of neurasthenic, invalid women—which syndrome, at least in Cassandra's case, is due to a profound ignorance of the physiological and resulting psychological influences of sexuality on women. He has seen it all repeatedly; and if his language is taken literally, his prognosis for Cassandra's future, notwithstanding her counter-affirmation to look after her health, is scarcely hopeful. Interestingly enough, however, Cassandra will live up to her declaration over the course of the novel. When she next requires medical attention, no vague or imagined reasons are at issue.

After Cassandra is injured in the violent, sexually charged accident produced by Charles, who is unable to manage the uncontrollable stallion that symbolizes the erotic fury he tries to suppress, a Dr. White attends her. If Dr. White is indeed the doctor who previously diagnosed Cassandra's bedridden condition as a product of her naive, sexually engendered temperament, his bedside manner has become altogether transformed as he treats the injured young woman. When Cassandra regains consciousness, Dr. White says by way of comfort, "You crawled out of a small hole, my child." Cassandra shortly cries out, asking if Charles was killed in the accident. Dr. White whispers, "He is dead." Cassandra's maniacal laugh in response to this information evidently causes Dr. White to react in a surprisingly unprofessional manner, for Cassandra observes, "You are crying, Doctor," while her own "eyes feel dry." To which Dr. White says, "Pooh, pooh, little one. Now I am going to set your arm; simple fracture, that's all. The blow was tempered, but you are paralyzed by the shock" (121). Clearly enough,

Dr. White's emotional identification with Cassandra's physical and psychological pain in the episode suggests once again the role of physician-as-father, inasmuch as he treats her as if she were his own child.

Resembling Dr. White, Mr. Bond in *Ruth Hall,* and Dr. Jeremy in *The Lamplighter* are two prominent male physicians in Augusta Jane Evans's *St. Elmo* (1866). The first one tenderly treats the young Edna Earl when she is injured in a train wreck. Many years later, when Edna collapses after completing her magnum opus, she is attended by the physician of the Andrews family, a Dr. Howell. He questions Edna about her family medical history, her previous treatment for fainting spells, and her symptoms related to the paroxysms leading to her collapse. After feeling her pulse and listening to her chest, he diagnoses "hypertrophy of the heart" (281). Edna wants to know if she will live, and Dr. Howell says:

> "Miss Earl, I never deceive my patients. It is useless to dose you with medicine, and drug you into semi-insensibility. You must have rest and quiet; rest for the mind as well as body; there must be no more teaching and writing. You are overworked, and incessant, mental labour has hastened the approach of a disease which, under other circumstances, might have encroached very slowly and imperceptibly. If latent (which is barely possible) it has contributed to a fearfully rapid development. Refrain from study, avoid all excitement, exercise moderately but regularly in the open air; and above all things, do not tax your brain. If you carefully observe these directions, you may live to be as old as your grandfather." (281)

It might sound as if Dr. Howell merely echoes a conventional patriarchal critique of a woman's limited mind, convinced of Edna's incapacity to undertake the sort of rigorous intellectual efforts that belong to men alone. But that is patently not the case. Edna does tax her mental and physical strength, working late into the night week after week, often going without any sleep at all. Furthermore, as the novel frequently mentions, she doesn't eat enough to sustain the demands exerted on her body. Most of all, however, to see Dr. Howell falling into the familiar historical pattern of disparaging the mental ability of women is erroneous because, as he honestly declares, he values Edna's writing and considers himself one of her greatest literary admirers. His pleading with her, therefore, reveals a humane response to what would seem to be an accurate diagnosis of Edna's condition.

Without discounting any of the previous novels discussed here, E.D.E.N. Southworth's *The Hidden Hand* (1859) adds more demonstrable support to my suspicion that women writers posit male physicians as idealized projections of the way men ought to be, whether as father figures, potential husbands, or, quite simply, friends. Two doctors figure prominently in the novel's subplot. The first is Dr. Day, who takes pity on Marah Rocke and rescues her from poverty. His compassion and Christian charity receive far more attention than do his skills as a physician. But Dr. Day serves a more significant function in the novel by providing Marah Rocke's son, Traverse, the means by which to receive his own medical training, first under the tutelage of Dr. Day himself and then under the most distinguished professors at Washington College in St. Louis. For it is Traverse who best exemplifies the sympathy that, historically, women often found missing in male physicians in the nineteenth century. Strong of will but exceedingly gentle in his feelings for others, Traverse may seem too good to be true, the antithesis of the attractive villain Black Donald with whom the central figure, Capitola, becomes adventurously involved; but he serves as Southworth's idealized norm for middle-class men, one who imbibes the self-sacrificing nurture of his mother as the only example by which he can live. First in St. Louis and then in New Orleans, Traverse establishes his medical practice, serving the poor with the same kind of tireless devotion and love that he received and continues to count on from his mother. Through him, the subplot finally converges with the main plot when he is invited to join the staff at an insane asylum near East Feliciana, where, through his sympathetic powers of divination, he believes what other male physicians have diagnosed as a hallucinatory tale told by a woman who turns out to be Capitola's mother, thus leading to her release from the asylum and to a long-awaited reunion with her daughter. As a man who possesses the emotional and selfless qualities traditionally ascribed to women, Traverse clearly represents Southworth's embodiment of what a physician—and a man—ought to be.

I should like to conclude this survey of novels with some attention to Chopin's *The Awakening* (1899). It cannot be said with certainty that Chopin suggests an increased respect for male physicians on the part of women at the end of the century; but it can be said with confidence that Dr. Mandelet appears as the only unqualified male figure in the novel. We first see him when Leonce consults the doctor about Edna's strange behavior after the Pontelliers' return to New Orleans from their summer retreat at Grand Isle. The doctor, we learn, "bore a reputation for wisdom rather than skill" (62), and his behavior with Leonce and Edna confirms this reputation. When Leonce offers the example of Edna's allowing "housekeeping to go to the dickens," Dr. Mandelet observes: "Well, well; women are not all alike, my dear Pontellier." Somewhat more telling is the doctor's reaction to Leonce's summary account of Edna: "Her whole attitude—toward me and everybody and everything—has changed. . . . She's making it devilishly uncomfortable for me. . . . She's got some sort of notion in her head concerning the eternal rights of women; and—you understand—we meet in the morning at the breakfast table." Rather than take sides with Leonce in this man-to-man confession, Dr. Mandelet reveals an obvious leaning toward Edna: "What have you been doing to her, Pontellier?" (63).

It is of course true that Dr. Mandelet tells Leonce that a woman is a "very peculiar and delicate organism" and that "most women are moody and whimsical" (63–64). Nevertheless, the extent to which these comments express Dr. Mandelet's true views of women remains in doubt. We might say on the one hand that his science is suspect when he seems content to overlook the cause or causes of Edna's recent defiance of conventions; and yet it would be hard on the other hand to gainsay his point that, from a male point of view at the end of the nineteenth century, it would take an "inspired psychologist" to fathom women generally and Edna particularly (64). Based upon Dr. Mandelet's final encounter with Edna, it would seem fair to say that the family physician treads a delicate balance between his allegiances to Leonce and Edna. Taking up Edna's part when he suspects Leonce of mistreating her, the doctor then offers the unhappy husband a patriarchal, sugar-coated pill—the old saw about women's delicate, highly organized constitution, their whimsicality and moodiness: in other words, their feminine irrationality. In any event, the scene closes with the doctor promising to pay a visit to the Pontelliers in order to observe Edna.

Just how wise Dr. Mandelet is can be witnessed in two later scenes. First, when he visits the Pontelliers, he correctly detects in Edna "a subtle change which had transformed her from the listless woman he had known into a being who, for the moment, seemed palpitant with the forces of life. Her speech was warm and energetic. There was no repression in her glance or gesture. She reminded him of some beautiful, sleek animal waking up in the sun" (67). Of course, the doctor's insight here is correct, and its importance is strengthened by the fact that Chopin conveys it omnisciently through the doctor's mind, a narrative strategy nowhere else applied to any character other than Edna. Adding emphasis to Dr. Mandelet's insight is his fear, which will soon prove well grounded, that Edna is having an affair with Alcée Arobin.

The second and more significant example of the doctor's wisdom and sympathy for women appears near the close of the novel, after Edna has been traumatized by the painful labor and birthing of Adèle Ratignolle. When the doctor and Edna leave what Edna considers this "scene [of] torture" (104), Dr. Mandelet responds to Edna's depressed reaction to the birthing: "'The trouble is,' sighed the Doctor, grasping her meaning intuitively, 'that youth is given up to illusions. It seems to be a provision of Nature; a decoy to secure mothers for the race. And Nature takes no account of moral consequences, of arbitrary conditions which we create, and which we feel obliged to maintain at any cost' " (105).

In this passage, Dr. Mandelet implicitly critiques the "arbitrary" cultural conventions that compound women's natural enslavement with their biological function of propagating the species. His psychological understanding of the importance that love plays as the seemingly necessary illusion by which women are lured into entrapped roles of motherhood only adds gravity to his credentials as an unusual male sympathizer for a sex not his own, but one which, evidently based upon many years of delivering babies and attending to mothers, he has come to comprehend quite well. We are therefore prepared for Dr. Mandelet's offer to Edna: " 'It seems to me, my dear child,' said the Doctor, holding her hand, 'you seem to be in trouble. I am not going to ask for your confidence. I will only say that if ever you feel moved to give it to me, perhaps I might help you. I know I would understand, and I tell you there are not many who would—not many, my dear.' " He then bids her goodnight, saying, "I will blame you if you don't come and see me soon. It will do us both good. I don't want you to blame yourself, whatever comes" (105).

I take Dr. Mandelet's offer as a genuine expression of an understanding of Edna and of women generally that is far more sensitive to the condition of woman in the nineteenth century than permitted by our usual view of patriarchy and its large cast of adherents. Such understanding also extends beyond what the historical record normally reveals about male physicians' sensitivity to their women patients. Charlotte Perkins Gilman would not have had an autobiographical basis for "The Yellow Wall Paper" if she had been fortunate enough to have been placed in the care of a physician like Dr. Mandelet or, perchance, any of the other medicine men I have mentioned here. What I am therefore tempted to argue is the hypothesis that women writers who represent male doctors in a positive light do so because they imagine, by virtue of the intimacy with which doctors in the extratextual world come to know the minds and bodies of the opposite sex, that such men might well respond sympathetically to the biological and cultural constraints and restraints imposed on women. A sympathetic response might then prove instructive to the husbands and sons throughout the republic, resulting, at the very least, in a greater measure of psychic health in wives, daughters, and unmarried women. That this fictionalized hope for male physicians to exert a feminizing influence on the patriarchal status quo largely turned out, in the historical case, to be merely wishful thinking may well suggest the last patient investment that many women writers would place in men before they and their female readership would assume responsibility for healing the republic in a new way—prescribing to men a homeopathic dose of their own powerful medicine.

Notes

1. For the rise of male physicians and the controversy over the establishment of their power through such means as scientific knowledge, medical schools, and professional organizations, see Rothstein; and Starr 3–197.

2. For an incisive account of the role played by male physicians in promoting the view that women were mentally and physically inferior to men, see Ehrenreich and English.

3. See Wood 25–52 and Herndl 20–74. For information on the argument that women were inferior to men because of their having smaller brains, see Haller and Haller's chapter "The Lesser Man" (47–87). Behind Herndl's study and my own lies a massive body of material impossible to cite here. Interested readers might well begin with the substantial studies of Carroll Smith-Rosenberg and Charles Rosenberg; a good place to begin might be their essay "The Female Animal: Medical and Biological Views of Woman and Her Role in Nineteenth-Century America" in Leavitt 12–27. Wood's essay may be also be found in this collection (222–38).

4. For the relation between the cult of domesticity and women's inferiority, see Harris 32–72.

5. Cogan's study, of course, itemizes many advice books for women that did not assume feminine weakness. For a view, suppressed in feminist literary studies, that the cult of domesticity and its corollary, the angel in the house, had a liberating effect on middle-class women, see Achterberg 134–36.

6. Because it embraces medical circumstances of men and women, I exclude from consideration Joan Burbick's *Healing the Republic.*

7. For critiques of the invasive practices of male physicians and discussions, along with medical reform movements and self-help programs sponsored by women, see Risse et al.

8. Evidently, around midcentury there was a fairly strong movement to encourage women to enter the medical profession, judging from the number of articles in magazines that promoted the issue or gave attention to it. See "Female Doctors"; "Females as Physicians"; "Female Medical Schools"; Dowler; Gross; King; and Wilson.

9. Mitchell, trained in neurology and a believer in somatic causes of psychological disorders, has somewhat unfairly won a bad reputation as a result of the widespread critical attention given to Gilman's story. For a balanced treatment of the man and his work, see Poirier.

10. According to Rothstein, evidence suggests that women interested in medi-

cine were more attracted to homeopathy and more welcomed by the homeopathic schools than by regular medicine. The popularity of homeopathy for women rose steadily throughout the latter half of the century. "Homeopathy, like the other non-regular sects, had many more female practitioners than regular medicine did. In 1900, women constituted 5 percent of the students in regular medical schools, 9 percent of the students in eclectic schools, and 17 percent of the students in homeopathic schools. . . . In the same year, 12 percent of all homeopathic physicians were women" (300–301, n. 5). For further information on women's attraction to homeopathy, see Hurd-Mead and Moldow.

11. See Walsh 106–46 for the reactionary efforts of male doctors to solidify their power under the threat, beginning in the 1870s, of women seeking to enter the profession and feminize it.

12. Buell and Zagarell declare (255, n. 32) that this man is Dr. White, the family physician of Charles Morgeson who is so named before the episode at hand and later in the novel when he attends Cassandra after the accident that results in Charles's death.

Works Cited

Abram, Ruth J. *"Send Us a Lady Physician": Women Doctors in America, 1835–1920* New York: Norton, 1985.

Achterberg, Jeanne. *Woman as Healer.* Boston: Shambhala, 1990.

Burbick, Joan. *Healing the Republic: The Language of Health and the Culture of Nationalism in Nineteenth-Century America.* New York: Cambridge UP, 1994.

Chopin, Kate. *The Awakening.* 2nd ed. Ed. Margo Culley. New York: Norton, 1994.

Cogan, Frances B. *All-American Girl: The Ideal of Real Womanhood in Mid-Nineteenth-Century America.* Athens: U of Georgia P, 1989.

Cummins, Maria Susanna. *The Lamplighter.* Ed. Nina Baym. American Women Writers Series. New Brunswick, NJ: Rutgers UP, 1988.

Dowler, B. "Female Physicians, Medical Colleges, and Medical Ethics." *New Orleans Medical and Surgical Journal* 17 (1860): 908–11.

Ehrenreich, Barbara and Deirdre English. *Complaints and Disorders: The Sexual Politics of Sickness.* Glass Mountain Pamphlet No. 2. Old Westbury, NY: Feminist P, 1973.

Evans, Augusta Jane. *St. Elmo.* Ed. Diane Roberts. Tuscaloosa: U of Alabama P, 1992.

"Female Doctors." *Buffalo Medical Journal* 13 (1857/1858): 191.

"Female Medical Schools." *Boston Medical and Surgical Journal* 51 (1854/1855): 263–64.

"Females as Physicians." *Boston Medical and Surgical Journal* 53 (1855/1856): 292–94.

Fern, Fanny. *Ruth Hall and Other Writings.* Ed. Joyce W. Warren. American Women Writers Series. New Brunswick, NJ: Rutgers UP, 1986.

[Gross, Samuel]. "Female Medical Colleges and Female Doctors." *North American Medico-Chirurgical Review* 1 (1857): 942–47.

Haller, John S., Jr., and Robin M. Haller. *The Physician and Sexuality in Victorian America*. Urbana: U of Illinois P, 1974.

Harris, Barbara J. *Beyond Her Sphere: Women and the Professions in American History*. Contributions in Women's Studies, Number 4. Westport, CT: Greenwood Press, 1978.

Herndl, Diane Price. *Invalid Women: Figuring Feminine Illness in American Fiction and Culture, 1840–1940*. Chapel Hill: U of North Carolina P, 1993.

Hurd-Mead, Kate Campbell. *A History of Women in Medicine from the Earliest Times to the Beginning of the Nineteenth Century*. Haddam, CT: Haddam P, 1938.

King, Dan. *Quackery Unmasked*. Boston: Clapp, 1858.

Leavitt, Judith Walzer. *Women and Health in America: Historical Readings*. Madison: U of Wisconsin P, 1984.

Moldow, Gloria. *Women Doctors in Gilded Age Washington: Race, Gender, and Professionalization*. Urbana: Illinois UP, 1987.

Poirier, Suzanne. "The Weir Mitchell Rest Cure: Doctor and Patients." *Women's Studies* 10 (1983): 15–40.

Risse, Guenter, et al., eds. *Medicine without Doctors: Home Health Care in American History*. New York: Science History Publications, 1977.

Rothstein, William G. *American Physicians in the Nineteenth Century: From Sects to Science*. Baltimore: Johns Hopkins UP, 1972.

Smith-Rosenberg, Carol and Charles Rosenberg. "The Female Animal: Medical and Biological Views of Woman and Her Role in Nineteenth-Century America." *Journal of American History* 60 (1973): 332–56.

Southworth, E.D.E.N. *The Hidden Hand: or, Capitola the Madcap*. Ed. Joanne Dobson. American Women Writers Series. New Brunswick, NJ: Rutgers UP, 1988.

Starr, Paul. *The Social Transformation of American Medicine*. New York: Basic Books, 1982.

Stoddard, Elizabeth. *The Morgesons and Other Writings, Published and Unpublished, by Elizabeth Stoddard*. Ed. Lawrence Buell and Sandra A. Zagarell. Philadelphia: U of Pennsylvania P, 1984.

Walsh, Mary Roth. *"Doctors Wanted: No Women Need Apply": Sexual Barriers in the Medical Profession, 1835–1975*. New Haven: Yale UP, 1975.

Wilson, Stainback. "Female Medical Education." *Southern Medical and Surgical Journal* ns 10 (1854): 6–10.

Wood, Ann Douglas. "'The Fashionable Diseases': Women's Complaints and Their Treatment in Nineteenth-Century America." *Journal of Interdisciplinary History* 4 (1973): 25–52.

7

Gender Bending: Two Role-Reversal Utopias by Nineteenth-Century Women

DARBY LEWES

For centuries, the creators of fictional utopias have proposed myriad alternatives to their societies—everything from the left of anarchy to the right of fascism. Yet all of these schemes invariably start out by asking "what if?" What would happen if, for example, a republic were governed by the principles of temperance, courage, wisdom, and justice? or if an island were peopled by pagans who were somehow more Christian than Christians? or if totalitarianism were given such free rein that the state controlled the way people thought? For many nineteenth-century women, the "what if" question pertained to gender-specific roles: men had been in charge since the beginning of time, after all, and it might be argued that there was considerable room for improvement. What if the supposed "separate spheres" imprisoning women and men alike were suddenly reversed?

Two nineteenth-century women answered this question in their utopian fictions. In 1870, Annie Denton Cridge published a short work entitled *Man's Rights; or, How Would You Like It?* consisting of five "dream visions" detailing life on the topsy-turvy world of Mars, where women rule the country and men remain at home to mind the children. Later that year, Cridge published a serialized version of the text in *Woodhull and Claflin's Weekly,* adding four "visions." The narrative first offers a sympathetic portrait of housebound men trapped in an endless loop of domestic drudgery, then explains how a Man's Rights movement eventually succeeds in creating an equitable society in which both genders move freely between the public and private spheres. Twelve years later, Mrs. J. Wood published *Pan-*

Portions of this essay first appeared in *Paradoxa* 3.1–2 (1997): 286–303 in "[C]Loathing Womanhood: Two Role-Reversal Utopias by Nineteenth-Century Women."

taletta: A Romance of Sheheland (1882), a novel that also employed the role-reversal model to make its satiric point. Wood's narrative, however, is an antifeminist dystopian satire, detailing the exploits of a disoriented American aviator who happens to land in Petticotia—a society composed of effete, enslaved males ("heshes") and dominant females ("shehes") who smoke and drink while secretly hungering for the attentions of an old-fashioned, "manly" man. Thanks to the hero's machismo and the longings of the man-hungry females, the "natural" order of things is eventually reinstated.

Little is known about either author. Cridge was the sister of William Denton: a geology professor and the original publisher of *Man's Rights,* he was also an authority on psychometry (the ability to sense people and events by holding inanimate objects). Cridge was herself a gifted psychometer, and the *Encyclopedia of Occultism and Parapsychology* cites several of her "readings" at some length (Shepard). In addition, an 1868 *Boston Investigator* article suggests that she and her husband, Alfred, lived in Washington, D.C., and promoted social reforms such as cooperative kitchens and workshops. Nevertheless, she remains an elusive figure: even her dates of birth and death are unknown (although in 1884 her son Alfred Denton Cridge referred to her as the "late" Mrs. Cridge in his *Utopia, or the History of an Extinct Planet*). Still less is known about Mrs. J. Wood: aside from the fact that she wrote an antifeminist utopia, she exists only as an initial sandwiched between the marital honorific and her husband's name—and even that single initial might be his.

The texts that these women produced share a good deal of common ground: both were written by nineteenth-century women, and were published within a span of only twelve years; both employ the utopian genre; and both employ role reversals to make their satiric point. Yet they express diametrically opposed political philosophies: Cridge's inverted society is a place of justice and order managed by responsible, reasonable women, while Petticotia is a chaotic madhouse, run by jealous, strident harridans. These oppositions reflect nineteenth-century women's differing individual perceptions of their own nature, as well as their role and place in society. Both works address specifically feminist concerns: the need to blur the notion of separate spheres in order to provide equal access to education, equal work and pay, and equal participation in public political matters.

In the nineteenth century, these concerns were all linked by a single element—clothing—which accentuated, reinforced, and promoted gender difference. Fashion determined that the female image should epitomize aesthetic sensibility, physical delicacy, and womanly grace. These apparently innocuous qualities had dire consequences for women who wished to vote, obtain higher education, or work. Aesthetic sensibility translated into a preoccupation with frippery, frills, and other non-essentials, and perpetuated the view of women as frivolous, light-minded creatures. The myth of women's physical delicacy, resulting in part from the physical constraints of women's fashion, precluded any sort of strenuous activity—physical or mental—and was used as an argument against female higher education. Of course, without advanced training, women were effectively barred from any lucrative profession. Fashion thus tacitly forced women to remain in the domestic sphere, the ideal frame for their natural grace and moral superiority. It is no wonder that feminists such as Annie Denton Cridge argued for dress reform which blurred gender difference; it was the first step toward increased political, educational, and occupational opportunity for women. Nor is it surprising that Mrs. J. Wood's antifeminist novel ridiculed all of these issues, using satire, exaggeration, pseudoscience, and false logic.

Fashion has always been an oppressive tyrant—especially women's fashion. Any twentieth-century woman who has struggled into a girdle or hobbled after a taxi in high heels and a long, tight skirt can readily identify with nineteenth-century women's complaints about their clothing. The more exaggerated styles of late-nineteenth-century middle-class women bordered on torture: vise-like corsets; long, dragging gowns (made of highly delicate fabric which could easily be ripped or stained); tiny, narrow, pinching shoes with precariously high heels; bulky headgear perched atop complex hairdos. These clothes were not only obviously inconvenient; they were also implicitly absurd. Women who preferred a sixteen-inch waist to breathing, whose clothes prevented them from walking any distance or raising their arms above their shoulders, whose feet were deformed by shoes several sizes too small, and whose internal organs were compressed out of shape by steel-reinforced corsets—such were hopeless slaves to fashion who could hardly be taken seriously as intellectual beings.

Neither can the men of Cridge's Marsian [sic] society. Although they still wear the pants in the family, they do so with a difference: their suits are monuments to excess and frivolity. Men are all but unrecognizable beneath masses of brightly colored garb, smothered in lace, embroidery, bows, and streamers. They peer out at the world from beneath fantastic headgear, covered in "flowers, bits of lace, tulle or blonde, feathers, and even birds" (13–14) and topped with ribbon, tinsel, and glitter. Maneuvering in such a getup is difficult at best, and the men have been forced to develop a swinging gait, "something like that of a sailor, that made their coat-tails move to and fro as they walked" (14). As if all this were not sufficiently demanding, they must also "carefully and daintily" hoist their trouser legs as they attempt to navigate the city boulevards, lest "the laces, ribbons, embroidery, or ruffles . . . come in contact with the mud of the streets" (14). Marsian women, on the other hand, dress simply in "plain, substantial clothing." Like nineteenth-century men, Cridge's women are not expected to define themselves through fashionable dress. Nor is their power dependent upon their physical attractiveness: as the narrator is quick to point out, there is "something about them far more beautiful than beauty" (13). Unencumbered by frippery, they move gracefully through the streets, physically, morally, intellectually, and politically powerful beings.

Cridge's text demonstrates that notions of a specifically male or female "nature" are essentially a question of convention. She does not ridicule the wretched men who are trapped in her reversal of social norms; instead, she finds them pitiable. A fashionable Marsian male, teetering on his high heels as he struggles to keep his ludicrous hat on his head with one hand while clutching his fantastically decorated trousers in the other, is not comical. He is instead a tragic figure, a degraded human being who has been stripped not only of personal dignity but of his own humanity as well: "a monkey standing on two feet" (34). His degraded state is not due to any personal shortcoming, but rather is the result a humiliating costuming *designed* to make him appear foolish, childish—even infantile. Such garb is a cultural marker, indicating that the wearer is to be patronized (or, in this case, matronized), petted, and spoiled. His fragility is emphasized by the diminutives that characterize his clothing: "little ruffles . . . round the bottom of the pants," "rows of small ruffles" on the vest, "little flat hats" with childish "ribbon streamers" (13), his "little green velvet cap" and "tiny porte-monnaie" decorated with the emblem of his servitude: "little chains" (35).

The men of Mrs. J. Wood's *Pantaletta* are even more degraded—they, after all, do not even have the consolation of trousers, but must drag about in skirts. They have one dubious comfort, however. Since everyone in Petticotia cross-dresses, everyone is ridiculous. Mrs. Wood has little compassion for any gender that persists in behaving in a perverse, unnatural fashion. Instead, she exploits the comic possibilities of transvestitism: her men are grotesque parodies of women, and her women hideous travesties of men: indeed, they are no longer "women" and "men," but androgynous "shehes" and "heshes." Shehes sport preposterous false beards and moustaches; they have traded away their glorious womanhood for a chance to be false men. They have been encouraged to do so by females who have proven inadequate as women: few of them "have ever been married, and those who [are] so fortunate have been, with few exceptions, childless or unhappy in their family relationships. Their milk of human kindness is somewhat soured" (84). In this new world order, however, the most masculine females are perceived as the most attractive. The result is a grotesque amalgam of "exaggerated pantaloons, stiff dress-coats, high collars, low foreheads, short noses, bulging eyes, and other strange physical proportions" (190). Petticotian males' attempts at ersatz womanhood are equally futile. No amount of shaving or cosmetics will make even the most effeminate heshe womanly, so the result is an equally ridiculous "medley of giraffe-like beings in petticoats, endowed with roman, aquiline and mongrel noses of generous proportions, big chins and inexpressive eyes" (190).

The nineteenth-century debate over dress reform notwithstanding, Wood sees nothing wrong with women's fashions per se. Indeed, she values them as a reassuring part of the natural order of things: flounces and frills, corsets and crinolines do not demean, nor do they indicate an essentially frivolous nature. Such niceties are merely a reflection of a cultured woman's taste for beautiful things, a genteel sensibility that even a male should be able to appreciate. When Wood's American intruder is forced into female garb, he feels "ill at ease, to say the least." Yet his primary concern has relatively little to do with fashion, and a great deal to do with role-shifting: he is terrified that someone will charge him "with being a fraud and a vile not-what-I-seemed" (100). The clothes themselves do not upset him overmuch: he remarks that his wig is a bit unwieldy, that he cannot feel his hat through all the extra hair, and that his corset hugs him "rather closely." His only real complaint is that his artificial inflatable rubber breasts (which, like the women's false beards and moustaches, emphasize the unnaturalness of Petticotian arrangements) sit "like a late supper upon [his] chest." Otherwise, the experience is "not as dreadful as [he] expected" (100). Later in the novel, he even goes so far as to describe his satin and velvet ball gown in fairly approbatory terms. The implication is of course that feminists have no real basis for complaint about fashion. Still, he feels uncomfortable and unnatural in women's clothes; they act as a litmus test of Real Manhood. The parallel test of a True Woman is her distaste for trousers, and the lovesick, pantalooned President of Petticotia passes with flying colors. When she attempts to attract the American by bejeweling and gowning herself—"in all a [traditional nineteenth-century] woman's splendour" (81)—she immediately notices the comfort of dressing as nature meant her to: she is "greatly relieved by this change from the uncomfortable garments [i.e., trousers] which the law assigned to her sex" (85). Her relief is understandable; in her pre-unisex era, after all, dress is a very real indication of gender—and gender difference. Skirts are a synecdoche for femaleness; trousers represent everything masculine. Any deviation from gender-specific clothing seems perverted and unnatural (which may be why Cridge avoids any reference to cross-dressing in her narrative).

Yet her relief also reflects the late-nineteenth-century nexus between helplessness, femininity, and social status. These elements were so tightly linked that anything which gave women physical freedom was immediately perceived as not only unfeminine, but a touch déclassé. Dress was a cultural signifier, after all, a marker of one's social position: even lower-class women tried to look as if they were members of the "carriage class." A protected, beloved household goddess did not need to breathe deeply, since her movements were invariably (and unavoidably) graceful and stately—nothing to put one out of breath. Nor would she need to bend over, since her servants would presumably attend to her every need. Any woman who wished to be fashionable must at least *look* as if she spent her days moving from parlor to carriage and back. Complaining about an inability to perform rigorous activity was tantamount to confessing one's failure as a female: either the complainer was insufficiently attractive to secure male protection, or she was one of those "mannish" feminist types—the same thing, really. For many women, the very word "healthful" was linked with a dangerous androgyny, one that threatened to blur the separate spheres. As Kate Gannett Wells asserted in 1850, "instead of grace, there has come in many women an affectation of mannishness, as is shown in hats, jackets, long strides, and a healthful swinging of the arms in walking" (qtd. in Kinnard 194). How much more ladylike to luxuriate in one's delightful helplessness, to enjoy what one 1870 woman termed the "delicious sensation of perfect compression" afforded by stays—a sensation so delightful that "when once accustomed to it," women would corset themselves tightly even "if appearance were no consideration at all" (qtd. in Murray 67).

Yet appearance *was* a consideration—a consideration so important that nineteenth-century women were willing to risk their very lives in the name of fashion. The long, trailing skirts that provided a feminine aura of grace and dignity were not only inconvenient; they could be dangerously unhealthy as well. As the nineteenth century progressed, walking skirts ballooned into tents generally four to five yards around; ball gowns were so huge that an average room could hold no more than two. Many a careless woman strayed too close to the fireplace and went up in flames: an 1865 English newspaper lamented that "not a year passes but in this country alone hundreds suffer death by burning through crinoline" (qtd. in Cunnington 221). The longer, trailing skirts that replaced it, however, were even more uncomfortable and difficult to maneuver: in 1878, Margaret Oliphant complained that "no-one but a woman knows how her dress twists around her knees, doubles her fatigue, and arrests her locomotive powers" (qtd. in Gernsheim 65). The narrower skirt had yet another disadvantage, however: it required severely tight-laced corsets to maintain the illusion of a tiny waist (the crinoline had been so voluminous that *any* waist looked small by comparison). These whalebone-and-steel contraptions were not merely painful; they could be lethal. By forcing women's bodies into unnatural contours, corsets often caused the uterus to prolapse. This complaint became so common that "pessaries" (devices to hold internal organs in place) became a regular, albeit unmentionable, fashion accessory. Additionally, corsets not only tended to force ribs to grow directly into the lungs, but could so weaken the spine that many women had to wear "night stays" in order to sit upright in bed. Even champions of clothing that emphasized the separate spheres were troubled by the more exaggerated fashions—although their concern was for the most part limited to domestic issues such as motherhood and housekeeping. Stays, for example, were criticized not for their effect on the woman who wore them, but because they could render her incapable of producing children. Fashion must not deny a woman her natural, divinely ordained function in life. Antifeminists also condemned long, trailing skirts—again, not because of an individual woman's convenience or health, but rather out of a concern that such fashions were unhygienic, since long skirts tended to pick up mud and germs and bring them into the home, contaminating the family sanctuary.

Yet women's fashions threatened even more than physical health. They took an emotional toll as well. Corsets, huge skirts, and crippling shoes could make even the healthiest woman not only appear frail, but *feel* frail. In many cases, this ingrained sense of personal infirmity had been encouraged since early childhood, when she had been conditioned to accept the middle-class aversion to female exercise: anything vigorous enough to raise perspiration was at best undignified and at worst unnaturally "mannish." Proper young girls remained inside, sewing or playing with dolls, while young men were free to engage in rough-and-tumble play. Proper young ladies were trained to enjoy "feminine" pursuits designed to help them acquire a husband and the financial security he would bring. As Harriet Martineau noted in *Society in America,* "the sum and substance of female education . . . is training women to consider marriage as the sole object in life" (2: 47). Young women were encouraged to appear as fragile and delicate—as feminine—as possible. Even had their clothing permitted unladylike vigorous activity, such exertion could only repel a potential suitor. Unfortunate young women who had physical heartiness thrust upon them by an overly resilient constitution generally tried to conceal the fact.

After all, antifeminists argued, physical delicacy was a natural—even essential—component of the female constitution, meant to complement male strength. A strong, physically powerful woman, they argued, was a freakish androgyne who, if she did somehow manage to attract a husband, should certainly not be encouraged to reproduce. The feminist/antifeminist clash over woman's physical nature is dramatically illustrated in *Man's Rights* and

Pantaletta. Indeed, the role-reversal mechanism—in which women behave like men and vice versa—is especially relevant in an age that hotly disputed exactly how women and men *should* behave.

Cridge argues that nature does not produce frail people. It is fashion and convention that give such an impression, and thus fashion and convention must be defied. Resisting social norms will enable nature to generate healthy, strong men *and* women. Supporting such perverse norms, on the other hand, will result in feeble weaklings such as Cridge's young male Marsians, imprisoned by their upbringing and clothing. A Marsian boy must be confined to "over-heated rooms," since his inadequate clothing—"flimsy pants of white muslin" and a "flimsy jacket and paper shoes"—provides little protection from the elements. He is expected to be "a dear little gentleman" and not spoil his delicate clothes, while his sister frolics outside in her "warm cloth dress" and "substantial over-garments, and thick shoes. . . . The girl may romp and play in the snow, climb fences and trees, and thus strengthen every muscle; while the little pale-faced boy presses his nose against the window-pane, and wishes—alas! vainly—that he, too, had been a girl" (26). Cridge argues that a childhood based on the notion of separate spheres dooms young Marsian men to a life of poor health, a painful existence composed of weakness, disease, and poor muscular development. Most maddening is the fact that such frailty is perceived as a natural thing, when in reality it is "ignorance and custom" that are "the foundation for bodily weakness . . . dependence and mental imbecility." "Were boys subject to the same physical training as girls," she asserts, "the result would prove that no natural inferiority exists" (27).

For Wood, however, physical inferiority is an innate part of womanliness. In Petticotia, only ugly and mannish females enjoy physical strength—although since these females now breed, their type is increasing with alarming rapidity. (Happily, the few True Women who remain have managed to retain their delicate and sensitive nature despite perverted social norms that demand female health and vigor.) Wood presents physical strength as an inherently male quality, and one that should remain exclusively so: anything else is abnormal and degenerate. Petticotian history exemplifies the danger of perverting this natural order of things: the founder of the female republic was a monstrous, man-hating freak known as "Tyrania the Strong" (151), "a man in all but sex," (153) who was so physically powerful that "half-a-dozen ordinary men would be to her in single-handed combat as a litter of pups, tossed with ease wherever she pleased to bestow their insensible remains" (152). She used her strength to challenge the patriarchal order of things, and plunged the nation into civil war. The result was a political bloodbath, described with horrific revolutionary imagery: tumbrels rolling through the streets, mass beheadings, and so forth. Tyrania has little in common with the beautiful President of Petticotia (the True Woman who assumed female garb in order to seduce the American visitor). Despite her feminist conditioning, the President remains "a creature all softness and sensibility, bearing happiness meekly and sorrow with fortitude: gentle, mild, submissive" (183)—and she invariably drops into a dead faint when excited.

Such a woman reflects the stereotypical image of the Victorian belle-ideal: an innocent darling clad in adorably frivolous frills and furbelows, too weak to even pick up her own dropped handkerchief, obviously in need of a big, strong man to protect her—and unwilling to challenge him in anything. The portrait in itself might be seen as an amusing period piece, the harmless stuff of nostalgic Victoriana. But the effect of such a portrait on actual women's lives was insidious. Women imprisoned in awkward clothing and denied exercise since earliest childhood could be convinced fairly readily that they were far too fragile to withstand the rigors of any activity outside the shelter of the domestic sphere. And this myth of inherent physical frailty prohibited them from obtaining an education, from engaging in profitable work, and from taking part in politics.

Late-nineteenth-century America witnessed an ongoing debate about exactly how much exertion members of the frail sex could endure, and—more importantly—about precisely what *kind* of exertion best suited them. Feminists such as Cridge regarded female frailty as a direct result of the physical constraints placed upon women, and many argued that the myth of inherent female infirmity was engendered and enforced by those who wished to keep women confined to the domestic sphere. It was a powerful myth indeed, and one that was the basis of powerful arguments against female education, since it was used to keep them not only from rigorous exercise, but from rigorous study as well.

Many renowned male scientists were quick to explain that all work outside the home—including intellectual activity—was terribly dangerous and debilitating for women, since it made unnatural demands upon them. Dr. Edward H. Clarke, for example, a member of the Massachusetts Medical Society, a fellow of the American Academy of Arts and Sciences, and a professor of medicine at Harvard, expounded at some length on typical examples of educated or independent women. "Miss A——" was a brilliant scholar whose erudition resulted in chorea, "prolonged dyspepsia, neuralgia, and dysmenorrhoea" (69). "Miss B——" was a successful actress who "persisted in the slow suicide of frequent hemorrhages"—in fact, she even "encouraged them" by her determination to work "in a man's sustained way" (73)—and eventually fell victim to heart palpitation, difficulties in breathing, "dizziness, semi-consciousness . . . anemia and epileptiform attacks"

(74). "Miss C——" was a bookkeeper whose refusal to make "allowance for the periodicity of her organization" and "shape of her skeleton" resulted in "neuralgia, backache, menorrhagia, leucorrhoea, and general disability" (77). Dr. Clarke was finally forced "to consign her to an asylum" (87). The good doctor continues through a substantial portion of the alphabet in this fashion, tossing out abstruse scientific terms dexter and sinister. The medical jargon alone would have been enough to intimidate a woman denied specific medical training: impressive statistics seem even more impressive when they are incomprehensible.

But intimidation was precisely the idea. Women had to be frightened away from specific medical training—or any training that could draw them away from the domestic sphere with the promise of lucrative and stimulating work. This need to keep women in the home generated article after article, and book after book, all "proving" "scientifically" that female education was directly linked to female illness. Dr. Clarke cited cases of young women who "graduated from school or college excellent scholars, but with undeveloped ovaries. Later they became sterile" (39). Noted gynecologists such as Dr. William Goodell asserted definitively that female "boarding-schools and public schools . . . breed a host of sickly girls" plagued by "manifold diseases, both functional and structural" including "neuralgic pains," "amenorrhoea," "irregular menstruation," "spinal irritation, leucorrhoea, irritable bladder, pruritus vulvae, painful ovaries, a bearing-down feeling, and various pelvic aches and congestions" (Goodell et al. 669). The famed neurologist S. Weir Mitchell argued that intellectual work is "dangerous" for women, "sexually incapacitative to a varying amount," and the cause of "hysteria, or hysterical hypochondriasis" or "neurasthenia" (Goodell et al. 672). Sir James Crichton Browne declared (in the medical journal *Lancet,* no less) that education causes women's brains to consume themselves, resulting in "nervous disturbances, insomnia, anaemia . . . general delicacy," and "anorexia scholastica" (qtd. in Kinnard 256). Women were clearly too frail to undergo the specialized training that would enable them to debunk the very same pseudoscience that prevented them from getting that training.

Women could not even be sure of reassurance from other members of their gender: some of the most violent antifeminists were women—and ironically, many were highly educated, well-paid career women (Eliza Lynn Linton was a noted author, Sarah Josepha Hale the editor of the popular and influential *Godey's Lady's Book*). All, however, were quick to jump on the scientific bandwagon. Those who lacked medical training relied on questionable logic: Miss M. A. Hardaker, for example, argued in 1882 that since the male brain is larger than that of the female, one can establish "an exact correspondence between brain-substance and intelligence," since "in the case of every other organ of the body we know there is an ascertainable correspondence between size and condition, and the amount of work that an organ can do" (578). Just as a larger heart will pump more blood than a small one, a larger brain will pump more intelligence. Eliza Lynn Linton pointed out that education took both a moral and physical toll on women: it not only made women "arrogant, pretentious, [and] vain," but "ruin[ed] them for pregnancy, lactation, and child rearing" (qtd. in Kinnard 232). She condemns the young intellectual woman who selfishly risks her reproductive organs, and suggests that she not taint the race with her brain-damaged body: "Let her then dedicate herself from the beginning as the Vestal of Knowledge, and forego the exercise of that function the perfection of which her own self-improvement has destroyed" ("Higher Education" 818). In other words, a woman's intellect was not merely incompatible with her biological imperative, but its direct negation. The desire to educate or support oneself was not a noble effort, but an indication of hormonal deficiency. Either one was a "womanly" woman, whose happy ovaries generated a healthy maternal urge, or an unnatural "mannish" female, whose natural instincts had been perverted into a craving for "public applause, an audience, excitement, notoriety." Lacking the warm love and validation provided by a husband and children, such failed women could only hope to be "lecturers, professors, entitled to wear gowns and hoods, and put letters after their names" (Linton, "Revolt" 201). They are more to be pitied than despised, since their personal ambition exposes their deficiency of womanly grace and force.

Antifeminists were not anti-woman, by any means—as long as one accepted their rather narrow definition of the term. A True Woman was a highly moral, impeccably chaste, invariably noble creature who devoted herself selflessly to her husband and family. The domestic sphere was her glory and her protection, and she would leave it only on missions of charity, in order to extend its benefits to those less fortunate than she. She was a fragile being, but not a weak one; although unnatural activities such as education would rob her of her strength, a woman who lived according to God and nature—whose priorities were centered on her own biology—could draw upon her own huge reservoirs of moral and spiritual power. This might explain how a nineteenth-century woman managed labors that would daunt even the most aerobically fit twentieth-century matron: shopping at a bewildering variety of stores (and a thrifty housewife would make it a point of pride to discover the establishments which offered the best value that day), doing the necessary baking, canning, and preserving (with fruits and vegetables grown in her own garden), dressing slaughtered meat, churning butter, laundering (a chore that involved sorting, carrying buckets of hot water, scrubbing clothing on a washboard, and ironing), floor-scrubbing and sweeping, rug-beating, furniture-dusting, dishwashing, bed-making, window-washing, sewing and mending clothing and undergarments, knitting scarves and socks—assuming, that is, she had put the children to bed and had no invalids to nurse. The wealthiest of women could afford the battalions of servants needed to perform such tasks (and overseeing servants is in itself a fairly exhausting activity, requiring interviews, hiring, firing, upholding high moral standards, planning, and ceaseless supervision); most middle-class housewives struggled to maintain the illusion of a grand establishment with a single housemaid and a cook; the less fortunate were left with no resources except their own two hands. Yet, while such an extraordinary level of activity might be expected to kill a physically frail creature, Truly Womanly women apparently drew strength from their household devotions: ironically, managing such a grueling regimen was seen not as evidence of innate female vigor, but as proof that they were doing the work for which they were best suited. Indeed, such work was perceived as actually *beneficial* to women because it was a natural, womanly occupation. Woman's natural place in society was the defining criterion. Intellectual exertion was deadly because it was outside women's natural ability. Such *un*natural activities as formal education, and the manly activities to which it would lead (earning money or taking part in political action), were the real threat. Such endeavors would take the woman out of the domestic sphere, away from home: the source of her joy and fulfillment and the site of whatever power she had managed to obtain.

Feminists who had encountered all this supposed joy and fulfillment firsthand were a trifle skeptical, however. Annie Denton Cridge presents a more realistic portrait of domestic bliss and its effect on the housebound spouse. Marsian men tend to be "very pale, and somewhat nervous" (3), "stoop-shouldered . . . weak and complaining," "pale and haggard" (4), "poor, sickly" (7), "very feeble . . . suffering from dyspepsia" (6) and a host of other ills. Their fragile state is not the result of excessive study, however; like American women, Marsian men are discouraged from attempting higher education or entering the business world. Their poor health is a direct result of their crushing domestic workload, their "long and weary battling with the cares of the household" (4). The poorer Marsian male must arise at dawn in order to tend to the fire and prepare breakfast. He must hurry, hurry, hurry, trying to get as much as possible accomplished before the baby wakes—for of course he then must continue his chores "with baby in his arms, carrying it around with him" as he "rake[s] the fire, frie[s] the meat, and set[s] the table for breakfast" (4). At some point during all this frenzy of activity, he must see that his older children are washed and dressed. No wonder his appetite is gone as, "pale and nervous," he finally sits down to his meal, still holding the baby in his arms. Throughout all of this, his wife has sat "quietly and composedly" (4) drinking her morning coffee and reading the morning paper, "apparently oblivious of the trials of her poor husband, and of all he had to endure in connection with his household cares" (4–5). His day has only just begun, however. When his wife leaves for work, he must do the laundry while the baby sleeps, rocking the cradle and washing at the same time. He must then perform his daily chores, "running and hurrying here and there about the house; while in his poor, disturbed mind revolve[s] the thought of the sewing that ought to be done, and only his own hands to do it" (5). After dinner, the husband sits late into the night, "darning stockings and mending the children's clothes after the hard day's washing." Unfortunately, the clothesline breaks and drops the clothes he has so painfully washed into the mud of the yard; "the poor man [has] a terrible time rinsing some and washing others over again" (5). Finally, he soaks the laundry in tubs filled "with water he had brought from a square distant" (5–6). Throughout all of this, his wife, "in comfortable slippers" (6), sits reading by the fire.

Things are not much better in the homes of the wealthy. Upper-class gentleman-housekeepers, just as "pale and unhappy" as their poorer brothers, do the best they can to manage their household, but the result is a round of "bad coffee, burned meat, and heavy biscuits." The lady of the house chastises her husband, telling him he "ought to attend to things better" (6). Yet good help is hard to come by, even on Mars; too delicate and too uneducated to direct his domestic staff properly, the husband is frequently terrified of his own servants, "crushed and held by his help." If anything, the level of anxiety increases with the number of servants that are kept; they bring him no relief, but only trouble: "trouble about washing, trouble about ironing, trouble about children; there was waste, there was thieving" (7).

Cridge argues that the dismal situation of these men has nothing to do with supposedly natural inferiority. The "beautiful, noble" (19) Martian women would have been in exactly the same degraded condition had they been "trained and educated as these degraded men,—without a motive in life, limited in education and culture, shut out of every path to honor or emolument, and reduced to the condition of paupers on the bounty of the opposite sex" (19). Men's lack of education has excluded them from "nearly all avenues to pecuniary independence." No wonder that marriage is "necessarily their highest ambition," for there is "no other way for them to obtain wealth or a home." Their only hope is to devote "all their powers to the one grand object of catching a woman with money" (19). Ultimately, both spouses can suffer from such arrangements, since women are frequently "trapped into marriage by one of these silly, worthless men, who [has] learned well the arts and schemes of wife-catching" (19–20).

Even a woman burdened with such a mate, however, can find some consolation in her work, which is bound to be far more manageable, far more lucrative, and infinitely more satisfying than his. Women are the movers and shakers on Mars—and are clearly in a position to keep things that way. They hold all legal and political power, and "every office of honor and emolument"; they control "all colleges and literary institutions," which, "with very few exceptions," have been "built for women, and only open to women" (16). Their physical appearance reflects their physical and intellectual freedom: healthy, happy, relaxed, and powerful, they are "almost divine" (16). Students, professors, lawyers, judges, and jurors, they can be found in the "lecture-room and the pulpit, the house of representatives and the senate-chamber,—yea, everywhere" (16–17). In a world in which women determine their own "natural" abilities, it seems as if "Nature had intended—in this part of the world at least—that woman, and only woman, should legislate and govern; and that here, if nowhere else, woman should be superior to man" (17).

Petticotian arrangements, however, suggest that female superiority has not worked out particularly well there. In order to show the unnaturalness of male domesticity, Wood depicts heshes not as housebound drudges—no man is capable of running a house or rearing children properly—but as vacuous, bubbleheaded flirts. In order to attract beaux, heshes "rub villainous snuff on their gums, chew fatty and resinous substances, paint their faces," and "eat arsenic for the complexion" (177). Thanks to technology, they have the leisure to do so: even degraded males remain good with machinery. In order to be able to devote themselves "to lives of voluptuous ease and fashion," they have invented "curious appliances and machines for domestic use, which reduced their tasks materially." Heshes with children are still housebound, but the "thousands who had no babes to watch·over" now "pass half their time in reading novels, thrumming insipid music, studying the latest styles of trains, or acquiring the fascinating art of flirting" (171). If men are not permitted to be men, Wood suggests, they will be as frivolous and flighty—and promiscuous—as women. Indeed, the problem of heshe promiscuity is so great that fairly draconian laws regarding male morality have been enacted. Males must testify as to the state of their chastity each year. Those heshes found guilty of perjury are beheaded; those who confess openly to a fallen state are immediately sent to a brothel.

There is a lively trade in such places, for shehes have adapted "all the vices and wickedness of men" (176) along with their trousers. In addition to whoring, Petticotian females drink, gamble, smoke, chew tobacco, and take snuff; they indulge in "racing, prize fighting, stocks, and other costly iniquities" (176). Yet although they have abandoned their womanly natures, they have managed to retain such "womanish" characteristics as jealousy, envy, backbiting, and greed. Physically, they are caricatures of the nineteenth-century feminists: "tall, angular, ugly-faced" (33), prematurely gray, bitter, and man-hating. Their unnatural way of life has marred them physically; their mannish behavior has stripped them of whatever feminine charm they might have once possessed. It has marred them ethically as well—their abandonment of female morality leads them to participate in such unlady-like activities as murder, treason, and perjury. A number are mentally crip-pled as well: General Pantaletta, the title character, is an ugly androgyne who has been driven nearly mad by her consuming ambition. As a result, she behaves irrationally, and her speech frequently deteriorates into incoher-ent, rambling, Lady Macbeth–like soliloquies.

To be sure, there are a number of True Women left in Petticotia who manage to withstand their conditioning; all they need is a Real Man to set them straight. The American visitor is just such a type: even his low-cut gown, wig, petticoat, and falsies cannot obscure his virility (although per-haps the fact that he has managed to retain his moustache helps somewhat). His masculinity strikes a responsive feminine chord in the young President, who ultimately repudiates her rank and power in favor of docile submission: "I lay my presidency—all that I possess of honors or riches—at your feet," she cries. "Share them with your devoted slave and speak but one kind word that her pain may be turned to joy . . . I love you, love you—yes adore you" (89). Wood's philosophy is readily apparent: women only *think* they want public lives because they have not met the right man; once they do, condi-tioning is no match for biology. The aviator realizes this, forgives the Presi-dent her unnatural (and unwanted) position of political power, and lauds her essential being as the quintessence of his own version of the domestic ideal: "a sweet tempered, laughing-eyed little woman, whose face is full of intelligence and refinement," who "steps out in the hallway and meets the loving eyes of him for whom her heart beats first and last" (141).

Such an ideal was seen as positive: even the staunchest feminist found it difficult to criticize the "womanly" woman whose high moral standards ensured her modesty and chastity, and whose maternal instincts were the source of her noble selflessness and gentleness. A model of grace, decorum, and gentility, she functioned as a moral exemplar to all who were fortunate enough to enter her sphere. Yet, feminists such as Cridge argued, were not her virtues the best argument for female suffrage? Surely such a paragon would have a decidedly positive influence on worldly, corrupt males.

Cridge's depiction of Marsian social arrangements suggests that female government might improve things anywhere—precisely because women are endowed with such strong moral force. Her paragons of womanhood do not drink or smoke, and while they may not be particularly helpful around the house, no instances of husband- or child-beating are reported. Women are the soul of chivalry; they courteously open doors and give up train seats to the weaker sex—and invariably rise when a male enters the room. They occupy themselves with refined pursuits, and are respectable and civic-minded. Their leisure time is devoted to self-improvement, or to their spouses and families: women escort their gentlemen to church or to the theater, perhaps take them to an "ice-cream saloon" (18) for refreshment, and gallantly see them "safely home" (18) afterwards (although, in this community of order and decency, one wonders what the men are being kept safe *from*). The matriarchal society of Mars certainly appears to be better run than its terrestrial patriarchal counterpart.

Indeed, the only real shortcoming of Marsian women is their myopic inattention to their husbands' oppression. Even this, however, is eventually overcome by the innate female sense of fair play, and a willingness to blur or even dissolve the restrictions of separate spheres. First, women invent machines "that cook, wash, and iron for hundreds of people at once" (9), eliminating all heavy labor and greatly easing their husbands' domestic burdens. In Petticotia, such machinery resulted in lazy, bored, flirtatious male belles; on Mars, however, the benefits of female technology are directed toward a higher goal. Marsian men use their surplus time and energy to organize a Man's Rights movement. Their arguments are so persuasive and their evidence so compelling that women are speedily won over to the cause. Marsian females are not so jealous of their power that they will refuse to share it; instead, they demonstrate "a profound respect for the rights of man, and a sincere desire that man should enjoy every right equally with themselves" (24).

Antifeminists, however, had a rebuttal for such thinking. A True Woman effected social change from within her proper sphere: the home. A wife could wish no more than to be a moral and spiritual exemplar to her husband and children. Any other arrangement was doomed—as antifeminist tracts were quick to point out. Wood, for example, portrays nondomestic women as monstrous, selfish freaks who have abandoned not only their husbands and families but their moral imperative as well. No wonder Petticotia has become ethically, economically, and politically bankrupt under the rule of women. The shehes, after all, have defied nature and God by refusing to be meek and submissive, and have degenerated into jealous, petty viragos, driven by emotion. Religion has become a sham: there is indeed "a fashionable sort of gewgaw which passes for public worship, but it is rather a concert in which the choir displays its culture, the clergywoman her gorgeous vestments, and imbecile man the thing he once ridiculed, namely, a bonnet" (171). The Bible, along with all history and literature, has been rewritten to suit the times and justify female rule. Financially, the country is at the point of collapse; the entire economy is based upon worthless paper money that citizens will not use and outsiders are beginning to suspect. The government is impossibly corrupt, and, racked with political infighting and partisan struggle, teeters on the brink of revolution. Without the guiding presence of Real Men and the moral influence of True Women, the situation is hopeless. Order will be restored in Petticotia only when the natural order of separate spheres is restored also. Fortunately, the American aviator manages to escape, and plans just such a restoration.

Ultimately, both *Man's Rights* and *Pantaletta* close with what their authors see as a return to a natural order, although their perceptions of exactly what constitutes "natural" are diametrically opposed. Cridge's negative exemplar argues that a natural balance can exist only when society eliminates gender division and advances to egalitarian social arrangements, while Wood's topsy-turvy novel closes with the replacement of an "unnatural" gynocentric hierarchy with a "natural" androcentric one. Cridge's *Man's Rights* demonstrates the unfairness of such arrangements, and offers a tantalizing view of a world in which femininity is a powerful force for good, a gentle strength directed away from control, toward nurture, peaceful coexistence, and egalitarian harmony. Wood's *Pantaletta* presents a worldview in which woman can only be fulfilled when she seeks and gains the protection of a strong male. Ironically, her dogged defense of customary arrangements might have inadvertently subverted its own agenda. Although she would probably have been horrified by the notion, some women might well have read her powerful women as an intriguing alternative to the nineteenth-century status quo; others might have considered that the pathetic situation of males trapped in the domestic sphere in no way enhances its appeal. Ultimately, however, both texts reflect the philosophical and social divisions that characterized nineteenth-century female experience, and, many might argue, are still being debated even today.

Works Cited

Clarke, Edward H., M.D. *Sex in Education; or, A Fair Chance for the Girls.* Boston: James R. Osgood, 1873.

Cridge, Annie Denton. *Man's Rights; or, How Would You Like It? Comprising Dreams.* Boston: William Denton, 1870.

Cunnington, C. Willett. *English Women's Clothing in the Nineteenth Century.* 1937. New York: Dover, 1990.

Gernsheim, Alison. *Victorian and Edwardian Fashion.* New York: Dover, 1981.

Goodell, William, M.D., with T. Gaillard Thomas, M.D., James R. Chadwick, M.D., S. Weir Mitchell, M.D., M. Allen Starr, M.D., and J. J. Putnam, M.D. "Co-Education and the Higher Education of Women: A Symposium." *Medical News* 14 December 1889: 667–73.

Hardaker, Miss M. A. "Science and the Woman Question." *Popular Science Monthly* March 1882: 577–84.

Kinnard, Cynthia D. *Antifeminism in American Thought: An Annotated Bibliography.* Boston: G. K. Hall, 1986.

Linton, E[liza] Lynn. "The Higher Education of Women." *Eclectic Magazine of Foreign Literature* December 1886: 812–20.

——. "The Modern Revolt." *Eclectic Magazine of Foreign Literature* February 1871: 196–203.

Martineau, Harriet. *Society in America.* 2 vols. 1837. New York: AMS Press, 1966.

Murray, Janet Horowitz. *Strong-Minded Women, and Other Lost Voices from Nineteenth-Century England.* New York: Pantheon Books, 1982.

Shepard, Leslie A., ed. *Encyclopedia of Occultism and Parapsychology.* 2 vols. Detroit: Gale Research, 1991.

Wood, Mrs. J. *Pantaletta: A Romance of Sheheland.* New York: American News Company, 1882.

PART III

On the Home Front and Beyond:
Domesticity and the Marketplace

8

A Homely Business: Melusina Fay Peirce and Late-Nineteenth-Century Cooperative Housekeeping

Lisette Nadine Gibson

Their domestic life was so harmonious and perfect that it was a perpetual pleasure to contemplate. . . . Human nature finds its sweetest pleasure, its happiest content, within its own home circle; and in Mizora I found no exception to the rule. . . . To purchase anything for merely outside show . . . was never thought of by an inhabitant of Mizora.

—Mary E. Bradley Lane, *Mizora: A Prophecy*

I
Domesticity Enlarged

In her feminist utopian novel *Mizora: A Prophecy,* Mary Bradley Lane describes an ideal future world made up entirely of (blonde) women living in domestic bliss, a climate-controlled paradise at the North Pole purified of all traces of racial darkness and maleness. In the highly technologized Mizoran culture, even the need for real food has been circumvented with the invention of "purer" artificial foodstuffs. In fact, the Mizorans take this quest for purity even farther; in an inexorable process of a racial and cultural evolution, the separate race of men has been eradicated. Not only has the male race been extinguished as a result of natural selection, but as Mizora's spokeswoman says, they believe that "the highest excellence of moral and mental character is alone attainable by a fair race. The elements of evil belong to the dark race" (92).

The utopian vision captured in Lane's depiction of Mizora provides a troubling reminder of the often obscured connections, in the second half of the nineteenth century, among the cultures of women based in the domestic sphere, the operations of a new market economy, and evolving social scientific paradigms. While a once-conventional history of nineteenth-century domesticity stresses its antagonism toward the public, economic spheres, *Mizora* reveals how much these spheres of life in nineteenth-century culture were mutually legitimating. In fact, much popular domestic writing, particularly after the Civil War, brought the idealized model of a secure, emotionally protected home life alongside the technologies of a new industrialized worldview.

These two aspects of late-nineteenth-century life are drawn together in the project of cooperative housekeeping propounded just after the Civil War by Melusina Fay Peirce, conservative feminist and an influential champion of domestic reform. In her manifesto entitled "Cooperative Housekeeping," Peirce vigorously confirms the importance of the sphere of women at a time when its influence was diminishing, even as she deplores its institutional backwardness. The first wife of philosopher Charles Sanders Peirce, "Zina" Peirce, as she was widely known, published this work as a series in the *Atlantic Monthly* (1868–69). After this first publishing foray and an ambitious (although ultimately unsuccessful) attempt to keep alive a pilot cooperative in Cambridge, Massachusetts, she later revised these ideas in an expanded book-length version of the series: *Co-Operative Housekeeping; How Not to Do It and How to Do It; A Study in Sociology* (1884).[1]

I have orchestrated this brief meeting between Lane and Peirce because their works serve as domestic barometers, of a sort, after the Civil War. Peirce provides a particularly significant example, for she works in the pliant space between the disciplines of sociology (and more generally scientism) and literature. Mediating allegiances both to ideals of republican womanhood and to business management models as a source for domestic reform, her ambitious proposal explores possible interpenetrations between the new marketplace technologies and the values of a feminized society characterized by homely virtues. The relationship is a reciprocal one, wherein industrial or time-saving strategies discipline domestic labor and feminized virtues can be exported to the marketplace.

Peirce's observations in the first and last articles of this series highlight this reciprocity between spheres. In the first installment she emphasizes the value of a smoothly running domestic machinery, yet in the later issues she employs an idealized rhetoric of home life instead. In her first article in the November 1868 issue of *Atlantic Monthly,* Peirce offers these observations: "In these days of strain and struggle and desire, who of us is there that understands how to live? who is it that possesses a domestic machinery so perfectly balanced, so nicely adjusted, so exquisitely oiled and polished, that every duty and every pleasure glide from it noiseless and complete as the separate marvels that fall from the crafty wheels and lathes of this modern era?" (33).[2] In this first article, Peirce's rhetoric describes the work of domesticity not as an unquestionable effect of a woman's physically determined nature, but as a technology or a machine. Insofar as it is like a machine that can be balanced and adjusted, domesticity appears to be rational and manageable. In her final article, she returns to a more idyllic and utopian vision of domestic stability. The bright cheer of a truly feminine home is opposed to the somber rectitude of a patriarchal future: "A wonderful land called The Future [holds] the structure of the feminine civilization . . . [in] bright contrast to the vast, time-worn towers and somber splendors of its frowning brother. . . . It is an opposing citadel or a true *home,* created by love, whither every man may come to find refreshing, peace, and joy" (*AM,* March 1869: 296). These concluding words rely on the premises of a feminized culture and on the promise of domestic power.

After briefly describing Peirce's Cambridge Housekeeping Association and her published reform tracts, in the following pages I discuss the connections between cooperative housekeeping and contemporaneous reform movements. The final sections of this chapter address Peirce's vision of reformed gender relations. Foremost among the problems I will address here is the extent to which her cooperative housekeeping venture and theories, correctly viewed as part of a nationalist project, were implicated with her assumptions about the importance of a national, raced identity.

While Peirce has received recent attention, critical appraisals of her work have not sufficiently examined either the sociopolitical implications of her work and thought nor their implications for the study of women's and reform cultures in the second half of the nineteenth century. In the discussion that follows I focus on Peirce's description of a domesticated workplace as well as on her paradoxical argument for a homeplace unfettered and yet disciplined by the practices of business. While fighting for the improved work conditions for women both within and without the home, an effort reflecting the possible egalitarian, even utopian extensions of her work, she also relies on late-nineteenth-century systematized work models for her program. Her program simultaneously critiques women's roles as consumers and embraces the kind of streamlined and regimented household work that could be supported most persuasively in the context of a new monopoly capitalism.

Peirce molds the rhetoric of domesticity to new demands on women in an increasingly rationalized industrial marketplace; in this her project is by turns revisionist and highly conservative. She insists upon social reform, yet does not question the validity of the new order of business practices. Particularly important here are the junctures between women's social reform movements and the deeply entrenched discourses of racial and class difference of the nineteenth century. In addition to this program's mixed investments in reform and technological progress, the utopian and basically egalitarian aspects of cooperative household reform are in fact implicated in what Lynn Wardley has called the "race work" of the nineteenth-century middle-class woman. This "race work" refers, in other words, to the self-conscious work of middle-class women to support and shape a national culture. The cooperative housekeeping movement that Peirce spearheaded attests to the continuing appeal and utility of normative domestic ideology even as its meaning changed in the last third of the nineteenth century.

Peirce's work belongs in the tradition codified by Catharine Beecher in *A Treatise on Domestic Economy for the Use of Young Ladies at Home and at School* (1849). Beecher's revision (with her sister Harriet Beecher Stowe) to this work, *The American Woman's Home; Or, Principles of Domestic Science; Being a Guide to the Formation and Maintenance of Economical, Healthful, Beautiful and Christian Homes,* was published in 1869, contemporaneously to Peirce's *Atlantic Monthly* articles. One of the most important aspects of Beecher's work was her insistence that household work was not simply an expression of women's natures, but was also a potentially scientific technology to be mastered. Peirce was joined in reformulating arguments like those of Beecher by reformers such as Abby Morton Diaz, the onetime member of Brook Farm who insisted on the importance of developing a scientific basis for women's work. Peirce challenges the divisions between private and public worlds, at least insofar as they demarcate home from marketplace, distinguishing hers from earlier critiques by assigning a heightened importance to women's productive labor, crisscrossing the powerful language of "home" with the rhetoric of business and political economy. She is not positioned simply as a spokeswoman for domestic values, but relies on the legitimizing authority of the discipline of social science.

Peirce's recognition of the financial contributions of women has led to the recent rediscovery of her work by historians eager to trace the development of materialist feminism in the United States. Viewed from this perspective, she belongs in the ranks of the feminists working in the transitional period between that of antebellum domestic theorists and the more modern utopian appeals of writers such as Mary Bradley Lane and Charlotte Perkins Gilman.[3] However, Peirce considered herself a sociologist following in the scientific tradition of the famed Louis Agassiz and in her lifetime gained notoriety for her reformist ardor.[4] After the collapse of her first and only cooperative venture, the Cambridge Association, Peirce continued her work in the flexible disciplinary zone of reform traditions and the increasingly self-conscious scientific arena of sociology. The title of her 1884 publication, *Co-Operative Housekeeping; How Not to Do It and How to Do It; A Study in Sociology,* marks the location of this disciplinary crossroads. While her management program remains largely unchanged in the 1884 edition, the influence of racialist social theories on her program becomes more pronounced.[5] The pungency of her attitudes is sharp enough to have provoked Norma Pereira Atkinson's suggestion that "it is unfortunate that Zina did not stop her writing career with the publication of her articles and pamphlets on cooperative housekeeping, for in them all of her important ideas, which she explored at greater length later, are included, and her pet obsessions [including an anti-immigrationist nativism] are held in check" (204).[6]

II
A Plan for Cooperation and Its Contemporary Responses

Melusina Fay Peirce's project first reached a public forum when it was serially published in the *Atlantic Monthly* beginning in 1868. By 1869 she had assembled a number of her Cambridge supporters to begin a housekeeping cooperative. The new venture would export women's basic housekeeping jobs—including cooking, sewing, and laundry—out of the home and to a central production location.

From a notable New England family, Melusina Fay finished her formal education at the Louis Agassiz School for Young Ladies and in 1862 married philosopher Charles Sanders Peirce, who had also studied with Agassiz.[7] In July 1869, Peirce, with her husband, his family, and several Harvard professors numbered among her supporters, organized the cooperative called the Cambridge Housekeeping Association.[8] Despite its backers' enthusiasm, the venture did not long survive. Vexed from the beginning by management conflicts, power struggles, and a lack of capital, the association was permanently dissolved in 1871. Peirce attributed some of these problems to the Council of Gentlemen's (the husbands') excessive interference in the association. Her absence from the cooperative also contributed to its demise; during this period she traveled to Sicily to view a solar eclipse with her husband. When Peirce later described the association's problems, she complained that "a few men sustained the attempt most loyally, but most of the men laughed good-naturedly at the whole thing, prophesied its failure, and put their wives out of heart and out of conceit with it from the beginning, while the husband of the chief promoter and responsible officer of the whole undertaking, the treasurer [Peirce], kept writing to her so continually from Europe . . . that at last she felt forced to go and leave the Association to get on without her as best it might" (*Co-Operative Housekeeping* 109). After the Cambridge Housekeeping Association's anticlimactic demise, Peirce never again founded a cooperative. However, despite the association's practical failure, she never gave up her belief in the value of group housekeeping, maintaining a measure of notoriety and celebrity in reform circles for years after the experiment.[9]

According to the plan, cooperative members would share their work in a organization that demonstrated the compatibility between basic Yankee virtues and new models of industrial efficiency. In the introductory *Atlantic Monthly* treatise, Peirce suggests that groups of twelve to fifty women join together in cooperative ventures to tame the more egregious of their household chores.[10] Participants would make capital investments for their families in the bulk purchases of commonly needed goods. In addition to increasing the collective's power as purchasing agent for its members, this would reduce household chores. A core group of members working at the site of the cooperative would provide the principal meals for member families, along with basic sewing and laundry services.

The *Atlantic Monthly* series assures readers that joint housekeeping would help them to maintain a balanced "domestic machinery." The benefits of this system would be many and varied. Member families, for example, could count on receiving inexpensive food of consistently high quality. The system also would relieve women of the burden imposed by the dictates of European-imported fashion: women would be fitted at the cooperative with attractive, simply designed clothing made by the cooperative's hired seamstresses. Thus the cooperative system also would participate in the contemporary clothing reform movement.[11] Finally, in providing such commodities and services for families, the cooperative system could bring far-reaching economic benefits to women of all classes. Economic freedom could also confer another kind of liberation for cooperative participants: women no longer need be confined to the alternatives of going out alone into the marketplace or being forced into the marriage market. Unmarried women, especially those of middle- and upper-class origins, would have a safe, socially legitimate outlet for their talents. Poor women factory workers employed by the cooperative would see their working conditions ameliorated through the beneficence of its managers. Finally, and most politically important for Peirce, women members would have a means to develop a personal savings by accruing cooperative stocks.

In addition to these ample economic benefits, cooperative housekeeping gained impetus from the diminishing social value of women's roles in the postwar economy. Holding up a standard of effortless and thorough housekeeping made familiar by conservative proponents of domestic science, Peirce lays the blame for women's failure to attain this high standard on their new roles as consumers. Cooperative housekeeping would provide the necessary antidote to women's ills, effecting a return to accepted values of Yankee efficiency. Peirce's ideal housekeeper of the past lived in a spotless, sunny home uncluttered by ornamentation and consumerist affectation, where "nothing was for show, and but little for pure ornament." This paragon is praised for the "comprehension in her eye, a firmness in her mouth, [and] a concentrated and disciplined energy" (*AM*, November 1868: 514). This woman's virtues, however, had been lost in the scattered frenzy of contemporary life in which women tried to do all, and mastered none, of their household duties. As a result, women ceded a significant portion of their authority in province of cultural and aesthetic experience. The feminist writer Abby Morton Diaz asserted the importance of this female cultural authority even more directly in 1874 when she asked, "Simplify cookery, thus reducing the cost of living, and how many longing individuals, now forbidden, would thereby be enabled to afford themselves the pleasures of culture?" (*The Schoolmaster's Trunk* 114–15).

Although nostalgic desire for the ideological power of republican motherhood provides the motive force behind cooperative housekeeping, at the same time the project reveals a future-directed movement toward ideals of efficiency later characteristic of the domestic science movement. The translation of republican ideals into a "scientific" form could be a profoundly appealing combination, as Abby Morton Diaz's writings show. In *The Schoolmaster's Trunk*, Diaz's narrator states that he is working "as an investigator, investigating the very important subject of domestic affairs. Why not call it a scientific subject? . . . My science has the forces of Nature in it too (human nature), and a motive-power. Their motive powers act on machinery, mine acts on human beings" (36).

Peirce not only plays the same themes, but goes so far as to claim a central role in shaping literary visions of technology. In *New York: A Symphonic Study in Three Parts,* for example, she suggests that Edward Bellamy's technological fantasy, *Looking Backward* (1888), had been indebted to her theories of cooperative housekeeping. *Looking Backward* "had an immense vogue," Peirce writes, "because of its vision of a frictionless and faultless push-the-button housekeeping. . . . [I]t is perhaps natural for me to flatter myself that in some way my plea for organized (and therefore perfected) housekeeping had been brought into the focus of the Bellamy imagination" (13–14). In the same section, Peirce contends that Charlotte Perkins Gilman stole a number of her ideas (15–16). Whether or not Bellamy and other participants in the nationalist movement were directly influenced by cooperative housekeeping experiments, Peirce's perception of her own influence reflects the continued viability of industrial and scientific models for domestic work earlier in the century.[12]

Peirce's real contribution is to have contextualized the changing priorities and responsibilities of women as belonging in an explicitly financial domestic economy: "Because women once found an ample sphere and an absorbing vocation within the walls of their home, it is believed that they can find them there still, though that vocation has been taken almost entirely away, and to their larger mental growth that sphere is narrowing frightfully around them" (*AM*, November 1868: 521). Such a challenge to the paradigms of public and private spheres, based on an analysis of women as consumers, casts women's labor as distinct from the marketplace. However, Peirce does not reject the market altogether; instead, her critique is based on recognizing the importance of women's economic contributions. Her appeal for the importance of domestic virtues is conceived of as a hedge against the encroachment of a consumer market that is just becoming recognizable at this time. Or, to be more specific, it is a hedge against the negative effects of the consumer market.

III
Reform and the Social Evolution of the Race

Critics like historian Dolores Hayden have emphasized Peirce's intellectual connections to U.S. social and labor reform.[13] Hayden's study *The Grand Domestic Revolution: A History of Feminist Designs for American Homes, Neighborhoods, and Cities* is the work most responsible for linking Peirce to the lost tradition of materialist feminism. In the interests of retrieving the valuable aspects of Peirce's economic and social analyses, however, Hayden elides the more problematic aspects of Peirce's work. While she does characterize Peirce as an "angry housewife," Hayden takes her work seriously as social critique, conservative though that work might at times have been (67). Other appraisals have been more dismissive than critical. Carl Guarneri refers to Peirce as a "respectable Harvard faculty wife who attached the label 'cooperative housekeeping' to groups of women who performed all their domestic work collectively—and charged their husbands for it" (398).[14] In effect, if not intention, Guarneri dismisses her project as the idiosyncratic product of a housewife's boredom.

Peirce's project reveals the extent to which Fourierism and other related social theories wending their way through the working-class labor movement in the United States and Europe could become reconciled and shaped to the outlines of mainstream domestic norms. Hence Peirce was operating somewhere within the range of recognizable reform strategies when she proposed that women join together to work. Her network of allegiances could be staunchly conservative as well. Peirce had access and exposure to intellectual and elitist reform movements, with all of their attendant contradictions. As I have already discussed, as a privileged (although not wealthy by the standards of her social circle) member of Cambridge society, Peirce was allied with white middle-class reform movements and belonged to social circles including luminaries like Ralph Waldo Emerson and William Dean Howells, among others.[15] However, her interest in cooperative housekeeping indicates the extent to which workers' reform programs could be assimilated and accepted in an arguably more conventional milieu. The English working-class collective, the Rochdale Society of Equitable Pioneers or Rochdale Pioneers, was especially responsible for her interest in cooperative housekeeping.

The Rochdale Pioneers became well known around 1863, when news of the successful cooperative store movement in England made its way across Europe and the Atlantic. In 1871, Eugen Richter publicized the "supposed crack-brained enterprise" of a group of English weavers. "All over England, France, and Germany, the Rochdale Pioneers are famous as the men who . . . have given the world a splendid example of the great results which even the humblest may bring about without external aid, merely by co-operation" (Richter 5). After opening their first store in 1844 with twenty-eight member families, by 1865 the Rochdale Society had 5,326 members, earning an 11.3 percent profit in the first quarter of 1866 (5). The gradual progress of the society led to the opening of a whole network of similar societies, spurred on by the kind of success that gave the original group enough capital to open its own cotton factory in 1855 and to establish various forms of insurance and home builder's financing for its members. The goal of these associations was at first simple: in times of job insecurity, workers could jointly assume the costs and profits of the sales of necessary food and clothing. Supporters like Richter especially noted the Rochdale Pioneers' reputation for fair dealing and quality.

A cooperative store movement in the United States had been crippled in its infancy by the economic instability of the 1850s. Before long, however, public accounts of the success of the Rochdale stores revived dormant interest in cooperative projects. The British idea proved so compelling to Americans that "between 1863 and 1865, Rochdale stores were set up all over the east, and the Massachusetts legislature passed a special act for their incorporation" (Fogarty 40). "By 1860, there were over eight hundred Protective Unions [or consumer's cooperatives] in New York, New England, and the Midwest" (Hayden, *American Utopias* 77). The appeal of these economic ventures was not immediately apparent to women, and in fact these U.S. cooperatives were connected predominantly to the laboring class, as in England, rather than to women. Guarneri describes a similar pattern of affiliation organized around class divisions; his example is American Fourierism. Guarneri claims that in Boston, "working-class Associationists committed themselves disproportionately to such cooperative experiments as Brook Farm and the Protective Union Stores, while white-collar Fourierists wrote for communitarian journals, ran local clubs, or helped to sustain Fourierism through monetary contributions. A similar spectrum of affiliation obtained in Rochester, Cincinnati, and New York City" (243).

Peirce's innovation in this venture was to take an institution based on the self-identification of workers as a group and shape it to reflect the shared needs of women whose status as a collective economic entity was little recognized. Richter had already suggested that cooperatives were particularly suited to women's interests, writing that women "cannot be too interested in the undertaking [of beginning a cooperative store], since its object is so intimately related to their especial domain—housekeeping" (24). Where Richter argues for the urgency of women's involvement in cooperative ventures, he assumes that women's support is important because it is necessary for the success of tradesmen's cooperation. In contrast, Peirce shapes the concept of cooperation to fit women's specific needs. Where the labor unions reinforce a sense of commonality among the nation's workers, Peirce fosters women's recognition of their intertwined economic fates.

Peirce explores the possibilities of production as a means of legitimizing women politically as well as culturally, here anticipating Thorstein Veblen's now classic critique of women's role in consumer culture at the end of the century. In his retrospective turn-of-the-century account, Veblen characterizes women's roles as residual cultural traits, suggesting that "still the pervading principle and abiding test of good breeding is the requirement of a substantial and patent waste of time" (51). Enforced and conspicuous leisure, however, constitutes a form of alienated and unrecognized labor, for "the leisure of the lady and of the lackey differs from the leisure of the gentleman in its own right in that it is an occupation of an ostensibly laborious kind" (57). Although conspicuous consumption is typically associated with women's economic roles at the end of the century, Peirce's interest demonstrates how early could be recognized "a new class of unproductive consumers, i.e. of persons who do not pay back in mental or manual labor an equivalent for the necessities they use of the luxuries they enjoy" (*AM*, November 1868: 518).

In a dual critique, Peirce weighs the idle status of the leisure-class woman after the Civil War against the waning codes of productive womanhood sacrificed to the demands of the marketplace. The growth of a class of parasitic non-laborers constitutes for Peirce "one of the monstrous defects of modern civilization, and perhaps the most fruitful source of disorder, suffering, and demoralization that could possibly be devised" (518). Again foreshadowing Veblen's insights, Peirce's concerns are precipitated in an era in which middle- and upper-class women's labor is so far alienated as to no longer exist. Women who might otherwise be contented by sewing for themselves find their proper work stolen from their hands as a result of economic incentives: Irish sewing women can do the job more cheaply.[16] And, in commodifying domestic practices through industrial advances such as the sewing machine, men have taken away "this last corner of our once royal feminine domain" (518).

A social evolutionary model of political and social economy grounds this argument, as Peirce remodels the premises of Victorian womanhood in the light of a materialism legitimated by evolutionary discourse.[17] Peirce redefines the "TRUE FEMININE SPHERE" as that of manufacturing, for "throughout unnumbered centuries women assumed and . . . fulfilled the task of preparing the food and clothing of the race, out of the raw materials that man laid at her feet. . . . In that day, therefore, women must have created nearly half the wealth and supplies of the world, because they did one half of its necessary work. Hence every woman in her own home is *self-supporting*" (517). This story of origins is markedly similar to those offered by Engels about four years later in "The Origin of Family, Private Property, and the State" (1884). Here Engels writes, "In the old communistic household, which embraced numerous couples and their children, the administration of the household, entrusted to the women, was just as much a public, a socially necessary industry, as the providing of food by the men" (744). Whether or not Engels was familiar with Melusina Fay Peirce's work (he probably was not), the congruence between their ideas is suggestive of the extent to which these social evolutionary ideas had seeped throughout the mainstream intellectual life in the United States and Europe.

To combat the nineteenth-century scandal of nonproductivity, Peirce suggests that by reestablishing the domestic sphere's productive functions, women might work toward self-support (*AM*, November 1868: 519). "Men," Peirce complains, "have made women vain, they have made them frivolous, they have made them extravagant, they have made them burdens to society, and now they are repudiating them" (520).[18] Indeed, Peirce speculates that whether or not cooperative housekeeping is practical, women must organize themselves, and they must earn their own livings, for without this civilization cannot continue to develop properly (*AM*, March 1869: 297). "We deny, altogether," Peirce proclaims, "being the 'lesser man,' and are tired of the role of little brother. We are not an accident of nature, we are a necessity of Eternity. Our souls stamp the sex upon our bodies, not our bodies upon our souls. . . . It is not womanhood you get O men, by the conventional repressing process, but childhood; and thus it is that to this day there is not true marriage of the sexes, but a lonely and cruel lord stalks through the neglected and unfinished apartments of his ever-widening palace" (298–99).

The fact that women not suited for practical housewifery could be freed from those duties by unmarried and free women in the cooperative venture is a central appeal of the plan. "These unfortunates [the constrained housewives], if liberated from the prison of the household and freed from the fetters of the needle, the broom, and the receipt-book, would play the same noble part among women that the masculine leaders of knowledge, of art, of government, and of morality have enacted among men" (*AM,* February 1868: 161). That such women could be subjected to a life to which they are so obviously unsuited constitutes what Peirce calls a "bad economy" of feminine norms (162). On the face of it, this cooperative venture is egalitarian, allowing women to participate in it based on their ability to pay or to work, regardless of class status. Even working women could gain from the experiment with cooperative living, for the open policy of the cooperative should relieve them of domestic worry and enable them to work (for pay) in the protective environment of the cooperative itself.

By basing domesticity on production, Peirce extends its boundaries so that "woman's sphere" might encompass any place where women work. And this is the source of one of her more surprising paradoxes. How will women reorganize this sphere? Not by increasing the barriers around it, as one might expect in a similar project beginning earlier in the century, but by moving into the "RETAIL TRADE of the world" (*AM,* November 1868: 522). The world of domestic manufacturing comes to encompass the arena of retail sales. The implications of her small revolution in domestic science are so extensive, Peirce cautions her readers, that it would have to be gradual. Otherwise its effects would "cause this large body of [retail dealers] great embarrassment, if not suffering and ruin" (*AM,* January 1869: 29). Turning nineteenth-century assignments of gender against themselves, Peirce argues that the territory of retail sales belongs to women, a shift in areas of competence that could counterbalance the feminization of men who, "in the guise of clerks and small shopkeepers, have so long played at the spinning Achilles and Hercules that they have quite forgotten their natural vocation. . . . Give us the yardstick, O heroes," Peirce writes, "and let us relieve you behind the counter, that you may go behind the plough and be off to those fields" (30). The movement of women into the retail trade is accompanied by the return of men to a mythical condition of agrarian pursuits. According to her arithmetic, this shift will allow Americans to turn from their all-encompassing interest in trade and turn their attention to farming and becoming the "food producers of the world" (31). Thus her rather astonishing inversion of the conventional gendered arrangement of vocations situates women within the newly feminized realm of retail sales and allocates to men the pastoral pursuits of husbandry. This inversion derives its power from conventional arguments about the nature of women; their prized physical attributes would be lost in the hardscrabble labor of farming. The proper work of men and women is maintained within separate spheres, but with the feminine domestic sphere elastically embracing the business of sales. This adjusts antebellum northern ideals of gender to the new postwar, post-industrial economic context in a complex reassignation of gender values.

Peirce's reformed gender roles bear obvious contradictions. While she challenges women's parasitic consumerism—represented in her many references to the vacuity and uselessness of educated women's pursuits—she also suggests that women can reform their new roles in the consumer economy by holding fast to the ideal of frugal home management. In other words, *parasitic* consumption remains a problem even while involvement with productive consumption in the form of retail labor is laudable. Furthermore, the reformed sphere of women in trade is arranged in familial terms to ensure that it not duplicate the logic of the masculine order of business. As the first stages of the cooperative are described, women's movement into trade is legitimized as a movement into a "family" structure and the world of the marketplace is domesticated. Cooperative housekeeping programs can renovate the structure of domestic labor because they are based on a recognizable familial order. The cooperative itself will be a "family," organized so that working conditions can be closely arranged and watched over. In a division of women's labor that reflects the chief divisions of labor in the middle-class home, the cooperative's main departments are the kitchen, the laundry, and the sewing room. The familial arrangement of the home is a means of reforming working conditions for all classes of women. For example, the sewing section of the cooperative would occupy, she writes, a fairly large building, supplied with a dining room, a gymnasium, and a reading room. The whole establishment would be designed with "beauty," "health," and "cheerfulness" in mind.[19]

The design emphasizes the workers' mental and physical hygiene. For example, Peirce emphasizes the importance of exercise, a benefit that is not only permitted but "insisted on as a condition of [the workers'] employment; for constant sewing, as we all know, is the most killing of all feminine employments to youth, health and spirits. . . . It is high time that the free and favored of the sex . . . should feel a solicitude for these victims of the needle" (*AM,* December 1868: 691). This call for gymnasiums apparently reflects a benevolent dream of reform wherein all of American society could be renewed when governed as a family would be. On this point,

Peirce writes, "The race being considered as one family, and women the mistress of its home, what more beneficent enterprise can be imagined than one which seeks to organize that home so perfectly, that not alone the few in its drawing-rooms, but also the many in its garrets and cellars, will be clothed, fed, and sheltered in the manner most conducive to their moral and intellectual progress?" (689–90). In the collective, familial atmosphere of the cooperative, relations between classes would not have the "cold-hearted" feel of business transactions. With familial codes stretched to reach around the entire "race," parallel industrial reform might be effected. Thus the cooperative would become a mediating site, a kind of feminized business emphasizing women's material production.

IV
Disciplining the Social Body

Narratives in social science authorize Peirce's acknowledgment of women, with men, as part of the breed of *Homo œconomicus.* While familial models provide a basis for reform, they are not necessarily egalitarian and horizontal. In fact, the idea of "family" is compelling *because* it involves the stratification of function and hierarchies of power. This is important, as it indicates where the discourses of sociology and reform overlap.

The cooperative venture would assign the problem of women's working conditions to the managerial control of the "moneyed and employing class among women" (*AM,* December 1868: 691). While Peirce turns to cooperative housekeeping for legitimate feminist goals, cooperation also serves as the answer to class strife as it played out in the home. The democratizing potential of cooperation—as least as other social critics of the time conceived of it—sharply conflicts with her classist convictions. In the cooperative of Peirce's design, relations between working women and the "moneyed" class of women remain uneven. The middle-class woman retains her position as manager, while seamstresses, who we might imagine could ostensibly learn new forms of self-support at a cooperative, will do what they always have—the work of hands.

This controlling trope of the social family, sliding easily into identification with the figure of the social body, reveals in Peirce's hands a similar project of acculturation. The family itself, extended to encompass the race, has, as she puts it, its "head," its "heart," and, in the case of the workers, its "muscles, sinews, and hands." Following the model of the social family in its embodied condition, middle-class women in their reformed roles would oversee the physical as well as moral hygiene of the family. While Peirce assigns to her peers a place at the head of this family, working women in contrast are strictly equivalent to their embodied existence. The problematic reprise of the figure of the hierarchical family is clarified in the later publication of this series in book form: "Ah, thoughtless women! If your servants would bring to their work the quick and fine perceptions of a lady's educated brain, they would not have their own strong and enduring nerves and muscles with which to do it. The elements are not found together" (*Co-Operative Housekeeping* 31). Without any apparent irony, Peirce claims that if housekeepers would only organize their work, their servants would become as docile, honest, and plentiful as the "hands" in every other kind of manufacturing. The very real feminist aims of freeing women *from* unsuitable work and liberating them *to* other forms of work require a kind of dematerialization of the educated woman which does not extend to those of the laboring classes. In fact, the embodiment of working women is taken for granted as a necessary and even inescapable feature of civilized life.

The program is more than a system of labor reform and assistance to housekeepers. Cooperation would provide a way to blot out what Peirce calls, in familiar terms of the day, "the SERVANT PROBLEM" (*AM,* February 1869: 34). Peirce observes elsewhere that American democratization, along with the shock of emancipation after the war, has fostered a social disorganization of grand proportions against which "the domestic temple sways . . . on its ever-changing basis of ill-trained and unprincipled service" (*AM,* January 1869: 34). The spread of middle-class values had by this time made going into service suspect, and the expanding population of Irish immigrants, associated with heavy labor, minimal skills, and Catholicism, was widely distrusted. In a roughly contemporary work, *Forty Years of American Life* (1874), radical reformer T. L. Nichols observed that "[the Irish have] dug the canals, built the railways, and done the rough work of building the cities of the North and West" (274). It was perhaps because of the common association of the Irish with the rough labor of canal digging and railway building that Peirce so clearly dissociates herself from them. In a sympathetic description more the exception than the rule in this period (and exceptional in Nichols's work), Nichols goes on to claim that "the Irish in America have been a source of wealth and strength. One can hardly see how the heavy work of the country could have been done without them" (274).

Management is Peirce's answer to the social ill of bad "help." The material basis of her argument lends prerogative to her peers to "manage" the productive labor of their social and economic inferiors. Despite her emphasis on women's productive functions, women of the employing class would not themselves be laborers in any physical sense. Instead, they would assume the roles of overseer and organizer (*AM,* December 1868: 693).

In the new organization, Peirce envisions a hierarchical setting wherein "the same kind solicitude, life-long help and trust, and feeling of mutual interest which subsisted between mistress and servant under the old slave system, and veiled many of its deformities, might return, to make both happier and better than in the lawless selfishness of the present arrangement is possible" (*AM,* January 1869: 35). Indeed, the power of organization is particularly suited to southern domestic problems. "The slavery of an organization," Peirce claims, "must be substituted [for the slavery of a master] before such low-grade moral natures as those of the African can possibly be trained, disciplined, or controlled" ("Appendix," *Cooperative Housekeeping* 173). Uneasily, she combines a powerful trust in domestic nurturing with the prewar racist rhetoric (substituting, of course, the figure of woman alternately at heart and at head of the body).

Abby Morton Diaz made use of a similar logic in making a case for widespread radical domestic reform, writing that "an injury to one small bone in the foot may cause distress which shall be felt 'all over,' and shall disturb the operations of the lordly brain itself. So in the body social" (*A Domestic Problem* 54). In Diaz's neo-Lamarckian construction, ignorance begets unhygienic behavior, which will in turn reproduce itself to contaminate the whole of the body. Like the rapid self-duplication of a cancer, perversions might proliferate unchecked without public action—as in Diaz's apocryphal story about a woman set adrift in the world without benefit of home culture who went on to spawn in her descendants some two hundred criminals, plus diverse additional idiots, drunkards, and other transgressors. Far better, Diaz suggests, for the state to have spent money on this woman's development—possibly even sending her to Italy, should her interests and talents lie in an artistic direction (34).

Peirce's objective is somewhat different from Diaz's vision of social progress dependent upon the education of each of its members. Diaz's anecdote suggests that education can reform even a bad mother, with long-term effects on the moral and intellectual capacities of her progeny and, by extension, the race. Peirce seems equally indebted to another line of evolutionary thought championed by her teacher, Louis Agassiz. In a period during which evolutionary thought in the popular mind was dominated by the figures of Herbert Spencer and Charles Darwin, Agassiz remained a staunch and influential opponent of Darwinism and theories of natural selection. He was particularly opposed to the Spencerian maxim of the "survival of the fittest." Agassiz (who influenced Emerson and C. S. Peirce as well as Zina Peirce) was among the ranks of creationists in the period who held to polygenist theories. According to the polygenists, the human race did not evolve and differentiate into the distinct groups that became known as "races" in the nineteenth century; instead, they argued, there were many races from the beginning of time. This theory of separate (and unequal) races allowed for a variety of negative responses to people of non-British lineage, including the Irish and most especially African Americans.

As I have said, the trope of the social body—arranged in a reformed family hierarchy—assumes two things: the natural "mind-work" of "Educated Womanhood" and the physical orientation of the worker. All of this occurs in the name of civilization, or a civilizing process in which women must participate more fully.

V
Forging a Class of Women

Some of Peirce's last words to her sisters were: "*O Waiting Women of the World! Sisters Beloved!* AWAKE!—UNITE! You have everything to gain. You have nothing to lose but your chains—your vitriolic chains of flesh and sense" (*New York: A Symphonic Study in Three Parts* II 107). Based on the division between social head and hands, these "vitriolic chains of flesh and sense" are a problem of the educated class of women. Since working women are associated with "strong and enduring nerves and muscle," they clearly do not belong to the sisterhood of "World Women." Peirce's views on enfranchisement reinforce this division between "World Woman" and working woman. She suggests that through learning to cooperate, women could make strides toward an eventual international Woman's Parliament, a project with which she was briefly involved. No supporter of equal enfranchisement (she instead supported womanhood suffrage), Peirce argues that the international association could be a political forum parallel to masculine and national alliances. Womanhood suffrage would take the form of a separate vote in a Woman's Congress. In brief, womanhood suffrage would be a program designed to give women separate voting rights in a political forum distinct from that of men. An international congress made up of women could collectively assert feminized moral values. In this, Peirce remains a proponent of separate spheres of activity, although it is also clear that separate but parallel forms of political action are expected to guide the whole social "family."

This separation of genders would do more than maintain the purity of a distinctive feminine moral oversight. Assuming that women are confined to their economic circumstances, Peirce suggests that entitlement comes not from inherent right but from property. Her rejection of the doctrine of natural rights was an explicit rejection of the claims of more liberal feminists who, like Diaz, might find in neo-Lamarckian precepts hope of the betterment of all women. If a woman could be provided with the right amount of "culture," the benefits could be seen extending throughout future generations of her progeny. According to Peirce's argument, without the money with which comes extended education and influence, women would not be taken seriously in their efforts to gain the vote. For Peirce, economic privilege, not inborn right, is the real source of political enfranchisement. In essence, a person's social stake is limited to that with which she is born.

If economic privilege is the source of enfranchisement, economic growth should be women's primary goal. According to this argument, the real end of the collective movement is to establish the conditions for women's enfranchisement. Through economic independence, women could begin to support the kinds of educational infrastructure that would lead to the nurturing of a diverse and well-educated female populace to support the nation's full development. Peirce writes the following words on this note: "Never in the history of the race until this century have the mothers of a nation been generally enlightened by education, and I think we need seek no other cause for that brilliancy, invention and energy of American men which are astonishing the world, and for these beginnings of effort in every field of thought and action on the part of women which are almost alarming" (Co-Operative Housekeeping 105).

Thus collective organization, seen as one gradualist answer to the labor question, could apply to women's issues as well. "It has long been the theory that woman are incapable of organizing and working among themselves, and this alleged incapacity has been given as the reason why throughout the history of the other sex they have appeared as unorganized units or life-cells merely" (Co-Operative Housekeeping 102). In following this line of reasoning, Peirce again provides an evolutionary justification for a change in women's status. Her ideas in this regard bear comparison with those of August Bebel. In 1879, Bebel carefully explicated the potential for an alliance between the laboring classes and women in Woman under Socialism. Using then-popular narratives of social evolution to argue that woman was the first bondsperson in history, Bebel linked women and workingmen in their struggles to escape oppression. As Peirce reminds her reader, "There is no real chivalry in manhood toward womanhood on the grand scale. There never has been—never will be. Man has always expected woman to give him an industrial equivalent for all he vouchsafes her" (158).

Similar narratives of social evolution ground Bebel's and Peirce's insights about the material value of women's contributions to society. Peirce's program, however, would dictate selective enfranchisement. In other words, she rejects the idea of equal rights in order to assert the importance of women's distinct moral imperatives; separatism confirms the validity of women's special interests. When Peirce rejects the theory that women were "unorganized units or life-cells," she does not reject the diminishment of women to a single role. Instead, her argument suggests that these disparate parts will ideally be organized into a more streamlined whole. Thus Peirce turns to atomized notions of work, which the trope of the family's body seems to facilitate. As a body needs only one head, so society needs one class of educated women. Therefore, organizing women according to distinct roles in order to achieve an economy of scale and kind does not provide for the humanist goal of individual development, but instead for the better development of a highly differentiated whole. Around the question of labor, at least, the need to combine overshadows the desire for individuation. What women have failed to realize is that the technological setting or order of work might apply as well to the home. As Veblen later suggested when he speculated that social evolution would eventually favor not the hunter but rather the pack response in man, so Peirce recommends heightened socialization through structured organizations rather than individual self-management.[20] In essence, women become enfranchised not by becoming full economic participants but by developing a specialized role within the context of a larger social whole.

In claiming that women alone of the corporate and industrial body have shrouded themselves in "Cimmerian Darkness," Peirce reveals the tensions and contradictions in the social imaginary of her class. She yokes utopia and home under the strain of industrialization and nascent forms of incorporated subjectivities—subjectivities still over the horizon, as it were. Speaking to the often understated fact that individualism finds its most strident voices at the times when it is most tested, she turns to cooperation as the middle term between the socializing force of family and the subjectification of industry. Like the magnates of industry, Peirce asserts, women too can come together to provide opportunities for people to work. And only in cooperation can the ideals of individual will coexist with the needs of the many, as the "spirit of the age . . . revolts against the submission to an individual will, but freely subjects itself to the despotism of an organization" (*AM*, January 1869: 34). Insofar as she envisioned domesticity's expansion across economic boundaries, she paradoxically (although perhaps understandably) found in cooperation a link to the incipient corporatism of the late nineteenth century that might quell a destabilizing social chaos.

After the failure of the Cambridge Housekeeping Association, Peirce's plan for cooperative housekeeping seemed doomed to failure. In later writings she continued to insist that her vision of women working together was not simply a nostalgic or utopian dream: "This possible organization of the chaotic modern housekeeping is no theory, no Utopian vision merely. Its parallel exists in the world—a great, joyous, triumphant, almost miraculous FACT, which women have first simply to copy in the spirit and almost in the letter, and afterward to go a little farther along the same road, and the riddle is read—the problem solved—the uselessness and expensiveness of educated women to society and the consequent neglect and contempt of them by men, vanished" (*Co-Operative Housekeeping* 57). What her program, with all of its problems of exclusivity and entrenched class awareness, does provide for is a new vision—one that is inscribed firmly in the capitalist economy of the day, and one that strains against those boundaries. Her vision of the self in this new world of corporate adventures is one that can and must submit to that larger force, to the greater principle of "organization." Small communities of workers together will not simply harken back to an earlier day, but may, in the right hands, lend themselves to the future of a nation streamlined, organized, and efficiently moralized.

Notes

1. The flyleaf of the publication indicates that the substance of the study was read in 1880 in Chicago at an annual meeting of the Illinois Social Science Association.

2. Subsequent quotations from the *Atlantic Monthly* [*AM*] series will be referred to according to the date of publication, followed by the page number.

3. Gilman's *Herland,* featuring asexual forms of reproduction, an all-female society, and faith in the benefits of scientific progress, bears comparison to Lane's *Mizora*.

4. The *Dictionary of North American Authors Deceased before 1950* refers to Peirce as a reformer. Women's forums offered the more conservative interpretations of her work. For example, the 1914–15 edition of the *Woman's Who's Who of America: A Biographical Dictionary of Contemporary Women of the United States and Canada* lists Peirce as a writer and club woman. However, her affiliation to her husband and to Louis Agassiz places Peirce among Cambridge's intellectually privileged, particularly in the area of sociology. A relationship with Agassiz could confer a considerable degree of scientific authority. According to Laura Dassow Walls, "Agassiz amassed such a field of associates, allies, and material that even his most spectacular failure, his refusal to countenance Darwin's ideas, did not stop the spread of his influence and the confluence of his name with the power of modern science" (19).

5. Zina Peirce's relationships with Charles Peirce and Louis Agassiz seem to have supported her anti-immigrant and racist convictions. In such works as the revised *Co-Operative Housekeeping* and her novel *New York: A Symphonic Study in Three Parts,*

Peirce's racist ideas became more strident, making her feminism harder for later critics to support.

6. Peirce was sympathetic to nativism, a policy directed at favoring a country's prior inhabitants over immigrants. Catholics bore the brunt of the prejudice, and certainly conflicts over the Catholicism of the immigrant Irish played a large role in her disparagement. Peirce's views on immigrants coincided with the 1880s wave of nativist sentiment.

7. Born in 1836, Zina was the daughter of Rev. Charles Fay and the granddaughter of Rt. Rev. John Henry Hopkins, bishop of New Hampshire. She was involved in diverse reform movements, ranging from founding women's societies, the Daughters of the American Revolution, the Women's Philharmonic Society of New York, and the Poe Cottage Preservation Commission. Her marriage lasted twenty years; Charles Sanders Peirce divorced Zina in 1882, claiming that she had deserted him in 1876. Soon afterwards, according to his own report, Peirce married Juliette Froissy, of Nancy, France. Melusina Peirce never remarried.

The only substantial biography of Peirce is Norma Pereira Atkinson's 1983 dissertation, "An Examination of the Life and Thought of Zina Fay Peirce: An American Reformer and Feminist." Susan Mizrachi, who was related to the Fay family, died before her anticipated biography of Peirce could be completed. Joseph Brent's *Charles Sanders Peirce: A Life* also contains useful background to her life with the philosopher Peirce and their shared intellectual background.

8. The Cambridge Association was given the blessings of Horace Mann, Benjamin Peirce, William Dean Howells (then assistant editor of *Atlantic Monthly*), and Professors Francis J. Childs and Nathaniel S. Shaler.

9. Peirce's public persona developed gradually and often in contradictory directions. While working on the Cambridge Housekeeping Association, she also played a role in the 1869 efforts toward a Woman's Parliament along with Janice C. Croly. Croly was a well-known leader of the women's club movement and the founder of Sorosis, the New York Women's Club; she was also "Jennie June" from her column in the *New York World*. The first parliament was scheduled to meet in New York in October 1869. According to Atkinson, Croly and Peirce both envisioned the Woman's Parliament as a permanent adjunct to male political forums (62–75). However, probably because of ideological differences over the issue of the natural rights of women (which Peirce did not support), Peirce's involvement ended with the second congress.

10. In *New York: A Symphonic Study in Three Parts,* Peirce augments those numbers, suggesting that cooperatives consist of two hundred members. While logistical considerations support her argument for expansion, the increased numbers would be far more difficult to recruit. The objective of an expanded membership, far more difficult to achieve, suggests that the plan was becoming more of an ideal than a realizable goal.

11. Clothing reform would include dress and trouser combinations like those adopted earlier in the Oneida Community in central New York. While their attire was mildly controversial, the Oneidans and other reformers were simply institution-alizing more widespread experimentation with women's clothing. Elizabeth Stuart Phelps's reform tract *What to Wear?* further attests to the popular interest in the issue of dress reform.

12. The nationalist movement is associated with the post–*Looking Backward* evo-lutionary Christian socialism in the United States. The journal *The Nationalist* was one major mouthpiece for the movement. See Mark Pittenger, *American Socialists and Evolutionary Thought, 1870–1920.*

13. Other critics concur with this assessment. Peirce's biography is included in Robert Fogarty's 1980 *Dictionary of American Communal and Utopian History.*

14. Given that she was divorced by her husband in 1883 on the grounds of de-sertion, Peirce's respectability may not be as unquestioned as Guarneri implies.

15. Indeed, Peirce apparently wrote to Emerson in 1859 about the Agassiz School for Young Ladies before attending and had earlier offered him her ideas in a corre-spondence about millennialism (Atkinson 16).

16. The "foreign-born population in 1870 comprised 'one-seventh of the entire population' and performed 'one-fifth' of the work" (cited in Degler 303).

17. In her writings, Peirce refers to materialism as both the inverse of philo-sophical idealism and in the popular sense of the fetishization of objects.

18. Such a lost ideal of American womanhood is reminiscent of the ideal of republican womanhood, an inheritance from women "who encountered with true feminine fidelity the perils of wilderness and war by the side of the fathers of the nation" (*AM,* November 1867: 520).

19. Hayden's discussion of Peirce in *The Grand Domestic Revolution* is particularly attentive to the implications of the architectural designs of Peirce's cooperative housekeeping plans.

20. See especially chapter 9, "The Conservation of Archaic Traits," in Veblen's *Theory of the Leisure Class.*

Works Cited

Atkinson, Norma Pereira. "An Examination of the Life and Thought of Zina Fay Peirce, an American Reformer and Feminist." Diss. Ball State U, 1983.

Bebel, August. *Woman under Socialism.* 1897. N.p., 1903.

Beecher, Miss Catharine Esther. *A Treatise on Domestic Economy for the Use of Young Ladies at Home and at School.* Rev. ed. New York: Harper & Brothers, 1849.

Beecher, Catharine, and Harriet Beecher Stowe. *The American Woman's Home; Or, Principles of Domestic Science; Being a Guide to the Formation and Maintenance of Economical, Healthful, Beautiful and Christian Homes.* New York: J. B. Ford, 1869.

Bellamy, Edward. *Looking Backward: 2000–1887.* 1888. New York: Signet-New American, 1960.

Brent, Joseph. *Charles Sanders Peirce: A Life.* Bloomington and Indianapolis: Indiana UP, 1993.

"Charles Sanders Peirce." *Dictionary of American Biography.* Vol. 14. Ed. Dumas Malone. New York: Scribner's, 1928.

Degler, Carl. *Out of Our Past: The Forces That Shaped Modern America.* 3rd ed. New York: Harper Torchbooks, 1985.

Diaz, Abby M. "A Domestic Problem: Work and Culture in the Household." 1875. Rpt. in *Liberating the Home.* New York: Arno P, 1974.

———. *The Schoolmaster's Trunk Containing Papers on Home-Life in Tweenit.* Boston: James R. Osgood, 1874.

Engels, Friedrich. "The Origins of the Family, Private Property, and the State." *The Marx and Engels Reader.* Ed. Robert C. Tucker. New York and London: Norton, 1978. 734–59.

Fogarty, Robert S. *Dictionary of American Communal and Utopian History.* Westport, CT: Greenwood P, 1980.

Gilman, Charlotte Perkins. *Herland.* New York: Pantheon, 1979.

Guarneri, Carl J. *The Utopian Alternative: Fourierism in Nineteenth-Century America.* Ithaca and London: Cornell UP, 1991.

Hayden, Dolores. *The Grand Domestic Revolution: A History of Feminist Designs for American Homes, Neighborhoods, and Cities.* Cambridge: MIT P, 1995.

———. *Seven American Utopias: The Architecture of Communitarian Socialism, 1790–1975.* Cambridge: MIT P, 1976.

Lane, Mary E. Bradley. *Mizora: A Prophecy.* Gregg Press Science Fiction Series. Ed. Stuart A. Teilter and Kristine Anderson. 1890. Boston: Gregg P, 1975.

"Mrs. Charles Sanders Peirce." *Woman's Who's Who of America: A Biographical Dictionary of Contemporary Women of the United States and Canada.* Ed. John William Leonard. New York: American Commonwealth Company, 1914.

Nichols, T[homas] L[ow], M.D. *Forty Years of American Life.* London: Longmans, Green, 1874.

Peirce, Melusina Fay. "Co-Operative Housekeeping." *Atlantic Monthly* 22–23 (November 1868–March 1869): 513–24, 683–97, 29–39, 160–71, 286–99.

———. *Co-Operative Housekeeping; How Not to Do It and How to Do It; A Study in Sociology.* Boston: James R. Osgood, 1884.

———. *New York: A Symphonic Study in Three Parts.* 1892. New York: Neale, 1918.

Phelps, Elizabeth Stuart. *What to Wear?* Boston: J. R. Osgood, 1873.

Pittenger, Mark. *American Socialists and Evolutionary Thought, 1870–1920: History of American Thought and Culture.* Madison: U of Wisconsin P, 1993.

Richter, Eugen. *Cooperative Stores: Their History, Organization, and Management.* New York: Leypoldt & Holt, 1867.

Veblen, Thorstein. *The Theory of the Leisure Class.* New York: Penguin, 1974.

Walls, Laura Dassow. "Textbooks and Texts from the Brooks: Inventing Scientific Authority in America." *American Quarterly* 49.1 (1997): 1–26.

Wardley, Lynn. "American Fiction and the Civilizing House: 1850–1925." Diss. U of California, Berkeley, 1988.

9

Narratives of Domestic Imperialism: The African-American Home in the *Colored American Magazine* and the Novels of Pauline Hopkins, 1900–1903

DEBRA BERNARDI

In her 1998 essay "Manifest Domesticity," Amy Kaplan argues for the need to reconceptualize the idea of the "domestic" to signify both private household and national homeland. As Kaplan notes, domesticity not only helps to define the boundaries of the home and the nation, but becomes crucial in formulating shifting distinctions between the home and the foreign, concepts that loom large in the public consciousness during moments of national expansion. In this way, then, Kaplan lays the groundwork for examining connections between definitions of the American home and the project of U.S. imperialism. And imperialism is invariably about issues of home: the national homelands of colonized peoples are disrupted; colonizers extend their domestic borders as they appropriate so-called foreign homelands. Such a reformulation of the domestic, therefore, blurs distinctions between public and private, personal and political, national and international, and male and female spheres of concern.

Kaplan's work focuses on how white middle-class women participated in the American imperial project by attempting to expand their influence beyond the home and nation, while policing the boundaries of home against the threat of the foreign (585). But for African Americans at the turn of the twentieth century, the concerns of empire were weighted differently. Primary to representations of the black home at this historical moment is less the desire for expansion than the fear of invasion—a fear that emphasizes how private African-American family life was consistently linked to public political concerns. For example, the issue of lynch law focused attention on the national political dangers that threatened African-American homes and the bodies lodged there. Moreover, issues of racism within the nation paralleled international concerns, as anxieties about the black nuclear family echoed fears for the safety of an international family of color. Like the black nuclear family, the racial family, too, was vulnerable to invasion; by the turn of the century the United States occupied Cuba and Puerto Rico, as well as the Philippines, all acknowledged as homes of dark-skinned people with racial similarities to African Americans. A conjunction between the nuclear and the international family partly derived from the growing interest in pan-Africanism during the period, which redefined the black family as a multinational unit. In a paper delivered to the American Negro Academy, "The Conservation of Races" (1897), W. E. B. Du Bois conflates family and race, defining the latter as a "vast family of human beings, generally of common blood and language, always of common history, traditions and impulses, who are both voluntarily and involuntarily striving together for the accomplishment of certain more or less vividly conceived ideals of life" (76).

Within the context of local and international colonization, fears of invasion of both the private household and the larger racial family permeated African-American culture at the turn of the century. And, as this chapter will show, popular African-American formulations of the home often center around scenes of invasion, garnered from the imperialist, racial controversies of the day. For example, domestic invasions play such a large part in Pauline Hopkins's 1900 novel *Contending Forces* that advertisements for the novel feature an illustration of a white man attacking an African-American home: as the caption indicates, the invader "broke open the doors, seized my father and hung him to the nearest tree." From the outset, Hopkins positions her fictional households within the global context of imperialism, opening *Contending Forces* in a colonial space—Bermuda, home to British planter Charles Montfort. Transformed by the shadow of empire, the domestic sphere itself becomes a social space akin to the territories, lands, geographical domains, and other homelands invaded by the expanding nation, as much as it is a space vulnerable to American lynch law. Spatial invasion, then, becomes a pivotal trope in representations of the turn-of-the-century African-American home, acting as a metaphor for fears about the vulnerability of both private and extended families.

Given the climate of rampant racism at the turn of the century, a symbolic fear of domestic invasion is hardly surprising. But, in fact, figures of invasion signify more than fear: they also address African Americans' dual position toward their nation's expansionist policies. As historian Willard Gatewood has shown, while many blacks opposed U.S. colonization because of a sense of identification with people of color, they also participated in the nation's assault on other countries: African Americans served in the armed forces, and numerous writings by blacks encouraged civilian immigration to new U.S. territories, where it was believed blacks would mix well with the dark-skinned populations and escape local brands of racism. Such a conflicted role meant that although African Americans apprehended the threat of domestic invasions, they could also accept the strategic utility of such actions—reminiscent of the white domestic writers in Kaplan's study who followed "a double compulsion to conquer and domesticate the foreign" (591). However, the tropes of invasion used by black writers are not employed for purposes of "conquering" as much as for purposes of resisting attack; figures of invasion are specifically used for purposes of racial uplift, showing both the vulnerability of black families to invasion and the possibility that counter-invasive strategies might be used to secure domestic safety. Kevin Gaines has pointed out that "the rhetoric of racial uplift often resembled the imperialist notion of the 'civilizing mission'" (437). And surely these scenes of invasion prove his point: here are prospects of home life, rooted in the desire for racial uplift, that specifically employ descriptions of invasion and thereby echo the actions of empire.

These simultaneously frightening yet empowering invasionary images combine to form a popular paradigm of the turn-of-the-century African-American home which I am terming a model of "domestic imperialism." Appearing to identify with the societies under colonization as well as with the colonizers, turn-of-the-century African-American writers figure a domestic system—encompassing a nuclear and racial family—that is *both* invaded and invading. Homes are depicted as spaces vulnerable to racist invasion, while family members, in resistance to such dangers, counter-invade other spaces, other homes. The system of domestic imperialism that appears during the period creates a black family sphere that is subject to the menace of white invasion as it simultaneously partakes of the empowering aspects of invasive maneuvers.

This chapter will focus on narratives of domestic imperialism as they appeared to readers of the *Colored American Magazine,* a Boston journal of the period targeted at middle-class African Americans. The audience would have had good reason to apprehend domestic tales within the context of invasion, reading family stories alongside articles on African-American servicemen in the Philippines, the safety of the home in the face of lynching, and the shifting status of blacks in the Caribbean. While noting the invaded/invading nature of this model of the black home, this study also reveals the gendered nature of this system: throughout the *Colored American* and in the writings of other blacks often mentioned in its pages, the empowering potential of imperialism is given to men alone; black women appear as the victims of colonization, never the colonizers.

Moreover, this framework elucidates the fictions of Pauline Hopkins, editor of the *Colored American* from 1900 to 1903. Juxtaposing her first novel, *Contending Forces,* with her last, *Of One Blood* (1903), I argue that Hopkins's works, most commonly understood as black "domestic" fictions, engage with broad, interrelated political concerns by responding to the model of domestic imperialism. But Hopkins's narratives of invasion specifically feminize this model in an attempt to empower black women within the politics of empire. Such readings help us to see how Hopkins's visions of domesticity commented on the national political agenda. As Amy Kaplan writes, "Understanding the imperial reach of domesticity and its relation to the foreign should help remap the critical terrain upon which women's domestic fiction has been constructed. We can chart the broader international and national contexts in which unfold narratives of female development that at first glance seem anchored in local domestic spaces. We can see how such narratives imagine domestic locations in complex negotiations with the foreign" (600).

The model of African-American domesticity that inflects the works of Hopkins and the other writers in this study reveals, not surprisingly, the frightening, violent, annihilating aspects of imperialism—thus critiquing the effect U.S. foreign policy has on people of color. However, as part of the rhetoric of racial uplift, this model of home life also supports Gaines's assertion that such rhetoric tacitly endorses prevailing assumptions of racial and social hierarchy (449), which color the "civilizing mission" of U.S. imperialism. In employing invasive imagery as a means of securing black power and domestic safety, constructions of domestic imperialism indicate that invasions may have a purpose; such configurations thus support and even implicate blacks in the nation's colonial activities, notwithstanding widespread anti-expansionist sentiments among black Americans. As Edward Said has argued, "The enterprise of having an empire depends upon the *idea* of *having an empire,* . . . and all kinds of preparations are made for it within a culture" (Said's emphasis, 11). In this context, the invaded/invading model of the African-American home becomes one of these cultural preparations, indicating that all social groups—subordinate as well as dominant, black as well as white, women as well as men—help shape a nation for the experience of empire.

"We Shall Be Preserved": Domestic Imperialism and the *Colored American Magazine*

In its aim to introduce "a monthly magazine of merit into every Negro family" (May 1900), the *Colored American Magazine* was a venue for black writers to communicate ideas about the meanings of home to the newly literate black public. Founded in 1900, the magazine was part of a cooperative publishing venture attempting to reach a wide audience (readers could become members for an investment of over five dollars). Hazel Carby has speculated that the readership of the magazine included blacks in a variety of jobs: teachers and clergy, factory workers, blacksmiths and shoemakers, butchers, carpenters, millworkers, machinists and printers, railroad workers, female dressmakers, milliners, seamstresses, and household servants (127).

Writers whose works appear or are mentioned in the *Colored American Magazine* consistently figure the home as a system of domestic imperialism, in which the family—on multiple levels—is both invaded and invading. First, the magazine depicts black nuclear families threatened by violent white invasion such that they must embrace the tactics of white assault in order to survive. On another level, in attempting to formulate racial solidarity in opposition to white attack, writers in the *Colored American* transform these symbolic nuclear families into a family of the diaspora; domestic borders thereby extend to include other homes and other homelands (including those of people of color who expressly do *not* want to join in solidarity with American blacks). While such encroachment is more metaphoric than literal, it echoes U.S. expansion at this historical moment and invokes the invasive practices that make expansion possible. Moreover, members of this international racial family respond to white invasions with violent assaults of their own. And the *Colored American* ultimately expands this family again, in an effort to find a solution to global racism, formulating an interracial family. Containing both invaders and the invaded, the interracial family appears as a site of constant struggle between colonized and colonizer.

The vulnerability of the African-American nuclear family appears throughout the magazine—most obviously in numerous articles on the inadequacy of laws against lynching. As it assails current conditions, the *Colored American* underscores the destructive effect lynching has on the private home. In one exploration of the situation, "The Cure for Lynching," reprinted from the *Kansas City Star,* the *Colored American* considers possible legal recourses (455–59). This piece is then followed by an untitled essay that quotes the *Springfield Republican,* which argues that the nation is becoming immune to the horror of lynch law. These discussions of lynching close with a simple pen-and-ink drawing of an idyllic-looking country home. The juxtaposition of this happy home with lynch stories suggests that the depicted scene of safe-looking home life, while desirable, is not a reality for African Americans. Neither the familial nor the national home is safe from pervasive racist violence.

The effect of lynching on the African-American nuclear family is specifically addressed by Ida B. Wells-Barnett, a writer often referred to in the pages of the *Colored American* and probably read by the same audience. In *A Red Record* (1895), Wells-Barnett's graphic descriptions of actual lynchings frequently foreground acts of domestic invasion. Hamp Biscoe is only one of the many men who are taken from their homes by whites. In attempting to protect his home and family, Biscoe threatens a trespassing neighbor with "bitter oaths and violent threats" (159). As a consequence, the white neighbor secures a warrant for Biscoe's arrest: "Ford [the constable] . . . entered upon the premises. . . . Two other white men . . . forced the door of Biscoe's cabin and arrested him, his wife and thirteen-year-old son, and took them, together with a babe at the breast" (159). Another typical incident is that of Meredith Lewis, found innocent of murder. Still, a "mob gathered in his vicinity and went to his house. He was called, and suspecting nothing, went outside. He was seized and hurried off to a convenient spot and hanged by the neck" (175). Such invasions affect all family members: in one instance, Wells-Barnett establishes the number of widows and orphans that are "indebted to this mob for their condition" (239). Once their men are dead, female family members are especially vulnerable to white cruelty. Wells-Barnett writes, "wives and daughters of these lynched men were horribly and brutally outraged by the murderers of their husbands and fathers" (239). In these images of violation, the attack on the home is marked on the bodies within, via the lynching of the male body and literal invasion of the female body—that is, rape; domestic invasion in this narrative comes to carry a dual meaning of encroachment on property and bodily assault or attack.

Elsewhere, members of the black home participate in their own acts of invasion as they resist racist attack. Hamp Biscoe violently defends his home, firing upon the constable: "the load tore a part of [the constable's] clothes from his body, one shot going through his arm and entering his breast" (159). Biscoe's resistance is an act of bodily invasion, emphasized by Wells-Barnett's vivid description of the physical penetration of the constable's body. The *Colored American* further explores black resistance tactics, publishing fictional pieces that center on scenes of violent incursions. In "A Dash for Liberty," by Pauline Hopkins, a free black man attempts to emancipate his wife and in the process leads 134 slaves through a bloody battle. They escape by commandeering a ship—invading the decks and quarters designated for captain and crew—and eventually land at Nassau, New Providence—encroaching on a Caribbean island in order to establish their own homes. Hopkins ends her tale, based on a supposedly factual article in the *Atlantic Monthly,* by asserting, "Every act of oppression is a weapon for the oppressed" (243–47). The story advocates assault as a defense for blacks, their families, and their homes, if necessary. In "A Georgia Episode," by A. Gude Deekun, Russell Woodleigh takes revenge on whites for the rape and murder of his fiancée, first by "creeping" into the laundry in which the perpetrator works and then by blowing it up (3–7). Again, invasion is marked as a forceful act of resistance in the drive for domestic happiness.

The African-American home also attempts to stave off worldly threats by redrawing its boundaries beyond those of the nuclear family. In its first year of publication, the *Colored American* established a racial family through the promotion of pan-Africanism. In September 1900, the magazine published an account of the "First Pan-African Conference of the World." The conference attracted delegates from countries ranging from Abyssinia to Liberia and the British West Indies, "with the object of discussing and improving the condition of the colored race" (223). With this historical backdrop, the *Colored American* articulates its mission of formulating a racial sense of family: one of its purposes is to "intensify the bonds of that *racial brotherhood,* which alone can enable a people to assert their racial rights as men, and demand their privileges as citizens" (emphasis added). The racial family, then, is formulated to help resist racism. In fact, the pages of the *Colored American* look a lot like a family album, featuring numerous photos of successful, middle-class African Americans from around the country—perhaps, as Thomas Otten has suggested, in an attempt to culture the image of "the New Negro" (232). These photographic portraits create a community around the *Colored American;* readers become acquainted with other members of their "racial brotherhood."

Like the nuclear African-American family, the racial family is vulnerable to white power: after all, the United States is actively engaged in colonizing peoples of color during this period. Invasion takes on the third meaning here of entering a country or territory as an enemy. In an article about the role of Toussaint L'Ouverture in the Haitian fight against French colonization, Hopkins expresses her simultaneous hopes and fears for this reconfigured family unit. She writes, "As a race we shall be preserved, although annihilation sometimes seems very near" (24).

And opposing annihilation, the racial family, too, incorporates counter-invasive strategies of various forms. Hopkins compares African-American participation in the Civil War with the fight of Haitians against the French. She asserts, however, that such invasions—here, again, in the form of violent bodily assaults—are not natural to African Americans, who were "unaccustomed to arms" before the war; rather, these maneuvers are learned from whites when blacks are forced to arise in resistance ("Toussaint L'Ouverture" 24). Additionally, the very idea of the international racial family can be read as a concept of colonization—this expanded home integrates other nations, other families, some of whom are reluctant "family members." In fact, African-American desires for a racial family frequently contrasted with more local interests of other members of the African diaspora: as Major John Lynch observed after the U.S. occupation of Cuba, African Cubans had "no sympathetic feelings for colored Americans on account of race, for they had no race issue there such as we have in the States. . . . [The major concern of African Cubans] is not a question of race or color but of country" (qtd. in Gatewood 171).

The *Colored American Magazine* further broadens the familial circle, expanding to include other races, imagining an *interracial* brotherhood. Articles sketch, not a racial family, but "the essential unity of races, unvexed by arbitrary laws. . . . [T]he freshman, sophomore, junior and senior classes in the college of civilization are inseparably connected, and open to all classes and races who may desire to come" ("Wealth Makes Many Friends" 27). While this article uses collegiate rhetoric and does not create an interracial family per se, it inscribes the fluid nature of the racial family, which "essentially" unites with all races—even the white race that, as Hopkins notes, threatens peoples of color with annihilation. Complicating the idea of family by destabilizing its boundaries, the *Colored American* creates a new—potentially frightening—unity between colonized and colonizers, the invaded and the invaders. At this historical moment, African-American texts, unlike those by the white writers Kaplan studies, find more political power in destabilizing notions of domestic and foreign than in "generating notions of the foreign against which the nation can be imagined as home" (Kaplan 582).

This complicated domestic configuration partakes of the dual role African Americans are playing at this historical moment—understanding themselves as both under white assault and as part of the colonial forces invading other nations. Despite sympathies for nations that have attempted to stave off imperial forces (such as Haiti), the magazine also publishes articles that celebrate the African-American role in colonialism. In "Opportunities for Colored Americans in the East," the *Colored American* claims that Manila's "development has improved one thousand per cent. since American occupation. . . . Whenever a tourist steps off the lighter at the dock in Manila . . . he will undoubtedly say, 'The Americans did not take such a bad step after all'" (267–68). This article not only supports American military action on the islands, but encourages black civilian immigration, a form of invasion of the Caribbean and the Philippines popularized among African Americans. Further support of colonization is revealed in a May 1902 article, "The Enlisted Man in Action: Or, the Colored American Soldier in the Philippines." Here, Rienzi B. Lemus, a member of the 25th Infantry, describes his experiences fighting against Filipinos, in an effort to dispel any impression that the "enlisted man is always sullen, hard-hearted, and cold" (46). There is no reflection on who the enemy is or what the Filipinos are fighting for (freedom from U.S. domination); instead, the author gives a day-by-day account of his company's activities, including acts of bravery and kindness to one another. He ends his tribute to his comrades with this: "Thus we have seen the American Army enlisted man in action; always jolly and clad in his campaigning kit, ready to march where the will of his country demands him. Who knows where? To victory or destruction, which? 'The last time VICTORY!'" (55). The African Americans in this company are the colonizers here, as much as they, in other contexts, are victims of colonization.

These invaded/invading representations of domestic imperialism in the *Colored American* are, on the one hand, politically useful for African Americans in highlighting the dangerous aspects of colonialism for families of color while portraying black resistance to colonization—thereby articulating resentment toward and power against oppressive social practices. But, conversely, in picturing invasive practices as acceptable, the system of domestic imperialism undermines black power by supporting the often racist and violent policies of the nation's imperialist mission.

The model of domestic imperialism becomes more complex when the issue of gender is raised. It is first notable that while the *Colored American Magazine* shows the possibility of African-American resistance to white invasion of household, homeland, and body, it repeatedly gives that power specifically to black men. It is, after all, only "the enlisted *man*" who is part of the invading forces in the Philippines; a black *man* enters the laundry to gain revenge for a woman's rape and murder; a black *man* leads a slave insurrection while trying to free his wife, taking over a ship and settling on a Caribbean island; and Hamp Biscoe—not his wife—uses weapons to attack the intruders of the Biscoe household. When these males resist attack through invasion—in its varied meanings of encroachment on property, personal assault, and national offensive maneuvers—their actions echo the imperialist conduct of the United States. The power of imperialism, while sometimes violent and not always effective, can at times be usefully employed by African Americans, but seemingly only by African-American men. African-American women are left vulnerable to violence that will invade their homes, their bodies, and those of their children.

How, then, is women's power to derive from a system that consistently subjects homes to (male-dominated) invasions? While using a narrative strategy based on the invaded/invading model of domestic imperialism, the novels of Pauline Hopkins revise this configuration for women, creating an imperialism in which African Americans "invade" other homes, not through violence, but by the subtlety of influence. I am terming Hopkins's form of domestic imperialism an "invasion of influence." By gently penetrating other spaces and consequently changing white attitudes and improving black lives, Hopkins's African-American characters engage in conflict with the forces of white hegemony, but not through a violent, male-centered struggle. The model of invasion that organizes Hopkins's narratives registers black anxieties about white racism, but attempts (alas, not always success-fully) to invest black women with power for themselves.

Gentle Intrusions:
The "Invasion of Influence" in the Novels of Pauline Hopkins

Pauline Hopkins's novels are most often read as examples of African-Ameri-can domestic fiction, focusing on the desire for an ideal, stable, private home in the tradition of Harriet Jacobs.[1] But when understood as part of the system of domestic imperialism visible in the *Colored American Magazine,* which advertised and published Hopkins's work, these novels reveal that the boundaries of a safe, private home cannot be fixed during this period; African-American domesticity is consistently wracked by the fear and power of white racism and U.S. foreign policy, making a stable private sphere con-ceptually impossible.

In terms of plot, Hopkins's novels place African-American families within the experience of empire, indicating a relationship between the nu-clear and international families that I have been arguing marks the system of domestic imperialism. Hopkins's allusions to a broader stage of global activity are not always expansive, but, taken together, they constitute what Edward Said calls "a structure of attitude and reference" toward an impe-rialistic world (162); that is, Hopkins's references to international imperial-ism place private homes within the politics of empire. The private domestic sphere becomes an extension of national action. The home front in Hop-kins's work, then, is never a sphere outside imperialism.

The system of domestic imperialism does not simply appear in Hopkins's novels in terms of overt references to colonial activity. Rather, domestic imperialism inheres within the very narrative strategies that Hopkins em-ploys. Her novels can be read as narratives of invasion, narratives that are driven by spatial relocations, as one character invades a new social space, consequently propelling the plot. Social space in Hopkins's work comes to mean physical space used for social purposes—for example, actual house-holds—as well as the metonymically associated space of the body and, by extension, the psychic space of the mind. All function as sites of invasion that parallel the territories and lands that constitute the geographic fields of colonialism.

However, Hopkins's novels attempt to redefine domestic imperialism in such a way that the power of imperialist actions is not a power for males alone. Hopkins creates a model of imperialism as an invasion of influence that allows power to women as well. In nineteenth-century studies, women's influence typically refers to domestic acts designed to change the social world. When I employ the word "influence" I am specifically referring to a number of meanings in circulation in the nineteenth century: influence means "an act of flowing in"—suggesting a gentle form of invasion; it also means the flowing in from the stars or heavens of an ethereal fluid "acting on the character or destiny of men"—emphasizing a subtle invasion that changes the attitudes and lives of its objects. Hopkins's novels play on these definitions of influence, transforming the imagery of "invasion" from vicious representations of racist assault to figures of mild, nonviolent border crossings that result in changed lives and ideas. While transformed, these figures of invasion continue to carry the associations of the national and international political scene that surround them, and thus, like the more violent representations of invasion that appear in the *Colored American,* comment on domestic racism and the U.S. drive toward international dominance.

Taken together, Hopkins's novels can be read as an exploration of the domestic possibilities created by such an invasion of influence. In her first novel, *Contending Forces,* Hopkins advocates peaceful invasion, exploring the possibilities that African Americans—in particular, African-American women—may create satisfying domestic spaces for themselves by subtly colonizing the households of others. Here, I would argue, Hopkins supports the *concept* of invasion, while critiquing the violence associated with racist invasions of the period. In her final novel, *Of One Blood,* Hopkins investigates the power behind scientific (and pseudoscientific) invasive practices of the nineteenth century—in particular, medicine, archaeological expeditions, and mesmerism—as both physical and psychic invasions of influence. However, by the time *Of One Blood* is published, Hopkins's attitude changes: she seems unable to sustain her earlier optimistic views of the possibilities of invasive practices for women. Her final novel indicates an unwillingness to embrace fully even peaceful imperialist tactics as options for subordinate peoples, thus heightening a denunciation of U.S. imperialism as well as domestic racial assaults.

"Walking Nobly through Dark Gates": Physical Invasions of Space in *Contending Forces*

I have already noted the colonial references that open Hopkins's 1900 novel *Contending Forces* and place it within the framework of empire: the novel begins with the family of Charles Montfort, a British planter living on the island of Bermuda. *Contending Forces* immediately places familial concerns under a shadow of international imperialism *and* American racism: the Montfort family also owns slaves, a local form of injustice Hopkins's readers knew intimately. Later in the novel, one of Hopkins's black characters underscores this parallel between global expansion and American racism, explicitly establishing an affinity between African Americans and colonial subjects; at a political meeting, Luke Sawyer argues, "A tax too heavy placed on tea and things like that, made the American Colonies go to war with Great Britain to get their liberty. I ask you what you think the American Colonies would have done if they had suffered as we have suffered and are still suffering?" (262). When the British government threatens to end slavery in Bermuda, Montfort moves his household to the southern United States, entering a new territory in order to continue using slaves until he can retire to England. Within this frame of crossed national borders, slavery, and the practices of empire, invasions structure *Contending Forces,* motivating the plot and simultaneously echoing real-life attacks on the African-American nuclear family and the larger racial brotherhood.

The Montfort home participates in the invaded/invading model of domestic imperialism. Once in the United States, the colonial household itself becomes an invaded territory when the community suspects Charles's wife, Grace, of African ancestry. The narrator describes the disruption of the Montfort home as an act of invasion: "into this paradise of good feeling came [the Montfort's neighbor] Anson Pollack with his bitter envy and his unlawful love, and finally with his determination to possess the lovely Grace Montfort at all hazards" (45). As in contemporaneous accounts of invasion, bodies as well as homes are attacked; Charles is shot through the brain and Grace is whipped and raped: a lash cuts into her flesh, drawing "a long, raw gash across her tender white back. [Pollack's partner] Hank gazed at the cut with critical satisfaction, as he compared its depth with the skin and blood that encased the long, tapering lash. . . . Again and again was the outrage repeated" (69). While literally this describes a whipping, the word "outrage" is used as code for rape at this historic moment, and the whip reads as a phallic symbol, a "snaky leather thong [that] curled and writhed in its rapid, vengeful descent" (69). Grace Montfort's "cut," which Hank "gazed at," similarly signifies her genitalia. Finally, the "blood stood in a pool about [Grace's] feet" (69). As Hazel Carby writes, this is the final evidence that the "'outrage' that had been committed was rape" (132). The opening section of Hopkins's narrative thus parallels the scenes of invasion read elsewhere by the audience of the *Colored American Magazine*—incursions into nations, homes, and bodies.

Invasion as depicted in the early pages of *Contending Forces* is unequivo-cally racist and horrific. However, as Hopkins's novel continues, different styles of invasive practices appear useful to African Americans, who need to resist the dangers that threaten them. In this way, Hopkins imagines homes based on the invading/invaded model of domestic imperialism, but revises the imagery of invasion within the model. Following the attack, the Montfort son, Jesse, can only survive by intruding on the home of another family—yet his is a peaceful intrusion: "'Is Mr. Whitfield in?' [Jesse] asked, as he doffed his hat respectfully" (79). Jesse's invasion is an invasion of influence: he nonviolently enters the Whitfield home in order to save his life and ultimately creates his own domestic happiness by influencing the family, charming the Whitfields' daughter into marrying him. Jesse's inva-sion of influence is a method of resistance that Hopkins suggests is effective for African Americans' domestic happiness.

Throughout the novel Hopkins formulates gentle invasions that create rather than destroy, juxtaposing them with the deadly, violent attacks. Not only does Jesse save his own life, but his marriage to Elizabeth Whitfield brings about a new family and generates the narrative figures that drive the rest of the novel. The tragedy of the Montfort family, having taken place around 1800, gives way to the story of Jesse's progeny, living in Ma Smith's boardinghouse at the turn of the next century—the "present" for Hopkins's contemporaries. The very concept of a house of boarders, a home in which members constantly arrive and depart, underscores the instability of domes-tic borders in the tale, which comes to center around the newest arrival at Ma Smith's, the "beautiful mulatto" Sappho Clarke. Sappho, too, is only pre-sent in *Contending Forces* because of acts of gentle invasion: her life was saved by Luke Sawyer, who peacefully entered her home after his own was bru-tally attacked by whites (a drawing of which served as the aforementioned advertisement for Hopkins's novel).

Through the character of Sappho, *Contending Forces* explores the gender implications of such divergent strategies of invasion. Sappho's room is twice invaded by men who desire her. First, in an act of genuine concern, Will Smith surreptitiously enters to build a fire for Sappho and clean her hearth. This gentle intrusion is marked as feminine: Will wears "one of his mother's ample kitchen aprons for the protection of his clothing. . . . [T]he ample folds of the apron-skirt enveloped his limbs to his ankles; the long strings, crossed in the back, met in front in a huge bow-knot" (172). Such action contrasts markedly with those of John Langley, who bursts abruptly into Sappho's room: "I did not hear you knock, Mr. Langley," Sappho says. "I did not knock," he replies (316). John then threatens to ruin Sappho by revealing her secret past if she refuses to become his mistress. Reminiscent of the original vicious invasion of the Montfort home, John's attack is an invasion of space designed to result in the physical invasion of Sappho's body.

But by so abruptly entering Sappho's room, John gains no power over the woman he desires. Rather, it is Will's subtle, feminized invasion that succeeds, since Sappho agrees to marry him. John's violently coded actions are far from successful and, in fact, only cause Sappho to flee (also temporarily interrupting the union between Will and Sappho). Read in the context of the colonialism that opens the novel, as well as the violent invasions detailed in the *Colored American,* John's incursion into Sappho's room carries the specter of violent imperialist acts as well as the implications of racist invasions of African-American households. By John's failure, the novel suggests that (male-marked) violent colonization is ultimately an unsuccessful strategy; power cannot be gained from it.

Escaping John's lascivious advances, Sappho demonstrates the effectiveness of gentle, influential invasion—specifically for black women. At first she is furious with John: "revenge was all she craved; she shivered at the dark thoughts which came to her" (341). Presumably these "dark thoughts" concern violent attack—perhaps on John's home and body. But, rather than such an assault, Sappho chooses a mild entrance into a new home; she becomes a governess. Sappho's presence indeed affects all the members of this new household, as she "became the moving spirit of the home, warmly loved by her little charges and enthusiastically admired by the servants" (353). Resisting John and effecting an influence over others, Sappho is able to create a good domestic situation for herself. We are told, "Here, indeed, was peace" (354).

Sappho's entrance into this latest household allows her safety until her eventual reunion with Will Smith. The novel promises a blissful marriage for the couple. Yet the narrative, along with all the news articles of the period, suggests that home, whether household or homeland, is never secure from invasion. African-American family members must be prepared for assault, and, to survive, must themselves encroach on other homes. In fact, in the closing scene of the novel, Sappho and Will are moving from the American continent to Europe. The final words indicate that the African-American family will not be able to rest protected in one stable location:

My wife, my life, O, we will walk this world
Yoked in all exercise of noble end,
And so through those dark gates across the wild
That no man knows. . . .
Lay thy sweet hands in mine and trust to me. (402)

"Walk[ing] this world," passing "through . . . dark gates," this family is preparing to spend a lifetime crossing borders. But, as an "exercise of noble end," this will be a nonviolent invasion that promises a happy home to African Americans—in particular, African-American women—though home will never have stable boundaries. While careful to critique the violence of imperialism, Hopkins supports the idea of a transformed, peaceful entrance into new homes and homelands.

"Penetrating the Dark, Mysterious Forests": Bodily and National Invasions in *Of One Blood*

Where *Contending Forces* asserts the necessity of nonviolent spatial invasion for African Americans—a physical invasion of homes—*Of One Blood* explores the efficacy of simultaneous physical and psychological invasions. In this, her last novel, serialized in the *Colored American* (1902–3), Hopkins notes that dominant forces can invade bodies, minds, and nations through scientific and pseudoscientific means (scientific expeditions, medicine, and mesmerism), while also suggesting that these same methods can be harnessed by subordinate groups in an effort to create homes of their own. However, in *Of One Blood,* Hopkins's faith in the invasion of influence as a tactic of survival for African Americans—and African-American women in particular—seems to grow dim. The model of the invaded/invading home offers African Americans some possibilities for domestic felicity, but ultimately it cannot overcome the problems of its violent, racist roots. In *Of One Blood,* Hopkins can no longer fully support even "gentle" invasions— or even influence—as possible survival mechanisms, suggesting that the system of domestic imperialism and counter-invasion in general may eventually fail as a resistance strategy for subordinated peoples.

As in *Contending Forces,* international imperialism serves as the context for the narrative in *Of One Blood.* Though this is not apparent in the first section of the novel—which deals primarily with the life of the brilliant medical student Reuel Briggs—the second section focuses on a scientific expedition to Ethiopia, which Reuel joins upon becoming a doctor. The object of the British and American expedition is to "unearth buried cities and treasure which the shifting sands of Sahara have buried for centuries" (494). The aim, however, is not simply to "unearth," but to carry back home the Ethiopian treasures that are discovered. British and Americans, armed with guns and knives, invade the borders of African countries to steal relics of Africa's past. The menace of imperialism acts as the novel's backdrop.

Read within the shadow of colonial acts, the physical and psychic invasions of *Of One Blood* evoke these international invasions. In the first chapter, Reuel establishes a metonymic connection between nation and body: there is an "undiscovered country within ourselves," he tells his friend Aubrey Livingston—a "hidden self lying quiescent in every soul" (448). Further, where the novel's political invasions are undertaken for "scientific" purposes, bodily invasions, too, become associated with science. On one level, Reuel's work as a doctor paints him as a dominant social force with physical power over others. Working to save the life of an unconscious woman—Dianthe, another of Hopkins's "beautiful mulattas"—Reuel penetrates her body with a life-giving powder, administering this "subtile magnetic agent" that he considers the "secret of life" (468).

Reuel's invasion and colonization of Dianthe are accomplished through mesmerism, also called animal magnetism—a practice predicated on the idea of "influence." Mesmerism, popularized in the mid-nineteenth century, was based on the concept that human health is influenced by a magnetic fluid in the body that responds to planetary motion. The theories of Franz Anton Mesmer, on which mesmerism is founded, contend that "there is almost no change which happens in heavenly bodies without its influencing the fluids and solids of our earth in agreement. . . . The animal is part of the earth and is composed of fluids and solids, and when the proportion and equilibrium of these fluids and solids are modified to a certain degree, very perceptible effects will occur from this" (13). According to Mesmer, the entire human animal is susceptible to influence, is, in fact, always already influenced by the universe. Remember, too, that a nineteenth-century definition of "influence" directly corresponds to Mesmer's ideas: influence means the flowing in from the stars or heavens of an ethereal fluid acting on the character or destiny of men. Mesmerism, then, is a belief in the power of influence to affect the destinies of men and women.

The practicing mesmerist used this knowledge of influence to control his patients by invading their bodies with his own mental magnetic fluid, akin to Reuel's injection of Dianthe. As one magnetizer explained it, the subjects begin to feel "the irresistible effect of a superior mental power operating upon them . . . because the mental influence, or the nerve-aura of the operator controls directly the body of the subject" (Buchanan 252). The "superior mental power" of the mesmerist's magnetic fluid thus encroaches upon the magnetic fluids of the subjects. Mesmerism becomes an invasion of influence that is both psychic, due to mental influence, and physical, controlling the "body of the subject."

By depicting Reuel as a mesmerist, Hopkins suggests the power for subordinate peoples in peacefully invading other bodies and psyches. While Reuel's position in society—and especially vis-à-vis Dianthe—places him in a dominant role, the narrative reveals that he, like Dianthe, has an African heritage. Black Americans need not simply be the passive sites of imperialism to be penetrated, but can infiltrate other social spaces—in this case, bodies and minds. And this invasion can lead to domestic happiness as Reuel attempts to use his mesmeric power to establish a home for himself and Dianthe, saving her life and keeping her close to him. In fact, Reuel's very definition of love echoes invading practices, as he claims that when he loves a woman, "all the current of my being flows to her" (461).

These physical and psychic invasions parallel Reuel's later activities. When the bigotry of the medical establishment renders him unable to find work, he joins the scientific expedition to Ethiopia (before having the opportunity to consummate his marriage to Dianthe). Along the way, he continues to have mesmeric visions of what is happening back home—including Dianthe's death. This may mean the end of all hope of domestic happiness with Dianthe, but because he has taken part in an invasion of Ethiopia, Reuel is allowed a new chance at marital felicity. On the expedition, he stumbles upon his identity as the lost King Ergomenes of the ancient, hidden Ethiopian city of Telassar. Here, he will establish his true home: "United to [Queen] Candace, his days glide peacefully by in good works" (621). Claudia Tate notes that Reuel's ultimate happiness in Ethiopia may indicate Hopkins's inability to envision domestic peace for blacks in America (207), but I contend that this prospect of joy, obtained by entering foreign territory, indicates Hopkins's attraction to invasionary practices as ways African Americans may co-opt the dominant paradigm of imperial power.

Hopkins additionally appears to support the power of physical and psychic invasion by giving the power of mesmerism to her African-American heroine as well as to her hero. Early in the novel, Dianthe invades Reuel's mind by coming to him as a supernatural presence, in effect "haunting" him. Nineteenth-century mesmerists wrote that in trying to attune internal magnetic fluids with those outside the body, subjects could reach a state of "expanded interior perception"; telepathy, clairvoyance, and other feats of extrasensory perception are possible during this state (Fuller 45–46). Appearing to Reuel one stormy night in his home and, later, when he is visiting a friend, Dianthe, in this "expanded" state, uses her own mental powers of influence. She asks for Reuel's help; thus, when near the opening of the novel he sees her lying unconscious in the hospital, he is moved to save her life. Invaded and invading, Dianthe as an African-American woman uses an invasion of influence to achieve her own survival.

Similarly, it is Queen Candace's ability to "influence" that allows her domestic happiness with Reuel. Immediately Reuel notes a "sense of power" lurking in her "smile of grace and sweetness" (569), and while he originally had had "doubts and misgivings" over his Ethiopian adventures, "under

Queen Candace's magic influence, all doubts disappeared, and it seemed the most natural thing in the world to be sitting here . . . planning a union with a lovely woman, that should give to the world a dynasty of dark-skinned rulers, whose destiny should be to restore the prestige of an ancient people" (570). Her influence over the American doctor results in a type of colonization: slipping a ring onto his finger, the queen says, "Thus do I claim thee for all eternity" (571).

Yet Hopkins's vision of the usefulness of tactics of invasion, influence, and colonization finally falters for African-American women. Despite the fact that Dianthe, too, has mesmeric powers and that Reuel's mesmerism seems to promise conjugal happiness for them both in the first half of the novel, their relationship speaks of a troubling colonization from the start. Reuel controls Dianthe both physically and psychologically. After saving her, he refuses to search out her friends, houses her in the home of one of his own companions, and keeps all knowledge of her African past from her. In order for them both to "pass" in white society, he decides he must "marry her before she awakens to the consciousness of her identity" (479). The home Reuel plans is a site of domestic imperialism that is particularly oppressive to the woman: her mind is colonized, her identity is obscured, and she is physically removed from her old life in order to be absorbed into the life of another.

In fact, Dianthe is never able to find happiness within the system of domestic imperialism. While Reuel is in Ethiopia, his sinister friend Aubrey becomes obsessed with her and, ultimately, uses his mesmeric powers to control her and keep her prisoner in his home: "In vain the girl sought to throw off the numbing influence of the man's presence. In desperation she tried to defy him, but she knew that she had lost her will-power and was but a puppet in the hands of this false friend" (504). Dianthe is eventually driven to her death. While Hopkins attempts to make mesmerism possible as an invasionary practice open to her female characters as well as the males, this tactic eventually fails her women.

Finally, Hopkins retreats from fully embracing a paradigm of invasion for even her African-American male characters. Her novel ends on an ominous note when Reuel, from his new Ethiopian home with Queen Candace, "views with serious apprehension, the advance of mighty nations penetrating the dark mysterious forests of [Africa]. 'Where will it stop?'" he sadly asks. "But none save Omnipotence can solve the problem" (621). In *Of One Blood*, Hopkins seems more aware of the menacing problems of invasion and imperialism than in her earlier novel. She seems unconvinced that domestic imperialism is an effective familial system for African Americans—male or female.

But why does the paradigm of the invaded/invading home fail Hopkins?

We may speculate that she was so horrified by domestic racist assault and U.S. imperialism as to be finally unable to accept even transformed, gentler versions. Certainly Hopkins was aware of the racism underlying U.S. foreign policy; as she writes in a 1905 article in *Voice of the Negro,* "That the ultimate desire of the Anglo-Saxon is the complete subjugation of all dark races to themselves, there is no doubt" (qtd. in Gaines 449). Additionally, her choice of mesmerism as an invasionary strategy would have made a celebration of such activity difficult. If mesmerism is a paradigmatic physical and psychological invasion of influence, it also has numerous frightening associations within nineteenth-century culture—especially for women. As Robert Fuller notes in *Mesmerism and the American Cure of Souls,* mesmerism could be "an agent of great abuse and impropriety": it was feared that men, the usual practitioners, might use their mental powers to seduce their female patients (21, 32, 33–34). Even as Hopkins exploits the invasive powers of mesmerism as a way for Reuel to find (perhaps temporary) domestic happiness, certainly she and her readers would be aware of its menacing dimensions—so aware, in fact, that the entire vision of domestic imperialism becomes untenable, particularly for women.

Finally, then, the facts of empire and the use of mesmerism in *Of One Blood* seem to force Hopkins to recognize the threats of domestic imperialism more fully than in her previous work. In Hopkins's last novel, the death of Dianthe and the ominous future for Reuel and Queen Candace are inescapable indicators of the problems of colonizing practices. Moreover, crossed borders of empire lead to racial mixing and unclear bloodlines; and in *Of One Blood,* unclear bloodlines ultimately lead to incest. We discover at the novel's end that Reuel, Dianthe, and Aubrey are brothers and sister, conceived in slavery. The horror of having married one brother (Reuel) and (we assume) having had sexual union with the other (Aubrey) drives Dianthe to her death, illustrating the pain of familial ambiguity. Hopkins's previous attempt to find an invaded/invading system of domestic imperialism that may be positive for women as well as men seems to collapse under incest, the ultimate boundary violation. The concept of an international invaded/invading family takes on a sinister light: if boundaries between families are unfixed, if, as one character maintains, we are all "of one blood, descended from one common father" (585), incest is unavoidable. This is a horrific turn to the expanded, interracial family that was touted in the pages of the *Colored American*: to expand the family to incorporate other races, to erase the distinctions between domestic and foreign ends not as a utopia, but as an incestuous nightmare riddled with the threat of invading forces.

This study of African-American domestic representations suggests just how conflicted the response to colonialism can be among the subordinated people of an empire. African Americans writing in the *Colored American,* and Pauline Hopkins in particular, both support and oppose imperialist tactics, creating homes that both fall victim to and become victors by these tactics. As an African-American woman, Hopkins may have resisted the violent, male-oriented imperialist practices detailed in the *Colored American Magazine,* yet her formulations of domesticity support counter-invasions nonetheless. Even in *Of One Blood,* where Hopkins associates crossed boundaries with the horror of incest, she is able to point to some, albeit limited, positive possibilities of invasion for black American domestic happiness.

What becomes particularly important about the system of domestic imperialism is that such ambiguity resists the clear demarcation of ruler from ruled within an empire. This stands in contrast to Edward Said's argument that "imperialism acquires a kind of coherence, a set of experiences, and a presence of ruler and ruled alike within the culture" (11). While I would agree with Said that the *"idea* of *having an empire"* does indeed infiltrate all aspects of life in an imperial culture, I take exception to the notion that empire necessitates cultural "coherence": with the boundaries of the home changing, domestic imperialism blurs positions of the invaders and the invaded, the domestic and the foreign. As such it is a system that resists reinscribing African Americans into the territory of empire reserved by white American culture for subordination. It refuses simply to fix an African-American space in opposition to white hegemony. Where literary critics such as Claudia Tate and Ann duCille find African-American writers attempting to establish happy nuclear families for themselves, I would argue that in the writings in and around the *Colored American Magazine,* such a space does not seem fully desirable. Instead, the ability to reformulate boundaries and borders in the light of political anxieties fuels the desire behind these narratives. The resulting indeterminacy of the invaded/invading African-American home—familial, national, and international—is threatening and liberating.

Notes

For their help with this essay, I would like to thank Dale Bauer, Dawn Keetley, Susan Dunn, and Liz Cannon.

1. See, for example, Claudia Tate, who argues in *Domestic Allegories of Political Desire* that Hopkins uses the conventions of the domestic novel—in particular the narrative drive toward marriage—in an attempt to create a racialized ideal family (11). Similarly, Ann duCille explores Hopkins's use of the "coupling convention"— that is, the narrative desire for romantic relationships—in her fiction. Jane Campbell asserts that *Contending Forces,* in particular, abounds with "the trappings of domes-

tic fiction," in which "domestic scenes symbolize cosmic harmony" (33). While Elizabeth Ammons focuses on Hopkins's use of fantasy and allegory, she argues that Hopkins's novels are domestic fictions that use the supernatural as if it is part of the reality of day-to-day domestic life (84).

Works Cited

Ammons, Elizabeth. *Conflicting Stories: American Women Writers at the Turn of the Century.* New York: Oxford UP, 1992.

Buchanan, Joseph. *Neurological System of Anthropology.* Cincinnati, 1854.

Campbell, Jane. *Mythic Black Fiction: The Transformation of History.* Knoxville: U of Tennessee P, 1986.

Carby, Hazel. *Reconstructing Womanhood: The Emergence of the Afro-American Woman Novelist.* New York: Oxford UP, 1987.

"The Cure for Lynching." *Colored American Magazine* October 1901: 455–59.

Deekun, A. Gude. "A Georgia Episode." *Colored American Magazine* May 1901: 3–7.

Du Bois, W. E. B. "The Conservation of Races." *W. E. B. Du Bois Speaks: Speeches and Addresses, 1890–1919.* Ed. Philip Foner. New York: Pathfinder P, 1970.

duCille, Ann. *The Coupling Convention: Sex, Text, and Tradition in Black Women's Fiction.* New York: Oxford UP, 1993.

"The First Pan-African Conference of the World." *Colored American Magazine* September 1900: 223ff.

Fuller, Robert C. *Mesmerism and the American Cure of Souls.* Philadelphia: U of Pennsylvania P, 1982.

Gaines, Kevin. "Black Americans' Racial Uplift Ideology as 'Civilizing Mission': Pauline E. Hopkins on Race and Imperialism." *Cultures of United States Imperialism.* Ed. Amy Kaplan and Donald E. Pease. Durham, NC: Duke UP, 1993. 433–55.

Gatewood, Willard B. *Black Americans and the White Man's Burden, 1898–1903.* Chicago: U of Illinois P, 1975.

Hopkins, Pauline. *Contending Forces: A Romance Illustrative of Negro Life North and South.* 1900. Miami: Mnemosyne Publishing Co., 1969.

——. "A Dash for Liberty." *Colored American Magazine* August 1901: 243–47.

——. *Of One Blood, Or, the Hidden Self.* 1902–3. In *The Magazine Novels of Pauline Hopkins.* New York: Oxford UP, 1988.

——. "Toussaint L'Overture." *Colored American Magazine* November 1900: 9–24.

Kaplan, Amy. "Manifest Domesticity." *American Literature* September 1998: 581–606.

Lemus, Rienzi B. "The Enlisted Man in Action; Or the Colored American Soldier in the Philippines." *Colored American Magazine* May 1902: 46–55.

Mesmer, F. A. *Mesmerism.* Trans. and ed. George Bloch. Los Altos, CA: William Kaufmann, 1980.

"Opportunities for Colored Americans in the East." *Colored American Magazine* March 1902: 258–68.

Otten, Thomas J. "Pauline Hopkins and the Hidden Self of Race." *ELH* 59 (1992): 227–56.

Said, Edward. *Culture and Imperialism.* New York: Knopf, 1993.

Tate, Claudia. *Domestic Allegories of Political Desire: The Black Heroine's Text at the Turn of the Century.* New York: Oxford UP, 1992.

"Wealth Makes Many Friends." *Colored American Magazine* November 1900: 27.

Wells-Barnett, Ida B. *The Selected Works of Ida B. Wells-Barnett (1892–1900).* Ed. Trudier Harris. New York: Oxford UP, 1992.

10

Public Women, Private Acts: Gender and Theater in Turn-of-the-Century American Novels

Jennifer Costello Brezina

In a world ordered by sexual imbalance, pleasure in looking has been split between active/male and passive/female. The determining male gaze projects its phantasy on to the female figure which is styled accordingly. In their traditional exhibitionist role, women are simultaneously looked at and displayed, with their appearance coded for strong visual and erotic impact so that they can be said to connote to-be-looked-at-ness.

—Laura Mulvey, "Visual Pleasure and Narrative Cinema"

Maggie always departed with raised spirits from the showing places of the melodrama. She rejoiced at the way in which the poor and virtuous eventually surmounted the wealthy and the wicked. The theater made her think. She wondered if the culture and refinement she had seen imitated, perhaps grotesquely, by the heroine on the stage, could be acquired by a girl who lived in a tenement house and worked in a shirt factory.

—Stephen Crane, *Maggie: A Girl of the Streets*

While it may be a critical commonplace that nineteenth-century women were trapped by "separate sphere" ideology and were not able to successfully negotiate the public realm, many American novels published at the turn into the twentieth century problematize the public/private split by using female characters in public space to embody the powerful cultural shifts that modernity and rapid urbanization were bringing to American society. While it is clear that gendered space still existed at the close of the nineteenth century, many writers of urban fiction used their work to illustrate the blurring of the demarcation between the spheres that contemporaneous social movements were bringing to American culture. The theater, with its inherent emphasis on space and movement, serves as an apt metaphor for reworkings of the definitions of public and private, so it should come as no surprise that many writers of the time used the theater as a backdrop for the action of their novels when they wished to engage the intense cultural debates surrounding this uneasy triangle of women, modernity, and the city. The theater provided a unique setting that was simultaneously full of rich history yet absolutely contemporary. It was a public forum, but one that respectable women often frequented. The internal dynamics of the theater were also complex. While women onstage took part in erotic spectacles designed to titillate the male viewer, women in the audience looked both at the stage and each other, drawing pleasure from the experience. The actresses' position was not without gratification either; in addition to the obvious financial rewards, actresses wielded considerable cultural power. Women's acting is not confined to the literal stage in these novels as the ability to perform offstage is linked to social mobility, again blurring the boundaries between the public and private spheres.

At first, the image of the woman onstage may seem the antithesis of domesticity, and, in a sense, the very public role of actress seems to preclude her availability for a more private role, but when the novels are examined closely, this dichotomy does not hold up. It is through their public acts on the stage that the women of these novels are able to maintain and even control domestic space. Not only does the money earned through acting provide a material basis for private space, but the cultural capital earned carries over into the domestic as well. The theater itself, "home" to the actress, becomes a sort of virtual drawing room to the audiences as well, lending a vivid backdrop against which private dramas unfold. Finally, traditional domestic space is not immune from theater, as the performance of expected gender roles leads to a type of "offstage acting" that cuts across both spheres, appropriating the techniques of the stage to enhance domestic relationships.

All of the novels to be discussed in this chapter inspired intense reactions upon initial publication; through their sustained use of the theater as both setting and metaphor, their authors reflected the cultural impact that changing roles for women were bringing to their society. The troubled publication history of Dreiser's *Sister Carrie* (1900) is well documented, but the other novels I will discuss share the same type of uneven critical reception. Although it is now back in critical favor, Paul Laurence Dunbar's *The Sport of the Gods* (1902) was initially attacked as belonging to the plantation tradition, a mode of writing that glorified antebellum slavery and decried racial progress. And in spite of the fact that Frank Norris's *The Pit: A Story of Chicago* (1903) was a best-seller upon its publication in 1903 and was considered by many of Norris's contemporaries to be his finest work, it is now a mere footnote in literary history, replaced in the canon by his earlier novel *McTeague*. According to McElrath and Jones in their introduction to the recent Penguin Books edition of the text, the novel was so popular in its time that it inspired a myriad of reviews, a 1904 play, a 1917 silent film, and even a Parker Brothers card game. However, its popularity did not survive into the mid-twentieth century, and even now it does not receive the attention of Norris's other works. Finally, Ellen Glasgow's second novel, *Phases of an Inferior Planet* (1898), met with such disparaging reviews that it has not yet made its way back into print, in spite of the current Glasgow revival. What all of these novels share, in addition to their use of the theater as setting and metaphor, is their willingness to engage with one of the most controversial issues of their time: the place of women in public life.

Theater as Seduction:
Pleasure and the Triangulation of the Gaze

Gender is immediately implicit in the critical term "the gaze" as the power dynamics involved lead to the almost inevitable assumption that the gazer is male and the object of the gaze is female. As early as the 1860s, women's bodies were explicitly commodified and exploited for male theater audiences in what came to be called "leg shows." These shows, first developed by actress-turned-manager Laura Keene and perfected in the 1866 ballet *The Black Crook,* relied on capturing the male audience with displays of female flesh (tight-clad legs shown to mid-thigh) without alienating the female audience, which could enjoy the lavish scenery, dancing, and music (Dudden 7). In his article "The Culture of 'Leg-Work': The Transformation of Burlesque after the Civil War," Peter Buckley argues that these "leg shows" constituted a break with traditional American theater because of their lack of dramatic unity; the unity these shows did achieve was through their use of spectacle, costume, and women's bodies. He further asserts that these "representations of women's bodies and behavior absorbed and masked larger changes in the nature of the social body" (131).

This type of public male consumption of female images can be seen readily in novels such as Paul Laurence Dunbar's *The Sport of the Gods.* Mr. Thomas takes the Hamilton family to a "coon show," which, through its use of female performers in scanty costumes, could also readily be characterized as a "leg show." Although the dynamics of the gaze are significantly complicated by the fact that this display of African-American women is staged in large part for the white audience in attendance, Dunbar also emphasizes the increased opportunities for black spectatorship in the North as he makes sure to note that the Hamiltons have "good seats in the first balcony" in this New York theater, as opposed to the seats "far up in the peanut gallery in the place reserved for people of color" that they occupied in southern theaters (98). The reactions of the Hamiltons are very similar to those of the audiences of the early "leg shows"; while Joe Hamilton is mesmerized by the women onstage whose costumes "were not primarily intended for picnic going," his mother "was divided between shame at the clothes of some of the women and delight with the music" (102–3). The costumes clearly are thought by the narrator to be more proper for viewing in the private sphere (perhaps even only within the confines of the most private of spaces—marriage), but through their public display they become something else entirely. Joe, though, becomes so entranced by this public showing of female flesh that he enters his own private reverie within the public space of the theater. His mother, on the other hand, walks the tightrope between public pleasure and private shame, longing to lose her public identity as a woman in the beauty of the songs, but she is prevented from doing so by her own insistence on the propriety of the separate spheres. In another twist, Mr. Thomas, the Hamiltons' host for the evening, forgoes sharing Joe's consumption of the female spectacle onstage and instead turns Kitty into the sexualized object of his gaze, noting, "She was a pretty girl, little and dainty, but well developed for her age" (103). In this way, Dunbar draws attention to the implications of this public display of female bodies for the private sphere.

The recurrent emphasis on the female body in these novels can also be seen in the way these novels warn, both directly and indirectly, of the dangers for "proper women" in the world of the theater stemming from the seductive tendencies to identify with and try to emulate the actress onstage. Both Kitty in *Sport of the Gods* and Carrie in *Sister Carrie* are seduced into going on the stage largely because of its material associations, making their bodies available for public viewing to fulfill their private longings for status and glamour. For Carrie, the theater often prompts renewed concern with her physical appearance and an increased desire for material objects. When Drouet offers a last-minute invitation, Carrie asks him, "Shall I wear my hair as I did yesterday?" and comes out of her room "with several articles of apparel pending" (120). Her close identification of the theater with material wealth continues even after she goes onstage: "The flare of the gas jets, the open trunks suggestive of travel and display, the scattered contents of the makeup box . . . have a remarkable atmosphere of their own. . . . Here was no illusion. Here was an open door to see all of that. She had come upon it as one who stumbles upon a secret passage, and, behold, she was in the chamber of diamonds and delight" (191–92). Kitty is also seduced by the finery of the stage; she is not easily impressed by showy clothes on the street, but "take the same cheesecloth, put a little water and starch into it, and put it on the stage, and she could see only chiffon." Next, she comments, "This is grand. How I'd like to be an actress and be up there!" (102).

The splendor of the stage is a prime motivator for both women's decisions, but with some important differences. On the surface, Kitty is initially much less susceptible to this form of seduction because her family has long enjoyed an elite class standing among the African-American community in their small southern town which also subtly influences their social position in New York. It is only after Minty Brown's exposure of her father's crime, and the family's subsequent loss of respectability, that the public exposure of the stage seems to be a viable, even necessary, option. On the other hand, Carrie is already vulnerable to the power of the stage because of her precarious class position. And in spite of the fact that Kitty and Carrie seem to be making parallel journeys—from country to city and from private sphere to the public stage—the issue of race cannot be ignored. Carrie may be a sexualized commodity onstage, but Kitty is selling a racialized version of womanhood that is complicated by the fact that her offstage opportunities for financial reward are substantially limited by the same audience that readily consumes her onstage image.

But in addition to the more public danger that women may want to emulate the actresses they see onstage, the women of these novels also face an increased susceptibility to romantic seduction in the private sphere because of the heightened sensual awareness the theater produces. It is when she is at the theater that Carrie's attraction to Hurstwood solidifies. Carrie "was pleased beyond expression, and was really hypnotized by the environment, the trappings of the box, the elegance of her companion [Hurstwood]. . . . Drouet . . . was not in the least aware" (121). Another theater trip clinches Carrie's feelings: "If [Hurstwood] had been pleasing to Carrie before, how much more so was he now. His grace was more permeating because it had found a readier medium. Carrie watched his every movement with pleasure. She almost forget poor Drouet, who babbled on as if he were the host" (152).

Laura in *The Pit* is also more inclined to look favorably on Corthell's advances when she is under the spell of the theater. As she listens to the music, she "shut her eyes. Never had she felt so soothed, so cradled and lulled and languid. Ah, to love like that! To love and be loved" (22). When Corthell declares his love a short while later, Laura is still "all but hypnotized with this marvelous evening" and has difficulty summoning the proper response (23). Even though later, in the clear air of the street, Laura knows she does not love Corthell and has no intention of marrying him, in the romantic atmosphere of the theater she answers him warmly:

> This declaration of his love for her was the last touch to the greatest exhilaration of happiness she had ever known. Ah yes, she was loved, just as that young girl of the opera had been loved. . . .
>
> "Oh, I am glad, glad," she cried, "glad that you love me!" (24)

Later in the novel, when her husband is too busy to accompany her to the theater and she again relies on Corthell as an escort, an affair begins. At first they are just platonic members of the same theater party, but by the next night it leads to an evening visit where "neither [Corthell] nor Laura had spoken of Jadwin throughout the entire evening" (210). Soon, "by slow degrees the companionship trended towards intimacy. At the various theaters and concerts he was her escort. He called upon her two or three times each week. At his studio entertainments Laura was always present" (210). This affair is not long-lived, but the spell of the theater contributes to its viability. The couple's public visibility serves as a type of decoy or distraction from their private relationship, making possible a relationship that would have been unthinkable to Laura early in the novel.

And although it is true that many women became commodified objects of the gaze, it remains important to explore the many opportunities for spectatorship and public pleasure that women enjoyed in the world of the late-nineteenth- and early-twentieth-century theater. Women formed a major component of theater audiences and derived much pleasure from their experiences there. In Frank Norris's *The Pit,* Laura's first trip to the opera is a life-changing event: "The melody was simple, the tempo easily followed; it was not a very high order of music. But to Laura it was nothing short of a revelation. She sat spell-bound, her hands clasped tight, her every faculty of attention at its highest pitch. . . . Never, never was this night to be forgotten, this her first night of Grand Opera" (20–21). Similarly, in *The Sport of the Gods,* Kitty spends her first visit to the theater "enchanted. The airily dressed women seemed to her like creatures from fairy-land" (102). When Dreiser's Carrie Meeber attends the theater, "That spectacle pleased Carrie immensely. The color and grace of it caught her eye. She had vain imaginings about place and power, about far off lands and magnificent people" (87).

The feminine enjoyment of such spectacles, though, is often identified with private-sphere sentiment rather than artistry. In *The Pit,* Corthell, Laura's soon-to-be-erstwhile suitor, remarks, "I am so pleased that you are enjoying it all. . . . I knew you would. There is nothing like music such as this to appeal to the emotions, the heart—and with your temperament—" (31). But this comment only angers Laura, who refuses to have her pleasure reduced to mere feminine sensibility: "Straightway he made her feel her sex. Now she was just a woman again, with all a woman's limitations, and her relations with Corthell could never be—so she realized—any other than sex-relations" (31). The experience of the music had allowed Laura to transcend the limitations of her sex for a moment, to become almost disembodied, as she gave herself over to the pleasures of the ear and eye. She tries to resist the violent return to embodiment that Corthell's comments suggest, but she is not able to lose herself in the last act of the opera as she did with earlier acts. The spell is broken, but Laura carries the memory of pleasure and the moment of public triumph home with her.

The relation between the actress and the female spectator is more complex than this, though; the exchange of looks among the audience members is just as important as those directed toward the stage. Rather than being rendered as a straight line, the look is triangulated (if not further subdivided) as audience members watch each other watching the spectacle onstage. Additionally, the display of fashion among the women is a point of both competition and critique. Bruce McConachie writes: "Throughout the antebellum period it was customary to leave houselights on during the performance, partly to increase spectator visibility of the stage, but mostly to allow the audience to see one another. . . . In effect, the boxes became mini-stages designed to frame their fashionable spectators within small proscenia—stages the elite might use to attract the attention of others when they chose to do so" (50–51). From the very opening of *The Pit,* the focus is much more on the audience than on the stage. In spite of her best efforts, Laura's experience is constantly intruded upon by snatches of overheard conversation. During the intermissions, the "show" does not really stop as program sellers take up their cries and people-watching begins with a vengeance: "Who are those people down there in the third row of the parquet?—see, on the middle aisle—the woman is in red. Aren't those the Gretrys?" (30). And Laura's Aunt Wess finds much to be scandalized by:

> The audience itself had interested her, and the décolleté gowns had been particularly impressing.
>
> "I never saw such dressing in all my life," she declared. "And that woman in the box next to ours. Well! Did you notice *that?*" She raised her eyebrows and set her lips together. "Well, I don't want to say anything." (33)

At one point in *Sister Carrie,* Hurstwood asserts, "You ought to pay for seeing your old friends. Bother the show!" (195), explicitly foregrounding the private-sphere, social function of the theater at the expense of its ostensible public "art."

In *Phases of an Inferior Planet,* Glasgow manages to capture beautifully the interaction of the simultaneous displays of the audience and the stage. Near the end of the novel the main characters find themselves at the opera, and during the interlude between acts Mrs. Darcy turns to Nevins and asks, "Do tell me if that is Mrs. Gore across from us—the one in green and violets?" (256). As the women begin to implicitly criticize her, Algarcife defends the woman who, unbeknownst to the rest of his party, is his former wife. As the curtain rises, Algarcife tries to turn his attention back to the stage, but he cannot: "The figures [onstage] were blurred before his eyes and the glare tortured him. Across the circle of space he knew that Mariana was sitting, her head upraised, her cheek resting upon her hand, her face in the shadow. He could almost see her eyes growing rich and soft like green velvet" (256). As the soprano's voice swells, Algarcife remembers Mariana's passionate words to him so long ago, "I would give half my life for this—to sing with Alvary" (257). At this point, their eyes meet and his memories of their past meld with the story onstage: "The music had changed. It had deepened in color and a new note had throbbed into it—a note of flesh that weighed upon spirit—of disbelief that shadowed fate. The ideal was singing the old lesson of the real found wanting—of passion tarnished by the touch of clay. The ecstasy had fled. Love was not satisfied with itself. It craved knowledge, and the vision beautiful was fading before the eyes of earth. It was the song of the eternal vanquishment of love by distrust, of the eternal failure of faith" (258). The on- and offstage dramas merge, each becoming more powerful than it was standing alone. The spheres are no longer separate but conjoined; the private relationships are inflected by awareness of the public setting and the power of the music, and the events onstage seem a response to the characters' emotions rather than a distraction from them.

Power Plays:
Cultural Capital and the Authority of the Stage

Although the actress is often seen as the object of consumer desire, the pleasures experienced by women in the theater are not limited to those of the spectator. Actresses were powerful figures, both culturally and financially, and often received intangible benefits from their time onstage as well. In *Women in the American Theatre,* Faye Dudden writes of the economic power of actresses who often supported families and ran businesses either alone or in tandem with their husbands. As early as 1792, Susana Rowson, perhaps best known for her novel *Charlotte Temple: A Tale of Truth,* made her living on the stage because "writing books, even best sellers, did not yield a living income in those days" (Dudden 9). In the nineteenth century, figures such as Fanny Kemble, Charlotte Cushman, and Laura Keene parlayed their acting talents into national fame and fortune. With the advent of the mass press and the technological innovations in photography, inexpensive photographs of public figures such as actresses were collected by the public and contributed to "star" status for many performers (Dudden 6, 63, 160–61). In addition, the feelings of potency that come from being applauded by a live audience cannot be discounted. All these forms of power can be seen in the novels of the period, complicating the position of the actress as mere object of specular pleasure. Not only were these women able to successfully finance their private, family lives, they also had access to the public world of cultural power and influence that had seemed an exclusively masculine province.

Money is the most tangible reward of the actress, and this is a consistent theme in all of the novels being discussed. In spite of its dubious moral status, the stage was often the best opportunity for financial independence to many nineteenth-century American women (see Johnson 37–77). In *Women in American Theater,* Helen Chinoy emphasizes the financial rewards for nineteenth-century women of all class backgrounds: "For women of working class origins, the stage has always been a means of moving up socially and economically. In turn, 'ladies' fallen on hard times . . . found the theater, despite its taint of immorality, to be the only paying outlet for the good looks, genteel manners, musical skills, and elocution lessons that had been part of their social education" (58). The socioeconomic mobility experienced by actresses in the nineteenth century is mirrored in the literature of the time. Through her theatrical career, Carrie rises from the squalor of a small rented flat to life in a luxurious hotel that still does not touch her $150-a-week salary. Kitty of *The Sport of the Gods* also uses the stage as a vehicle to financial freedom, but Dunbar foregrounds other, more intangible benefits as well: "From the time that she went on the stage she had begun to live her own life, a life in which the chief aim was the possession of good clothes and the ability to attract the attention which she had learned to crave" (216). While the primary impetus that brings these women to the stage may be their financial survival, the fame they acquire through their theater careers becomes an important component to the power of the stage.

In some instances, fame leads to added financial value. Actresses at the turn of the century often lent their names to commercial products, appearing in national magazines to endorse them: "[Lily Langtry's] flawless complexion graced ads for Pears soap, a leading cosmetic at the time. Popular magazines carried article after article on beauty tips, some authored by such actresses as Billie Burke and Elsie Janis" (McArthur 42). Businesspeople of all types capitalized on women's desire to emulate their favorite stars, giving actresses greater financial power. Carrie herself benefits from this phenomenon as she receives free lodging at the Wellington because, as the manager puts it, "Your name is worth something to us. . . . Every hotel depends on the repute of its patrons. A well-known actress like yourself . . . draws attention to the hotel, and—although you may not believe it—patrons" (498). Her name has taken on a capitalistic value that at once provides her with indirect income and the hotel with more direct remuneration.

Although actresses were shunned by polite society throughout most of the nineteenth century, this attitude shifts at the dawn of the twentieth. While Sarah Bernhardt's 1880 reception was not attended by any society women, and Lillian Russell was asked to leave the clubhouse of Chicago's Washington Park racetrack in 1893, by the late 1890s actresses had become more accepted, even marrying into some of New York society's better families and wielding cultural power in their own right (McArthur 137–41). Along these lines, Carrie receives deferential treatment because of her new position. In striking contrast to the way she was treated by employers earlier in the novel, the cashier at the theater's office gives her the money "accompanied by a smile and a salutation" (505). This contrast is underlined when "one of the insignificant members of the company" behind her in line steps up: "'How much?' said the same cashier sharply" (505). Instead of "climbing several flights of steps" to a shared dressing room, Carrie enjoyed a large, private chamber where "gradually the deference and congratulation gave her a mental appreciation of her state. She was no longer ordered, but requested, and that politely" (496). And this change in treatment is not limited to those who have a financial stake in Carrie. She receives an influx of letters from wealthy men who want to "gratify [her] every desire" (503). Carrie intuitively knows the power of fame as she muses early on, "Ah, if she could only be an actress—a good one! This man [Ames] was wise—he knew—and he approved of it. If she were a fine actress, such men as he would approve of her" (358–59). In this way, the power of the actress in the public sphere spills over into the private, leading to ever-increasing opportunity and social mobility.

It is obvious in *Phases of an Inferior Planet* that the draw of the theater is more than financial for Mariana. From the opening of the novel, the stage is her greatest desire. She has already bought into the system of worship of stage personalities and idolizes the opera singer Alvary, mooning over his picture in the shop and dreaming yet despairing of ever singing grand opera with him. She continues her singing lessons even after her marriage, but turns down her first job offer in spite of the family's dire financial circumstances. A doctor had recently told the young family that their baby would not survive the sweltering New York City summer and needed to be taken to the seaside for relief, but they could not afford to go. Mariana sees this job as the only chance they have to take the baby away from the city, but her husband refuses to consider the possibility of his wife's going on the stage. Even though she frames her argument in terms of their financial needs and the baby's health and welfare, a personal note creeps in: "We need the money. It might take Isolde away—and it is a chance. I am so young, you see—and—" (151). She knows that her youth is a marketable commodity and that her chances of beginning a stage career are slipping away with each year. In fact, Mariana is being quite realistic; the chances of a stage career dropped dramatically for women after age 35. According to a 1900 census, 48.8 percent of actresses were between 16 and 24 and another 36.7 percent were between 25 and 34. Only 14.1 percent of actresses were over 35 (see McArthur 29). But her husband manages to convince her that her responsibilities in the private sphere preclude her participation in the public world of the stage, at least at that moment in her life.

After the death of her baby, however, Mariana can no longer tolerate life in the cramped apartment building with its ever-present smell of cabbage. She comes home from her voice lesson one day and tells Algarcife that she is leaving him to go on the road with a theater company. She explains, "It is not choice. . . . It is necessity. What else is there to do—except starve? Can we go on living like this, day after day, you killing yourself with work, I a drag?" (172). While again she foregrounds their lack of money, Glasgow also notes that she had come in from her voice lesson "cheerfully, and that a wave of her lost freshness had returned to her face" (168). While money is a powerful draw for Mariana, the fact that she does not leave the family earlier shows that it is not her sole concern. Their financial position is no worse than before, and possibly a bit better with the reduced household size, but this time it is different: "She wanted to flee from the sorrow she had known and all of its associations; she wanted to flee from poverty and ugliness to beauty and bright colors. The artistic genius of her nature was calling, calling, and she thrilled into an answering echo" (175). She talks of quitting the stage if she is successful enough, but Algarcife knows she will not return. Near the end of the novel he berates her for her choice, accusing, "Do you think . . . that I would have left you while there remained a crust to live on? Do you think that I would not have starved with you rather than have lived in luxury without you?" (293). There is a struggle for Mariana between the domestic sphere and the public world of the stage, but money alone is not enough to make her leave her home. It is only after the death of her child that the balance swings in favor of the stage; her husband, with his focus on the financial elements of her decision, misses the regenerative power that the stage holds for her in her grief. It allows her to escape her personal pain and believe, for a while at least, that "it would end well" (275).

Another often-neglected aspect of the stage is the personal power of the actress over the audience. Early on, Carrie imagines the power of acting, asking herself, "How often had she looked at the well-dressed actresses on the stage and wondered how she would look, how delightful she would feel if only she were in their place. The glamour, the tense situation, the fine clothes, the applause, these had lured her until she felt that she, too, could act—that she, too, could compel acknowledgment of power" (174). She thrives onstage and is transformed in Drouet's eyes: "She was more than the old Carrie" to him (204). While Carrie onstage is mesmerizing to both men, her power over them carries over into her offstage life: "They only saw their idol, moving about with appealing grace, continuing a power which to them was a revelation. Hurstwood resolved a thousand things, Drouet as well" (209). Carrie senses a shift in the balance of power almost immediately: "She was realizing now what it was to be petted. For once, she was the admired, the sought-for. The independence of success now made its first faint showing. With the tables turned, she was looking down, rather than up, to her lover" (210). The power of the stage gives her power over men, power that was not available to her as a poor factory girl.

And Carrie is not the only woman to experience this power. In *The Sport of the Gods,* Hattie and her onstage cohorts hold a power over Joe that is almost hypnotic: "He was lost, transfixed. His soul was floating on a sea of sense. He had eyes and ears and thoughts only for the stage. His nerves tingled and his hands twitched. Only to know one of those radiant creatures, to have her speak to him, smile at him! If ever a man was intoxicated, Joe was" (103). When he finally meets her, he is so overcome he is "near collapsing" (126). This inversion of the stereotype of the "fainting female" gives Hattie access to masculine power that is usually denied to women. But when Hattie the actress inevitably is converted to Hattie the mistress, the spell of the stage (and her hold over Joe) weakens. Although she is not able to maintain her influence within the private sphere, the onstage moments in this and other novels gave nineteenth-century women a hint of the public power that their male counterparts enjoyed as a matter of course.

Offstage Acting

As has just been shown, turn-of-the-century American women had some access to power through their theatrical performances. What is often overlooked, though, is the role of performance in the offstage lives of these women. While theorizing the role of the female spectator of modern-day cinema, Mary Ann Doane critiques Laura Mulvey's formulation of the female spectator as transvestite and foregrounds the role of the masquerade in the production of a feminine subject position:

The masquerade, in flaunting femininity, holds it at a distance. Woman-liness is a mask which can be worn or removed. The masquerade's re-sistance to patriarchal positioning would therefore lie in its denial of the production of femininity as closeness, as presence-to-itself, as, pre-cisely, imagistic. . . . To masquerade is to manufacture a lack in the form of a certain distance between oneself and one's image. . . . By destabilizing the image, the masquerade confounds this masculine structure of the look. It effects a destabilization of female iconography. (235)

In other words, by emphasizing the artificiality of the feminine, women can wield a certain type of destabilizing power. By "acting" their identities as though they were roles in a play, women undermine the essentialist no-tions of gender divisions and stereotypes. In essence, femininity becomes a public construct rather than an exemplum of private-sphere ideology. Judith Butler expands on this notion, arguing that the construction of gender itself is only attained through repeated social actions, explicitly tying what she terms "gender performance" to the rhetoric of theater criticism:

Gender reality is performative which means, quite simply, that it is real only to the extent that it is performed. . . . That gender reality is created through sustained social performances means that the very no-tions of an essentialist sex, a true or abiding masculinity or femininity, are also constituted as part of the strategy by which the performative aspect of gender is concealed. . . . As a consequence, gender cannot be understood as a *role* which either expresses or disguises an interior "self." . . . As a performance which is performative, gender is an "act," broadly construed which constructs the social fiction of its own psychological interiority. (527–28, emphasis Butler's)

In Butler's formulation, then, the notion of performance is primary to the formation of gender; men and women are created as gendered beings through the constitutive acts that comprise their gender roles. Read in this context, issues of theatricality and performance do not end at the wings of the stage; instead, the characters in these novels can be seen quite con-sciously playing "the masquerade" and performing their femininity in other places than the narrowly defined theater.

The concept of offstage acting is not a new one in the critical work analyzing Dreiser's *Sister Carrie*. In her article "Taking a Part: Actor and Audience in *Sister Carrie*," Deborah Garfield argues, "Dreiser labors to de-pict the city as a mega-stage, an extension of the theater . . . Dreiser blurs the distinction between theater and world through language which gradu- ally defines the two as twin spheres—each a reflection of the other" (224). Philip Gerber also explores the theatricality of the novel in his article "The Tangled Web: Offstage Acting in *Sister Carrie*," emphasizing Carrie's many changes in character and costume. But neither of these articles links Carrie's offstage performances to her specific subject position of a woman in search of socioeconomic mobility. Early in the novel, Carrie begins to mimic the mannerisms of other women she sees in order to improve her own station; Carrie "perceive[d] the nature and value of those little modish ways which women adopt when they would presume to be something. . . . She began to get the hang of those little things which the pretty woman who has vanity invariably adopts. In short, her knowledge of grace doubled, and with it her appearance changed. She became a girl of considerable taste" (116). By out- wardly performing the role of "stylish young woman," Carrie is able to become one, as shown by Hurstwood's initial reaction, "giv[ing] her credit for feelings superior to Drouet at the first glance" (117). Rather than being beneath Drouet socially as she was at the beginning of the novel, she is now ready to rise above him. Similarly, Carrie performs the roles of respectable wife and great actress; her ability to adapt to her changing circumstances, which often leads to the criticism that the character Dreiser created is in- herently unstable and flawed (see Witemeyer, Matheson, and Lehan for some examples of this argument), is crucial to her ability to rise socially and eco- nomically by the end of the novel. When viewed in the light of Doane's notion of the destabilizing qualities of the masquerade, Carrie's various per- sonae are simply more evidence of the power of offstage acting.

In *The Pit*, offstage acting appears in various guises. Norris often juxta- poses stage scenes with "real-life" dramas, emphasizing the theatricality of the larger world of the novel. The recurrence of scenes set within the theater in this novel that purports to expose the machinations of the wheat market is no accident. In the opening scene, the opera onstage is constantly interrupted by conversations about the day's activities in the commodities market:

> Close by—the lights were so low she could not tell where—a conver- sation, kept up in low whispers, began by degrees to intrude itself upon her attention. Try as she would she could not shut it out, and now, as the music died away fainter and fainter, till voice and orchestra blended together in a single, barely audible murmur, vibrating with emotion, with romance, and with sentiment, she heard, in a hoarse, masculine whisper, the words:

"The shortage is a million bushels at the very least. Two hundred carloads were to arrive from Milwaukee last night—" (22)

And only moments later:

The soprano vanished, only to reappear on the balcony of the pavilion, and while she declared that the stars and the night bird together sang "He loves thee," the voices close at hand continued:
"—one hundred and six carloads—"
"—paralyzed the bulls—"
"—fifty thousand dollars—" (23)

This motif of commodities talk alternated with theatrical performance draws attention to the high drama that surrounded the stock market, a place where fortunes were made and lost overnight. But Norris does not limit this technique to the drama of the wheat; he also draws attention to more personal dramas within the novel. Corthell first declares his love for Laura during a theatrical intermission. Likewise, Jadwin's proposal to Laura takes place in the middle of an amateur play rehearsal, Laura's first and only attempt at the actual stage. In this way, Norris draws parallels between onstage acting and the type that takes place offstage, allowing for a much broader definition of "theater" than is usually considered.

Laura ultimately chooses offstage acting over the world of the theater, but that does not mean that she stops thinking of herself as an actress:

She knew that there was another Laura Jadwin—the Laura Jadwin who might have been a great actress, who had a "temperament," who was impulsive. This was the Laura of the "grand manner," who played the role of the great lady from room to room of her vast house, . . . who affected black velvet, black jet, and black lace in her gowns, who was conscious and proud of her pale, stately beauty. (184–85)

She is uncomfortable with her husband's wealth at first, but she actively and consciously performs her role as a rich man's wife and finally comes to enjoy it:

Innocently enough, and with a harmless, almost childlike, affectation, she posed a little, and by so doing found the solution of the incongruity between herself—the "Laura of moderate means and quiet life"—and the massive luxury with which she was now surrounded. Without

> knowing it, she began to act the part of a great lady—and she acted it
> well. . . . She gave herself into the hands of her maid, not as Laura
> Jadwin of herself would have done it, clumsily and with the constraint
> of inexperience, but as she would have done it if she were acting the
> part on the stage, with an air, with all the nonchalance of a marquise,
> with—in fine—all the condescension of her "grand manner." (157)

Like Carrie, Laura is able to use her public, performative ability to achieve private class mobility. Her offstage acting serves her well as she attempts to renegotiate the boundaries of the private sphere.

At times, Laura's performances become even more obvious as she moves to regain the sentimental power over her husband that she held in the early days of their marriage. At first she is lost without her husband's attention and tries out new personae just as another woman might try on clothes, doing charity work, then, just as suddenly, putting on a "performance" at the racetrack (213). Her next whim includes building a stage in the ballroom of her house and rehearsing the part of Lady Macbeth "for three days uninterruptedly, dressed in elaborate costume, declaiming in chest tones to the empty room" (213). When next she appears in stage costume, she has "planned a little surprise" for her husband (225). When Jadwin arrives home after a long day, he finds Laura dressed as Bernhardt's Theodora, illuminated by a lamp, as if in a spotlight. Confused, he sputters, "But—Lord, what will you do next? Whatever put it into your head to get into this rig?" (226). But Laura is undaunted; she is sure that she can recapture her husband's love with this performance if only she can pick the right character. She abandons Theodora and, insisting, "I am anything I choose," assumes the role of Athalia, an Old Testament queen (226). Then, with a quick costume change, she becomes Carmen, dancing a seductive bolero for Jadwin. But, sadly, her ploy fails because Jadwin really prefers her in her domestic role, warning her, "I wouldn't . . . do too much of that. It's sort of overwrought—a little, and unnatural. I like you best when you are your old self, quiet and calm, dignified. It's when you are quiet that you are at your best" (228). What Jadwin does not realize is that the "quiet and calm" Laura is just as much of a performance as is her Carmen. The traditional boundaries of the private and public spheres collapse when seen in this light, forcing a redefinition of both.

In all of these novels, the authors tease apart the contradictions inherent in the public/private binary. While femininity is associated with the private sphere, paradoxically, it is only available through its public performance. Actresses themselves serve as a focal point for these contradictions because of their very embodiment of public femininity, yet the novels also show how the trope of acting pervades the private sphere as well as the public. The cultural and financial power that these women wield is quite public, yet it inflects their private-sphere relationships and living conditions. Finally, the theater itself serves as a locus of public spectatorship, of seeing and being seen, for nineteenth-century American women, intersecting the oft-cited boundary between the spheres.

Works Cited

Buckley, Peter G. "The Culture of 'Leg-Work': The Transformation of Burlesque after the Civil War." *The Mythmaking Frame of Mind.* Ed. James Gilbert, Amy Gilman, Donald M. Scott, and Joan Scott. Belmont, CA: Wadsworth, 1993. 113–34.

Butler, Judith. "Performative Acts and Gender Constitution: An Essay in Phenomenology and Feminist Theory." *Theatre Journal* 40 (1988): 519–31.

Chinoy, Helen Crida, and Linda Walsh Jenkins, eds. *Women in American Theater.* Rev. and expanded ed. New York: Theater Communications Group, 1987.

Crane, Stephen. *Maggie: A Girl of the Streets.* Ed. Thomas Gullason. New York: Norton, 1979.

Doane, Mary Ann. "Film and the Masquerade: Theorizing the Female Spectator." *The Sexual Subject: A Screen Reader in Sexuality.* New York: Routledge, 1992. 227–43.

Dreiser, Theodore. *Sister Carrie.* 1900. New York: Merrill, 1969.

Dudden, Faye E. *Women in the American Theatre: Actresses and Audiences, 1790–1870.* New Haven: Yale UP, 1994.

Dunbar, Paul Laurence. *The Sport of the Gods.* 1902. Miami: Mnemosyne, 1969.

Garfield, Deborah. "Taking a Part: Actor and Audience in *Sister Carrie.*" *American Literary Realism* 16.2 (1983): 223–39.

Gerber, Philip L. "The Tangled Web: Offstage Acting in *Sister Carrie.*" *Dreiser Newsletter* 17.2 (1986): 1–8.

Glasgow, Ellen. *Phases of an Inferior Planet.* New York: Harper and Brothers, 1898.

Johnson, Claudia D. *American Actress: Perspective on the Nineteenth Century.* Chicago: Nelson-Hall, 1984.

Lehan, Richard. "*Sister Carrie:* The City, the Self, and Modes of Narrative Discourse." *New Essays on Sister Carrie.* Ed. Donald Pizer. Cambridge: Harvard UP, 1991. 65–85.

Matheson, Terence J. "The Two Faces of *Sister Carrie:* The Characterization of Dreiser's First Heroine." *Ariel: A Review of International English Literature* 11.4 (1980): 71–86.

McArthur, Benjamin. *Actors and American Culture, 1880–1920.* Philadelphia: Temple UP, 1984.

McConachie, Bruce A. "Pacifying American Theatrical Audiences, 1820–1900." *For*

Fun and Profit: The Transformation of Leisure into Consumption. Ed. Richard Butsch. Philadelphia: Temple UP, 1990. 47–70.

McElrath, Joseph R., Jr., and Gwendolen Jones. Introduction. *The Pit: A Story of Chicago*. By Frank Norris. New York: Penguin Books, 1994. vii–xxx.

Mulvey, Laura. "Visual Pleasure and Narrative Cinema." *Visual and Other Pleasures*. Bloomington: Indiana UP, 1989. 14–28.

Norris, Frank. *The Pit*. New York: Collier, 1903.

Witemeyer, Hugh. "Gaslight and Magic Lamp in *Sister Carrie*." *PMLA* 86 (1971): 236–40.

PART IV

Sentimental Subversions

Gender Valences of Transcendentalism: The Pursuit of Idealism in Elizabeth Oakes-Smith's "The Sinless Child"

MARY LOUISE KETE

In 1841, an anonymous reviewer for the *Boston Notion* wrote the following summary of a long narrative poem that had recently appeared:

> The object of the writer appears to be the exhibition of a pure and gentle being, whose mind and affections are so harmoniously developed and so beautifully blended, that everything she sees takes the hue of her thoughts, and all outward nature moulds itself into accordance with her feelings; until the child, in her communings with nature, is supposed to see through the crust of creation, and to become cognizant of the spirit and moral meaning it contains. (34)

If it were not for the feminine pronouns, it would be easy to think the reviewer was discussing one of William Wordsworth's poems. In fact, this same reviewer makes this association explicit by explaining that the "poem strongly suggests to the mind the beautiful lines of Wordsworth, in which he sets platonism to sweeter music than it has found since the time of its founder." Given the propensity of nineteenth-century literary magazines to "puff" the work of authors, it is a surprise to find that the author of the poem being referred to does indeed describe the possibilities and the results of the pursuit of idealism. Like Wordsworth in his *Prelude* or in his "Ode: Intimations of Immortality," the author, Elizabeth Oakes-Smith, insists in "The Sinless Child" (1841) that this pursuit serves the growth of the poet's mind. I would like to suggest that Oakes-Smith (1806–93) is a full participant, with Ralph Waldo Emerson, Henry Thoreau, and Margaret Fuller, in the work of articulating the parameters of the American romantic movement. Sharing with these others the desire to articulate the personal and social possibilities of transcendence, Oakes-Smith refuses to abandon the possibilities of a subjectivity bound by the contingencies of both gender and nation.

In this way "The Sinless Child" asks us to reexamine the nature of the boundaries between the spheres of gender and genre that have been erected by nineteenth- and twentieth-century literary historians. I realize that in making this suggestion I am crossing several spheres that have been separated by the conventions of literary history: American romanticism and British romanticism, romanticism and sentimentalism, women's writing and men's writing, American women's writing and American men's writing. But as this collection (and as the recent "special issue" of *American Literature* on the topic of "No More Separate Spheres") shows, the revisions of literary history that have been under way since the mid-1970s are calling for a new set of paradigms as these older ones cease to be useful. From this brief discussion of Oakes-Smith's poem I hope to, at least, show that "The Sinless Child" is best understood as a transcendentalist, and thus romantic, text. It shares with Emerson and Thoreau a concern with interpretation and a set of assumptions about nature, self-creation, and the family. I also hope to show that the project of articulating a feminine transcendentalism was a problematic one for women writers. Oakes-Smith, for one, was unable or unwilling to succumb to the lure of giving up a relational conception of personal subjectivity that was, and remains, so vital a part of the ideology of femininity.

More importantly, I would like to suggest that our understanding of American transcendentalism is due to be reconfigured once we take the contributions of women writers seriously and once we set them beside those of their male contemporaries. This is not, of course, a new project but a continuation—with a difference—of the feminist revisions of American literary history that began in the late 1960s. As renewed interest (in the form of conferences, journal articles, and literary biographies) in the figures of Margaret Fuller, Lydia Maria Child, and Harriet Beecher Stowe testifies, these revisions have brought women writers into the foreground of academic attention.[1] Only now, after so many years of such work, has a critical mass of antebellum women writers begun to take shape: beyond the familiar figures, we now glimpse Lydia Sigourney, Harriet Jacobs, Fanny Osgood, Lydia Child, Frances Harper, Susan Warner, Harriet Wilson, Maria Cummins, Elizabeth Peabody, Elizabeth Stuart Phelps, Elizabeth Oakes-Smith, and others. The field of transcendentalist studies has been, perhaps, less affected by these revisions than others. But it is, perhaps, harder now to avoid teaching Fuller (at least) and easier for college students to understand the ongoing active role of women in shaping American culture.[2]

This kind of feminist activity, the primary scholarly work of revealing the contributions of women writers, editors, educators, and readers, needs to continue. However, while the project I am suggesting here relies on this kind of historical work, it differs from it significantly. If the work of one kind of feminist literary history has been to fill in the faces of Hawthorne's "damned mob of scribbling women," it is now possible to engage in another kind of feminist literary history by examining the nature and function of gender within various discourses and literary movements. The questions we can now begin to consider include the following: Is transcendentalism gendered—meaning, is it marked as feminine or masculine? Does transcendentalism carry only one gender marker—is, for example, transcendentalism a masculine discourse by definition, or can it carry the mark of either gender or even another gender? The question I am ultimately interested in is this: What work do these marks of gender do for the authors and for the project of transcendentalism?

In "The Sinless Child," Oakes-Smith both explores the foundations of poetic subjectivity and lays the groundwork for her own authority as a woman poet.[3] Oakes-Smith's contemporaries—Edgar Allan Poe, Rufus Griswold, Henry Tuckerman, and the anonymous reviewer cited above— recognized her role in the formation of the new social and aesthetic norms we now call romanticism. This has been more difficult for twentieth-century critics to see. The separation of American literary traditions, so nicely described by Joanne Dobson, into two binary categories—serious and masculine versus frivolous and feminine—posits a disjunction between Oakes-Smith's early "sentimental" works and her later role as a women's rights activist, and an even wider disjunction between the work of Oakes-Smith and the work of the male "Adamic" poets.[4] I have argued elsewhere that these conceptual categories do not help us understand Oakes-Smith's work that well at all.[5] I have become increasingly interested in the way this particular poem demonstrates one woman's effort to take up the challenge, posed by Emerson's *Nature,* of "restoring to the world original and eternal beauty" (*Selections* 55). "The Sinless Child" results from a struggle to articulate an American romanticism in response to British and Continental exemplars, a struggle that is no different from those which better-known figures such as Fuller, Emerson, Thoreau, and Marsh had with Goethe, Schiller, Swedenborg, and Coleridge. We might, then, expand Dobson's list of no-longer-operative binaries to include that of romanticism versus sentimentalism where romanticism becomes just one of the terms associated with and almost synonymous with "serious/masculine" literature and sentimental with "frivolous/feminine" literature (164). Like Emerson, Oakes-Smith offers a transcendentalist critique of materialist society by positing the salutary effect of a "lover of nature" whose "inward and outward senses are still truly adjusted to each other; who has retained the spirit of infancy even into the era of manhood" (*Selections* 23). Like Thoreau in *Walden* (and unlike Emerson and Fuller, who rely mainly on the nonfiction genre of the essay), Oakes-Smith turns to narrative to imagine the conditions under which these transcendentalist ideals of direct, unmediated communion with nature and soul can take place. But unlike Thoreau's hero of *Walden*, the protagonist of Oakes-Smith's transcendental adventure is an American girl; and that, as we shall see, makes all the difference.

Before going on, I would like to briefly introduce Elizabeth Oakes-Smith as a popular poet, novelist, speaker, and journalist who deserves more critical attention from those interested in nineteenth-century literature and culture. She has been the subject of an increasing amount of attention from feminist literary historians, and rightly so, for her career spanned almost the whole of the nineteenth century and nearly the entire spectrum of life-styles available to nineteenth-century white New England women.[6] Married at sixteen to the then-famous Seba Smith, who was twice her age, she was an eager autodidact whose literary talents maintained the family after (as was characteristic of Jacksonian America) her husband lost all his money in bad land speculations. As a writer she experimented with almost all the literary genres of the era: narrative poems, lyric poems, temperance tales, domestic novels, lyceum speeches, newspaper articles, didactic essays. She was active in many reform movements, and by the 1840s she had established herself as a leading figure in the literary salons of New York City. She counted both Poe and Emerson as friends and became a national celebrity as one of the earliest women to be featured on the lyceum circuit, where she argued for expanded rights and protections for women. She shocked her audiences by arguing for women's right to vote as well as for the rights of married women to control their own property. Horace Greeley printed her lyceum lectures as a series, "Woman and Her Needs," in his *New York Tribune,* and these were later issued in a popular book-length collection. In postwar New York, with her husband dead and her children grown, she became a founding member of the Sorosis Society (the first professional women's club) and ended her life as a minister to a congregation of Christian spiritualists.

Although Oakes-Smith had published numerous pieces in the 1830s, "The Sinless Child" established her reputation as a serious poet. It was published first by the *Southern Literary Messenger* (under Poe's aegis) in 1841 and was republished in at least three more editions during the following decade. The edition I have worked from was published by Wiley and Putnam of

New York and Ticknor of Boston in 1843 and inscribed by hand "with sisterly regards of the Author" to an unknown recipient in 1854. It was a popular and influential text, as evidenced by Stowe's use of "The Sinless Child" as the source for her figure of the saintly Eva in *Uncle Tom's Cabin*. One of the reasons for the poem's popularity was explained by contemporary reviewer Henry Tuckerman for *Graham's* magazine: Oakes-Smith had "long been a frequent and admired contributor to our literary periodicals," so her audience was predisposed to favor her attempt to develop the "abstract theory" of "Wordsworth's philosophy" (xxvii).But,Tuckerman stresses, her popularity derived from the combination of two particular traits: "the truly feminine" and the distinctly "American" character of "Mrs. Smith's genius" (xxviii, xxx).

"The Sinless Child" is written in rhymed octets (ABCBDEFE) and features all the conventions of romantic narrative verse: apostrophe, embellished language, poetic dialogue, embedded narratives. It is a narrative poem in seven cantos, each introduced by a prose precis (à la Wordsworth in *The Prelude*). The action of the poem, in brief, tells the story of a fatherless girl-child, Eva, who lives with her mother in a rural home until her death in young womanhood. However, the story of Eva's life and death is itself only a way of illustrating another story: how the narrator comes to be, herself, a poet. The cantos of the poem are preceded by a five-stanza apostrophe to the character Eva that explicitly links her protagonist with the first-person narrator. Eva, the protagonist, is the unnamed first-person omniscient narrator's own "spirit's cherished dream, / Its pure ideal birth" (Inscription 1.1–8 and 2.1). The character of Eva is the "Ideal" aspect of the narrator which "fosters" her "heart's pure, youthful dew" and, in turn, allows the narrator to minister to "kindred hearts" with the object of winning the "spirit back again, / To Love, and Peace, and Youth" (Inscription 4.3–5 and 5.4–8). Eva, the "Inscription" suggests, is also Oakes-Smith's version of the Emersonian poet imagined as a woman; she is the namer, the one who reconnects things to themselves and makes even the ugly beautiful. She is the aspect of the poet's self that allows the narrator to speak her "meter making arguments," arguments that are the vehicle for the restoration of several selves to themselves within the poem.

The action of the plot consists merely in Eva's growing to adulthood; her heroism is signaled by successful resistance to integration with the conventional social world. Oakes-Smith's sinless child "communes" directly with nature, learning its language even before her mother's tongue. Neither seeking nor having relationships with other children, she grows up accompanied by the spirits of the plants and forest creatures that surround her. The daughter of a widowed mother, Eva has no father. Like Hawthorne's Hester Prynne, Eva's mother is as unable to comprehend her daughter as she is unable to decipher the language of the flowers. Both her own daughter and the world of nature are equally obscure to the mother. Taking meaning neither from her filial relationship nor from a human cohort group, Eva remains incorruptibly "true" to herself and, on this basis, is able to minister to the benighted spirit of her poor and conventional mother. The explicitly gendered nature of Oakes-Smith's idealism becomes clearer once it is the "noonday of Eva's earthly existence" when "cometh the mystery of womanhood" (Precis 4). At this point, Eva's transcendental ministry extends to a young man who has been even more damaged by society than her mother. Oakes-Smith introduces the figure of the "hair-brained Albert Linne" whose dissolute life is changed by a brief encounter with Eva in the forest. This moment is the culmination of Eva's earthly life; for, having achieved a "marriage of souls" with Albert which returns him to himself, she returns to the spirit world by dying to Albert and her mother.

Much of the poem is devoted to the transcendentalist problematics of interpretation. The first canto illustrates the way Oakes-Smith characterizes Eva's interpretative powers: "she is gifted with the power of interpreting the beautiful mysteries of our earth" (Precis 1). The veins of flower petals and the songs of birds are transparent hieroglyphics (1.11). In true Swedenborgian tradition, the outer world, to Eva, is but a type of the "internal" through which she "beholds divine agency in all things" (Precis 1). Eva's interpretative powers stem from the fact that she lives in undisturbed sympathy with the natural world: her teachers are beneficent insects, and her playmates are songbirds. This sympathy is the foundation of her unmediated comprehension of the languages of nature: "For her a language was impressed / On every leaf that grew" (1.11.85–86) or "Each tiny leaf became a scroll / inscribed with holy truth" (1.12.89–90).

These things teach Eva of the reciprocity between the human and natural worlds. In her first speech, in fact, Eva explains that

> all noisome weeds
> Would pass from earth away,
> When virtue in the human heart
> Held its predestined way. (1.18.137–40)

Eva understands that it is possible to lose the ability to interpret nature correctly from her mother's constant mis-recognitions: where Eva lingering after dark in the woods sees and takes comfort in a "still moon in a saffron sky" (2.15.113) and experiences communion with "Ethereal forms with whom she talked" (2.18.141), her mother experiences something quite different:

> For every jagged limb to her
> A shadowy semblance hath,
> Of spectres and distorted shapes,
> That frown upon her path. (2.17.129–32)

The narrator's explanation, which Eva reiterates in a sermon later in the poem to her mother, is given in the last three lines of the octet:

> For when the soul is blind
> To freedom, truth and inward light,
> Vague fears debase the mind. (2.17.134–36)

Her mother, Eva knows, is bound by "the cords of earth" that deprive the human soul of all "its freshness" and freedom—and, most of all, of itself (2.3.18). The dangers of misinterpretation are clearly gendered. The most important type or figure of one whose perception of ideal reality has been corrupted is a mother. This corruption separates her from the solace of nature and from closeness with her daughter. Oakes-Smith depicts the figure of the mother as trying to corrupt the daughter by insisting that the daughter fulfill the conventional expectations of feminine behavior which have so crippled her. Eva's knowledge, which allows her to resist and to correct her mother, is authoritative in the best of all transcendentalist ways: it is immediate, unconventional, and stems from adherence both to nature and the self. In the third canto Eva encapsulates this knowledge:

> That union of the thought and soul
> With all that's good and bright,
> The blessedness of earth and sky,
> The growing truth and light. (3.15.17–20)

In contrast to Thoreau's efforts to achieve even a temporary sense of being able to translate through analogy the relationships between symbols, organic matter, and inorganic matter (as in the famous meditation on the melting bank from *Walden*), Eva does not translate at all—she immediately comprehends, without mediation, the "beauteous language" of nature.

"The Sinless Child" also participates in the transcendentalist project by imagining the conditions under which a person might achieve self-reliance. In this case, however, the endpoint of transcendental metamorphosis is not "manhood" but "womanhood." Like Thoreau, Emerson, and Fuller, Oakes-Smith stresses that one of the conditions of self-reliance is immersion in nature. Oakes-Smith's transcendent individual exists "without"—outside of—society. However, where the object of Thoreau's experiment at Walden Pond of his night in the Concord jail is to cantilever himself to a position "without society" so that he might begin to recover a direct, morning relation to the world, Eva begins in that relation and is never displaced from it. She has, and never loses, a morning knowledge.

Not only does Oakes-Smith place Eva deep in a forest away from neighbors and the corruption of social institutions such as schools and churches, but she also places Eva within a curiously fashioned family in which conventional power relations are absent or inverted. In contrast to much sentimental literature in which the relationship between parent and child (and in particular mother and daughter) is paramount, Oakes-Smith joins with the transcendentalists in eschewing parental influence. The poem depicts a conspicuous failure of communication between daughter and mother that at times comes to the brink of antagonism. It is not the mother who teaches the daughter, but nature; and later it is the daughter who protects and teaches the mother from the vantage point of her superior interpretative powers. Nature supplants the mother as teacher in this poem as the daughter later displaces the mother. If for Wordsworth the "child is the father of the man," for Oakes-Smith the child is the mother of the woman. Eva's self-authorizing authority is directly related to and dependent upon Eva's freedom from the interference of either mother or father.

Even more important to Oakes-Smith's project of imagining a transcendent woman is her choice to make Eva a fatherless child: "No Father's lip her brow had kissed, / Or breathed for her a prayer" (1.2.9–10). While the lack of a father causes her mother's "widowed breast" to heave with "doubt and care," it seems to liberate Eva as it leaves her open to the unmediated indoctrination of nature, for neither the name of the father nor the father's law is ever imposed on her (1.2.11–12). Eva herself realizes that the sublimation of the ordinary into transcendence is dependent upon her independence from human relationships. In response to her mother's urgings that she "learn to look and love, / And claim a lover's prayer" (3.12.93–94), Eva says "Nay Mother! I must be alone, / With no companion here" (3.13.97–98). Her own experience with her mother has taught her that "the gift of thought" causes people to "shrink away" (3.14.105–6). This protagonist, then, is in debt to no person as the "author" or authority of her interpretative strategies.

Thoreau explains in his narrative, *Walden,* that he went into the woods to try to live deliberately, to make sure that when he died he would not discover that he had not lived. Oakes-Smith's text poses a similar antagonism between the material world and the world of the ideal. This antagonism is played out as several battles of interpretation. First, as I mentioned before, there is the complex antagonism between mother and child. Where the mother interprets her own condition of widowhood as one of loss and loneliness, her infant daughter smiles and is at ease (Canto 1). This antagonism on the preverbal level is not resolved until the daughter has mastered both the language of nature *and* the language of her mother. These languages exist in a clear hierarchy: it is into nature's superior and antecedent language that Eva translates the language of society—the language her mother speaks. In this way, Eva is able to understand her mother's fears of the woods and darkness even as she tries to teach her mother the language that would enable her to translate the sounds and sights that scare her into the messages of solace they contain. Eva's superior powers of interpretation allow her to interpret society and its discourses better than her mother can even though Eva has had no direct social experience. Canto 4 takes the shape of a story told, but only partially understood, by the mother to Eva. As the precis explains, "Eva supplies portions [of the story] unknown to her mother, and enlarges" upon it so that it becomes an exemplum of the power of conscience and of the power of Eva as reader of "that mystic book—the human soul." The antagonism between the mother and the child is resolved by the mother's acquiescence to Eva's superior morality as manifested by her superior interpretations. Like the narrator, of whom Eva is a younger, re-membered version and for whom Eva serves as muse, the mother is left at the conclusion of the poem alone but with the solace of having learned the lessons Eva has taught her about the transcendence of souls and of the translatability of all signs. This interpretative agon between daughter and mother signals Oakes-Smith's discomfort with maternal collaborations with patriarchal society and rewrites what Emerson describes as the agon of the American scholar with the sepulchres of European culture as struggle between women.

However, Oakes-Smith poses a second conflict between the salutary idealism of Eva and the materialism of American society when she introduces a third character to the forest scene. This second order of interpretive conflict successfully contains the feminist impulse of the first while underscoring the transcendental import of Oakes-Smith's argument. Oakes-Smith is not attempting to escape from the bounds of gender into the boundless ideal, but to use the ideal to enforce what she sees as a more salutary set of gender parameters. Albert Linne, a hunter, comes upon Eva as she sleeps in the forest. He is not only "hair-brained" but "reckless" and violent toward women and toward the creatures of nature:

A reckless youth was Albert Linne,
With licensed oath and jest,
Who little cared for woman's fame,
Or peaceful maiden's rest. (6.9.65–68)

Oakes-Smith several times hints that Linne's wonted and socially "licensed" treatment of women is little different from what we would call rape. Women, the narrator attests, have been misinterpreted by Linne as things to by taken and wasted like the animals he carelessly hunts. This misinterpretation has been the source of Linne's alienation from his authentic self and has resulted in amoral, though socially approved, behavior. One look at Eva, however, causes Linne to look "within his very soul" and to reinterpret his past actions and correct his present ones. She has returned (or as Emerson would say adverted) him to himself. Oakes-Smith's poem concludes that this work—of returning others to themselves—is the ultimate work of Eva. The speaker of the poem—the teller of Eva's story—is healed of her own self-alienation just as Eva's mother and Albert Linne are: through Eva's idealized agency.

But Albert Linne also does important work for Eva. By this time in the story Oakes-Smith tells of her protagonist's development, Eva has attained what would seem to be transcendental perfection: "She hath held communion with all that is great and beautiful in nature, till it hath become a part of her being; till her spirit hath acquired strength and maturity, and been reared to a beautiful and harmonious temple, in which the true and the good delight to dwell" (Precis 5). Linne serves the necessary function of allowing Oakes-Smith to supplement the transcendental perfection of Eva by marking her with "the mystery of womanhood" (Precis 5). This mystery of womanhood comes from a "gentle going forth of the affections seeking for that holiest of companionship, a kindred spirit, responding to all its finer essences, and yet lifting it above itself" (Precis 5). Clearly, for Oakes-Smith, the conditions of femininity make visible the limitations of a transcendental subjectivity that is not contingent upon a relationship with another. In this way, Oakes-Smith tacitly critiques the self-reliant individual imagined by Emerson or Thoreau and even Fuller.[7]

Wanting to articulate the personal and social possibilities of a transcendent subjectivity, Oakes-Smith was not willing to abandon the potentialities of femininity. Instead, she attempts to graft the one to the other, creating a distinctively "feminine," yet transcendent, individual. The narrator offers this extended apostrophe to Eva as a means of justifying the introduction of this seemingly disruptive male presence into the narrative:

A woman, gentle Eva thou,
Thy lot were incomplete,
Did not all sympathies of soul
Within thy being meet. (6.18.141–44)

Albert Linne is the occasion for "all sympathies of soul" to meet in Eva.
And yet this "communion" with another is fatal to the self-reliance Eva
had previously cultivated. Eva, early on in the poem, had predicted this—
she understands that the emotional alienation between herself and her
mother stems from "the gift of thought, / Whence all will shrink away"
(3.14.105–6). Although the earlier episodes of the poem had celebrated this
gift of knowledge, the later ones suggest that such knowledge is only preliminary to a "deeper wisdom" of which Linne is the catalyst (6.24.192).
What the paragon, Eva, learns is to be "Content to feel!—care not to know"
(6.27.209). Oakes-Smith's narrator claims that a "deeper wisdom" is accessible through the feelings and that ideal transcendence (for both men and
women) is actually a process of sublimation through another:

Deep tenderness was in the glance
That rested on his face,
As if her woman-heart had found
Its own abiding place. (6.28.221–24)

Eva's "woman-heart" finds its "own abiding place" when looking at Linne's
face. She goes on to explain to an uncomprehending Linne that "thy thoughts
and mine are one" and that these commingled thoughts must "thy footsteps
guide / To life and mystery" (6.29.227, 231–32). What this means for Eva
is that she herself must physically die—or in the discourse of the poem,
"cease to be present" (Precis 7).

To cease to be present, then, is the ultimate sign of Eva's transcendence,
for to "cease to be present" is to continue to be ideal. Within the narrative,
it is explicit that Eva continues to act upon the lives of Albert Linne and
her unnamed mother as Eva also continues to affect the narrator. The narrator continually stresses that she "may not say farewell" to her character
because Eva's ideal life continues in what is imagined as the material life of
the poem's speaker (Inscription 5.33). Only because she is dead is Eva able
to continue her "mission high":

Did we but in the holy light
Of truth and goodness rise,

We might communion hold with God
And spirits from the skies. (7.11.93–96)

It is this lack of presence that allows her to actively work in the ongoing lives of those whom she touches, and it is this conclusion of the plot that paradoxically, yet most clearly, signals Oakes-Smith's feminization of the transcendentalist project.

Oakes-Smith, like Fuller in *Woman in the Nineteenth Century,* struggled with a problem that had very different parameters for them as women than for their male contemporaries. In this struggle, the idealism of transcendentalism is compounded by the idealism of femininity. Oakes-Smith dared to attempt to work through this equation, and in doing so she gained the privilege to act directly and forcibly upon the world. For the plot of Eva's life and death is the story of Oakes-Smith's self-authorization. In "The Sinless Child" Oakes-Smith justifies her right to call into being her own authorizing muse, Eva, whose power to inspire depends upon being both dead and beloved.[8] After all, the action of the poem is introduced with an extended apostrophe claiming her as the narrator's "spirit's cherished dream, / Its pure ideal birth" (Inscription 2.9–10). Eva, the narrator's ideal self, is responsible for teaching the contingent, non-ideal self "the language of the bird, / The mystery of the flower," and, more importantly, for winning the narrator's "spirit back again, / To Love, and Peace, and Youth" so that she may speak directly and publicly to an audience (Inscription 3.19–20 and Inscription 5.38–40). "The Sinless Child" is a bid, not for the self-reliance that would preoccupy Emerson and Thoreau and which Oakes-Smith shows to be an insufficient ideal for women under the conditions of nineteenth-century America, but for the ideal of what Elizabeth Cady Stanton would later call self-sovereignty.

So where do we stand in our project of understanding the gendered valences of transcendentalism? It has been difficult (as Dobson and others have argued) to see or read gender in the context of American studies because of the way the transcendentalist movement has been so consistently defined around a nexus of certain male writers. And, since the conventions of American literary history have tended to conflate sex, gender, and genre, it has been difficult to see any women writers (except for Fuller) as anything other than sentimentalists. But as Cathy Davidson has noted, the tendency for all antebellum American women writers to be described pejoratively as "sentimentalists" has been breaking down under the increasing weight of evidence that shows women writing in a plethora of literary genres and modes for a much wider set of literary markets than had earlier been supposed. This breakdown in the schema of literary history allows us not only to see previously obscured writers but to see familiar writers and familiar cultural movements in new light. The new light that feminist literary history has brought is the realization that many of the people who popularized and propagated the ideas and culture of transcendentalism were, in fact, women. Anne Mellor has argued persuasively that "a paradigm shift in our conceptual understanding of British Romanticism occurs when we give equal weight to the thought and writing of women of the period" (1), and a similar shift should be occurring in American studies of transcendentalism.

What happens if we let ourselves imagine that Margaret Fuller was not the only "important" woman transcendentalist writer? Many things *might* happen, but what I am interested in making happen is that we would begin to see the current conventional understanding of the parameters of American romanticism as incomplete. It has been built on too small a sample, a sample limited (with the exception of Fuller) to men. What we have been using as a working model of American romanticism *might* really be a definition of "masculine" romanticism. What would happen to our understanding of romanticism as a conceptual field if we broadened it to account for the expression of romanticism carrying a feminine inflection?[9] Or to put it another way, what would happen to our understanding of American romanticism if we began to admit that both women and men participated in the movement and that this movement was constituted by both transcendentalist and sentimentalist gestures? What if we began to recognize that the significant difference between these gestures is not the sex of the person making them? We cannot know the answer to this until we look carefully at the texts of a number of women romantics. Some, it will become clear, were participating in the transcendentalist project even if, as is the case of Elizabeth Oakes-Smith, literary history has not recognized them as such. Looking at women transcendentalists will enable us to discern the rhetorical function of gender—the function of masculinity and femininity—in the constitution and propagation of transcendentalist and romantic concerns within nineteenth-century America.

Notes

1. The 1990s have seen the production of several critically acclaimed biographies of these figures, signaling a new phase in feminist American studies. See, for example, Carolyn Karcher's biography of Lydia Maria Child, Joan Hedrick's of Harriet Beecher Stowe, and Charles Capper's of Margaret Fuller.

2. Of course, much credit for this is also due to Paul Lauter and the publishers of the *Heath Anthology of American Literature,* which makes a much wider and deeper selection of women writers available to students in the classroom.

258 • M<small>ARY</small> L<small>OUISE</small> K<small>ETE</small>

3. For two different discussions of the role of women authors in the project of imaging the American self, see Gillian Brown's *Domestic Individualism: Imagining Self in Nineteenth-Century America* and my own study *Sentimental Collaborations: Mourning and Middle-Class Identity in Nineteenth-Century America.* While the scope of this essay does not allow me to take up the question of class, I feel that this, too, provides an important and underanalyzed set of inflections of the American romantic movement.

4. This view informs especially the now out-of-date but still common reference works such as James's *Notable American Women* or Blain et al.'s *The Feminist Companion to Literature.* In content, these entries themselves seem derived from Rufus Griswold's mid-nineteenth-century *American Women Poets* and based almost exclusively on the extracts of Oakes-Smith's works that he includes.

5. In another essay, "From 'The Sinless Child' to the Voting Woman: Elizabeth Oakes-Smith and the Preface to Suffrage," I suggest that the figure of Eva, the sinless child, is what Derrida might call the "necessary predicate" to the figure of the voting woman as she is imagined by Oakes-Smith and those activists who followed her. In this companion piece, I begin to trace the way that Oakes-Smith's marriage of the cult of domesticity to Emersonian transcendentalism in "The Sinless Child" undermines the premises sustaining American women in the role of political idiot. This argument is, of course, a development of just one of the many valuable insights provided by Emily Stipes Watts's groundbreaking 1977 study *The Poetry of American Women from 1632 to 1945.*

6. My argument here is part of a general response and revision that has been going on for the last two decades. Every seven years or so Oakes-Smith's life is slightly revised, as in these three important works on American women poets: Emily Stipes Watts's *The Poetry of American Women from 1632 to 1945* (1977), Cheryl Walker's *The Nightingale's Burden* (1982), and Joyce Warren's collection *The (Other) American Traditions* (1993). A comparison of these revisions would itself map the topography of feminist biography over the past quarter-century. For briefer treatments, see Blain et al.'s *Feminist Companion to Literature in English* (1990) or Faust's *American Women Writers* (1979). Both of these have been superseded by Denise Knight's *Nineteenth-Century American Women Writers: A Bio-Bibliographical Critical Sourcebook* (1997) and Karen Kilcup's *Nineteenth-Century American Women Writers: A Critical Reader* (1998). Leigh Kirkland's dissertation, "A Human Life: Being the Autobiography of Elizabeth Oakes-Smith" (Georgia State University, 1994), promises to be the fullest treatment since Mary Alice Wyman's 1972 study, *Two American Pioneers: Seba Smith and Elizabeth Oakes Smith.* But Elizabeth Oakes-Smith herself left a fascinating autobiography of life on the nineteenth-century feminine vanguard.

7. Although Fuller's work has been paid much more (and more consistent) attention, Oakes-Smith was at least as interested as Fuller in making the potentialities

of transcendentalism available to women. Greater attention to Oakes-Smith's efforts would allow us to lift from Fuller's shoulders some of the pressure of being the representative "woman-thinking."

8. Oakes-Smith, then, would be another good example of Elizabeth Bronfen's argument about the difficulty for women of transforming oneself from "muse to creatrix."

9. For a full-length discussion of this problem, see Dobson's essay in Warren's *The (Other) American Tradition,* Buell's contribution to *American Literature's* special issue "No More Separate Spheres," and Cathy Davidson's preface to that issue.

Works Cited

Anonymous. "Frontmatter" to Oakes-Smith, *"The Sinless Child" and Other Poems.*

Blain, Elizabeth, et al., eds. *The Feminist Companion to Literature in English.* New Haven: Yale UP, 1990.

Bronfen, Elizabeth. *Over Her Dead Body: Death, Femininity, and the Aesthetic.* New York, Routledge, 1992.

Brown, Gillian. *Domestic Individualism: Imagining Self in Nineteenth-Century America.* Berkeley: U California P, 1990.

Buell, Lawrence. "Circling the Spheres: A Dialogue." Davidson 465–91.

Capper, Charles. *Margaret Fuller: An American Romantic Life.* New York: Oxford UP, 1992.

Davidson, Cathy, ed. *No More Separate Spheres!* Special issue of *American Literature* 70.3 (1998).

Dobson, Joanne. "The American Renaissance Reenvisioned." Warren 164–82.

Emerson, Ralph Waldo. *Selections from Ralph Waldo Emerson.* Ed. Stephen E. Whicher. Boston: Houghton Mifflin, 1960.

Faust, Langdon Lynne, ed. *American Women Writers: A Critical Reference from Colonial Times to the Present.* New York: Frederick Ungar, 1983.

Fuller, Margaret. *Woman in the Nineteenth Century.* New York: Norton, 1971.

Hedrick, Joan. *Harriet Beecher Stowe: A Life.* New York: Oxford UP, 1994.

James, Edward, ed. *Notable American Women.* Cambridge: Harvard UP, 1971.

Karcher, Carolyn. *The First Women of the Republic: A Cultural Biography of Lydia Maria Child.* Durham, NC: Duke UP, 1994.

Kete, Mary Louise. "From 'The Sinless Child' to the Voting Woman: Elizabeth Oakes-Smith and the Preface to Suffrage." Paper read at the Conference on the Canon and Marginality, SUNY Binghamton, 1991.

———. *Sentimental Collaborations: Mourning and Middle-Class Identity in Nineteenth-Century America.* Durham, NC: Duke UP, 2000.

Kilcup, Karen, ed. *Nineteenth-Century American Women Writers: A Critical Reader.* Oxford: Blackwell, 1998.

Kirkland, Leigh. "A Human Life: Being The Autobiography of Elizabeth Oakes Smith." Diss. Georgia State U, 1994.

Knight, Denise D., ed. *Nineteenth-Century American Women Writers: A Bio-Bibliographical Critical Sourcebook*. Westport, CN: Greenwood, 1997.

Mellor, Ann. *Romanticism and Gender*. New York and London: Routledge, 1993.

Oakes-Smith, Elizabeth. *Selections from the Autobiography of Elizabeth Oakes Prince Smith*. New York: Arno P, 1980.

——. *"The Sinless Child" and Other Poems*. Ed. John Keese. Boston: Ticknor, 1843.

Stowe, Harriet B. *A Key to Uncle Tom's Cabin*. Saint Clair Shores, MI: Scholarly P, 1970.

Thoreau, Henry David. *Walden and Civil Disobedience*. Ed. Owen Thomas. New York: Norton, 1966.

Tuckerman, Henry. "Frontmatter" to Oakes-Smith, *"The Sinless Child" and Other Poems*.

Walker, Cheryl. *The Nightingale's Burden*. Bloomington: Indiana UP, 1982.

Warren, Joyce, ed. *The (Other) American Tradition*. New Brunswick, NJ: Rutgers UP, 1993.

Watts, Emily Stipes. *The Poetry of American Women from 1632 to 1945*. Austin: U of Texas P, 1977.

Wyman, Mary Alice. *Two American Pioneers: Seba Smith and Elizabeth Oakes Smith*. New York: Columbia UP, 1927.

12

Sentimental Epistemologies in *Uncle Tom's Cabin* and *The House of the Seven Gables*

MARIANNE NOBLE

In the first chapter of *Sensational Designs,* Jane Tompkins points out that in the nineteenth century, *The House of the Seven Gables* was read as a sentimental novel. Rather than pondering its complex issues, such as its epistemological inquiries, its interrogation of the morality of property laws, or its psychological complexity, they enjoyed the book for its "tenderness and delicacy of sentiment" with a "moral constantly in view."[1] From the perspective of his contemporary readers, Tompkins points out, Hawthorne has more in common with the sentimental Susan Warner than with the abstruse Herman Melville. Indeed, Tompkins writes, "it is not that [genteel antebellum] critics couldn't *see* the difference between Warner's work and Hawthorne's, but that, given their way of seeing, there *was* no difference" (18). She emphasizes that it is twentieth-century criticism, still laboring under the sway of F. O. Matthiessen, that insists upon teasing out the connections between Hawthorne and Melville and ignoring those between Hawthorne and female writers.

Tompkins's argument makes a significant stride toward eroding the artificial barrier separating nineteenth-century men's and women's literature by demonstrating that many of the differences between authors we revere and those we revile lie in our own expectations, expectations that are shaped by literary history, academic structures, marketing, and the values of our own culture. But her thesis also opens up a new problem that in another way solidifies rather than erodes that boundary. Tompkins proposes that, in order to appreciate nineteenth-century women's literature, we need to cease reading as ourselves and instead read through other eyes, eyes that prize didacticism and unambiguous morality. "What Hawthorne's contemporaries saw when they read his work is not what we see now" (13). We are asked to ignore the tantalizing philosophical complexities of a Hawthorne in order to see him as an unambiguous moralist with clear prose. But such a positional shift on the part of modern readers can only partly succeed; while they can theoretically see Hawthorne through lenses informed by research into nineteenth-century domestic culture, at the same time, they are likely to perceive all the complexities that Tompkins would sever from their reading practices. And thus, while they can find material enabling them to classify Hawthorne as a novelist in the female tradition, they are also likely to keep in mind the psychological and philosophical darkness that they (as modern readers) cannot help but see in the text. And so, the material that must be ignored in order to see Hawthorne in the feminine tradition by default becomes the non-feminine, or the masculine. Thus, Tompkins's nineteenth-century classification system produces a secondary one that reifies gender boundaries: that which is male is psychologically and philosophically complex, while that which is female is unambiguous, stereotyped, and lovely. We moderns do not have to change to read women's sentimentality—which can be read "straight"—but in order to read male sentimentality, we must put on critical blinders.

But such a splitting is not necessary to recognize Hawthorne as a sentimental writer. Tompkins misrepresents sentimentalism by insisting that the sentimental precludes the philosophically and morally complex. It is true that sentimental moral philosophy optimistically affirms an essential goodness in human nature, but that affirmation is, in many instances, compatible with epistemological, ontological, and theological introspection of the type we moderns love to interrogate. In their eagerness to insist that books do not have to be philosophically complex in order to be good, feminist critics influenced by Tompkins have ignored the considerable philosophical introspection that in fact engaged their literary foremothers as well as forefathers. The philosophical tradition known as the Common Sense school of philosophy, whose principles provided the foundation of the early American education system, influenced many sentimental authors and provided a coherent intellectual foundation for much sentimental fiction, both male and female. In her journal, Susan Warner repeatedly mentions studying David Hume and Dugald Stewart of the Common Sense tradition. Harriet Beecher Stowe noted that Common Sense philosophers were some of her most formative influences. And since the father of Mary Virginia Terhune and her sister insisted that they be educated as if they were boys and preparing for college, their training doubtless exposed them to the Scottish philosophy that has been widely viewed as the most important intellectual development in the American Enlightenment.

In this chapter I read Hawthorne as a sentimental author by focusing squarely upon his philosophical introspection, which is very much within the tradition of Common Sense philosophy. Comparison of his sentimental epistemology with that of arguably the most famous American sentimental author—Harriet Beecher Stowe—demonstrates that sentimentality can be— and in *The House of the Seven Gables* and *Uncle Tom's Cabin* is—philosophically complex. Both of these texts are centrally concerned with questions of epistemological doubt, and in response, both affirm an optimistic belief in an innate moral sense accessed through feelings, an affirmation that reflects their interest in and allegiance to Common Sense philosophy. *The House of the Seven Gables* cannot be read as a pure affirmation of sentimental aesthetics, however; it is concerned about the potential political pitfalls of an aesthetic centered upon the production of physical affect. The problems relating to sentimental affect that Hawthorne poses as theoretical possibilities in *The House of the Seven Gables* actually occurred in some readers' responses to *Uncle Tom's Cabin,* suggesting that our modern skepticism about the value of sentimental literature is not *simply* a critical bias imposed by modernist standards of literary value but rather is anticipated by the enthusiastic but critical engagement of sentimental authors within their own genre.

I
The Philosophical Foundations of Sentimentalism

The stream of recent, increasingly sophisticated critical speculations upon the meaning of the word "sentimental" has produced something like a consensus on at least one point: sentimentalism is about a desire for union, what Dobson calls "an irresistible impulse toward human connection; sentimentalism in its pure essence envisions—indeed, *desires*—the self-in-relation" (170–71).[2] Sentimental literature privileges visions of such connections, invents language to characterize that primary vision, articulates moral outrage over social injustices that violate it, and strives to move readers toward a more humanitarian stance by making them *feel* the pain of separation and associate their own pain with that of the suffering others. A number of studies, including those of Gregg Camfield, Elizabeth Barnes, and David Denby, have shown that this aesthetic movement is rooted in Enlightenment philosophy. Denby points to the roots of French sentimentalism in Rousseau and Diderot; Camfield and Barnes indicate the roots of the American tradition in Scottish philosophy of the Common Sense tradition, in the writings of such thinkers as Adam Smith, Frances Hutcheson, Dugald Stewart, Hugh Blair, Archibald Alison, and others.

Common Sense philosophy is the disgruntled heir of Lockean empiricism. Its adherents share with Locke a belief in the primacy of sense experience for all knowledge, but they challenge his notion of the *tabula rasa* on the grounds of an implicit threat of atheism and solipsism in it. They worry that if the human mind is a blank sheet that is defined only by the sense impressions it receives, and if all ideas derive from those sense experiences, then human beings have no real access to each other or the world, and no standards of morality, apart from ideas and beliefs of their own devising. Common Sense philosophy attempts to reason its way out of this impasse. It blends the idea that our sensations are our most fundamental and reliable source of insight with a belief gained from experience that human nature inclines to virtuous actions because of the pleasurable feelings such actions generate. Out of this blend emerges a theory of an innate moral sense, more akin to intuition than to reason, an additional human faculty that instinctively perceives right and wrong by allowing one person to experience another's pains and pleasures through the power of sympathy and thereby to gain moral knowledge intuitively and experientially rather than through reason. Common Sense philosophers see logic as a secondary process erected upon an embodied, feeling-based, primary response to the world.

Common Sense philosophers idealize sympathy as a privileged cognitive device. Adam Smith, not only a famous economist but also a renowned philosopher of the Common Sense school, explains in the opening of his 1759 text *The Theory of Moral Sentiments*: "As we have no immediate experience of what other men feel, we can form no idea of the manner in which they are affected, but by conceiving what we ourselves should feel in the like situation. . . . By the imagination we place ourselves in his situation, we conceive ourselves enduring all the same torments, we enter as it were into his body, and become in some measure the same person with him, and thence form some idea of his sensations, and even feel something which, though weaker in degree, is not altogether unlike them" (73–74). Because knowledge gained in this way is grounded in the senses (accessed by the imagination), it is prior to knowledge that might be gained through logic and, at least in cases of human nature, more reliable than that secondary form of thought. And a society in which sympathy governs human relations is likely to have a morally upright, humanitarian character. Sympathy spontaneously produces benevolent behavior; one does unto one's neighbor as unto oneself because one's neighbor *is*, in a sense, oneself. Sympathy thereby promotes social cohesion, an effect that was highly valued in young America, where it was unclear how a society devoted to individual rights would unite into a community. Common Sense philosophy proposed that sympathy would serve as a crucial form of social glue.

Sympathy serves as the link between Common Sense moral philosophy and sentimental literature; it is the foundation, then, both of a theory of social organization and of a theory of aesthetic value.[3] The Common Sense image of a naturally benevolent streak in human nature, painted by theorists such as Smith, characterizes sentimental literature, which both portrays and presumes the beneficial workings of spectatorial sympathy. Sentimental authors portray sympathetic characters who are moved to humanitarian actions by the sight of suffering; they also presume that that same dynamic will apply to readers faced with the sufferings of fictional characters. Their sentimental literary plots model appropriate social behavior for readers. This feature of sentimental aesthetics leads to the curiously anti-realistic form of realism that contemporary critics have observed in nineteenth-century sentimental literature. The philosophical position that the senses are our primary avenue toward knowledge leads theorists of Common Sense aesthetics to emphasize the importance of realistic descriptions, but the moral imperative that art model right behavior leads simultaneously to a strain of idealism (Camfield 47). A literature of the ideal grounded in the real was seen not only as "beautiful" but as moral.

II
Stowe's Sentimental Epistemology

Like many authors whom today we call "sentimental," Harriet Beecher Stowe was suspicious of sentimentality. When she wrote that its authors "talk what they cannot have felt," she was reiterating a widely held belief that sentimentality traffics in unearned displays of emotion.[4] However, she also recognized that the epithet "sentimental" was all too frequently used to dismiss anyone who placed a high value on individual feelings. In *Uncle Tom's Cabin,* for example, Senator Bird ridicules "all sentimental weakness of those who would put the welfare of a few miserable fugitives before great state interests" (155). Likewise, St. Clare recalls that his brother had accused him of "a womanish sentimentalism" for sympathizing with slaves (342). Stowe values a certain form of sentimentality, that which Paula Bennett calls "high sentimentality," which she describes as "an epistemologically based discourse" that bases judgments of character and ethics on feelings, intuition, and spirituality rather than on abstract logic (593). Stowe found in high sentimentality a redress for the cognitive failures of abstract analysis. As Mrs. Bird puts it, "I hate reasoning . . . on such subjects. There's a way you political folks have of coming round and round a plain right thing; and you don't believe in it yourselves when it comes to practice" (145). She advocates a sentimental alternative: "Your heart is better than your head, in this case" (153).[5]

This appeal to the heart over the head is grounded in the sentimental philosophies of the Common Sense school. Gregg Camfield demonstrates that in *Uncle Tom's Cabin*, "Stowe seems to be engaged in a serious intellectual defense of the sentimental ideal; she is trying to explain how naturally good human beings can lose their sensitivities to goodness" (26). This question, he demonstrates, is rooted both in Stowe's readings of the Scottish philosophers and in her opposition to the Calvinistic doctrines of both her husband and her father. In 1831, Stowe's sister Catherine Beecher had written a textbook of moral philosophy on the Scottish model, and Stowe reiterates in her fiction her sister's optimistic perspective on morality, rejecting her male relations' doctrines of innate depravity and attributing evil to social customs that alienate people from their feelings. Her basic educational training emphasized Common Sense principles of morality and aesthetics. In an autobiographical sketch of 1863, she cites influential thinkers of the Common Sense school as important formative influences: "Much of the training and inspiration of my early days consisted . . . in such works as Paley's 'Moral Philosophy,' Blair's 'Rhetoric,' Alison 'On Taste'" (qtd. in Camfield 36).

The Common Sense privilege of sympathy over detached reason is central to Stowe's work. The epistemological problems with unsympathetic pure reason are vividly exemplified in an 1852 review of *Uncle Tom's Cabin* written by George F. Holmes, a noted essayist with the *Southern Literary Messenger* and the first president of the University of Mississippi. Deriding Stowe's contention that "there is no law that amounts to anything" to protect slaves from abusive masters, Holmes pointed out that southern legislators had passed many laws whose specific intent was to protect "the negro's safety in life and limb." The Louisiana Code Noir, passed that very year, went so far as to protect slaves even in the eventuality that there were no witnesses of the abuse. He quoted it in his review:

> If any slave be mutilated, beaten, or ill-treated contrary to the true intent and meaning of this section, when no one shall be present, in such case the owner or other person having the charge or management of said slave thus mutilated shall be deemed responsible and guilty of the said offence, and shall be prosecuted without further evidence, unless the said owner, or other person so as aforesaid, can prove the contrary by means of good and sufficient evidence, or can clear himself by his own oath, which said oath every Court under the cognizance of which such offence shall have been examined and tried is by this Act authorised to administer. (474–75)

Stowe found it ludicrous that a law intended to protect slaves' physical safety would define an abstract oath as more compelling evidence than a concrete, mutilated body:

> Would one have supposed that sensible people could ever publish as a law such a specimen of utter legislative nonsense—so ridiculous on the very face of it!
>
> The object is to bring to justice those fiendish people who burn, scald, mutilate, &c. How is this done? Why, it is enacted that the fact of finding the slave in this condition shall be held presumption against the owner or overseer, unless—unless what? Why, unless he will prove to the contrary—or swear to the contrary, it is no matter which— either will answer the purpose. (*Key* 168)

"Sensible people" like Holmes are not innately depraved, as a Calvinist might believe; rather, they have a cognitive problem, as a Common Sense philosopher might suggest. They do not think clearly because they think in abstractions divorced from sensory experience. The rhetorical circumlocutions and twisted syntax in the legal code prevent basically good-hearted but misguided people from apprehending the absurdity that her simple, body-centered form of expression makes so vivid.

Uncle Tom's Cabin uses a "high sentimental" aesthetic, focusing upon that abused body in order to restore it to public consciousness through sympathy.[6] People like Holmes have lost touch with their innate moral sense, and they need—not to be reasoned with—but to be touched at the level of their feelings. Stowe vowed to "make this whole nation *feel* what an accursed thing slavery is," and she wrote in the end of the book: "there is one thing everyone can do and that is *feel* right" (624).[7] This assertion is part of the Common Sense belief that identification with suffering others through sympathetic self-extension would naturally produce the morally correct response of a desire to alleviate that suffering. Sentimental authors interested in humanitarian relief encouraged readers to seek the truth of a book through emotional and physical identification with the suffering of the other. They both portrayed and invited their readers to use an epistemology that was neither purely intellectual nor purely sensual but rather a blend of both that was best—though imperfectly—understood as "intuition," consultation with the "heart," or simply "feeling." We can see the Common Sense roots of *Uncle Tom's Cabin* when Stowe sarcastically describes a "poor heathenish Kentuckian" who assists Eliza in her escape because he "had not been instructed in his constitutional relations, and consequently was betrayed into acting in a sort of Christianized manner, which, if he had been better situated and more enlightened, he would not have been left to do" (119). According to Common Sense epistemologies, intuitive thinking—thinking governed by an untaught response of sympathy—will be morally sound, while more abstract thought governed by legal codes will be less reliable because it is more distant from innate morality.

As is customary in a "high sentimental" aesthetic, Stowe not only portrays characters who appropriately perform benevolent actions after witnessing others' suffering, but she specifically directs her audience to do the same. She urges them to identify with the tortured characters in *Uncle Tom's Cabin,* to feel their pain through an imagined projection into their situation, and to respond accordingly. When Tom is torn from his wife and children, for instance, Stowe writes: "Sobs, heavy, hoarse, and loud, shook the chair, and great tears fell through his fingers on the floor; just such tears, sir, as you dropped into the coffin where lay your first born son; such tears, woman, as you shed when you heard the cries of your dying babe. For, sir, he was a man,—and you are but another man. And, woman, though dressed in silk and jewels, you are but a woman, and, in life's great straits and mighty grief, ye feel but one sorrow!" (90–91). She facilitates readers' efforts to put themselves in the shoes of the slaves by reinvigorating their personal anguished memories of bereavement and separation, enabling them to understand the pain of slavery at a gut level. In doing so, she exemplifies the Common Sense, sentimental belief that vicarious experiences of others' suffering will produce humanitarian reform and thereby a consolidation of the community.[8]

But her method for provoking sympathy is frequently more subtle. The Senator Bird chapters provide a *mise-en-scène* illustrating Stowe's own authorial strategy of producing sympathy.[9] Senator Bird supports the Fugitive Slave Law because of an epistemological failure; he thinks in dehumanizing abstractions that enable him to think of "fugitives" without ever considering the emotions of the human beings involved in the discussion: "His idea of a fugitive was only an idea of the letters that spell the word,—or at the most, the image of a little newspaper picture of a man with a stick and bundle with 'Ran away from the subscriber' under it. The magic of the real presence of distress,—the imploring human eye, the frail, trembling human hand, the despairing appeal of helpless agony,—these he had never tried" (156). These kinds of abstract representations of slaves erase the actual human beings concerned, in the very act of invoking them, as does the Code Noir. The senator, Stowe sentimentally maintains, will be restored to his innately good heart if he can be made to stop intellectualizing and instead to sympathize with a real, live human slave. Eliza Harris appears in his kitchen as though to test the fundamental principles of an epistemology based upon sympathy. When the senator asks a series of fact-based questions designed to make Eliza explain why she ran away from "a good home," she interrupts with a question of her own that shifts the epistemological basis of the discussion from his logic to her feelings. She asks if the Birds have ever lost a child, a question that was "thrust on a new wound." When the Birds answer yes, Eliza explains, "Then you will feel for me. I have lost two" (148). She stimulates their preexisting wound in order to enable (force) them to "enter as it were into [her] body, and become in some measure the same person with" her, as Adam Smith had put it. This scene offers a fictional example of Stowe's own literary method; like Eliza, she reinvigorates readers' preexisting wounds, forcing them to "feel for" slaves by reexperiencing their own painful separations and other forms of suffering. Wounding forces a new mode of cognition upon readers, who understand slavery through their gut memories of sorrow rather than their sense of reason, and thereby apprehend the "plain right thing" that logic conceals.

For Stowe, a sentimental epistemology is characteristically female. In *Uncle Tom's Cabin,* men are frequently detached individualists, self-absorbed and inclined to attempt to understand other human beings by transforming them into abstractions rather than encountering them as living presences. Because others never become living presences to them, such men run the risk of solipsism, living isolated in their own mental reconstructions of the world with little access to unmediated, direct contact with the world and its inhabitants. Following a scene featuring the slaves as embodied, sympathizing people interconnected through physical and emotional self-extensions, Stowe describes a slave trade that is remarkable above all for its high level of abstraction: "The trader and Mr. Shelby were seated together in the dining room afore-named, at a table covered with papers and writing utensils. . . . Mr. Shelby hastily drew the bills of sale towards him, and signed them, like a man that hurries over some disagreeable business, and then pushed them over with the money. Haley produced . . . a parchment, which after looking over it a moment, he handed to Mr. Shelby, who took it with a gesture of suppressed eagerness" (79–80). The mediated, symbolic nature of this exchange erases the bodies in question, enabling Mr. Shelby to remain emotionally detached from the transaction, which he would not be able to do if Tom were present. After desecrating his dining room table by covering it with abstract symbols of home and living people rather than with life-giving food, he abstractly says, "I hope you'll remember that you promised on your honor, you wouldn't sell Tom, without knowing what sort of hands he's going into." Haley points out, "Why you've just done it sir." Though Haley agrees to do his best, "Mr. Shelby did not feel particularly reassured by [Haley's] declarations, but, as they were the best comfort the case admitted of, he allowed the trader to depart in silence, and betook himself to a solitary cigar" (80). Stowe emphasizes his isolation. Having violated his human relations because his is a detached world experienced via symbols and reason, Shelby is left to a lonely state of alienation from meaningful human contact.

Stowe's "high sentimental" effort to describe ways of apprehending the "real presence" of another in his or her emotional or spiritual dimension and her efforts to activate a sense of that "real presence" in readers deserve more serious attention than critics have heretofore given it. Her struggle to represent the role of the senses and feelings in cognition and her insistence upon the morality of a cognition grounded in feeling represent a complex epistemology with respected philosophical antecedents. In the hands of skillful sentimental authors like Stowe and Hawthorne, sentimentality informed by Common Sense philosophy represents an attempt to put into language the relationship of body and feelings to personal identity and to affirm the body and the feelings as effective and moral instruments for interpreting the world.

III
Sentimental Hawthorne

Like Stowe, Nathaniel Hawthorne studied Common Sense philosophy; and not surprisingly, given the presuppositions of the scholars reading them, his interest is better documented than hers.[10] History-of-ideas studies from the late 1960s and early 1970s reveal that he studied Dugald Stewart, Hugh Blair, and Locke while studying at Bowdoin, from 1821 to 1825. He also took classes there with the seminal theorist of Common Sense psychology, Thomas Upham. And in 1827, while in Salem, he read, in order, Adam Smith, Thomas Brown, Lord Kames, Dugald Stewart, Frances Hutcheson, and Archibald Alison. His uses of sentimentalism are also well documented, in feminist-informed studies of the 1980s and early 1990s.[11] Lora Romero, for example, points out that "Hawthorne's relentless and gendered opposition of public and private spheres, his hostility toward the Puritan patriarch, and his representation of imperiled womanhood are precisely the materials of the domestic novel" (112). *The House of the Seven Gables* in particular has been treated as sentimental based upon its domestic setting, its foregrounding of a typical "angel in the house"–type heroine, and its unrealistically happy ending. But the relationship between Hawthorne's philosophical inquiries and his sentimentalism has gone unaddressed, perhaps because the two modes of discourse have consistently been presumed to be diametrically opposed to each other. I want now to suggest that the epistemological questions in *The House of the Seven Gables* and the answers to them are themselves sentimental. In this respect, the book resembles *Uncle Tom's Cabin,* whose epistemological questions and answers are likewise sentimental.

It is certainly true that Hawthorne denigrated "the damned mob of scribbling women" who were outselling him. But as those who have read *The Lamplighter* (which elicited the "scribbling women" remark) will concede, it is indeed bad writing, overtly derivative of *The Wide, Wide World,* while lacking the psychological realism that makes Warner so interesting— or the humorous social realism and impassioned humanitarianism of Stowe, or the feisty adventure plotting of Southworth, or the unconventional female heroines of Sedgwick, or the erudition of Evans. The "scribbler" remark does not mean that Hawthorne disliked sentimental literature; rather, it means that he disliked the fact that the American consumer seemed to value bad writing. As his favorable responses to Fanny Fern and Julia Ward Howe suggest, Hawthorne was not blind to the worth of women's sentimental discourse when it was well written.[12] Fanny Fern showed herself a sentimentalist in the Common Sense tradition when, in the dedication to *Rose Clark,* she identified her ideal reader as one who read with body and heart rather than mere intellect: "Should any dictionary on legs rap inopportunely at the door for admittance, send him away to the groaning shelves of some musty library, where 'literature' lies embalmed, with its stony eyes, fleshless joints, and ossified heart, in faultless preservation." Hawthorne admired her efforts to write a literature of heart and body, observing that she wrote "in little more than her bare bones, her heart pulsating visibly and indecently in its cage of ribs. Still there are ribs, and there is a heart" (2 February 1855, *Letters* 17: 307–8). In using the metaphor of a living, pulsating body to capture the intensity of Fern's writing about human emotion, Hawthorne is drawing attention to, and appreciating, a sentimental privilege of embodied feelings over detached analysis, the same kind of privilege that, as we have seen, was Harriet Beecher Stowe's central concern.[13]

Like *Uncle Tom's Cabin, The House of the Seven Gables* suggests that the heart and the gut are better cognitive instruments than the head. This belief responds to the epistemological uncertainty that is a central theme of the book: how are we to apprehend the truth given the unreliability of the information we receive from our senses? To all the world, Hepzibah Pyncheon looks like an angry woman harboring ill will toward all, but the reader knows that in fact, her scowl is caused by nearsightedness. Likewise, Judge Pyncheon looks like the essence of benevolence, while the truth is that he is both criminal and cruel. When appearances are so deceiving, Hawthorne seems to be asking, how are human beings to find the truth in questions of human nature?

His answer to this epistemological question is taken directly from sentimental tradition: use sympathy. As Holgrave says, "one never can be certain that he really knows [others]; nor ever guess what they have been, from what he sees them to be, now. Judge Pyncheon! Clifford! What a complex riddle—a complexity of complexities—do they present! It requires intuitive sympathy, like a young girl's, to solve it. A mere observer, like myself, (who never have any intuitions, and am, at best, only subtile and acute,) is pretty certain to go astray" (158–59). One could hardly find a more vivid description of a sentimental epistemology. Like Stowe, Holgrave contrasts detached male analysis with sympathetic female self-extension, and he proposes that the insight into the human heart derived from intuitive sympathy is more reliable than that obtained from disinterested observation, no matter how "subtile and acute."

Even if such information were not more reliable, it would still be preferable to a purely intellectual epistemology, for as Holgrave says—and as Hawthorne regularly suggests—detached abstraction erodes the human community. In a self-critical, introspective moment, Holgrave later tells Phoebe, "It is not my impulse—as regards these two individuals [Hepzibah and Clifford]—either to help or hinder; but to look on, to analyze, to explain matters to myself, and to comprehend the drama . . . Providence sent you hither to help, and sends me only as a privileged and meet spectator" (191). Phoebe is "perplexed and displeased" by his lack of sympathy: "I wish that you would . . . feel more like a Christian and a human being! How is it possible to see people in distress, without desiring, more than anything else, to help and comfort them?" (191). This response could have been spoken by virtually any of the Common Sense philosophers, who, as we have seen, maintained that it is human nature to respond to the sight of another's pain with benevolent actions. As Smith writes in the first line of *The Theory of Moral Sentiments:* "How selfish soever man may be supposed, there are evidently some principles in his nature which interest him in the fortune of others and render their happiness necessary to him, though he derives nothing from it except the pleasure of seeing it" (73). The kind of behavior Holgrave ascribes to himself—a willingness to watch others suffering without helping them—is unnatural, arising from an unwillingness or inability to feel one's own feelings. In this he resembles Stowe's Senator Bird, while Phoebe resembles Mary Bird. And in both novels, the female sentimental characters are affirmed as sites of moral authority and happiness.

If sympathy is the source of happiness, Stowe and Hawthorne suggest detachment is the source of unhappiness. Not only does it undermine Holgrave's study of human nature, but it leads to solipsistic isolation, as it does for Senator Bird. Phoebe argues that Holgrave exploits the suffering of the two old people for his own intellectual amusement: "You talk as if this old house were a theatre; and you seem to look at Hepzibah's and Clifford's misfortunes, and those of generations before them, as a tragedy, such as I have seen acted in the hall of a country-hotel; only the present one appears to be played exclusively for your amusement! I do not like this. The play costs the performers too much—and the audience is too cold-hearted!" (191–92). The metaphor of mind-as-theater echoes the skeptic Hume, who posited that "The mind is a kind of theatre, where several perceptions successively make their appearance" (253), an approach that created what Scheick describes as an "unbridgeable gap between the external world of matter and the internal world of the registering mind" (133). The alienation from the human community in Humean or Holgravean skepticism is precisely that which spurred the development of Common Sense epistemologies. Common Sense philosophers proposed that we can in fact be confident of the reality of our sensory impressions of the world by checking our experiences against those of others. But in treating Clifford and Hepzibah not as suffering fellow human beings but as objects of intellectual interest, Holgrave deprives himself of the opportunity to know his own reality, to be an engaged participant in life rather than only a spectator of it.

The story of Clifford exemplifies the Common Sense postulate that shared experiences with other people are necessary for individuals to feel that the material world is in fact real beyond the confines of their own minds. Deprived of human contact in prison for thirty years, Clifford lived in his imagination only, which became as real to him as the physical world, so that upon his return to the world outside his prison he can no longer distinguish between the real and the imaginary:

> He was seeking to make himself more fully sensible of the scene around him; or perhaps, dreading it to be a dream, or a play of imagination, was vexing the fair moment with a struggle for some added brilliancy and more durable illusion.
> "How pleasant!—how delightful! . . . Will it last? . . . Aah; this must be all a dream!" (109)

As the inscrutability of Judge and Hepzibah Pyncheon demonstrates, Hawthorne believes that such anxieties regarding the illusory nature of the visible world vex us all, not just the mentally unstable. Indeed, just as

Hepzibah asks "Is not this a dream?" and Clifford wonders "Is it a fact—or have I dreamt it" (264), Hawthorne himself wrote in a letter to his wife: "Nothing else is real, except the bond between thee and me. The people around me are but shadows. I am myself but a shadow, till thou takest me in thy arms, and convertest me into substance. Till thou comest back, I do but walk in a dream" (7 April 1856, *Letters* 17: 465). In response to his own skepticism, Hawthorne also reiterates the sentimental, Common Sense assurance that extension to others through sympathy and physical contact releases people from skeptical doubt, enabling them to be "substance," people actually interacting with the physical world and others outside of themselves.

The House of the Seven Gables illustrates the same principle. When Clifford mourns, "I want my happiness!" the narrator comments: "Fate has no happiness in store for you; unless your quiet home in the old family residence, with the faithful Hepzibah, and your long summer-afternoons with Phoebe, and these Sabbath festivals with Uncle Venner and the Daguerreotypist, deserve to be called happiness! Why not? If not the thing itself, it is marvellously like it, and the more so for that ethereal and intangible quality, which causes it all to vanish, at too close an introspection. Take it therefore, while you may. Murmur not—question not—but make the most of it!" (141). The unsatisfying resolution to skeptical doubt posed here ("If not the thing itself, it is marvellously like it") is precisely the resolution offered by Common Sense philosophy, which insists that "common sense" tells us that that which surrounds us is real. Thomas Reid, credited as the founder of Common Sense philosophy, wrote that the consent of ages and nations is sufficient assurance of the reliability of the visible, and he insisted that if philosophers reject common sense, then "I despise Philosophy, and renounce its guidance—let my soul dwell with Common Sense" (18). Like Reid, Hawthorne's narrator advocates a faithful, though unverifiable, trust in the realness of the world because human happiness lies only in such acceptance. Solipsistic skepticism—the anxiety that our experiences are not "the thing itself" but only a figment of our imagination—isolates people, preventing the encounters with the real outside the mind, encounters that are most fully available in sympathetic extension of the self to others, as in the Pyncheon Sabbath parties. Though ultimately unverifiable, the experience of physical and sympathetic communion is the most reliable mode of access we have to the reality of the external world. When Hawthorne affirms a trusting, anti-skeptical reliance upon one's feelings of connectedness with the physical world and with other people, he is affirming a sentimental epistemology.

IV
The Problematic Pleasures of Sentimental Affect

And yet, while *The House of the Seven Gables* endorses a sentimental epistemology, that endorsement does not necessarily translate into an unqualified
embrace of sentimental fiction. Hawthorne shares with many of his contemporaries the anxious suspicion that the spectacle of human suffering that
one observes in sentimental fiction merely gratifies the reader's base lust for
stimulation rather than leading him or her to a more humanized—because
genuinely intersubjective—stance, such as real encounters with suffering are
supposed to produce. It is upon precisely those grounds that Phoebe criticized Holgrave for enjoying the spectacle of Hepzibah and Clifford's suffering for his own amusement. And upon similar grounds, when Clifford angrily commands Phoebe not to read light fiction that makes her cry, the
narrator moralizes, "And wisely too! Is not the world sad enough, in genuine earnest, without making a pastime of mock sorrows?" (131). Sentimental
fiction runs the risk of exploiting "mock sorrows" for the idle, and private,
pleasures of the reader. Witnessing others' suffering may not effect the genuine human contact and moral awakening that was supposedly inevitable,
given human nature; after all, Holgrave himself merely enjoys the spectacles
of suffering without being moved to action. Ironically, then, sentimental
fiction runs the risk of being unsentimental, if by sentimentalism we mean
an epistemology of sympathetic self-extension.

Hawthorne presents a more fully developed consideration of this problematic pleasure of sentimental affect in the chapter "Alice Pyncheon."
Holgrave introduces that chapter as a tale he has written for *Graham's* or
Godey's, prominent publishers of sentimental fiction and other works appropriate for genteel women. (Hawthorne had published in both.) He has been
well received in these, he says, because "in the humorous line, I am thought
to have a very pretty way with me; and as for pathos, I am as provocative of
tears as an onion" (165). In comparing the effects of his sentimental fiction
to the merely mechanical stimulation of an onion, Holgrave sneers at his
own willingness to "scribble" a literature valued primarily for its physical
affect.

The tale-within-a-tale—Holgrave's story "Alice Pyncheon"—can be
read as an exploration of the problems with sentimental affect. In it, when
Alice is mesmerized by Holgrave's ancestor, Matthew Maule, she is hence-
forth "Maule's slave, in a bondage more humiliating, a thousand-fold, than
that which binds its chain around the body. . . . 'Alice, laugh!'—the carpen-
ter, beside his hearth, would say; or perhaps intensely will it, without a spo-

ken word. And, even were it prayer-time, or at a funeral, Alice must break
into wild laughter. 'Alice, be sad!'—and, at the instant, down would come
her tears, quenching all the mirth of those around her" (185). Alice's humiliating response to Maule's mesmerism is set in precise apposition to the
reader's response to Holgrave's sentimental fiction. His readers, like Alice,
are compelled by a force beyond their control to produce an outpouring of
laughs and tears with no legitimate cause. Their response, like hers, Hawthorne
implies, is degrading.

This control of the reader's emotional and bodily responses actually is
characteristic of sentimental fiction. Reports of the effects of *Uncle Tom's
Cabin* consistently refer to the compulsive, hypnotic effects of reading it.
According to George Templeton Strong, a prominent New York lawyer and
diarist, *Uncle Tom's Cabin* "set all Northern women crying and sobbing over
the sorrows of Sambo" (Gossett 168). Rev. Henry Clarke Wright observed,
"It has fascinated and repulsed me at the same time, as a reptile that enchants
you, while it excites your loathing and abhorrence . . . moving and melting
and swaying my heart and sympathies" (Gossett 170–71). Horace Greeley's
tears were so uncontrollable that he had to interrupt a trip from Boston to
Washington to spend the night in a hotel—presumably crying in private.[14]
How different is he from Alice Pyncheon? or Phoebe Pyncheon? And
Hawthorne's critique of sentimental affect on the grounds that it might not,
in fact, lead to benevolent actions that widened the circle of human community but instead might exploit the occasion of fictional suffering for private pleasure also has some basis in fact. When Wendell Phillips writes,
"There is many a man who weeps over Uncle Tom and swears by the [pro-
slavery New York] *Herald,*" he indicts those multitudes of people who enjoy
the intense emotional stimulation of the book without being persuaded by
its appeal to their moral sense (Gossett 168).

As we have seen, Hawthorne does not oppose literary appeals to the
body. The problem with some sentimental works, he intimates in "Alice
Pyncheon," is that they appeal *only* to the body, incapacitating their readers
for thoughtful responses. It is a physical addiction rather than a communally
centered moral activity. And, Hawthorne suggests, there is an air of sexual
danger about this readerly enslavement to physical stimulation. The encounter between Alice and Maule is eroticized, limned in sexual words and
phrases. First Maule says he wants Alice's "pure and virgin intelligence,"
then Alice is "struck with admiration—which she made no attempt to conceal—of the remarkable comeliness, strength, and energy of Maule's figure."
When he hypnotizes her, she believes that she can withstand his "evil potency [which] was now striving to pass her barriers" because of her own
"high unsullied purity, and the preservative force of womanhood" (177,

178, 180). The relationship between Holgrave and Phoebe—who is hypnotized by Holgrave's story—is also sexual. Holgrave, Hawthorne writes, is tempted by the "seductive" opportunity to "complete his mastery over Phoebe's yet free and virgin spirit" (187). The seduction, imperiled virginity, and threatened rape he associates with sentimental literature implies a concern on Hawthorne's part that the sentimental reader—who does not read with an alert, critical mind—is too vulnerable to the will of the author and could as easily be corrupted as morally improved.[15]

He would have been horrified (but not surprised, I suspect) by a certain strain of reader responses to *Uncle Tom's Cabin*. The powerful, involuntary simulation produced by Stowe's sentimentalism lent itself to the eroticization of sympathy. As the burgeoning psychoanalytic movement began intensifying its efforts to induce people to talk about their secret sexual selves, many confessed that they had been erotically aroused by the representations of suffering in *Uncle Tom's Cabin*. Both Sigmund Freud and Richard Krafft-Ebing, the Victorian sex researcher who coined the term "masochism," explicitly mention *Uncle Tom's Cabin* as a novel their patients read while masturbating, deriving sexual excitement from its representations of torture and unlimited power over life and death. Such responses clearly vitiate the sentimental ideal; scenes that are supposed to provoke public actions of benevolence in fact exploit others' suffering for private pleasures, contracting rather than widening the community.[16]

Hawthorne's critique of sentimentalism in *The House of the Seven Gables* could be seen as suggesting a certain conservatism on his part, in that it advises a cautionary stance toward humanitarian causes and disparages qualities of many female-authored texts. But as David Reynolds has shown, those qualities also characterized a great many male-authored popular texts. And surely Hawthorne's critique of the potential for humanitarian representations of suffering to exploit the pain of victimized others for the private pleasures of middle-class readers—all in the name of altruism—is hardly conservative. Overall, the verdict of *The House of the Seven Gables* on the question of sentimentalism is ambivalent: while on the one hand, like *Uncle Tom's Cabin,* it idealizes sympathy as a reliable and ethical way to seek the truth of the human heart, on the other hand, it recognizes the potential for representations of spectacles of suffering to exploit their objects of sympathy in ways that detract from the overall goals of social cohesion.

Contemporary critics need to take sentimental literature seriously enough to criticize it.[17] To identify its shortcomings is not to promote a patriarchal literary canon, but to address questions raised by what is clearly one of the most important major philosophical and literary movements in American literary history. Hawthorne's meditations upon the possible negative effects of sentimental affect, combined with his idealization of sympathy as an antidote to solipsism, make his book a particularly useful contribution to the American sentimental literary tradition. Reading the book as an exploration of a sentimental epistemology helps contemporary critics recognize sentimentality as the major philosophical and literary movement that it was. Doing so gives us new cause to respect nineteenth-century sentimental literature by men *and* women, and new critical tools for interpreting it. It also demonstrates that the separation of men's and women's spheres is, in many cases, a fiction produced by twentieth-century historiography.

Notes

1. Tompkins 18. The first quotation is from Evert Augustus Duyckink's 1851 review; the second is from an unsigned review in the May 1851 *Christian Examiner.*

2. Among these studies, see Harris, Bennett, Herget, and Samuels.

3. For genealogies of the roots of sentimentalism in Common Sense moral philosophy, see Camfield, Barnes, and Alkana.

4. Quoted in Rugoff 111.

5. On these grounds, Margaret Fuller can be read as a "high sentimental" author. See Sandra Gustafsen's study of Fuller's uses of sentimentalism.

6. See Brodhead, Laqueur, Halttunen, and Cvetkovich for analyses of representations of abused bodies in *Uncle Tom's Cabin* in particular and in narratives of humanitarian relief in general.

7. The story of Stowe's vow is widely reported; see, for example, Douglas's introduction to *Uncle Tom's Cabin.*

8. See Nudelman's analysis of the sentimental abolitionists' ideal of a community of free and enslaved women bonded through suffering.

9. See O'Connell's discussion of this *mise-en-scène.*

10. For discussions of the influence of Common Sense philosophy on Hawthorne, see Alkana, Scheick, Simpson, Franzosa, Pancost, and Howard.

11. In addition to Tompkins, see Brown, Gallagher, and Pfister.

12. Wallace points out that Hawthorne appreciated these authors for their daring explorations of embodied passions but also scorned them because—as women—their self-exposure was, he felt, inexcusable. His article is a clear and nuanced appraisal of Hawthorne's mixed relationship to women's sentimentalism.

13. See Wallace's discussions of this letter.

14. Ammons's preface to the Norton edition of *Uncle Tom's Cabin.*

15. In objecting to sentimental fiction on the grounds of a potentially enslaving sexuality associated with its production of affect, Hawthorne is reiterating objections to such fiction that were commonplace by the mid-1800s. See, for example, Haller and Haller 102–3, Cvetkovich's chapter on Stowe, and Halttunen. Hawthorne

also participates in a discourse that, as Barnes has shown, is associated with the founding republic, in which seduction and rape were metaphors for threats to the national body, the loving bonds of the national family.

16. For extensive elaboration of this point, see Noble and Reynolds.

17. There is ample precedent for doing so. See, for example, Armstrong and many of the essays in Samuels's collection.

Works Cited

Alkana, Joseph. *The Social Self: Hawthorne, Howells, William James, and Nineteenth-Century Psychology.* Lexington: UP of Kentucky, 1997.

Ammons, Elizabeth, ed. *Uncle Tom's Cabin.* Norton Critical Edition. New York: Norton, 1994.

Armstrong, Nancy. *Desire and Domestic Fiction: A Political History of the Novel.* New York: Oxford UP, 1987.

Barnes, Elizabeth. *States of Sympathy: Seduction and Democracy in the American Novel.* New York: Columbia UP, 1997.

Bennett, Paula. "'The Descent of the Angel': Interrogating Domestic Ideology in American Women's Poetry, 1858–1890." *American Literary History* 7.4 (1995): 591–610.

Brodhead, Richard. "Sparing the Rod: Discipline and Fiction in Antebellum America." *Representations* 21 (Winter 1988): 67–95.

Brown, Gillian. *Domestic Individualism: Imaging Self in Nineteenth-Century America.* Berkeley: U of California P, 1990.

Camfield, Gregg. *Sentimental Twain: Samuel Clemens in the Maze of Moral Philosophy.* Philadelphia: U of Pennsylvania P, 1994.

Cvetkovich, Ann. *Mixed Feelings: Feminism, Mass Culture, and Victorian Sensationalism.* New Brunswick, NJ: Rutgers UP, 1992.

Denby, David. *Sentimental Narrative and the Social Order in France, 1760–1820.* Cambridge UP, 1994.

Dobson, Joanne. "The American Renaissance Reenvisioned." *The (Other) American Traditions: Nineteenth-Century Women Writers.* Ed. Joyce Warren. New Brunswick, NJ: Rutgers UP, 1993. 164–83.

Fern, Fanny. *Rose Clark.* New York: Mason, 1856.

Franzosa, John. "Locke's Kinsman, William Molyneux: The Philosophical Context of Hawthorne's Early Tales." *Emerson Studies Quarterly* 29.1 (1983): 1–15.

Gallagher, Susan Van Zanten. "A Domestic Reading of *The House of the Seven Gables.*" *Studies in the Novel* 21.1 (1989): 2–13.

Gossett, Thomas F. *Uncle Tom's Cabin and American Culture.* Dallas: Southern Methodist UP, 1985.

Gustafsen, Sandra M. "Choosing a Medium: Margaret Fuller and the Forms of Sentiment." *American Quarterly* 47.1 (1995): 34–65.

Haller, John S., and Robin M. Haller. *The Physician and Sexuality in Victorian America.* Urbana: U of Illinois P, 1974.

Halttunen, Karen. "Humanitarianism and the Pornography of Pain in Anglo-American Culture." *American Historical Review* April 1995: 303–35.

Harris, Susan K. *Nineteenth-Century American Women's Novels: Interpretive Strategies.* New York: Cambridge UP, 1990.

Hawthorne, Nathaniel. *The House of the Seven Gables.* New York: Signet, 1961.

———. *The Letters, 1853–1856.* Centenary Edition. Vol. 17. Columbus: Ohio State UP, 1987.

Herget, Winfried, ed. *Sentimentality in Modern Literature and Popular Culture.* Tübingen: Gunter Narr Verlag, 1991.

Holmes, George F. Rev. of *Uncle Tom's Cabin,* by Harriet Beecher Stowe. *Southern Literary Messenger* 18 (1852). Reprinted in Ammons 467–77.

Howard, Leon. *Literature and the American Tradition.* New York: Doubleday, 1960.

Hume, David. *A Treatise of Human Nature.* Ed. L. A. Selby-Bigge. 1888. Oxford: Clarendon, 1958.

Laqueur, Thomas. "Bodies, Details, and the Humanitarian Narrative." *The New Cultural History.* Berkeley: U of California P, 1989. 175–205.

Noble, Marianne. "Ecstasies of Sentimental Wounding in *Uncle Tom's Cabin.*" *Yale Journal of Criticism* 10.2 (1997): 295–320.

Nudelman, Franny. "Harriet Jacobs and the Sentimental Politics of Female Suffering." *ELH* 59 (1992): 939–64.

O'Connell, Catharine. "The Magic of the Real Presence of Distress: Sentimentality and the Competing Rhetorics of Authority." *The Stowe Debate: Rhetorical Strategies in Uncle Tom's Cabin.* Ed. Mason I. Lowance, Jr., et al. Amherst: U of Massachusetts P, 1994. 13–36.

Pancost, David W. "Hawthorne's Epistemology and Ontology." *Emerson Studies Quarterly* 19.1 (1973): 8–13.

Pfister, Joel. *The Production of Personal Life: Class, Gender, and the Psychological in Hawthorne's Fiction.* Stanford: Stanford UP, 1991.

Reid, Thomas. *An Inquiry into the Human Mind.* Ed. Derek R. Brookes. University Park: Pennsylvania State UP, 1997.

Reynolds, David S. *Beneath the American Renaissance: The Subversive Imagination in the Age of Emerson and Melville.* New York: Knopf, 1988.

Romero, Lora. "Domesticity and Fiction." *The Columbia History of the American Novel.* New York: Columbia UP, 1991. 110–29.

Rugoff, Milton. *The Beechers: An American Family in the Nineteenth Century.* New York: Harper & Row, 1981.

Samuels, Shirley, ed. *The Culture of Sentiment: Race, Gender, and Sentimentality in Nineteenth-Century America.* New York: Oxford UP, 1992.

Scheick, William J. "The Author's Corpse and the Humean Problem of Personal Identity in Hawthorne's *The House of the Seven Gables.*" *Studies in the Novel* 24.2 (1992): 131–53.

Simpson, Lewis David. "The Relationship of Common Sense Philosophy to Hawthorne, Poe and Melville." Diss. Ohio State U, 1987.

Smith, Adam. *The Theory of Moral Sentiments,* in *Adam Smith's Moral and Political Philosophy.* Ed. Herbert W. Schneider. New York: Hafner, 1948.

Stowe, Harriet Beecher. *The Key to Uncle Tom's Cabin.* London: Clarke, Beeson, 1853.

———. *Uncle Tom's Cabin, or Life among the Lowly.* 1851. Ed. Ann Douglas. New York: Viking Penguin, 1981.

Tompkins, Jane. *Sensational Designs: The Cultural Work of American Fiction, 1790–1860.* New York: Oxford UP, 1985.

Wallace, James D. "Hawthorne and the Scribbling Women Reconsidered." *American Literature* 62.2 (1990): 201–22.

13
"I Try to Make the Reader Feel": The Resurrection of Bess Streeter Aldrich's *A Lantern in Her Hand* and the Politics of the Literary Canon

DENISE D. KNIGHT

Few contemporary scholars of early-twentieth-century literature were familiar with the name Bess Streeter Aldrich (1881–1954) until her 1928 novel, *A Lantern in Her Hand,* was reissued in late 1994. Likewise, when the novel was first published on the eve of the Great Depression, critics took little notice. Within eighteen months of its original release, however, *A Lantern in Her Hand* was in its twenty-first printing. Today, more than seventy years after it first appeared, the novel has been translated into over twenty languages. Yet regardless of its timeless appeal—it is touted for having "outlasted literary fashions to touch generations of readers"[1]—the novel is still relegated to the margins of American literary history, a position in which it seems destined to remain.

The politics of canonization are, of course, enormously complex. And while *A Lantern in Her Hand* defies easy classification—as recently as 1995 scholars were still struggling to define Aldrich's work—it is heavily steeped in the tradition of nineteenth-century sentimentalism. Set in the Midwest prairies, the novel pulls the reader into the human dramas that befall the heroine—the death of her newborn infant, the destruction of her crops, the sacrifice of her dreams. Despite the contemporary dismissal of sentimentalism as a literary convention that has outlived its usefulness, it is precisely that—the novel's ability to raise one's sensibilities—which accounts for its power "to touch generations of readers." Addressing her critics some sixty years ago, Aldrich noted, "If one writer does not see life in terms of grime and dirt, adulteries and debaucheries, it does not follow that those sordid things do not exist. If another does not see life in terms of faith and love, sympathy and good deeds, it does not follow that those characteristics do not exist. I grow weary of hearing the sordid spoken of as real life, the wholesome as Pollyanna stuff. I contend that a writer may portray some of the decent things of life around him and reserve the privilege to call that real life too. And if this be literary treason, make the most of it" (qtd. in Martin 21). Yet it is the undercurrent of sentimentalism in *A Lantern in Her Hand* that has, ironically, confined this work of popular fiction to the periphery of American literature.

The marginalization of *A Lantern in Her Hand* is in no small way the result of its being labeled a "woman's book," a perception perpetuated by a March 1939 Gallup poll listing the novel as "one of the ten books most read by American *women*" (emphasis added) and crediting it as being "among the first ten in point of sales to women readers" (Petersen 89). Even the well-meaning praise of Bessie Rowe, editor of *Farmer's Wife Magazine,* who wrote that "Aldrich had shown women could 'love the soil' as much as men were purported to" (qtd. in Petersen 89), undoubtedly reinforced the early characterization of the novel as a "woman's book."

Even more potentially damning was the ideological view promoting a cultural assumption about the existence of a "woman's sphere" and relegating women writers to an obscure and largely separate position in the landscape of American literary history. The segregation of women's texts—and the insistence that the domestic sphere is a separate and inferior realm in which women writers "belong"—effectively eclipses our appreciation of that type of literature which often transcends the boundaries arbitrarily created by the dominant culture. In fact, while *A Lantern in Her Hand* may indeed invoke sentimentalism, it also challenges assumptions about women's roles and reveals much about nineteenth-century domestic life, social history, and material culture. Moreover, while the novel borrows some of the conventions of nineteenth-century sentimentalism, it undeniably blends elements from several other literary -isms, including realism and naturalism, which are themselves no longer automatically viewed as separate entities. As Carol Miles Petersen notes in her biography of Aldrich, there is an ongoing debate about how to characterize Aldrich's work: "There were those who spoke of [Aldrich's] work as that of a Romantic; others argued that she was a Realist. . . . I believe that her writing has connections to both schools, and that her life, viewed as if it were fiction, melds both elements. . . . I have come to see her and her life as exemplars of the Romantic Realist" (xv, xvii). It is, however, the label of sentimentalism that has clung most tenaciously since the novel first appeared.

As critic Paul Lauter observes in his landmark revisionist book *Canons and Contexts,* "the dominant view [this century] has been suspicion of literary sentiment; indeed, among the most damning terms in a critic's arsenal has been 'sentimental.' We have much preferred the detachment and aesthetic distance of irony . . . and [have learned] to busy ourselves in cerebral linguistic enterprises" (106). Rejecting the traditional view of sentimentalism as a literary convention with no redeeming value, Lauter asks the reader to reconsider both the aesthetic function and the value of works that have been historically marginalized for their perceived shortcomings—for their failure to adhere to elitist standards of literary "excellence."

By way of example, Lauter notes that a work such as Stowe's *Uncle Tom's Cabin,* once relegated to the most distant margins of the literary canon, has now been restored "to a degree of literary grace." This is not because of "a shift in our literary aesthetic"; rather, its restoration in the 1960s marks the "impact of the civil rights movement," which, in turn, affects our literary tastes. In other words, "standards of literary merit are not absolute but contingent," and as a result, "we need constantly to reexamine our cultural yardstick" (107). In the case of *Uncle Tom's Cabin,* the social interest in the condition of African Americans that emerged in the 1960s had a direct bearing on the renewed interest in and subsequent reassimilation of the novel into the literary canon. Similarly, the 1960s saw the rebirth in popularity of Thoreau's *Walden* as "flower children" sought peace in nature and exchanged the trappings of materialism for a simpler way of life. Lauter also argues that "it is not merely literary concepts and historical configurations that are undergoing reconstruction; it is our *consciousness,* that set of internal assumptions . . . that forms what we see, or even what we look at" (116).

Using Lauter's paradigm of cultural aesthetics and consciousness, we can better understand the enduring power and appeal of *A Lantern in Her Hand.* While it is easy to repudiate sentimentalism or, as Harold Bloom does in *The Western Canon,* to dismiss those "sadly inadequate women writers" whose works are "as imaginatively dated now as they were already enfeebled when they first came into existence" (540), it is the unique aesthetic formula of sentimental fiction—its ability to evoke basic human emotions—that lends its appeal. Bloom maintains that we should "not read to unpack our hearts" (523) but rather "to confront greatness" (524). His aesthetic standards of "greatness," however, are deeply rooted in the Shakespearean tradition; hence they embody the traditional values of a decidedly masculine and archaic culture. If, on the other hand, as Lauter argues, our literary and aesthetic standards are "contingent" upon our cultural values and the "merit resides as importantly in the capacity of a work to move us, [and] to evoke authentic feelings" (105), then we must challenge the modernist rejection of sentimentalism as an inferior convention devoid of genuine aesthetic value.

If we examine Aldrich's fiction alongside that of her contemporary Hamlin Garland (1860–1940), himself a Midwestern writer, the distinctions between the two are rather nebulous. Both writers examine common American themes (the often-elusive pursuit of the American dream, including owning a home, attaining self-fulfillment, and creating a better life for one's children), and both document the extraordinary hardships of farm life in the Midwest. There are, perhaps, more thematic and stylistic similarities between the two writers than there are differences. But although Garland exercises his own "considerable sentimentalization of the facts" (Schorer 260), he is typically hailed as a "local colorist" or "regional realist," while Aldrich, whose fictional settings are likewise confined to the Midwestern prairies, is summarily dismissed as either a sentimentalist or, at best, a "romantic realist." Despite Garland's "proclivity for sentiment" (Schorer 267), not unlike Aldrich's, his work has been embraced by the academic community, and even with its apparent shortcomings, it is firmly assimilated into the American literary canon. Aldrich, on the other hand, remains precariously perched on the outside, looking in.

Even scholars and critics who tout the "importance" of Garland's writing are quick to acknowledge its deficiencies. Donald Pizer, in *Realism and Naturalism in Nineteenth-Century American Literature,* maintains that "Garland's weaknesses as a writer of fiction . . . are readily apparent," that all of the stories in *Main-Travelled Roads* "have major flaws," and that many of his stories "are marred by melodramatic and sentimental touches" (137–38). Likewise, in the afterword to the Signet edition of *Main-Travelled Roads,* Mark Schorer concedes that "Garland's literary faults are well enough known. . . . Not one of our great exciting writers, and sometimes a plain boring one, he is nevertheless important in ways not merely historical" (268–69).

What accounts for the privileging of Garland's fiction over Aldrich's, and what is implied, then, by the distinction in the relative "value" placed on each writer? How is it that Garland, a "weak," "flawed," "marred," "boring" writer, has come to be regarded as one "of the major figures of the age" (Pizer 157)? Certainly Garland's friendship with the enormously influential author and editor William Dean Howells, who publicly praised *Main-Travelled Roads,* helped not only to promote his writing but also to secure his place in American literary history. Howells, after all, helped to launch the careers of countless young writers. But other factors besides earning Howells's endorsement seem to elevate the appreciation of Garland's work above that of Aldrich's.

First, it is likely that there is a perception among readers—albeit an ill-founded one—that Garland's work boasts an authenticity that is lacking in Aldrich's fiction. Since Garland himself was the son of a farmer, he could presumably write with authority about the hardships endured on the Midwestern farm. Aldrich, on the other hand, "was not a farm child and never knew at first hand any of the experiences" confronting the prairie farmer (*Lantern* v). But like Hawthorne, whose childhood introduction to the tales of his ancestry compelled him to set his fiction in Puritan New England, Aldrich too was regaled with so many ancestral stories that the episodes, she said, "became a part of my knowledge, even though they had happened so many years before I was born" (vi). Before she commenced writing *A Lantern in Her Hand,* Aldrich also solicited "authentic historical material" from early pioneers to supplement the "childhood memories of my own hardy forebears [that] gave the keys to the pioneer character" (viii). Her goal was to present a realistic depiction of the pioneer woman: "to catch in the pages of a book the spirit of such a woman" and to do so with "historical accuracy" (vii). The result, *A Lantern in Her Hand,* was a resounding success and remained on the American best-seller list for more than two years (Petersen 88).

Indeed, according to aesthetic standards proposed by Daniel L. Marsh, president of Boston University in the late 1950s, the American literary canon is composed of "certain American writings so significant, so inspired, so esteemed by Americans, so durably valuable to the American people, so pregnant with the essence of American spirit, so revelatory of the genius of America, that, taken together, they constitute the authoritative rule of Americanism" (qtd. in Quick and Scharnhorst 13). Certainly with its depiction of the indomitable pioneer spirit, the pursuit of the American dream, and its extraordinary popularity, *A Lantern in Her Hand* would seem to meet Marsh's criteria—dubious though they may be. The novel was lauded, in fact, by an English reviewer as being "if not actually the best, certainly one of the best novels to come from America. A story told with beauty and distinction that has in it the ring of real literature" (qtd. in Petersen 91). Despite Aldrich's realistic depiction of life on the prairie, "simply placing women into the dominantly male tradition is clearly [an] inadequate step" in canon reformation, as Lauter acknowledges (117). The inherent prejudice against women's texts results in the exclusion of a number of fine literary works.

A more significant factor in comparing the relative status accorded the two writers is that prairie fiction was, and still is (Cather notwithstanding), perceived as *primarily* the domain of the male writer. As Petersen argues, "Frontiering was seen as a male enterprise, and the Western women of the time were either Calamity Janes or prostitutes" (79). Eventually, "the female picture was softened to allow women to become either the self-effacing Madonnas of the Prairie, or, at the other end of the spectrum and equally inaccurate, the heroic pioneer mother, combating white- or red-skinned marauders" (79). Aldrich, however, took pains to break the dominant stereotypes of women in the Midwest and to show her protagonist's vital connection to the prairie. Still, as Lauter observes, the term "frontier spirit" has been traditionally associated with *male* valor: "The phrase came to be defined in terms exalting male individualism, physical courage, and the honor code of the 'lone cowhand' heroically confronting and triumphing over savagery. . . . Although . . . recent scholarship has quite altered understanding of the history of the frontier, it is not at all clear that a category like the 'Frontier Spirit' could, even now, be freed of its chauvinist cultural baggage and be used to validate a significantly different canon" (38–39).

For a short time, in fact, *A Lantern in Her Hand* did enjoy canonical status. By 1942 the novel had been added to "other classics for classroom use in the Modern Literature Series," which also featured Crane's *The Red Badge of Courage* and Wharton's *The Age of Innocence* (Petersen 89). Eventually, however, the long-held academic bias against sentimentalism pushed the novel into relative obscurity until it was reissued in 1994. Even as scholars continue the process of literary retrieval, though, the inherent devaluation of sentimentalism limits its appreciation.

However, as Aldrich insisted, without apology, "My type of story is a story of emotion rather than of intellect. I try to make the reader feel" (*Collected Short Works* xii). Indeed, Aldrich's novels, including *A Lantern in Her Hand, The Lieutenant's Lady, The Rim of the Prairie,* and *A White Bird Flying,* are conspicuously out of place when viewed alongside those of some of her contemporaries—Hemingway, Fitzgerald, and Faulkner, for example. Petersen observes that "there is no swearing in Aldrich's stories, no sex, no divorce, none of the seamy side of life" that we would typically find in the works of Hemingway and Fitzgerald (xi). Aldrich also rejected as irrelevant academic classifications of literature and argued that like it or not, "sentiment" was a significant part of reality. "Sentiment doesn't lie in the soil, or in climate, or latitude, or longitude," Aldrich wrote. "It lies in the hearts of people. Wherever there are folks who live and work and love and die, whether they raise hogs in Iowa or oranges in California or the sails of a pleasure boat at Palm Beach, there is the stuff of which stories are made" (qtd. in Lambert 299).

Despite the stigma attached to Aldrich's fiction, boundaries between her work and Garland's become increasingly blurred when we examine it alongside Garland's most frequently anthologized short story, "Under the Lion's Paw," in which he effectively portrays the struggles of the human spirit when an honest, hardworking farmer who has endured years of grueling labor is exploited by a greedy capitalistic landowner. Just as the enraged farmer is about to attack the landowner with a pitchfork, he hears "a

gush of faint, childish laughter, and then across the range of his vision . . .
he saw the sun-bright head of his baby girl as, with the pretty tottering run
of a two-year-old, she moved across the grass of the dooryard" (155). The
sight of his daughter causes the farmer to drop the pitchfork, and the landowner escapes unharmed. This touch of sentimentalism at a critical junc-
ture in the story—a device that is repeated many times in Garland's fiction—both tempers its impact and compromises the realism. Still, Garland
remains a permanent fixture in the American canon; he has not been subjected to the culturally elitist bias that haunts Aldrich and other women
writers whose alignment with a "woman's sphere" has caused them to be
deemed somehow "lesser than" the male writers.

While a critical assessment of Aldrich's work is just starting to emerge
following the republication of *Lantern*, Petersen's biography of Aldrich ten-
tatively characterizes her as a "Romantic Realist" (xvii). In an article published in 1933, however, Aldrich took exception at being pigeonholed into
one school or another. Clearly, she understood that the boundaries between
various literary movements were far more fluid than conventional critical
wisdom allowed: "Why quarrel with a writer over realism and idealism?
After all, an author is glass through which a picture of life is projected. The
picture falls upon the pages of the writer's manuscript according to the
mental and emotional contours of that writer. It is useless to try to change
those patterns" (qtd. in Martin 21).

Aldrich's protests aside, one could argue that in addition to the realism
and sentimentalism that permeate the text, there is also a strong naturalistic
strain in her writing, similar to that found in any number of American
naturalist writers. (In this way, too, Aldrich's work subverts the popular notion that naturalism is the province of the nineteenth-century male writer.)
The utter randomness of nature is noted in several passages. For example, in
describing a grasshopper infestation in the crops, Aldrich writes, "By the
next night the stalks of field corn were skeletons, a few delicate veins of
leaves left, like so many white bones bleaching on the desert of the fields.
At the end of three days the oat field was stripped almost as bare as the day
the plow had finished its work. The young orchard was a graveyard of hopes.
. . . It was as though the little grayish-green fiends became a composite
whole,—one colossal insect into whose grinding maw went all the green of
the fields and the gardens" (103). The passage is reminiscent of Garland's
description of a grasshopper plague in "Under the Lion's Paw": "They
wiped us out. They chawed everything that was green. . . . I ust t' dream of
'em sitt'n 'round on the bedpost, six feet long, workin' their jaws" (144).
Similarly, the cosmic irony characteristic of nature in the fiction of such
naturalists as Crane and London becomes, in Aldrich's novel, "Nature's little

joke, as though she were laughing at the settlers for their pains" (132). Another tenet of naturalistic fiction—nature's ability to be absolutely indifferent to the plight of man—is also seen frequently in *A Lantern in Her Hand*.[2]

In addition to Petersen's work on Aldrich, a recent study by Abigail Ann Martin concludes that "if [Aldrich's] vision has been affected by her own sunny disposition . . . she is no different from many other earnest writers of fiction. She has a right to be called a realist . . . but the term is not technically applicable to her work" (33). Martin cites Aldrich's "irritating tendency toward didacticism" and her inability to refrain from "pointing [out] a moral—and [usually] it is a moral that readers are quite capable of finding for themselves" as deficiencies in Aldrich's writing. "Further, most of her 'moral' passages are interwoven with a sugary sentimentalism quite unworthy of so gifted a teller of tales," Martin argues (32).

What Martin has apparently missed in her assessment of this "sugary sentimentalism" is that Aldrich intentionally capitalized on human drama as a significant and successful ingredient in her aesthetic formula. By placing ordinary human beings—farmers, housewives, pioneers, and children—in situations that test their courage, expose their weaknesses, and reveal their strengths, she was able to invoke universal themes that readers could readily embrace. Moreover, if we apply Lauter's argument that current social and cultural conditions affect our literary tastes and shape our aesthetic values, then we need not look far to determine the reasons for the renewal of interest in Aldrich and her literature. In a cultural climate characterized by airline disasters, domestic terrorism, racial and serial murders, and drive-by shootings, her "sugary sentimentalism" offers the reader an escape to a time when traditional values still loomed large.

Significantly, Garland, too, has been criticized for his occasional tendency toward didacticism: "The fact is that the effect of the echoes of Garland's theories is sometimes to give his stories a curiously schoolmasterish tone, as if he is instructing some uninformed person in the anthropology of the frontier, lecturing him on sociological injustices while showing lantern slides of picturesque native habits" (Schorer 262). Yet his status as a writer of great import is secure because "his stories are often moving in a peculiarly American way, in their allegiance to what we can only hope is a still persisting democratic trust, in their allegiance to a native locale that, for all its harshness, they cannot relinquish" (268–69). Compare that assessment of Garland's fiction with the following praise of Aldrich's novel: "Aldrich has infused *A Lantern in Her Hand* with some of the rugged spirit of the earlier West. . . . One likes the Plains states better, and has more faith in the United States, for reading the book [which] is so true, so natural, and so American. . . . [It is] a picture as thrilling and joyously fresh as the prairie sky. A most welcome addition to those . . . documents that recount the development of our national consciousness" (qtd. in Petersen 87). Still, Aldrich's writing is depreciated in large part because of the premium automatically accorded frontier literature written by men.

If there is one thing, however, that should redeem Aldrich's novel in the eyes of contemporary critics, it is the deliberate and painstaking effort she took to ensure the historical accuracy of her works, not unlike Garland's historical rendering of "the privations and hardships of the men and women who subdued the midland wilderness" (Garland xi). As she was writing *A Lantern in Her Hand,* Aldrich invited anecdotes from early settlers who could provide authentic details about life on the Nebraska prairie. (Likewise, Garland interviewed his neighbors in South Dakota.) The response to her solicitation was enormous: so many diaries, letters, newspapers clippings, and scrapbooks flooded her home that it took her fourteen months to sort through it. Infused in the novel, too, are allusions to such actual historical and political events as slavery, secessionism, the Civil War, Lincoln's election and assassination, Native American treaties, and the Spanish-American War. The result of her research was so compelling, in fact, that in 1949 *A Lantern in Her Hand* was named one of the top ten books in rendering an accurate depiction of American life (Martin 41).

This is high praise indeed, particularly considering that it was given near the end of World War II, when the spirit of the nation was inevitably shattered by the horrific consequences of the war. But Aldrich had little interest in writing fiction that focused exclusively on the political climate of the nation. Rather, she explored the day-to-day struggles of her protagonist, Abbie Deal, as she attempts to define her "self" in a chaotic and indifferent world. She particularly wanted to avoid "that type of woman" which "other writers had depicted in the Midwest's early days . . . gaunt, browbeaten creatures, despairing women whom life seemed to defeat" (*Lantern* vii). One is reminded of Martin's allusion to the "sunny disposition" in Aldrich's writing, apparently stemming from a too-superficial reading of the novel in which Martin confuses "sunniness" with valor. In fact, the character of Abbie Deal endures enormous pain, but her invincible courage, like that of many of Garland's protagonists, allows her to triumph over every adversity, including droughts, prairie fires, snakebites, and blinding blizzards. It is not bright optimism, but rather a carefully created, gender-neutral form of independence that allows Abbie Deal to survive the many trials.

Some contemporary critics, including Suzanne Clark in *Sentimental Modernism,* argue that "the modernist revulsion against sentimentality was not really so reasonable as its invective against emotion would imply. The sentimental is at issue because no discourse can escape appealing to the emotions of its audience, and yet modernist criticism pretended to do so" (5–6). Clark also refuses to see sentimentalism and modernism as opposite art forms, arguing instead that modernism is "an extension of attention to the uncanny sentimentality it has always tried to deny" (15). Therefore, she holds the conviction that "we need to restore the sentimental to modernist literary history" (15) in order to adequately judge the contributions of women writers who have been marginalized.

Harold Bloom, on the other hand, maintains that in reading so-called "marginal" works, among which he would include sentimental fiction, "we are destroying all intellectual and aesthetic standards" (35) because only "true" canonical works can manifest "aesthetic dignity" (36). One of the problems with noncanonical literature, including sentimental fiction, according to Bloom, is that it derives its aesthetic value from an individual's "class struggle" with society (23). True "aesthetic value," Bloom argues, "emanates from the struggle between texts: in the reader, in language, in the classroom" (38).

Bloom is actually restating a long-held view; even as early as 1928, the year *A Lantern in Her Hand* was originally published, critic Norman Foerster, in his introduction to *The Reinterpretation of American Literature,* argued that good literature must adhere to a high aesthetic standard, and therefore "a focus on domesticity and family, on education and marriage, even on 'love and money' . . . would not do. . . . The tension for the 'new woman' between work life and family life would also not suffice as a topic of high national seriousness" (qtd. in Lauter 32). But as Lauter and others point out, aesthetic values must be constantly redefined so that the exploration of female experience emerges as a valid topic for reading and discussion. For many "female writers," Lauter argues, "removal to the frontier represents a tearing up of roots; their concern is less self-discovery or conquest of new territory than the reestablishment of family, community, and a socially productive way of life. To the extent that we concentrate primarily on work from the antisocial escapist tradition in [American literature], we keep our students from learning of that more socially-focused tradition concerned with how to make life work in the here and now" (103). Moreover, while we generally "talk about 'literary' or 'aesthetic' merit, we are speaking of the interest the form and language of a text hold for us. . . . What if one were to argue," Lauter asks, "that merit resides as importantly in the capacity of a work to move us, to evoke authentic feelings, even to prod us into action?" (105).

The reconfigured aesthetic concerns that Lauter proposes can be easily applied to Aldrich's fiction. For example, universal themes that move the reader and "evoke authentic feelings" are woven throughout *A Lantern in*

Her Hand, beginning with a scene in which Abbie Deal's adult children gather in their mother's home after learning of her death. Structurally similar to Robert James Waller's best-selling novel, *The Bridges of Madison County,* the remainder of the work is a reconstruction of her life from the age of eight. One of the major thematic emphases embedded in the novel is the fear of death, which stems from a traumatic episode in Abbie's early childhood. Death is never far from her thoughts; she seems, in fact, to spend a lifetime preparing for it. Her fear of death, and the subsequent and deliberate cultivation of an independent spirit in which she consciously distances herself from emotional involvement in relationships, both humanizes Abbie and renders her sympathetic to the reader.

Aldrich irreverently states at the beginning of the novel (which takes place between 1854 and 1926), "This is the story of the old lady who died while the meat burned [in the kitchen] and the children played 'Run, Sheep, Run,' across her yard" (6). As her middle-aged children—a banker, a state legislator, a professional singer, a university professor, and a homemaker—come together in "the old parlor with its familiar objects" (6), the pathos of the situation is apparent. Consumed by grief and overcome by guilt that their mother died alone, one of her children articulates what they all seem to be thinking: "Isn't it *dreadful?* Poor mother! So many of us . . . and not one of us here just when she needed us" (6). Abbie Deal's young granddaughter, Laura, in whom Abbie has confided her deepest fears and regrets, interrupts: "*I* don't think it was so dreadful. I think it was kind of nice. Maybe she didn't miss you. . . . When you think about it, maybe she didn't miss you *at all*" (6).

Indeed, only her twelve-year-old granddaughter possesses the wisdom that allows her to view the death without the sentiment that clouds the perceptions of Abbie's adult children. This simple but astute statement is one of the keys to understanding Abbie's character, and it illuminates an important subtext in the novel: Abbie's ability to detach herself from emotional entanglements with others. Still, the power of sentiment in the novel cannot be overlooked. While Martin insists that Abbie finds her greatest satisfaction in being a loyal daughter, devoted wife, and strict and compassionate mother (25), the subtext suggests instead a character who *accepts* her station in life but certainly does not embrace it. One aspect of Abbie's character that Aldrich does not oversentimentalize, in fact, is her relationship to her children. Despite her obvious love for them, for example, Abbie describes herself, in the language of painful self-sacrifice, as being "like an old mother partridge who had plucked all the feathers from her breast for the nest of her young" (298). At the same time, Abbie maintains an emotional distance from her loved ones, insulating herself against the seemingly inevitable pain of hurt, betrayal, and disappointment. Like the enormously conflicted Francesca Johnson in *The Bridges of Madison County,* Aldrich has depicted in Abbie Deal's farmwife character the dramatic entanglements that lie beneath the quiet reserve. But her self-protective emotional armor ultimately sustains her.

It is in the safety and privacy of a fantasy world that Abbie rejects the conventional roles of wife, daughter, and mother that dominate the "woman's sphere." We see Abbie's repudiation of those roles reinforced in both the interior monologues and the third-person narrative summaries that occur throughout the novel. On the surface, Abbie projects a cheerful persona, but her character also harbors enormous resentment about lost opportunities and bitterly regrets some of the choices she has made.

One of her biggest regrets is that her greatest dreams, which had their genesis in her childhood, go unfulfilled: "Some day she was going to be a big person. She could feel it in her—that she was going to do great things, sing before vast audiences, and paint lovely pictures in frames and write things in a book" (39). But those dreams never reach fruition; her bitter disappointment, while concealed from her family, is obvious to the reader. Aldrich writes, "Abbie Deal [lived] two lives; one within herself, wracked and tortured,—the other, an outward one which met all the old duties and trivial obligations with composure" (176). This duality between the "tortured" and "composed" selves, or the private and public personae, is seen frequently throughout the novel. Her bitter regret over the sacrifice of her own dreams for the benefit of others is a recurring theme. One by one, her children, and later her grandchildren, appropriate Abbie's dreams: to be a singer, artist, and writer. Shortly before her death, she cries bitter tears: "It just came over me . . . in a sort of wave . . . all of the wonderful things I planned to do when I was young . . . and never did" (293, Aldrich's ellipses).

Although she accepts her maternal role, motherhood was never part of Abbie's dream. Her ambivalence toward motherhood, in fact, is striking. During her fourth pregnancy, for example, she becomes physically abusive toward her young children. Aldrich writes, "All through August, Abbie went about in a dull, stupid way, depressed by the last hard luck that had descended upon them and the knowledge that her fourth child was coming. She was nervous—cross to [her husband] Will and to the children. Sometimes, in a temper, she jerked one of her little tots by the arm or spanked one angrily" (104). By this point in the novel, Abbie has endured an endless amount of adversity; the cause and effect of her impatience with her children is obvious to the reader. Moreover, when Aldrich remarks that Abbie "seemed [to be] doing things she did not want to do" (105), the double meaning, with its allusions to both harming her children and adhering to traditional roles, is obvious. As her thoughts drift, the regrets begin to crystallize. One particularly revealing passage that combines sentimentalism with the ability to evoke the "authentic feelings" advocated by Lauter merits quotation:

> If she had known—if she could have foreseen—the drought and grasshoppers—the blizzards and the winds that were never still—the hard work—and the privations—the song that might never be sung—the four babies in eight years. "No! . . . No!" She pulled herself out of the dream. "Don't let me think it. Don't let me *think* of thinking it. It's wicked. There's nobody but Will. It's just the crop failures and the terrible hard luck that made me think it. Those things have nothing to do with love." But even as she said it, Abbie knew that it was not true. Abbie knew that unless you are very strong, those things have something to do with love. . . . The thought that she probably would never be able now to do anything [now] that another child was coming,— they all harassed and tormented her. (105–6; 107–8)

Aldrich's frank depiction of Abbie's resistance to her role as mother and the oppression that stems from the loss of her dreams authenticates Abbie's experience and appeals to the basic human emotion of sympathy. The power of sympathy enables the reader to view Abbie as a woman "harassed and tormented" but not utterly defeated, for as long as she acknowledges her anger, she has at least some degree of control. When the baby is stillborn, Abbie is tortured by guilt. "It was because I didn't want him at first," she confesses to her husband, insisting that the infant's death is her punishment (121). Later that day, she sees her husband drive by in the lumber-wagon with her neighbor holding across her lap the little wooden box that contains the remains of her dead son. In the context of other events in the novel, the little stillborn body represents the death of yet another of Abbie's dreams.

By the time her own death occurs, some thirty years later, the eighty-year-old Abbie Deal has mastered the art of emotional insulation. Despite repeated invitations from her grown children to come and live with them, Abbie prefers to live alone. Her twelve-year-old granddaughter's comment on her death, that "Maybe she didn't miss you. . . . Maybe she didn't miss you *at all,*" is right on the mark. Abbie dies from coronary failure—in sentimental terms, from a broken heart—and the thoughts that visit her during her dying moments are significant: "That queer thought of death intruded itself again, but she reasoned, slowly and simply, with it. If death were near she would be frightened. Death was her enemy. All her life she had hated death and feared it." And then the denial, "But Death was not near" (304), followed by a fantasy not unlike the one Hemingway provides for the disillusioned Harry at the end of "The Snows of Kilimanjaro" when he, too, would prefer to deny, rather than confront, imminent death. In her reverie, Abbie imagines her family peacefully gathered together one last time. The beauty of her perception is ultimately an illusion; as her senses rapidly fail and she makes the transition from life to death, Abbie imagines herself walking with her husband hand in hand, "past the old poplars, through the deepening prairie twilight—into the shadows" (306). The ending of the novel is sentimentalized as Abbie finally lets go of the fears that have bound her for much of her life.

In the final analysis, *A Lantern in Her Hand* operates on several levels: the novel tells a story of strength and courage, of the beauty and devastation of nature, of a woman whose fear of intimacy leaves her strong but emotionally unfulfilled. Still, Abbie Deal is never presented as a pathetic figure; rather, she is a stoic woman who finds a way to survive. In addition to operating on various levels, the novel is a classic example of a work that demonstrates that the often-arbitrary distinctions between men and women writers—and their characters—are not so clearly delineated as some critics would claim. While *A Lantern in Her Hand* does not come close to fulfilling Bloom's aesthetic standards of "excellence," the novel is finding a new generation of readers more than seventy years after its original publication.

In her essay "The Story behind *A Lantern in Her Hand,*" Bess Streeter Aldrich urged promising young writers to ignore literary conventions: "Regardless of the popular literary trend of the times," she implored, "write the thing which lies close to your heart" (*Lantern* ix). In the end, Aldrich's failure to conform to those popular literary trends, and to write, instead, the thing that lay closest to her heart, might just explain the timeless appeal of *A Lantern in Her Hand.*

Notes

1. Aldrich, *A Lantern in Her Hand,* dustjacket.

2. For example, Aldrich writes: "The small grain amounted to very little. The corn began to curl and brown and bake on its roots. Crops were stillborn in the womb of Nature" (172). A passage later in the novel shows nature's bounty: "Nature began to seem less parsimonious with her rains. No longer was the sky a dry blue bowl turned over the dry brown earth. Heavy with moisture, the clouds gathered and fell in a blessing of light showers or heavy, soaking rains. Out of Nature's benediction grew fine crops, better times, high land prices" (207). Certainly the naturalism in these passages rivals some of those of such "mainstream" American naturalist writers as Dreiser, Crane, Norris, London, and Garland, the last of whom Pizer

identifies as one of "the earliest representatives of American literary naturalism" (97). Despite the pioneering work of Judith Fetterley, Marjorie Pryse, Paul Lauter, and countless others to expand canonical margins and retrieve lost texts, few, if any, women writers have been identified as naturalists. And while Aldrich cannot be considered a mainstream naturalist, the naturalistic strain in her writing is evident. The power of nature to wreak havoc or to bestow blessings in the lives of humans is a major theme in her fiction.

Works Cited

Aldrich, Bess Streeter. *Bess Streeter Aldrich: The Collected Short Works, 1907–1919*. Ed. and intro. Carol Miles Petersen. Lincoln: U of Nebraska P, 1995.

———. *A Lantern in Her Hand*. 1928. Lincoln: U of Nebraska P, 1994.

Bloom, Harold. *The Western Canon*. New York: Harcourt Brace, 1994.

Clark, Suzanne. *Sentimental Modernism: Women Writers and the Revolution of the Word*. Bloomington: Indiana UP, 1991.

Fetterley, Judith, and Marjorie Pryse, eds. *American Women Regionalists, 1860–1910*. New York: Norton, 1992.

Garland, Hamlin. *Main-Travelled Roads*. New York: Signet, 1962.

Lambert, Lillian. "Bess Streeter Aldrich." *Midland Schools* [Des Moines, Iowa] 42.8 (1928): 299.

Lauter, Paul. *Canons and Contexts*. New York: Oxford UP, 1991.

Martin, Abigail Ann. *Bess Streeter Aldrich*. Western Writers Ser. 104. Boise: Boise State UP, 1992.

Petersen, Carol Miles. *Bess Streeter Aldrich*. Lincoln: U of Nebraska P, 1995.

Pizer, Donald. *Realism and Naturalism in Nineteenth-Century American Literature*. 2nd ed. Carbondale: Southern Illinois UP, 1984.

Quirk, Tom, and Gary Scharnhorst, eds. *American Realism and the Canon*. Newark: U of Delaware P, 1994.

Schorer, Mark. Afterword. *Main-Travelled Roads*. By Hamlin Garland. New York: Signet, 1962.

Waller, Robert James. *The Bridges of Madison County*. New York: Warner Books, 1992.

Contributors

Debra Bernardi is assistant professor of English at Carroll College in Helena, Montana. She is currently working on a book about the political and social horrors that affected popular representations of the American home in the nineteenth century; her essay on "Domestic Horror and the Politics of Genre" appeared in the journal *Legacy*.

Jennifer Costello Brezina is lecturer of English at the University of California, Riverside. Her current projects include an exploration of the interrelation of different types of urban public space for American women at the close of the nineteenth century.

Lucinda L. Damon-Bach is assistant professor of English at Salem State College. Founder of the Catharine Maria Sedgwick Society and organizer of the Sedgwick Symposium, she has written and lectured extensively on Sedgwick and Susan Warner. She is currently editing a Sedgwick reader and collection of criticism.

Monika M. Elbert is associate professor of English at Montclair State University and associate editor of the *Nathaniel Hawthorne Review*. She has published extensively on nineteenth-century American authors. Among her works is *Encoding the Letter "A": Gender and Authority in Hawthorne's Early Fiction*.

Lisette Nadine Gibson holds a part-time faculty position and teaches at Syracuse University. She is working on a study of post–Civil War women writers.

Dawn Keetley is visiting assistant professor at Lehigh University. She has published essays on antebellum women in *Legacy, a/b: Auto/Biography Studies, ESQ,* and *American Quarterly* and is currently working on a book on homicidal insanity in nineteenth-century law and fiction.

Mary Louise Kete is associate professor of English at the University of Vermont, where she teaches both English and Women's Studies. She is the author of several works on sentimentality and American culture, including *Sentimental Collaborations: Mourning and Middle-Class Identity in Nineteenth-Century America.*

Denise D. Knight is professor of English at the State University of New York College at Cortland. Among her numerous studies are *Charlotte Perkins Gilman: A Study of the Short Fiction, The Later Poetry of Charlotte Perkins Gilman, The Diaries of Charlotte Perkins Gilman,* and *Nineteenth-Century American Women Writers: A Bio-Bibliographical Sourcebook.*

Darby Lewes is associate professor of English at Lycoming College. She is the author of *Dream Revisionaries: Gender and Genre in Women's Utopian Fiction, 1870–1920* and *Nudes from Nowhere: Utopian Sexual Landscapes.*

Frederick Newberry is professor of English at Duquesne University. Having published essays on nineteenth-century American writers, he is also the author of *Hawthorne's Divided Loyalties: England and America in His Works* and the editor of the *Nathaniel Hawthorne Review.*

Marianne Noble is associate professor of literature at American University. She has published articles in the *Yale Journal of Criticism,* the *Emily Dickinson Journal,* and *MLA Approaches to Teaching "Uncle Tom's Cabin."* Her recently published book is entitled *The Masochistic Pleasures of Sentimental Literature.*

Karen S. Nulton holds her Ph.D. in American literature from Rutgers University and works at Educational Testing Service in Princeton, New Jersey. In addition to parenting four sons, she actively supports the revisioning of public education in New Jersey.

Katharine Rodier is assistant professor of English at Marshall University. A co-editor of *American Women Prose Writers, 1820–1870,* a forthcoming volume of the *Dictionary of Literary Biography,* she has published many essays on

American women writers. Her poems have appeared in various journals, such as the *Virginia Quarterly Review* and the *Antioch Review.*

Karen E. Waldron is professor of Literature and Writing and Associate Dean for Academic Affairs at College of the Atlantic in Bar Harbor, Maine. Her published work focuses on nineteenth- and twentieth-century women's and minority literatures and on American novels and narrative form.